CW01512876

A SHELLSHOCKED NATION

A SHELLSHOCKED NATION

BRITAIN BETWEEN THE WARS

ALWYN TURNER

Profile Books

First published in Great Britain in 2026 by
Profile Books Ltd
29 Cloth Fair
London
ECIA 7JQ
www.profilebooks.com

1 3 5 7 9 10 8 6 4 2

Typeset in Garamond by MacGuru Ltd
Printed and bound in Great Britain by
CPI Group (UK) Ltd, Croydon CR0 4YY

A CIP catalogue record for this book is available from the British Library.

Our product safety representative in the EU is BGC Sustainability
& Compliance, 7 avenue du Général Leclerc, Paris, 75014,
France https://baldwinglobalconsulting.com

ISBN 978 1 80522 187 6
eISBN 978 1 80522 189 0

This book is dedicated to Brian Freeborn,
even if it is before his time.

'There's an east wind coming, Watson.'

'I think not, Holmes. It is very warm.'

'Good old Watson! You are the one fixed point in a changing age. There's an east wind coming all the same, such a wind as never blew on England yet. It will be cold and bitter, Watson, and a good many of us may wither before its blast. But it's God's own wind none the less, and a cleaner, better, stronger land will lie in the sunshine when the storm has cleared.'

Arthur Conan Doyle, 'His Last Bow', 1917[1]

The new world they were creating, the world of bonds and debts and mortgages, massive industry and wild speculation, was bringing with it a new set of traditions, a new standard of values, as it had brought new art and music, the jazz band, the mass-production cinema.

Ellen Wilkinson, *The Division Bell Mystery*, 1932[2]

CONTENTS

NOTE ON CURRENCY AND INCOMES

The UK's pre-decimal currency was a little convoluted. There were twelve pennies to a shilling, and twenty shillings to the pound, so a pound was the equivalent of 240 pence. Prices tended to be written in the form £2 12s 6d, representing two pounds, twelve shillings and sixpence. To confuse matters, there were also standard units of a crown (five shillings) and half-a-crown (two shillings and sixpence). And some payments were made not in pounds but in guineas, with a guinea being one pound and one shilling.

In the mid-1920s the average weekly wage of a male manual worker was under £3, while a waitress in a good restaurant might be on £1 a week (plus meals). A wage of £5 to £10 would put someone in the lower middle class. A study in Sheffield in 1931 concluded that a married couple with two children would need a minimum of £1 11s 10d a week to pay for rent, food and fuel. The Working Men's Club and Institute Union calculated that the average annual expenditure on alcohol was £8 10s per head of the population. For most of this period, MPs were paid £400 a year.

SILENCE

Oliver Cromwell: I have a faith that the people of this country are born to be, under God, a free people. That is the fundamental principle of this English life.

John Drinkwater, *Oliver Cromwell*, 1921[1]

I look around me and daily I see
Thousands and thousands of fellows a lot worse off than me.
In Piccadilly, friends pass me by,
I'm absolutely stranded in the Strand.
But I confess I was contented, more or less,
When I was stony broke in No Man's Land.

Frank Miller, 'Stony Broke in No Man's Land', 1921[2]

George V lays a wreath at the Cenotaph on Armistice Day, 1919

AT THE ELEVENTH HOUR OF THE ELEVENTH DAY OF THE ELEVENTH MONTH, Britain fell silent. It was 1919, exactly a year since the Armistice, the ceasefire that had brought to an end the war to end all wars, and King George V had asked that there should be a two-minute pause in the life of the nation. 'All work, all sound, and all locomotion should cease, so that, in perfect stillness, the thoughts of everyone may be concentrated on reverent remembrance of the Glorious Dead.'[3]

The idea was extraordinary, the realisation powerful beyond expectation. In cities, towns and villages across the country, millions gathered to pay tribute; life came to a standstill in shops and factories, in schools, prisons and courts; public transport stopped, and passengers stood in reverence; telephone exchanges noted that not a single call was made. 'It was a stillness that could be felt,' marvelled one reporter, 'broken only by the sobs of women who could not restrain their grief, and the soft whirr of wings of a covey of pigeons who hovered overhead.'[4]

It was a communal experience that was also intensely personal, for there was scarcely a family in the country untouched by the conflict. 'For two brief minutes I saw again the distorted horizon of northern France, and the last resting-place of so many of my gallant comrades,' reflected a soldier.[5] At Crewe station, 'one old gentleman, who had lost four sons in the war, knelt in silent prayer'.[6] In the Sailors' Orphan Home in Hull, 'three hundred children stood to attention; most of them were there as a direct result of the war'.[7] And among the vast crowds in Whitehall, a ten-year-old boy looked at the Cenotaph and asked his mourning mother, 'Is daddy in there?'[8]

'London was like a dead city,' it was reported.[9] 'An unearthly strange stillness fell upon the shops, they were like the petrified cities of Pompeii.'[10] It became known as the Great Silence, and nothing like it had been experienced before.

Nor would it ever be replicated, for thereafter Armistice Day was increasingly to become a ritual, formalised by officialdom. But this first year, there was no standard service or ceremony, no structure; the start and the end were marked by maroons being fired, church bells being rung, workplace hooters being sounded, and that was all. The rest was Silence.

Some felt that the moment encapsulated the change in the country. 'It is a strong national trait that we do not carry our hearts on our sleeves,' observed the *Newsman*; 'anything like a display of emotion is, and was, particularly in pre-war days, quite foreign to the British character, but the Great War has changed the outlook on many things.'[11] But the dominant note, as the *Cheshire Observer* pointed out, was not 'a display of emotion' so much as 'a feeling of suppressed emotion'.[12] Despite the novelty of the moment, the idea of expressing grief through silence seemed entirely appropriate for a race renowned for its reticence. 'In that great hush,' said the *Lincolnshire Echo*, 'lies our strength; and in it all there was a glimpse into the soul of the nation.'[13]

When the Silence ended, normal life resumed, but it would never be the same. Due tribute had been paid to the dead and would be paid again at the same time next year, and every year thereafter. Now it was time for the country to put the war behind it, or at least to put it aside. The focus was on rebuilding, not reflection. And so there descended a Cultural Silence, in which the war was not to be discussed.

This was a question of demand rather than supply, for there was no shortage of literature on the subject – and particularly of poetry. The conflict, said veteran writer Edmund Gosse in January 1918, had produced 'a flood of verse' with 'more than five hundred volumes of new and original poetry'.[14] By 1920, Birmingham Public Library could claim to have 1,100 books of war poems, most of them British but with representation from America, Argentina, Barbados, Belgium, British Columbia, Canada, Egypt, France, India, Italy, Malta and Norway.[15] If more recent enemies were noticeably absent from that list, still there was a sense of the human experience transcending national – and, by implication, nationalistic – boundaries.

There was, however, no obvious public appetite for accounts of the horrors witnessed in those blighted years. Those who had served needed no reminding, while those who had not were more concerned with their own lives. One publisher said in 1919 that he had 'half a dozen long shelves' of war poetry, books that should each retail at 3s 6d, but which he couldn't get rid of even when discounted to threepence.[16] A man invited to give a lecture to the Southampton Rotary Club that year said he'd been undecided whether to speak on war poetry or tea, and had fixed upon the latter, because 'whereas war poetry would interest probably only a few, a cup of tea appealed to everyone'. There were cries of 'Hear, hear.'[17] The only war poet whose work really commanded public attention in the post-war years was Rupert Brooke, and he was a special case; he had died of septicaemia in April 1915, en route for Gallipoli, and was preserved in the aspic of idealism and beauty, untouched by images of the trenches.

As the volumes continued to appear, despite poor sales, indifference turned to impatience. In A. S. M. Hutchinson's novel *One Increasing Purpose* (1925) a veteran cries, 'Why was I spared?' to which the *Sketch*'s reviewer tetchily pointed out 'the obvious fact that he was spared because he wasn't hit'.[18] 'Most people are tired of books about the great World Struggle, whether they be in poetry or prose,' sighed the book reviewer of the *Western Mail*.[19]

The war books that had sold well during hostilities were the adventure stories. John Buchan's *The Thirty-Nine Steps*, published in the summer of 1915 and set a year earlier, established the template for the war thriller: Richard Hannay, an ordinary – if remarkably resourceful – chap finds himself caught up in a battle of wills and weapons as he's chased by enemy agents. Hannay returned to the fray in *Greenmantle* (1916), now in uniform, but called away from his regiment to undertake a secret mission. There's talk of an Islamic rising in the Ottoman Empire, the advent of a foretold prophet, backed by Germany. 'There is a dry wind blowing through the East, and the parched grasses wait the spark,' Hannay is told. The compass point is significant. In such thrillers, the Western

Front did not loom large; romance, adventure and heroism were to the fore, not artillery attrition. Many other novels followed the Buchan formula, including John Ferguson's *Stealthy Terror* (1917) and *The Man with the Clubfoot* (1918) by Valentine Williams, who had served in France and been awarded the Military Cross.*

A war setting was also acceptable for a comedy or romance. Cartoonist Bruce Bairnsfather (wounded at Ypres) turned his character Old Bill into a musical comedy, *The Better 'Ole* (1917), which ran in the West End for over 800 performances. In *Alf's Button* (1919), by W. A. Darlington (wounded at Arras), a piece of Aladdin's lamp resurfaces in a brass button on a soldier's uniform; when rubbed, it unleashes a genie who can grant any wish, and farcical escapades ensue. The book sold in the hundreds of thousands and was swiftly turned into a film.†

This trend continued into peacetime. Ethyl Smyth's opera *Entente Cordiale* (1925) was set in France in 1919 and centred around a comic misunderstanding of a British soldier's appalling French accent. Or there was Harry Wall's play *Havoc* (1924), a hit on the London stage and then again in New York and Paris, before being filmed in Hollywood; the story was a simple love triangle with two officers on the front and a girl back home. But when the *Observer* drama critic Hubert Griffith, who'd served through the war, wrote a play, *Tunnel Trench* (1924), intended to reveal 'the utter futility of war', it received just a single, amateur performance.[20] 'We should like in our moral cowardice to forget what war is and what men suffered in it,' wrote novelist Arnold Bennett. 'We are tired of being grateful to the sufferers.'[21]

The war poets were, in short, out of tune with their times. 'The

---

* The fiendish German agent Clubfoot returned for a further six volumes, up to *Courier to Marrakesh* (1944), by which time he was serving Hitler, rather than the Kaiser.
† Cecil Hepworth's 1920 silent movie was remade with sound by W. P. Kellino in 1930. A third version, Marcel Varnel's *Alf's Button Afloat* (1938), starred comedy team the Crazy Gang.

vocal people were apt to be damaged sensitives, who were scarcely typical of the average man,' argued one of John Buchan's heroes. 'There were horrors enough, God knows, but in most people's recollections these were overlaid by the fierce interest and excitement, even by the comedy of it.'[22] Charlie Melvin of Kirriemuir, Angus, who served with the Black Watch and won the Victoria Cross in Mesopotamia, shared that perspective. 'I've read too many war novels,' he said. 'They're overdrawn. Too much hysteria and drinking. There were people whose nerves gave way, but that wasn't general.'[23]

Instead, concepts of honour and duty remained, a shared culture seeking to make sense of individual tragedy. The music-hall star Sir Harry Lauder (knighted for his charitable work during the war) reflected on his son, Captain John Lauder, who'd been killed in December 1916: 'I am glad that he and I lived in those days when men were patriotic and brave and kind and willing.'[24] He wrote 'Keep Right On to the End of the Road' (1924), a song of stoical acceptance, in tribute to his lost boy, and it became one of his best-known pieces:

> If you're tired and weary, still journey on
> Till you come to your happy abode,
> Where all you love and you're dreaming of
> Will be there at the end of the road.[25]

ii

Even when it went unspoken, the war shaded these years. And if the conflict itself wasn't always apparent, that was largely because so much else was changing in its wake. Most obviously, politics was utterly transformed by the expansion of the franchise. The House of Commons at the time of the Armistice was the product of the last pre-war election, when fewer than five million men voted; barely a decade later, in the 1929 poll, all men and women over the age of twenty-one were entitled to vote, and some twenty-two million did so. Politicians now had to appeal to an electorate that had more than quadrupled.

The adjustment was not entirely straightforward. There were general elections in each of three consecutive years, 1922–4 (with four prime ministers), and most of the 1920s and 30s was spent under either a coalition or minority government. In the process, the Liberal Party was replaced by the Labour Party as a pretender to government. Yet the single most striking political feature of the age was the strange survival of the Conservative Party, adapting to this new democratic order – the dawning of which it had feared so much – with remarkable ease. There were seven general elections between the wars, and in every single one of them the Conservatives won the largest share of the vote. That wasn't always enough, and Labour did form two short-lived minority governments, but there was no real doubt that Britain remained an essentially conservative nation.

There was, though, a redefinition of what being conservative meant in political terms. Lady Eleanor Smith, socialite daughter of the Tory grandee Lord Birkenhead, argued in 1929 that the Liberals had become irrelevant, since 'the present Conservative government is far to the left of any pre-war Liberal platform'.[26] The evidence was to be seen in the extension of the state's involvement in everyday life, with increased spending on pensions, welfare benefits and education, and subsidies for housebuilding and struggling industries. In 1913 expenditure by central government had stood at 8 per cent of gross domestic product, rising dramatically during the war; it fell a little in peace, but never returned to its pre-war level, and throughout the 1920s and 30s it hovered around 25 per cent of GDP. Much of this was an attempt to address relative economic decline in the face of international competition, and to respond to an ageing population: at the beginning of the century there were 1.75 million people over the age of sixty-five; by 1937, there were 3.75 million.

All the while, technology was transforming society, with strange, synthetic materials: Bakelite, cellophane, reinforced concrete, foam rubber, nylon, Perspex, polystyrene, PVC. The modern, middle-class home was far less likely to have a live-in maid than before the war, but the twentieth century (so the adverts said) was 'the Electric Era,'[27] and there was now an impressive range of labour-saving electrical appliances, from bacon-slicers to bed-warmers, washing machines and dishwashers to coffee percolators, sunray lamps and trouser presses. Newly invented items became household names: the Aga cooker, the Anglepoise lamp, the Ascot water heater, the Bush radio, the Goblin Teasmade, Pyrex dishes. It was an increasingly consumerist society, so that something like chocolate, once a luxury, could become an affordable treat, and shelves were filled with new British products: Aero, Black Magic, Chocolate Homewheat Digestive, Chocolate Orange, Crunchie, Fruit & Nut, Kit-Kat, Maltesers, Mars bars, Quality Street, Rolos, Roses and Smarties. Even the staples of life were reinvented, with the advent of sliced bread, 'cut by special machinery and wrapped in an airtight packet'. ('Another Yankee idea!' exclaimed the press.)[28]

Outside the home, the world shrank with cars, motor bicycles and aeroplanes, and the impact of mechanised transport was felt in unexpected ways; it encouraged the spread of suburbs, and there was much public concern over ribbon developments that stretched along arterial roads rather than grouped around communal services.

There was concern too over culture becoming passive, a fear that, with the rise of cinema, gramophone records and radio, people were consuming rather than participating. And yet there was a counter-current, the assertion of a communal spirit. It was manifest in the enthusiasm for community singing, particularly after the *Daily Express* began organising concerts at the Royal Albert Hall in 1926. The following year, the crowd at the FA Cup Final sang 'Abide with Me', and the hymn was henceforth folded into the annual ritual. The need to come together was still apparent.

Indeed, this was the great era of voluntary association. The Working Men's Club and Institute Union (CIU) had been founded back in 1862, but it was only in the aftermath of the war that the network really grew. By 1922, its diamond jubilee year, the 2,300 clubs affiliated to the CIU boasted well over a million members. Non-native initiatives were welcomed too. The Women's Institute, founded in Canada, reached Britain during the war and in 1936 had over 300,000 members, while Rotary Clubs, founded in Chicago, had around 19,000, and the League of Nations Union 500,000. Perhaps most important of all was the British Legion, which merged various veterans' groups in 1921 and within a decade had a membership of 300,000, around one in ten ex-servicemen.

There were also political clubs – some two thousand Conservative, nearly a thousand Liberal, the early stirrings of Labour – but it was the non-party institutions that really mattered. Membership was often rooted in class, of course, and there were biases: the League of Nations Union primarily attracted Liberals, while the British Legion branches, said War Secretary Duff Cooper, were essentially 'Conservative working men's clubs'.[29] But the non-aligned status of the various societies allowed for diversity of opinion, and for finding common cause beyond politics. That helped foster the feeling of national unity, of cooperation and coalition. So too the trade unions, membership of which, even at the lowest point following the defeat of the 1926 General Strike, stood at around five million; it was that failure that killed the dream of unions as a revolutionary force, and thereafter the main characteristic of the movement was compromise. Some believed that these voluntary associations ensured a continuing faith in liberty and tolerance. Three-time Tory prime minister Stanley Baldwin argued that the people had learned from trade unions and friendly societies 'the elements and principles of a democracy' which 'they will never let go'.[30]

Conservative and communal, Britain experienced a degree of domestic security and stability that was exceptional in an increasingly volatile world. There was much disruption, events so significant that their initials were capitalised – the General Strike, the Depression, the Abdication – but they were dwarfed by comparison with what was happening in other countries. Unemployment, inflation and industrial slumps were less marked than in most of Europe and beyond. The Irish War of Independence cost 2,000 lives, but the Spanish Civil War cost 400,000. The 'distressed areas' in northern England and in South Wales saw much hardship, but not on the scale of America's Dust Bowl, let alone the Holodomor, the Ukrainian famine engineered by the Soviet Union, in which perhaps as many as eight million people died, including 2,500 peasants executed for resorting to cannibalism.

Above all, in an era of dictators, Britain failed to produce a credible candidate. Though there were plenty of men who seemed to have the right autocratic tendencies and credentials, they were mostly to be found running their own fiefdoms: Lord Beaverbrook in Fleet Street, John Reith at the BBC, Ernest Bevin in the trade unions. There were British fascists and communists, but they were barely a shadow of their European contemporaries, and there was no equivalent to paramilitary groups such as La Cagoule in France or the Ku Klux Klan in America. While Europe was being reshaped by Mussolini, Stalin and Hitler, the dominant force in British politics was Stanley Baldwin – 'honest, pipe-smoking, straightforward Baldwin', in the words of the *Liverpool Echo*[31] – a public-spirited man who in 1919 anonymously donated a fifth of his personal wealth, some £120,000, to the nation, as a contribution towards paying off the war debt. 'Anybody more temperamentally indisposed to be a dictator can hardly be imagined,' observed Labour politician Lord Ponsonby.[32]

Even moral panics over the state of modern youth seemed less than shocking. The Reverend C. Ensor Walters, president of the Methodist Conference, was far from alone in denouncing the 'decadent Bright Young Things' as they chased a life of 'cocktail and sherry parties, cabarets and midnight revelries'.[33] But it all looked a bit tame when one could also read – in a review of Erich Kästner's novel *Fabian* (1931) – about 'the hysterical gaiety of Berlin nightlife in which perverts, erotomaniacs, half-starved prostitutes, society gluttons and lunatic cabaret players mingle in a mad dance of impending death'.[34] Britain couldn't compete with that sort of thing.

Nor did it wish to. This was a respectable country, an increasingly middle-class, suburban country, with rising levels of home ownership, a distrust of authoritarians and utopians and an attachment to institutions. 'In our democracy,' wrote Herbert Thomas, veteran editor of the *Cornishman*, in 1934, 'we have not discarded the monarchy, Parliament, trade unionism, nor the freedom of the churches.'[35] Despite the troubles that periodically visited the nation, it was possible to feel broadly optimistic about the direction of travel – so long as one didn't look abroad.

iii

In 1925 the journalist James Agate, theatre critic for the *Sunday Times*, published a collection of his more general essays under the title *Agate's Folly*. It was mostly well received. His writing was 'often whimsical, but acutely sagacious under their fashion of gaiety', said the reviewers;[36] 'he says many a serious thing jestingly'.[37] There was, though, a lone dissenting voice. The reviewer in the *Guardian*, a small-circulation Church of England publication,* evinced no love for Agate: 'the fact that he is now regarded as one of our leading drama critics illustrates how pitifully that important branch of criticism has deteriorated, and explains a great deal that is wrong with the modern stage'.[38]

That was a little harsh for such a lightweight volume – and not strictly relevant, since these pieces did not concern the theatre – but it was part of the rough-and-tumble of reviewing, as Agate presumably knew; he was a critic himself, and not one known for pulling his punches.† It was, therefore, a strange decision on his part to sue the *Guardian* for libel. The result was perhaps the most

---

* Not to be confused with the paper then called the *Manchester Guardian*, which changed its title to the *Guardian* in 1959.

† 'This is not a play,' Agate wrote of Terence Rattigan's first big hit, *French Without Tears* (1936). 'It is nothing. It is not witty. It has no plot. It is almost without characterisation.'

trivial trial of the decade, with even the judge grumbling about 'the thin skins of dramatic critics'; although Agate won, the jury awarded him a derisory farthing in damages, and he was left to pay his legal costs.[39] Amid the foolishness, one moment encapsulated the cultural tenor of the times. The theatrical producer (and former wrestling promotor) Charles B. Cochran was asked in cross-examination: 'Are you on the side of the highbrows or the lowbrows?' He hedged his bets. 'I am,' he declared, 'what is called a high lowbrow.'[40]

It was a live debate at the time, this business of highbrows and lowbrows, at least among those who identified with the former group. It reflected a nervousness about the rise of mass culture, with a publishing boom in thrillers, detective fiction and romance at the expense of serious literature. Worse yet was the influence of America, the first child of the imperial family to have struck out on its own; having outgrown its parent economically, it now threatened to do the same culturally. The young and the working class of Britain were enthralled by the adolescent joy of Hollywood movies and jazz music, and their enthusiasm was thought to jeopardise the fine arts of European civilisation.

In response, the highbrows withdrew into their ivory towers, making a virtue of their limited appeal. In his pamphlet *Hunting the Highbrow* (1927), Leonard Woolf explained why the 'first-rate novelist' (by which he meant he meant the likes of his wife, Virginia) tended not to be very popular: 'the aesthetic necessities involved in good novel-writing make it impossible for the writer to concentrate his attention on producing a good story and interesting characters'.[41] Regrettably, most of the reading public rather liked good stories and interesting characters.

Into this increasingly polarised atmosphere came the BBC, the most significant cultural development of the time, seeking to satisfy all sides. Pianist Fred Hartley, a regular broadcaster with his Novelty Quintet, said he was 'neither highbrow, nor lowbrow, but broadbrow, as one must be in catering for the great wireless audience'.[42] *Punch* magazine joked that the BBC aimed at the 'middlebrow', those 'people who are hoping that someday they will get used to the stuff they ought to like'.[43]

A typical Friday evening's radio schedule in 1930 opened with talks by Commander Stephen King-Hall (a 'summary of the week's news') and Mrs E. Lucas ('some ways of cooking onions') and there were further talks later from missionary Dr Donald Fraser, science writer Gerald Heard and gossip columnist Harold Nicolson. The main feature was a production of Oscar Wilde's comedy *The Importance of Being Earnest*, and there was a range of music, from pianist Maurice Cole playing Bach, through the light music of Katharine Parker and Gershom Parkington's Orchestra, to the dance band of Eddie Gross-Bart, live from the Ambassador Club in London. The fixed points were the news, weather, shipping forecast, reports from the stock markets in London and New York, and 'fat stock prices for farmers'.[44] Like the voluntary societies, this all spoke of non-denominational diversity and tolerance.

Similarly, the entertainment industry made less distinction between high and low than some might have wished. Sergei Diaghilev brought his Russian Ballet to London's Coliseum Theatre in 1924, performing new work including *Le Train Bleu* by Jean Cocteau with music by Darius Milhaud; it was presented on a bill that also featured the magician Edgar Benyon, Eric Randolph ('the Romany Tenor'), and comedian Harry Tate. Diaghilev returned the following year, this time sharing the stage with Hilda Ward's Lady Syncopators, hoop jugglers Stylo and Sonny, and Bi Bo Bi, who played the sleigh bells. There was also – in case the audience took the art too seriously – comedy double act Nervo and Knox, 'with their screamingly funny burlesque of ballet dancing'.[45]

In this book, highbrows and lowbrows live cheek by jowl, rubbing along with politicians, priests and pressmen. There is, though, a bias towards the popular. As with its predecessor, *Little Englanders: Britain in the Edwardian Era*, the intention is to try to take the temperature of the nation, so that Agatha Christie looms larger than Virginia Woolf and Henry Hall means more than Benjamin Britten, while figures such as holiday-camp king Billy Butlin and the thief known as Lady Jack – even Gef the talking mongoose – warrant more attention than many, far more worthy, politicians. Much of the story is also shaped by the increasingly noisy newspapers, which were frequently determined not merely to report the news, but to make it.

In 1937 Arthur Wontner starred in the film *Silver Blaze*, his fifth and final screen appearance as Sherlock Holmes. It was a rather pedestrian movie, but it did at least retain the most famous lines of dialogue from the original story. Holmes draws attention to 'the curious incident of the dog in the night-time', and when Inspector Lestrade shrugs that the dog did nothing, the great detective retorts: 'That was the curious incident.' The dog that didn't bark in the Britain of the 1920s and 30s was political extremism, and – perhaps, more than anything else – it is that curious absence that underlies the following pages.

1

SICKNESS AND CURES

Ten million young men were laid dead upon the ground.
Twice as many were mutilated. That was God's first warning
to mankind. But it was vain. The same dull materialism
prevailed as before.

Arthur Conan Doyle, *The Land of Mist*, 1926[1]

When the local train loafed in I got into it, with a stiff upper
lip and a bleeding heart, and set out on as eventful and
strange a journey as ever a man took.

P. C. Wren, *Beau Geste*, 1924[2]

A. A. Milne, Christopher Robin and Winnie-the-Pooh

THE NUMBERS WERE KNOWN, BUT THE COST COULD NEVER BE TRULY CALCULATED. The United Kingdom of Great Britain and Ireland lost nearly a million lives in the Great War: around 888,000 military personnel and 107,000 civilians died. Up to two million more were wounded. Nearly half of those who served in the army were either killed, wounded or taken prisoner.

The vast majority of the casualties were men, and the country was changed as a result. In the 1911 census, females outnumbered males by 3.5 percentage points; ten years later that had risen to 4.8 points, and the differential was greatest for those aged thirty to thirty-five, those born around the time of Queen Victoria's Golden Jubilee in 1887: one in six men in that cohort had lost his life. And the damage was still being done; in years to come, a disproportionate number of veterans would die at an early age.

The impact was felt right across society, though particularly at the higher end. The death rate was 17 per cent for officers and 12 per cent for other ranks; of the 5,650 Old Etonians to serve, one in five was dead. Nor were politicians spared: 264 sitting MPs and 323 members of the House of the Lords served, with forty-six parliamentarians killed in action. At the outbreak of war in 1914, the main British parties were led by H. H. Asquith (Liberal), Andrew Bonar Law (Conservative), Arthur Henderson (Labour) and John Redmond (Irish); of these men, the first three each lost a son in the conflict – two in Bonar Law's case – while the fourth lost his brother, the MP Willie Redmond.

And so it was across the country. Even those who had not personally suffered a family bereavement knew others who had. In 1936 the writer Arthur Mee coined the expression Thankful Village to refer to those places 'where all the men came back'.[3] He could identify just thirty-two such villages.*

In the context of the other great powers in Europe, the figures

---

* Later research has expanded this number to fifty-three.

were not extreme. Austria, France, Germany and Italy suffered much greater losses, and the east fared worst of all, both numerically – Russia and the Ottoman Empire each saw around three million deaths – and proportionally: Serbia's population fell by around 16 per cent. Such comparisons, of course, meant little in Britain.

Nor, even, did the national statistics. The scale of the fatalities was mostly marked by an absence at the heart of families and communities. 'Forty-two were killed from this village and they'd be men of thirty-five and forty by now,' says a regular in a rural pub in A. G. Macdonell's *England, Their England* (1933), in explanation of why all the drinkers are old men. ('Ah! That War didn't do any of us any good,' adds another.) In the face of such ravages, the country's inclination was to withdraw into itself, as it had a century earlier, after the defeat of Napoleon. A period of isolation, of recuperation, was needed, while – as Lord Beaverbrook, proprietor of the *Daily Express* put it – 'leaving Europe to the Europeans'.[4]

To compound the losses, the last months of conflict had also seen the outbreak of a killer epidemic. The first reports of Spanish influenza reached Britain in June 1918, though the name was not yet fixed; it was also referred to in the early days as Russian Flu or Flanders Fever. Nor was the designation accurate, for the disease was manifest around the world, from Ireland to India, Sweden to South Africa, but since Spain was not a combatant nation – and therefore had less press censorship than other countries – that was where the news was first heard.

With government attention focused on the war, there was no nationally coordinated response when the virus arrived in Britain in July, and local authorities responded piecemeal. Many closed schools, sometimes because of a shortage of staff, sometimes as a precautionary measure, while others, such as Richmond in Yorkshire, also closed cinemas and theatres. The number of staff absences through illness severely disrupted business and industry, as well as public services, with a shortage of policemen, firemen, doctors and nurses. Restaurants shut due to cooks being ill. In

Manchester, 220 tram drivers and guards were off sick on a single day, and forty cars were unable to run.

Official advice was not especially helpful. The *British Medical Journal* suggested that the simplest answer was for everyone to cover their mouth and nose when sneezing or coughing; this should be taught in childhood 'with the thoroughness engendered by the fear of, say, an instant smacking'.[5] In the absence of anything more immediate, queues formed outside chemists to buy products said to be effective in combatting the flu: 'ammoniated quinine, eucalyptus oil, sweet nitre and Turkish rhubarb'.[6] Pharmacies weren't the only businesses that took commercial advantage of the emergency. 'You don't want Spanish Influenza,' ran the advert for Howarths, which sold umbrellas in its shop on Bull Street in Birmingham; 'avoid the chills that follow rain-sodden clothes.'[7]

Not everyone shared this urgency. 'It is not a serious malady,' said Dr René Legroux of the Pasteur Institute, Paris in a widely reported interview. 'The Spaniards made a great fuss about it; but for that, it would not be noticed today.'[8] A leader column in the *Daily Mirror*, headlined DON'T THINK ABOUT IT, recommended that 'all mention of this new offensive of Nature's' should be banned by the government. 'You may have observed that the plague frequently falls upon those who brood over it – that those who don't think of it don't get it.'[9] If that was a little Pollyannaish, it was certainly true that at this stage the fatality rate among the infected was not high. For most people, life carried on, however inconvenient the adjustments one had to make. 'Last night I cooked my own dinner for the first time in my life,' said a man in north London. 'My wife and daughters are all down, the war has left us servantless, and the "char" only comes in twice a week as a great favour.' He ate ham, potatoes and peas.[10]

The epidemic receded in the summer of 1918, only to return with deadlier force in the autumn, peaking in November as peace broke out. School attendances plummeted, gardeners from municipal parks had to be called in to dig graves (though there was also a shortage of coffins) and even the prime minister, David Lloyd

George, was confined to his rooms for a week. Precautions were more serious this time, though that didn't stop the Armistice Day celebrations, with perhaps predictable results: a week on from jubilant scenes in Albert Square, the *Manchester Evening News* reported that the number of deaths in the city had more than doubled. The experience reported by Dr D. J. Thomas, the medical officer for Acton, west London, was typical: the first wave had killed ten residents in the borough; the second saw fewer infections but a far greater number of fatalities, with 177 deaths.[11]

Again there was a lull before, in January 1919, there came a third, final wave of 'considerable virulence', as *The Times* put it. The advice from the paper was to avoid crowded places and all contact with the infected, to wear 'a mask of gauze (a handkerchief serves very well)', and to keep enclosed spaces well ventilated: 'fresh air is most valuable'.[12]

All told, the Spanish flu killed up to a quarter of a million Britons, including hundreds who committed suicide, suffering from the depression that often followed infection. Globally, the death toll was anything up to 50 million, far in excess of the fatalities in the war. This loss was also swallowed up in the post-war silence, leaving behind virtually no cultural trace. Within a few years, the deadly disease had become little more than a jokey metaphor. 'I'm peevish and feverish like folks with the flu,' sang male impersonator Ella Shields in 'Why Did I Kiss that Girl?' (1924),[13] before moving on to more pressing questions: 'If her kiss did that, what would her huggin' do?'*

'Never since the Black Death has such a plague swept over the face of the world,' observed *The Times*; 'never, perhaps, has a plague been more stoically accepted.'[14]

---

* There was the occasional mention of Spanish flu in a few novels, including Aleister Crowley's *Diary of a Drug Fiend* (1922), R. H. Mottram's *The English Miss* (1928) and T. H. White's *Farewell Victoria* (1934), but it tends to be minor characters who die, their deaths taking little more than a sentence.

ii

Beyond the numbers, there was a deeper, less defined feeling that something had been irrevocably changed by the conflict, that the loss was not just of life, but of a *way* of life, of certainty and stability. 'Sometimes it feels as if we comfortable people are walking in a flowery meadow that is really a great quaking morass, and underneath there is black slime full of unimaginable horrors,' reflects the heroine of O. Douglas's novel *Penny Plain* (1920). 'The War made a tremendous crack. It seemed then as if we were all to be drawn into the slime, as if cruelty had got its fangs into the heart of the world.'

Some saw a moral infection, resulting from lowered standards during the war. There had been a rise in divorce cases, in the number of children born outside wedlock, and in prostitution, and there were fears that these changes might become permanent. There had also been a blurring of labour divisions between the sexes, a confusion of social expectations: women had worked in munitions factories, on public transport and in the police force, while men had learned domesticity in the army, responsible for sewing, cleaning, cooking and laundry. Old roles and rules were losing their sway, and young women in particular were a worry, as they became – at least so far as their elders were concerned – bolder and more outrageous in their dress, their expectations and their behaviour.

Cosmo Gordon Lang, the Archbishop of York, blamed the war for having 'gradually intensified the dangers of a moral corruption among all classes' on sexual matters. 'There has been a very general breakdown of the old restraints and ideals, not least among girls who are almost children,' he observed.[15] The Reverend Harry Pearson of the London Police Court Mission, who worked with the destitute and the criminal classes, came to the same conclusion: 'Our social workers have found that young girls and young women have as great a knowledge of the world, and of evil in particular, as grown women.'[16] There were, in the early years of peace, many such warnings in church circles. 'Immorality is stronger and more rife than it has ever been in the history of the country,' said Caroline Abraham, wife of the Bishop of Derby;[17] it was 'all too common amongst young folk', agreed Methodist minister Reverend W. H. Heap of Hull, adding ominously: 'That way lies destruction.'[18]

Again it went back to the war. Young women were more forward than previously because the loss of so many men of marriageable age meant husbands were in short supply, thereby making the Victorian ideal of demure maidenhood something of a social handicap – or else they simply didn't care any more. The *Daily Mail* ran a series of reports from seaside resorts in 1920 about the scandalously scanty clothing worn by young people as they engaged in mixed bathing: 'The modern girl has so poor a chance of marriage, owing to the scarcity of men, that it does not matter what she looks like when bathing.'[19]

One option for women was to advertise for male companionship, and local newspapers published notices so long as they were respectably worded: 'Lady (24), Clifton, would like correspondence with gentlemanly young man with a view to closer relations.'[20] Less modestly, there was *Link* magazine, 'a monthly social medium for lonely people', owned and edited since 1915 by Alfred Barrett, an experienced journalist who'd once been on the staff of the *Christian World*. Adverts here were more forthright. 'Bit of fluff (London, SE), 19, very lonely, invites dark sporty Adam to write her,' read one; 'Two breezy boys, just back from Japan, experts at having a good time, wish to meet two sporty girls,' said another; and a third: 'Widow (London, W), interested in discipline questions, would like to meet others, either sex, similarly interested.'[21] This was considered to overstep the mark, and in 1921 Barrett found himself in the dock of the Old Bailey, charged with conspiring to corrupt public morals. The hostile tone of the trial was set when counsel for the Crown Sir Richard Muir successfully argued for an all-male jury, saying he doubted 'whether any woman, excepting, perhaps, one off the streets, could even understand the case'.[22] Although the defence produced an anonymous Mrs X to testify that she'd made a happy marriage as a result of advertising in the

Link, neither the jury nor the judge were impressed. Barrett was sentenced to two years, and the judge expressed his regret that it couldn't be penal servitude.

Further evidence of moral decay came with the rise of birth control. Contraceptive sheaths had been encountered by soldiers serving in France, and the availability of the product grew rapidly back home. 'Every village chemist is selling them,' it was reported in 1919,[23] and it wasn't long before they were being advertised in the more raffish papers, such as the *Sporting Times*.* Alternatively, a Nurse Adams in Smethwick sold by mail order 'Dutch pessary', which used *Moringa oleifera*, the 'best contraceptive known'.[24] Awareness of contraception was spread further by Marie Stopes, who in 1921 opened the Mothers' Clinic in Holloway, north London, the first birth-control clinic in Britain, and whose book on the subject, *Married Love* (1918), sold three quarters of a million copies in twelve years.† By the mid-1930s, there were automatic vending machines on the streets, dispensing sheaths.

The churches were divided in their response to birth control. The Catholics were adamantly opposed – Jesuit priest Father Henry Day warned a congregation in Glasgow that contraception amounted to 'the unnatural vice of conjugal masturbation'[25] – while the 1930 Lambeth Conference of Anglican bishops settled for fudging the issue. 'The conference was unable to condemn the use of artificial methods of birth prevention,' said Cosmo Gordon Lang, now Archbishop of Canterbury, 'but it held that their use was permissible only in exceptional cases.'[26]

In truth, the state of public morality was not as hazardous as

---

* The Cygnet Surgical Company of south London offered 'superior quality teat end' for 3s 6d a dozen, and 'Paragon washable sheaths' at prices ranging from 1s 3d to 4s each.

† Stopes was seen by some as breaking all moral codes – her play *Vectia* (1923) was banned – but she had definite limits. Oral and anal sex were 'disgusting and cruel', she said; 'acts of such gross indecency that they undoubtedly amount to cruelty mentally to any refined or sensitive woman'.

the churchmen claimed, and the disruption of the war years largely passed. While there were five times as many divorces in the 1920s as there had been in the pre-war years, it was still a tiny minority of marriages that broke up, and the rate didn't rise any further. The number of illegitimate births peaked in 1920 before returning to Edwardian levels. Likewise, there were over a million of cases of venereal disease treated in 1919, but the numbers reduced steadily in the 1920s; the infant mortality rate from congenital syphilis fell by 90 per cent in two decades from its wartime peak.

Also falling was the birth rate. In reaction to the war, 1920 saw the highest number of live births ever recorded in the UK: 1.3 million babies, with a slight imbalance in favour of boys,* but the boom was brief; a decade on, that figure had halved. Partly this was the consequence of better healthcare – infant mortality in the 1920s was half the level it had been at the start of the century – but easier access to contraception also played its part.

iii

Perhaps the overreaction of the churches to the supposed erosion of moral standards was a symptom of their own waning position in the life of the nation. 'People are saying that Christianity has struck a bad patch,' admitted Samuel Knight, the Bishop of Jarrow; 'they talk about the decline of Christianity.'[27] Knight was inclined to be optimistic, but others were less confident. The Methodist Church noted falling numbers in 1920, and by the end of the decade was calling the decline a 'crisis'.[28] Baptists were similarly reporting a reduction in worshippers. 'If the deplorable drift continues for another ten years,' said Dr Douglas Brown, president of the Baptist Union, in 1930, 'organised religion for all practical purposes will be as dead as a dodo.'[29]

---

* The rise of male births after a war had first been noted by scientists in the nineteenth century, though it remained unexplained. In 1920 the boy–girl ratio of live births was 51.3 per cent to 48.7.

Broadly, the country still considered itself to be Christian. Baptism was the norm, with three in four infants being christened, and in 1928 there were said to be around 4.75 million children attending an Anglican or Free Church Sunday school. This latter figure, however, had fallen by a quarter in twenty-five years; the structures were still standing, but participation was declining.[30] On paper, around two thirds of the country – some 25.8 million people – were members of the Anglican Church, but fewer than one in ten of those took Easter Day communion in 1931.* When the sociologist Seebohm Rowntree undertook *Poverty and Progress*, a survey in York in 1935, he found that the proportion of adults attending church had halved since the start of the century.

'Why are the churches empty?' asked the *Daily Chronicle* in 1930,[31] and much of the answer lay, inevitably, in the war. Attendances had risen at the outbreak of hostilities and then fallen as the years wore on. And peace had brought a rival to organised religion, as remembrance spilled onto the streets in an act of secular spirituality that went beyond official structures. 'Those who went to church,' the *Daily Express* had said of the Silence in 1919, 'missed the stupendous thrill and mystery of the greater service in which men and women confronted their God, held communion without the hindrance of formula.'[32] The Cenotaph, which bore no religious or patriotic inscriptions, was now the people's sacred site of mourning, far more so than the Tomb of the Unknown Warrior in Westminster Abbey, with its references to God and nation, its talk of 'His Majesty King George V, his ministers of state, the chiefs of his forces'.

This shift in spiritual authority was recognised and resented by the establishment. When Armistice Day fell on a Sunday for the first time in 1923, the government announced that there would be no ceremony at the Cenotaph that year, replaced by a service in Westminster Abbey. This was met with a storm of outrage.

---

* The next largest denominations, as estimated in 1931, were Methodists (7.5 per cent of the population), Catholics (5.5 per cent) and Congregationalists (2.7 per cent).

CENOTAPH PLAN MUST BE AMENDED, read the *Daily Mirror* headline; WHOLE COUNTRY DISMAYED AT OFFICIAL BLUNDER. The *Western Daily Press* denounced an 'amazingly fatuous suggestion', and the *Dundee Courier* talked of how the commemoration had 'become sanctified into a kind of public sacrament'.[33] The government backed down, and both services were held, the king and queen going to Westminster Abbey, the Prince of Wales to the Cenotaph. Lessons were learned; the next time Armistice Day fell on a Sunday, in 1928, there was no such attempt to sideline the Cenotaph.

Again, though, the secularisation of remembrance was not the real issue, just one more expression of the disruption wrought by the war. There were others, for this was a world in search of reassurance and meaning, and finding it in unlikely places. 'The churches are losing ground, the quack religions are making rapid headway', wrote journalist John England. 'Perhaps it is a symptom of a sick age, of an age harrowed by war and suffering.'[34]

The 'quack religions' cited most often included not just the likes of 'the so-called Tantrik Love Cult' led by American yogi Pierre Bernard – a man sometimes known as 'The Loving Guru' or 'Oom the Omnipotent'[35] – but older, more established sects such as Christian Science, Mormonism and Theosophy, all enjoying a new lease of life. Spiritualism too was at its peak, there being so many bereaved wishing to contact loved ones who had passed over, even if some regarded it as beyond the pale: 'identical with devil-worship, with black magic, with the necromancy of the past, the continuation of Satan's revolt against God', according to Father Henry Day.[36]

There was even actual devil-worship, according to some. 'Satanism is practised in England at the present day',[37] wrote Montague Summers, an authority on Restoration drama, Gothic fiction and pederasty, who made his name with *The History of Witchcraft and Demonology* (1926), and maintained it with a carefully cultivated image. Often wearing the garb of a Catholic priest, he had the 'general air of having stepped out, all alive, from an eighteenth-century ecclesiastical engraving', according to one society hostess.[38] Or he was 'a fruity unfrocked cleric of the Nineties', in the words of writer Cyril Connolly, 'like an old toad'.[39] He insisted that evil still existed in all its traditional forms; modern churches tended to downplay the existence of demons, vampires and werewolves, but Summers never admitted a hint of doubt that they still walked the earth.*

Also thriving was the British Israel movement, which believed that the Anglo-Saxon race was directly descended from the Lost Tribes of Israel; Britons were, in essence, God's chosen people.[†] British Israelism had been around since the late nineteenth century, attracting support from, in the words of the *Catholic News*, 'people with lively imagination and little learning',[40] and it was reinvigorated by the proselytising of Cornish-born Canadian William Pascoe Goard. He'd been a Salvation Army officer, then a Methodist minister, before returning to Britain to found the British Israel World Federation in 1919. The movement became, for a while at least, very fashionable; Princess Alice (granddaughter of Queen Victoria) was a patron of the federation, as were the 7th Duke of Buccleuch, the 9th Earl of Dysart, and Norman de Jersey, Bishop of the Falkland Islands. It gained further publicity when Christabel Pankhurst, former leader of the Suffragettes, was reported in 1922 to be a convert, though she didn't remain in the movement for long.[‡]

---

* There were also reports in 1921 that the Russian Bolshevik leader Leon Trotsky had attended a Black Mass, at which 'the Evil One was worshipped and invoked to grant victory to the Red Army'. These stories originated in the exiled Russian press and may not have been strictly accurate.

† To be clear, this did not mean that the British were Jewish. 'It has been reiterated to the point of weariness,' wrote a frustrated British Israelist in St Leonards-on-Sea, Sussex to his local paper, 'that though the Jews are Israelites, all Israelites are not Jews.'

‡ 'Those days of the suffrage campaign were the days of political childhood,' wrote Pankhurst in 1924. Now it was time 'to abandon the childish, nay foolish dreams of a human-made Utopia, and in its stead hold fast, rejoicing, to the certainty that the Lord cometh'.

As a character in John Buchan's novel *The Three Hostages* (1924) observed, the war had caused 'a dislocation of the mechanism of human reasoning, a general loosening of screws'. *Guidance from Beyond* (1923) was a volume of automatic writing, in which various spirit guides channelled their thoughts from the Other Side through the pen of Miss K. Wingfield. The advice offered was not distinguished by great insight – it was observed that Christmas seems to come round earlier every year[41] – but the book was taken seriously in some circles: there was a preface by the Countess of Radnor, widow of a former Conservative MP, and an introduction by Sir Edward Marshall Hall, the most famous barrister of his (pre-war) generation. The latter summed up his own position, and that of many other seekers of consolation in these uneasy times: 'My knowledge is nil, my belief strong, my hope infinite.'[42] Sales of the book were good enough to warrant a sequel, *More Guidance from Beyond* (1925). Less noticed, but equally characteristic, was Colin Bennett's *Practical Time-Travel: How to Reach Back to Past Lives by Occult Means* (1937). Reincarnation being taken as read, the book explored how to use various techniques – astrology, crystals, hypnosis – to recover one's 'pre-natal' history.

There seemed no limit to what might be believed. One afternoon in July 1917, sixteen-year-old Elsie Wright of Cottingley in west Yorkshire had borrowed her father's camera, and returned with a photograph of her nine-year-old cousin, Frances Griffiths, surrounded by dancing fairies. A couple of months later came a second photograph, this time showing Elsie with a gnome. The pictures were nothing more than a childish joke, the girls posing with cardboard cutouts of the supposed fairies, and they were treated as such by Elsie's father. Her mother, though, wasn't so sure and showed them to a member of the Theosophical Society, whence they eventually came to the attention of the writer Arthur Conan Doyle. In December 1920 Doyle sensationally revealed them to the world in the *Strand* magazine, under the unequivocal headline PHOTOGRAPHING FAIRIES. The pictures proved, he concluded, 'that there is a glamour and mystery to life'. A further three pictures featured in a second article, and all appeared in Doyle's subsequent book *The Coming of the Fairies* (1922).

At the time, Doyle was one of a handful of literary figures – along with Rudyard Kipling, Arnold Bennett and H. G. Wells – whose mass appeal transcended age and class, a genuine literary celebrity. His fame rested chiefly on the creation of Sherlock Holmes, the man described by his chronicler Dr Watson as 'an automaton, a calculating-machine',[43] and the public assumed that this reflected Doyle himself; he too was seen as a man of logic, reason and intellect, so his endorsement of the Cottingley fairies was taken more seriously than it might otherwise have been.

It wasn't quite enough, though, for a press that remained sceptical. Although Elsie Wright had 'always been a truthful girl', according to her mother, she was described as 'dreamy' by a former teacher, and it was noted that having worked for a photographer in Bradford for a few months after leaving school, she was no stranger to cameras. Now, backed into a corner, she felt obliged to keep the charade going, though when she was interviewed by a reporter from the *Westminster Gazette*, his questions 'were only answered with smiles and a final significant remark: "You don't understand."'[44]

A more spectacular apparition yet was the 1933 sighting in a Scottish lake of a huge beast, the existence of which had long been rumoured. THAT LOCH NESS 'MONSTER'! STURGEON, EEL OR UPTURNED BOAT? read the headlines,[45] and whatever it was, it was the sensation of the season. A Grand Aquatic Gala at the public baths in Nairn was advertised as having 'Humorous Events, including First Appearance of the Loch Ness Monster',[46] and the Ness District Fishery Board ensured newspaper coverage of the angling industry by solemnly proclaiming that they might have to 'take steps' to protect the plentiful supplies of salmon from the monster.[47]

There was further excitement in 1936 when a farmer on the Isle of Man discovered a talking mongoose living behind a panelled wall in his farmhouse. The animal, who was named Gef, claimed to have been born in Delhi in 1852 and to be able to speak a number of languages, including English, Welsh, Flemish, Arabic, Hebrew and Hindustani. It required a certain leap of faith to believe in the mongoose, however, or in his linguistic abilities, since no one outside the farmer's family ever saw Gef. Hair samples were produced, but they turned out to have come from the family sheepdog. Nonetheless, the story attracted several psychic investigators, including Harry Price and Richard S. Lambert (founding editor of the *Listener* magazine), who co-wrote a book on the phenomenon.

There was, in short, much credulity, gullibility and downright delusion in these years, along with a self-conscious awareness that it was all a bit silly. When the Duchess of York had her second child, Margaret, in 1930, the *Sunday Express* marked the occasion by getting the astrologer R. H. Naylor to cast her horoscope, which was published only semi-seriously: the princess would have an 'eventful life', he suggested, offering few hostages to fortune.[48] By the end of the year, Naylor had a weekly column – the first in any newspaper – telling readers what the stars said about their future, and popularising the idea of sun signs. For those who wished to delve deeper into such arcane matters, there was a thriving circuit of psychics and fortune-tellers, the likes of Madame Honri of Birkenhead in Cheshire, who advertised tarot-card readings by post, and Madame Mary Stanley-Shute of Mevagissey in Cornwall, who charged five shillings for a Ouija board reading.[49]

Such things became part of the cultural texture. The mystery of the tarot, for example, was familiar from the pages of fiction, including Helen Simpson's *Cups, Wands and Swords* (1927), Charles Williams's *The Greater Trumps* (1932)* and David Magarshack's *Death Cuts a Caper* (1935). The latter was a detective novel, and crime stories in particular had a deep fondness for the quasi-fantastic paraphernalia of table-turning and the like, from Agatha Christie's *The Sittaford Mystery* (1931) to Graham Greene's

---

* Charles Williams's earlier novel *War in Heaven* (1930) had seen the Holy Grail surface in a country church.

Brighton Rock (1938). It wasn't always taken seriously, though. 'I can't approve of this modern craze for the supernatural,' says Aunt Lilian in Georgette Heyer's *Footsteps in the Dark* (1932). 'I once spent a whole hour with a Ouija board, and the only thing it wrote was M about a hundred times, and then something that looked like Mother's Marmalade.'

If all else failed, there was still primitive superstition to fall back on, tales of ancient evil loosed into the world. The excavation in 1923 of the tomb of the Egyptian pharaoh Tutankhamun, sealed for over 3,000 years, was led by British archaeologist Howard Carter, and funded by the 5th Earl of Carnarvon. When the latter died of blood poisoning, reportedly after a mosquito bite, there was much dark talk of a curse. Novelist Marie Corelli said it had been dangerous to enter the tomb, and Arthur Conan Doyle was inclined to agree: 'An evil elemental may have caused Lord Carnarvon's fatal illness.'[50] Elsewhere, the idea was pooh-poohed. 'With all the gods of the underworld at his disposal,' mocked the *Belfast Telegraph*, 'is it credible that Tutankhamen would employ a mosquito to poison an enemy?'[51]

There were similar, if smaller, stories at home. In 1936 the East Grinstead Cottage Hospital moved to new premises in the Sussex town, renaming itself the Queen Victoria Hospital. 'We had a very wet day for the opening,' commented Captain Joseph Price, hospital secretary, 'and that very day Miss Garnett, the matron, was taken ill. Since then two patients have died.'[52] It didn't seem much of a run of bad luck, given that this was a hospital and that Garnett recovered. Nonetheless, the story spread that there was a curse, and blame was directed to a sculpture of the Rod of Asclepius, a serpent-entwined staff, which had been installed on the outside of the new building: clearly, this was a snake of ill omen. As *Truth* drily observed, 'the victory of science over superstition is by no means complete'.[53] There were calls for the piece to be taken down, but Price explained that the hospital had debts of £3,000 and couldn't afford the £63 removal cost. So the sculpture remained in place, and the curse was soon forgotten. 'I don't think anyone fears the serpent,' reassured Garnett, a year later. 'Most of the patients get better.'[54]

iv

'God as an all-wise Providence was dead,' wrote the poet Robert Graves in 1940, looking back on these years; 'blind Chance succeeded to the throne.'[55] If faith was floundering and fragmenting, it might have been expected that people would turn to technology and to science in the search for meaning. But there was little comfort here. Technological advances brought much that was good, yet the same ingenuity had recently introduced the world to machine guns, poison gas, submarines and tanks. In the light of such developments, it was hard to pin one's faith on progress.

As for science, the frontiers were being pushed so far and so fast that they were scarcely visible to the naked eye. Back in 1912 Gustav Dalén had won the Nobel Prize in Physics for inventing a new kind of lamp for use in lighthouses. Ten years later, the award went to theoretical physicist Niels Bohr in recognition of his work on the structure of the atom – no doubt it was all very important, but it was not so readily understood by the layperson. 'This Einstein theory,' bemoans a woman in Aldous Huxley's novel *Crome Yellow* (1921); 'it makes me so worried about my horoscopes.'

Psychology, the newly fashionable branch of medicine, did at least diagnose and treat the mental impact of mechanised warfare. Shellshock – or 'war neurosis', as a 1922 War Office committee of enquiry said it should be called[56] – was now a recognised condition that required psychoanalysis and psychotherapy. Even for those who were well but struggling to cope with the stress of modern life, help was forthcoming. French psychologist Émile Coué published *Self-Mastery through Conscious Auto-Suggestion* (1922) and spoke at venues from the Royal Albert Hall to Eton College to propound the virtues of his system. 'Every day, in every way, I'm getting better and better,' was his mantra, and it was heard widely as 'the vogue for auto-suggestion' swept through society.[57]

One could restructure one's thinking, just as one could restructure one's posture by using the celebrated Technique of the Australian F. Matthias Alexander.

Yet there was also a darker side to this growing scientific interest in the mind, seen in the new approaches for treating more serious ailments such as schizophrenia. 'So far,' said Dr P. K. McCowan, physician superintendent of the Crichton Royal Institution in Dumfries, as he presented his report for 1938, 'we have only used convulsive therapy, but I propose introducing insulin therapy in the coming year.'[58] Convulsion therapy was rooted in the belief that since schizophrenia and epilepsy were never found in the same person, it might be that inducing epileptic-type seizures could cure the schizophrenic patient.* Insulin therapy required doses of the recently discovered hormone to be injected, sending the patient into a coma, followed by large quantities of glucose to bring them back, a process that was repeated daily over a period of weeks and sometimes months. Neither technique proved effective, but there was hope on the horizon: doctors in Europe and America were pioneering psychosurgery, cutting connections in the brain in an operation known as a lobotomy.

With so much to be scared of in modernity, there came a redis-covery of pre-science, pre-Christian myths and legends. A public appeal raised money for the land around Stonehenge to be bought, with the National Trust taking over responsibility for the mon-ument. New excavations challenged existing assumptions about the ancient nature of the stones, wrote R. H. Cunnington in his book *Stonehenge and Its Date* (1935),[59] arguing that they had been erected as recently as the fourth or fifth century BC. It was a shame to lose 'the far distant and mysterious Stone Age', he admitted, but 'it may be some compensation to feel that it was a people of our own blood who built it'.† The renewed attention inspired Susan

---

* It turned out to be untrue that epilepsy and schizophrenia were mutually exclusive.
† Stonehenge is now generally accepted to date to at least 2400 BC, and possibly earlier.

Spain-Dunk's symphonic poem *Stonehenge* (1929), an impressively murky and mystical orchestral piece intended to evoke the raising of the stones ('a gloomy work', said the *Daily News*).[60] When the Shell petrol company commissioned posters to encourage drivers to 'See Britain First on Shell' in 1931, American-born artist Edward McKnight Kauffer contributed a depiction of Stonehenge. It was now a fixed part of the tourist map of the country.

Forty miles to the west, John Cowper Powys's novel *A Glastonbury Romance* (1933) told of a place sacred to Joseph of Arimathea, to King Arthur, Merlin and the Druids, to 'the religion of the people who lived *before* the Ancient Britons; perhaps even before the Neolithic Men'. Glastonbury here embodies the pagan and Christian soul of England, attracting cranks, obsessives and monomaniacs, from mystics to anarchists and communists. At the centre of it all is John Geard, who becomes mayor of the town and sets about constructing a new religious cult, worshipping the Holy Grail.

The Old Straight Track (1925) was also concerned with prehistoric Britons. Seventy-year-old amateur archaeologist Alfred Watkins had discovered that churches, ancient mounds, standing stones, beacons, barrows, hill notches and other sites could be connected via a network of straight lines: ley lines, as he called them. These, he argued, were the human trackways and trade routes of prehistory, dating back to 25,000 BC, when Britain was still covered by forests.*

Children's literature embraced English legends with Geoffrey Trease's *Bows Against the Barons* (1934), which recast Robin Hood as a radical left-wing hero, and T. H. White's *The Sword in the Stone* (1938), telling of the magical childhood of King Arthur. More elevated culture addressed the same material in Laurence Binyon's *King Arthur* (1923), a verse drama with music by Edward Elgar. Composer Rutland Boughton, the self-taught son of an Aylesbury

---

* In a later, even more credulous, age, ley lines were discovered to be an expression of the spiritual energy of the earth and/or navigational aids for UFOs.

grocer, helped found the Glastonbury Festival in 1914, where a piano version of his opera *The Immortal Hour* was first heard. It was in 1922, however, in a production at the Regent Theatre in King's Cross that the work took off, running for 212 consecutive performances – a world record for a serious opera – with revivals following in 1923 (another 160 performances), 1926 and 1932. Adapted from an 1899 verse play by Fiona Macleod, it was rooted in Celtic mythology: immortal, god-like fairies co-existed with humanity in what the critics[61] called 'a dream-world peopled with curious phantoms, animated by elusive motives, perplexed by strange problems'.*

Some even tried to bring these traditions into the modern world. Inspired by Arthurian mythology, Frederick Thomas Glasscock founded the Fellowship of the Knights of the Round Table in Tintagel, Cornwall in 1927, to encourage chivalry and good works. Six years later, he opened King Arthur's Hall, newly built to house the Order, in a ceremony of great solemnity. 'To the strains of *Tannhäuser* the robed knights escorted the white-clad founder to a granite throne,' intoned the press.[62] It was a long way from Glasscock's previous life as a businessman, making custards and jellies with Monkhouse & Glasscock of Bermondsey, south London.†

And somewhere in the midst of it all, trying to make sense of the strangeness in the world, was Charles Fort, an American para-scientist who specialised in collecting stories and data about unexplained phenomena, from ghosts and vampires to the mystery of the *Mary Celeste* and showers of frogs falling from the sky. He admitted that a good deal of what he wrote about might seem preposterous, before asserting that science was, in any case,

---

* Boughton was also in the midst of writing a five-opera Arthurian cycle that started with *The Birth of Arthur* (1909) and ended with *Avalon* (1945). None of these was performed in his lifetime.

† John Monkhouse, the Methodist co-founder of the firm, was the grandfather of comedian Bob Monkhouse.

only 'established preposterousness'.[63] He spent much of the 1920s in London, scouring the darkest recesses of the British Museum archives for new material, until he emerged, stumbling into the light, clutching his masterpiece *Lo!* (1931). Outlining his theories of teleportation (a word of his own coining) and cosmology (the Earth is stationary), it was, wrote one reviewer, 'an astonishing book', though 'what it is all about is quite beyond me'.[64]

v

At the Monmouth Assizes in June 1921, a jury of seven men and five women found Harold Jones, a fifteen-year-old shop-boy from Abertillery, not guilty of the sexual assault and murder of an eight-year-old girl. The verdict was greeted with jubilation by crowds outside the courthouse, and there were more celebrations when he returned home to streets that were 'gaily decorated with bunting'.[65] A fund was set up, headed by local councillors, to pay Jones's legal bills. No one believed that this popular boy, a miner's son who played the organ in chapel, could have committed such crimes. He'd carried himself well in court, impressed onlookers with his calm maturity, and, said his employer, there'd be a promotion for him if he returned to work. While on remand, he told the press, he had read *Oliver Twist*.

Seventeen days later, he murdered an eleven-year-old girl. This time he pleaded guilty, and also confessed to the first killing. Too young to hang, he was sentenced to detention at His Majesty's pleasure.* His father, who was allowed to see him before he was taken to jail, was asked how the boy was bearing up. 'Champion,' he replied. 'I cannot understand it at all.'[66] Nor could anyone else. What would cause a child to do such evil things? Was the prosecution right to suggest that 'some sort of perverted lust played a part'? Jones's own explanation of his actions was simpler: he had 'a desire to kill'.[67]

---

* Jones served twenty years, and died in 1971.

The same questions were asked in 1924. What possessed fourteen-year-old servant girl Violet Shaw of Gleason, Lancashire to entice the seven-year-old Florence Whittaker into a cornfield and slit her throat with a razor bought for that purpose? Shaw had no history of crime, and the doctor who examined her said she wasn't insane, though she was disturbed. 'Mentally, she was below normal, unstable and very emotional, and at certain times excitable and uncontrollable.' She was apparently depressed following the death of a favourite dog, had become interested in a recent murder case in Langney, East Sussex and – during her time on remand – twice attempted suicide. Fortunately, Florence survived the attack, though she was terribly scarred, and Shaw was ordered to be detained for four years. 'It was a daft thing to do,' she admitted. 'I wish I had not done it.'[68]

Harold Jones and Violet Shaw were highly unusual, of course, extreme cases, but there was no doubt that their generation – those who were under the age of majority at the time of the Armistice – was adversely affected by the war. The most obvious impact was in the number of fatherless children: the 1921 census recorded the words 'Father dead' next to nearly three quarters of a million of those aged fourteen and under, and there were many more who were now in their late teens.

There was a wider sense of disturbance as well. It could be seen in the number of suicides among the under-twenty-fives; the rate rose by 60 per cent in the ten years from 1921. And in rising criminality: according to government figures, serious crime stood at 2,700 offences per million of the population before the war, remaining thereabouts until 1921 when it began to go up, reaching 3,700 per million in 1930. Much of this increase was driven by those born around the turn of the century, the likes of James Murphy, twenty-four, a ship's fireman, and Arthur Ray, twenty-three, salesman, who were each given four years' penal servitude for the armed robbery of a newsagent in 1924.[69] Murphy also received twenty strokes with the cat o' nine tails, since he'd been carrying the revolver. In sentencing, Sir Ernest Wild, Recorder at the Old Bailey, said that 'there was a spirit of lawlessness about in young men nowadays'.*

'We represent a lost generation, neither pre-war nor post-war,' argued the writer Ethel Mannin, born in 1900. 'We had been adolescent children when it began, and now we were young adults, but there had always been a war.'[70] When the *Daily News* ran an article in 1927 that was critical of the younger generation, the paper was deluged with responses. Some reflected the familiar impatience of youth. 'The middle-aged and elderly cling grimly to the seats of the mighty, and youth cannot get a look in,' insisted Paul, a correspondent from Cambridge. 'It is sheer lack of opportunity that makes us careless, selfish and flippant.' Others thought that they'd been shaped by their wartime childhood. 'This is probably the most independent and self-reliant (if somewhat opinionated) youth there has ever been,' one young woman said; they'd grown up in 'a scrimmage between mother's war work and father's leaves, and they had more or less to fish for themselves'. For Betty in Chelmsford, it looked bleak: 'This is an age of disillusion and we are all the children of disillusion.'[71]

If there was any hope to be found, it lay surely with the youngest in the land, the post-war generation, crowned by those 1.3 million babies born in 1920. Here was the possibility of renewal, and perhaps of a rediscovery of innocence in a battle-scarred world. And to articulate this rebirth of a nation came a wave of children's literature that looked back to better times.

Hugh Lofting served in the Irish Guards until he was invalided out in 1918 with a shrapnel wound. He'd been an engineer in civilian life, and only turned to fiction because there was nothing else to say when writing home from the trenches. 'The news was either

---

* A less noted feature of the time was the decline in numbers of female prisoners. In the first two decades of the century, women had accounted for around 15 per cent of the prison population; by the 1930s, that had fallen to 6 per cent. The reduction was such that Hull closed its female section, leaving just six jails in England and Wales that held women.

too horrible or too dull,' he shrugged. 'And it was all censored.' So he started making up stories for his two young children. Struck by the horses, mules and dogs that were part of the war effort, and by the lack of medical care they received, he created a doctor who could talk with animals, illustrating his letters with drawings.[72] By the end of the war, he later explained, he'd become 'definitely anti-militarist' and saw his character as a chance to preach peace to the next generation.[73] *The Story of Doctor Doolittle* was published in 1920 to great success, followed by a further nine volumes; by 1927 it was being said that 'Dr Doolittle has established himself in popular favour as strongly as Peter Pan.'[74]

The story was set a century in the past, in a village named Puddleby-on-the-Marsh, where the local doctor learns how to speak to animals, and opens his practice to non-human patients. He has money problems (African monkeys call the world of white people 'the Land Where You Pay to Eat'), but there are compensations, for this is a world drenched in pastoral Englishness. 'Old yellow bricks, crumbling with age in a garden-wall,' sniffs a dog, picking up the various smells of the village; 'the sweet breath of young cows standing in a mountain-stream; the lead roof of a dove-cote – or perhaps a granary – with the midday sun on it.'

That same year, 1920, saw the first appearance in the pages of the *Daily Express* of Rupert Bear, resident of Nutwood, another idyllic village. Thereafter came a host of enduring characters in children's fiction: *Just William* by Richmal Compton (1922); *The Midnight Folk* by John Masefield (1927); *Tarka the Otter* by Henry Williamson (1927); *Milly-Molly-Mandy Stories* by Joyce Lankester Brisley (1928); *The Squirrel, The Hare and the Little Grey Rabbit* by Margaret Tempest (1929); *Swallows and Amazons* by Arthur Ransome (1930); Biggles in *The Camels Are Coming* by W. E. Johns (1932); *The Incredible Adventures of Professor Branestawm* by Norman Hunter (1933); *Mary Poppins* by P. L. Travers (1934); *Worzel Gummidge* by Barbara Euphan Todd (1936); *The Hobbit* by J. R. R. Tolkein (1937). There was also *Child Whispers* (1922), a book of poetry for children from a school mistress named Enid

Blyton who would become particularly prolific; she averaged six books a year in the 1930s. And Dundee publisher D. C. Thomson revolutionised British comics with the launch of the *Dandy* (1937) – featuring Desperate Dan and Korky the Cat – and then the *Beano* (1938), with Lord Snooty and His Pals and Pansy Potter the Strong Man's Daughter.*

Chief among all of these, the universally acknowledged boy-leader of the new generation, was the fictional incarnation of the real-life Christopher Robin Milne. One of the multitude born in 1920, Milne was an only child, much attached to his toy animals. 'The hours he spent with them were golden ones,' said his mother, Daphne, 'stimulating his imagination and engaging his interests.'[75] Those hours were subsequently shared with the nation, documented by his father in two books of poems – *When We Were Very Young* (1924), *Now We Are Six* (1927) – and two of short stories: *Winnie-the-Pooh* (1926) and *The House at Pooh Corner* (1928).

Like Hugh Lofting, A. A. Milne had served in the trenches and had come to loathe war. The world he created in the Pooh books was an English Eden – complete with rain and snow, and honey still for tea – evoking that which had been lost. He 'permits grown-ups to glimpse this forgotten world again', said the critics, 'and to discover that deep within them is something which is eternally young'.[76] That forgotten world glowed even more golden in the wake of the Great War. 'Milne is our Lewis Carroll,' said the *Illustrated London News*;[77] perhaps he was, but his appeal was very different. Carroll's mid-Victorian tales of Alice are witty, intellectual excursions to a dreamland, a place where logic and language dissolve into absurdity, and authority is undermined. The Pooh books have none of that brittle brilliance; they're warm, reassuring, safe. There is wisdom here rather than cleverness.

It's a world so perfect that it can never change – which ultimately means that we shall have to leave it behind, because Christopher

---

* The rhyme in Pansy Potter the Strong Man's Daughter depended on a Dundee accent.

Robin himself is growing up. The beautifully elegiac final scene in *The House at Pooh Corner* sees him saying goodbye to Pooh and to the glorious days of doing Nothing; it's the best thing in the world to do, he explains, but when you get older, 'They don't let you.' He has to leave Hundred Acre Wood, sent away to school, to the outside world, where there are 'People called Kings and Queens and something called Factors, and a place called Europe'. It didn't sound as though any good would come of it.

vi

If there was a political symbol of the country withdrawing into its shell, it came with the response to a proposed tunnel under the English Channel, linking Britain to France. This wasn't a new idea. There had been talk of it way back in 1751, and Napoleon had got as far as preliminary borings in 1802 before abandoning the idea. Seventy years after that, an agreement was struck between the French and British governments, and a start was made. Then concerns over defence were expressed, prompting Britain to pull out. In the thirty years before 1914, there were thirteen attempts in Parliament to get the tunnel restarted, all opposed by the government of the day.

When the suggestion resurfaced in 1919, however, the cabinet was more receptive. There was 'a prejudice in favour of the construction of a tunnel', said Lloyd George, 'largely due to the atmosphere resulting from the war'.[78] It was now seen as a way to help rebuild the European economy after all the destruction. It would be beneficial to trade and tourism, and although it would be a major expense – the cost was estimated at around £30 million, with an annual profit of £2.5 million – it was the kind of infrastructure project that would provide employment for demobilised soldiers.

But the old doubts swiftly resurfaced. France might have been Britain's ally in the recent conflict, but that hadn't always been the case. Lord Curzon, the foreign secretary, said that his opposition to the scheme came from observing 'the instability of the

Continental outlook, and remembering the teachings of history'.[79] A Foreign Office memo spelled it out more directly: 'Our relations with France never have been, are not, and probably never will be, sufficiently stable and friendly to justify the construction of a Channel Tunnel.'[80] By 1920 the political will had melted away and the plans were shelved once more.*

Instead, the grand project of the time turned out to be much more parochial, situated in Wembley, a pleasant if unremarkable suburb in north-west London where, in April 1923, the FA Cup final was staged in a newly built stadium. The structure itself was regarded as something of a wonder. It resembled the Colosseum in Rome, said the press, except that it was bigger, and the papers revelled in the scale of the enterprise: it had a capacity of 127,000 – mostly standing, though there were 35,000 seats – with prices ranging from two shillings on the terraces up to a guinea for the most expensive seats. A banqueting hall, big enough for 'an indoor football ground, so immense are the dimensions of everything connected with this building', could seat 1,000 people, and for the day of the final, the various refreshment stands had laid in 120,000 bottles of beer, 500 gallons each of tea and coffee and 200,000 sandwiches. At least 120 trains would bring fans to London, and more than 300 police would be on duty.[81]

These latter were soon called into action. Crowds arrived in far larger numbers than had been anticipated and somewhere near double the supposed capacity got inside the stadium, with tens of thousands more outside. The police patiently cleared the pitch of spectators, so that the match might proceed, allowing Bolton

---

* Also perhaps reflecting British withdrawal from Europe, it was striking how many novels opened onboard a ship, preferably a cross-Channel ferry, bringing travellers back home to Britain: *The Big Four* by Agatha Christie (1927); *Mystery Mile* by Margery Allingham (1930); *Vile Bodies* by Evelyn Waugh (1930); *Let's Pretend* by Eleanor Rochester (1935). There's a variation on the theme in Bruce Graeme's *The Return of Blackshirt* (1927), which starts with the arrival in Calais of our honeymooning hero and his bride; after a terrible train crash, she is (apparently) burned to death on her wedding-day.

Wanderers, appearing in their third final, to win the tournament for the first time, beating debutants West Ham 2–0.* In the slightly murky film of the police operation, the nation's eyes were drawn to a white horse, ridden by PC George Scorey, who had served as a boy trumpeter in the Boer War and had fought right through the Great War. The White Horse Final was how it would later be remembered, though at the time it wasn't seen quite so positively. PANDEMONIUM AT WEMBLEY, read the headlines. THE CUP-TIE FIASCO.[82]

There were to be more cup finals – the Football Association had signed a twenty-one-year deal – and the stadium became primarily associated with football. It was constructed, however, to be the centrepiece of the 1924 Empire Exhibition. This was the biggest exhibition Britain had ever staged, a vast, sprawling network of streets, filled with pavilions and amusement parks and dance halls. The stadium was used to host a rodeo show, staged by American showman Tex Austin and British theatre impresario Charles B. Cochran. Unfortunately a steer had its leg broken in one of the performances and had to be shot; cruelty charges were brought against the promoters and the cowboy involved, and, although they were acquitted, it did rather take the gloss off the attraction.

Less controversially, there was a coal mine, complete with pit ponies, and the new steam locomotive the *Flying Scotsman*, pride of the London and North Eastern Railway. There was also the marvel of Queen Mary's dolls' house, designed by Edwin Lutyens, architect of the Cenotaph. It was fully equipped with electricity, running water and working lifts, and contained thousands of objects, both artistic and domestic, including a library of 200

---

* The first goal was scored by David Jack, who'd signed from Plymouth Argyle in 1920 for a world-record fee of £3,500. In 1928 he set a new record, the first five-figure transfer fee, when moving to Arsenal, where he won the FA Cup again, as well as three league titles, and became the first player to score 100 top-flight goals for each of two clubs.

miniature volumes, handwritten by some of the biggest names in British literature from Rudyard Kipling to Aldous Huxley.*

The Canadian pavilion had the best exhibit of all: a life-size effigy of the Prince of Wales and his horse, carved in butter. The intention was that when the exhibition ended, the model would be broken down and sold off in pots each weighing one pound. 'The model will make 3,500 pots,' boasted an official, 'so that the Prince of Wales will be in everybody's mouth.'[83] Regrettably, it turned out that sculpting-butter contained preservatives that made it inedible, and instead it was sold off to a railway company as wagon grease. When the exhibition returned for a second season the following year, Canada sent an even bigger statue: this time, three tons of butter were used to depict the prince in 'headdress and robes as Chief Morning Star of the Stoney Indians'.[84] Not to be outdone, the Australians contributed their own butter sculpture, though theirs was less reverential: a cricketing scene, with England's best batsman Jack Hobbs at the crease, having just been bowled out.

The Empire Exhibition cost £4.5 million to stage and made a loss of £1.5 million. But there were 27 million visits and it did what it was supposed to do: it cheered people up. This was a society traumatised by war, unsure where to turn, flirting with fringe faiths, doubting the old ways and the old conventions, yet yearning after them. The population was split by age into mutually distrustful groups: on the one side, those who had been too old to serve, on the other, those who had been too young, and between them a decimated generation of scarred men. For a while, Wembley brought people together, and the fun helped them forget.

It also reaffirmed the country's commitment to the imperial family. This wasn't a show for the world, as the Great Exhibition of 1851 had been. Rather, it was, wrote the American journalist Karl K. Kitchen, 'distinctly a British affair, and its appeal is only to the Britisher'.[85] That was the point. 'We have suffered much and

---

* George Bernard Shaw and Virginia Woolf were among those who declined the invitation to contribute.

suffered long since August 1914,' concluded writer Sarah A. Tooley. 'But the Empire lives. That is the great uplift of the Exhibition. It has been our family Thanksgiving for preservation and a reminder of our Imperial possessions.'[86]

2

REBELLIONS AND REASSURANCE

'There is a mighty Tory revival in sight, and it will want
leading. The newly enfranchised classes, especially the
women, will bring it about. The suffragists didn't know what
a tremendous force of conservatism they were releasing
when they won the vote for their sex.'

John Buchan, The Three Hostages, 1924[1]

It's the same the whole world over,
It's the poor what gets the blame,
It's the rich what gets the pleasure,
Isn't it a blooming shame?

Billy Bennett, 'She Was Poor But She Was Honest', 1930[2]

Stanley Baldwin, three-time prime minister

THE FIRST PERSON TO SING 'TILL THE BOYS COME HOME' was Sybil Vane ('the charming Welsh soprano'[3]) at the Alhambra Theatre in Leicester Square, London. It was an immediate success, the audience demanding nine encores before she was allowed to leave the stage. This was the autumn of 1914 and the song became the first new hit of the war, the simple hymn-like melody making a star of its twenty-one-year-old composer Ivor Novello. It was also he who had suggested to his lyricist, expatriate American Lena Guilbert Ford,* the opening line of the chorus, by which the piece became famous: 'Keep the Home Fires Burning'. The most popular song of the 1916 pantomime season, it stirred the hearts of many thousands of audiences in Britain and beyond. For pure drama, however, few performances could equal the one played on a pillaged piano to accompany the burning down of Luton Town Hall on Peace Day in July 1919.

The intention of Peace Day was to celebrate winning the war, which was now officially over. After months of negotiations between the victor nations, the terms of a settlement had been agreed: Germany would be obliged to accept responsibility for starting the conflict, and would be punished by losing territory and colonies, by disarming, and by paying reparations to its enemies. Threatened with an Allied invasion if it refused to accept these conditions, a reluctant Germany signed the Treaty of Versailles on 28 June 1919.

The agreement was not universally welcomed. Economist John Maynard Keynes, part of the British delegation, believed that the level of reparations was too high, and that it would harm the global economy as well as Germany. South African Jan Smuts was similarly disapproving, while French socialist Jean Longuet (Karl Marx's grandson) warned that it 'would sow the seeds of future

---

* Lena Ford did not survive the war, killed in a Zeppelin raid on London in March 1918.

wars'.[4] The American Senate refused to ratify the treaty at all. And in Germany, there was a good deal of anger. A grammar-school teacher in Essen was reported to have denounced 'the outrage and dishonour of Versailles' to his pupils: 'For us there can only be hatred, and from that hatred shall be born German daybreak and German freedom.'[5]

Among the British people, though, the treaty was popular. On the day of the signing, crowds gathered outside Buckingham Palace, and the king spoke from the balcony. 'So ends the greatest war in history,' he said. 'I join you in thanking God.'[6] These sentiments were not, in the public mind, incompatible with the belief that if Germany felt humiliated, it was no more than the 'brutish Boche' deserved.[7] That attitude was so widespread it even turned up in an advert for gramophones, sold by Frost's store on King Street in Great Yarmouth: 'The dirty beastly Hun, who well deserves his fate', should be made to 'pay, pay, pay'.[8]

So when the Peace Day victory parade was staged three weeks after Versailles, the six-mile route through the streets of London was packed. The crowds were reckoned to be bigger than those for the king's coronation, bigger even than for Queen Victoria's Diamond Jubilee in 1897, up to half a mile deep in places. It took over four hours for the parade to pass, with contingents from every part of the Empire, together with all its allies, from Belgium to Siam, led by the great generals: the American J. J. Pershing, Ferdinand Foch from France, and – getting the biggest cheers – Britain's own Douglas Haig.

Away from the formal events, there was an overspill into Hyde Park, where many of those who'd been lining the route ended up. There was a heavy rainstorm in the late afternoon, and queues at the refreshment tents stretched for up to a mile, but spirits were high and the mood was jubilant. 'This seems finer still,' said the *Manchester Guardian*, 'this gathering together of our people, this utterly mutual celebration of a great achievement.'[9] There was a concert in the park that evening, with a specially assembled 10,000-strong Imperial Choir of Peace, accompanied by the massed bands of the

Brigade of Guards, and there was a firework display. 'Rockets went up with the shock of heavy artillery, and high in the air exploded into great bursts of stars, with a roar like rapid musketry fire.'[10] The partying went on till three in the morning.

There were parades and events in towns and cities across the country. Amid the rejoicing, however, there was the occasional note of opposition. The majority of servicemen had now been demobilised, and many had returned home to find themselves out of work and with inadequate pensions. In Manchester, unemployed ex-soldiers, medal ribbons on their chests, marched with dignity, carrying banners that read: 'Honour the dead, remember the living.'[11] In Glasgow a similar demonstration was accompanied by women and children with placards: 'General's widow £25,000; Tommy's widow 13s 9d.'[12] (The reference was to the widow of Lieutenant-General Sir Stanley Maude; when he died of cholera in Iraq in 1917, she was awarded that sum in compensation for her loss.)

That night, and over subsequent days, the dissent broke out into violence and clashes with the police. There were disturbances that shaded into riots in several places, primarily in the Midlands – Bilston, Coventry, Leicester – but elsewhere too, in Swindon and Londonderry. In the latter incident, the Watt's Distillery was attacked and whiskey was liberally distributed. 'The whole district was in a state of terror, dozens of men roaming Bogside streets,' it was reported. 'Several children under sixteen were rolling drunk on the footpaths.'[13]

The worst of the troubles came in Luton in Bedfordshire, where ex-servicemen had requested the use of the park for a memorial service and been refused permission by the council. The anger boiled over as the mayor tried to deliver a Peace Day address from the steps of the Town Hall. His words were drowned out by booing and heckling from a crowd that then invaded the building and started smashing up the furniture and windows, before setting the place alight. When the fire brigade arrived, their vehicles were commandeered and their hoses cut. There was damage estimated at £250,000, a hundred people were injured in a truncheon charge by police, and the army had to be sent in to pacify the town. The riot was aided by strategic looting: a garage was raided for petrol to pour on the flames; a chemist for glass bottles to throw at the police; and a music shop for the piano on which 'Keep the Home Fires Burning' was played, to ironic cheers.

The war was over, the enemy had been made to pay, but there was, acknowledged the press, 'a sense of grievance and injustice'. The celebration of peace was seen by many as 'an affront and an offence', as a 'hollow mockery' of the suffering of ex-servicemen.[14] These were not encouraging signs.

ii

In *To Let* (1921), the third and final novel of John Galsworthy's Forsyte Saga, the solicitor Soames Forsyte, a relic of Victorian Britain, has given up the tall hat he used to wear and taken to a more humble Homburg. This was a different world now, he reflects, and his old upper-middle-class ways were no longer appropriate. 'It was no use attracting attention to wealth in days like these.'

His fears were a little exaggerated, but not unfounded. Wealth inequality reduced dramatically during the war and then fell still further. By 1940 the top tenth of society still enjoyed 34 per cent of the nation's income while the bottom half took just 20.5 per cent, but that gap of 13.5 points had narrowed considerably from the 42 points it had been at the start of the century.[15] Economically, the working classes were taking a larger slice of the national cake.

Politically, too. The general election of December 1918 marked a new era, the first under the recently passed Representation of the People Act, introducing universal male suffrage at the age of twenty-one, and votes for women at thirty. This was the biggest change to the franchise Britain had ever seen. At the last general election, in December 1910, the registered electorate had comprised 7.7 million men, just over a quarter of the adult population; eight years on, more than 21 million were on the rolls, 40 per cent of them women. A very low turnout meant that the number of ballots cast didn't increase in such dramatic fashion, but this was unmistakably a different electoral landscape.*

The expansion of the franchise saw the political system strain at the seams, as three national parties tried to fit into a voting method that could comfortably accommodate just two. Actually, it was more complicated than that. In 1916, a rebellion within the wartime coalition had seen H. H. Asquith forced out as prime minister. He remained as Liberal leader, however, and most of the party stayed loyal to him, despite a strong faction that owed allegiance to his successor in Downing Street, David Lloyd George, now the Liberal head of a new coalition dominated by Conservatives. Come the general election, Asquith's Liberals and Lloyd George's coalition Liberals fielded rival candidates.

The Labour Party, which had been a junior member of the coalition, withdrew from government at the end of the war, but a handful of ministers opted to stay where they were, and four were re-elected as coalition Labour candidates. Among them was George Barnes, who beat the official Labour candidate in Glasgow Gorbals, and was promptly expelled from the party he had once led.† Also elected were ten MPs from the National Democratic and Labour Party, a pro-coalition group on the Left, which subsequently dissolved into Lloyd George's Liberals.

Only the Conservatives presented a united front to the electorate, the largest partner in a coalition that proposed to continue into peacetime, in the interests of national rebuilding. And it was the Tories who did best in the 1918 election, winning 379 seats, enough to form a majority government on their own had they so wished. But the coalition continued, as promised, with Lloyd

---

* The 1918 Act also introduced a couple of war-related special classes: servicemen could vote at the age of nineteen, rather than twenty-one, while conscientious objectors were barred from voting for five years.
† The defeated candidate, John Maclean, later left Labour to help form the Communist Labour Party in 1920 and then the Scottish Workers' Republican Party in 1923.

George's own authority enhanced: his group trounced Asquith's Liberals, taking 127 seats to their 36, and he remained prime minister.* Between them, the coalition parties won over half the vote, and emerged with 520 MPs. Facing them were just 114 opposition members. (It would have been more, had Sinn Féin MPs not boycotted Parliament.)

The landslide vote of confidence meant the task of rebuilding the country could begin. During the election campaign, Lloyd George had promised that 'the laddies who fought and won' would come back to 'homes fit for heroes' in 'an ordered land of active, energetic, scientific, organised progress'.[16] The aspirations were great. 'No such opportunity has ever been given to a nation before,' the prime minister told the Reconstruction Committee, as it began its work; 'not even by the French Revolution.'[17] Regrettably, the results did not match the rhetoric.

With the ending of the wartime economy, the scale of the state was reduced somewhat. The coal and rail industries, brought under government control during the conflict, were restored to private hands. But there was no return to the pre-war order. In 1914 the top rate of income tax had been 1s 2d in the pound (just under 6 per cent); in 1918 the standard rate was 5s in the pound (25 per cent), and government finances became ever more dependent on the revenue – by the end of the Parliament, direct taxation accounted for half of the state's income, compared to a third pre-war. Other taxes also increased, most notably death duties. From 1919 there was a 40 per cent inheritance charge on estates valued at over £2 million, which contributed to a very substantial transfer of land ownership; millions of acres were sold, large estates broken up, and the shift from landed aristocracy to new money – evident since the turn of the century – was accelerated.

The money was needed to pay the wartime debts, but there were also additional calls on the public purse, as the government

---

* Asquith, who had been prime minister just two years earlier, lost his seat, subsequently returning to the Commons in a by-election.

picked up the thread of Liberal social reforms that had been lost at the outbreak of hostilities. The Education Act of 1918 raised the school-leaving age to fourteen and precipitated an extensive programme of building new schools and a doubling of teachers' pay. Old-age pensions were increased by nearly 80 per cent, and the Unemployment Insurance Act of 1920 introduced the dole, providing fifteen weeks' financial cover for those put out of work.

These were achievements that built on the pension and National Insurance schemes introduced by Asquith and Lloyd George, back when they had been cabinet colleagues. The real significance now was that the measures were being enacted by a Conservative-dominated government. The Tory response to the new times, to the enlarged electorate, was quietly to adopt much of the Liberals' approach to social policy, accepting that the state had a role to play in smoothing the rougher edges of capitalism. 'Every future government must be socialistic, in the sense in which our grandfathers used the word,' reflected Conservative cabinet minister Stanley Baldwin. 'Personally I don't know what socialism means, but I do know that if the Tory Party is to exist we must have a vital, democratic creed, and must be prepared to tackle the evils, social and economic, of our over-populated, over-industrialised country.'[18] The existence of the coalition enabled the Conservatives to ease into this readjustment under cover of Lloyd George.

Meanwhile, savings were made elsewhere. In 1919 the government adopted a policy, advocated by War Secretary Winston Churchill of the Liberal Party, that became known as the Ten Year Rule: the military budget would henceforth be based on the assumption that there would be no major war in the next decade.

Parallel to the expansion of the franchise, the trade union movement was growing rapidly; by 1921, membership stood at 8.3 million, more than double its pre-war peak, threatening – as the real-life equivalents of Soames Forsyte saw it – further upheaval and perhaps even revolution. The leaders of the unions, however, were less militant than their enemies feared and many of their activists desired. They tended to see their role as being to protect their own members, rather than to combine with others against capitalism. There had been a move towards solidarity when the three most powerful unions – representing rail, coal mining and transport – came together in 1914 in what was termed the Triple Alliance, but still they shied away from political confrontation.

When the Triple Alliance threatened joint strike action in 1919, the leaders met Lloyd George, and he called their bluff. 'We are at your mercy,' he admitted. If they struck, the elected government would be defeated. Had they, however, considered the consequences that would follow? 'If a force arises in the state which is stronger than the state itself,' he pointed out, 'then it must be ready to take on the functions of the state, or withdraw and accept the authority of the state.' How far were they prepared to go? They had no answer to his challenge. 'We were beaten and we knew we were,' reflected Robert Smillie of the Miners' Federation.[19]

When the economy took a serious downturn in 1921 – 'one of the worst years of depression since the Industrial Revolution', said the *Economist*[20] – the Triple Alliance was again activated, this time in support of the miners, who were threatened with wage cuts. A date was announced for the start of simultaneous strikes, only for the other unions to back out at the last minute, leaving the miners to face defeat alone. Militant trade unionists raged against this 'betrayal' by 'the Cripple Alliance',[21] but it was clear that the will to coordinate action, to confront the government, simply wasn't there.

The mining industry was hit hard by the recession, and even with the cut in pay, owners struggled to operate profitably. Coal exports had fallen to a third of their 1913 level, and although that did improve, there was never to be a return to pre-war prosperity. Production contracted, wages were squeezed, jobs were lost. The cotton industry suffered in much the same way, production in 1921 barely half that of 1913. These were long-term trends, as Britain struggled to adjust to the emergence of international rivals; Polish coal and Japanese cotton were making major inroads into markets once dominated by the British. Even when the economy recovered a little in the mid-1920s, coal exports were still a fifth down on pre-war levels, steel and cotton down a quarter and a third respectively.

Under these pressures, a geographical divide opened up, one that would continue to widen. Unemployment was concentrated in heavy industry – around a third of workers in shipbuilding, steel and engineering were out of work in 1921 – and many northern towns and cities built on manufacturing were hit hard. So was Wales, with its reliance on mining; according to the 1921 census, a third of the male workforce was employed in mines and quarries. The economy in London, on the other hand, was growing, and new industries were increasingly attracted to the south. Shipbuilding slumped in the 1920s, for example, using only around a fifth of capacity, so that in Hartlepool, County Durham, six out of ten were unemployed in 1921. But the manufacture of aircraft and cars was growing rapidly, and there were jobs to be had with the Bristol Aeroplane Company and with Morris Motors in Cowley, Oxfordshire.

Outside the declining industries, most of those who were in work saw an improvement in their living standards in the post-war years, particularly at the lower end of the income scale; even allowing for inflation, building labourers and railway porters earned a quarter more in 1920 than they had pre-war. This was a pattern that was to become familiar: the co-existence of relative comfort and misery.

iii

Despite the economic problems, Britain emerged from the war with its international status enhanced, while its European rivals were diminished. France was severely damaged, Russia had descended into revolution and civil war, and the Austro-Hungarian, German and Ottoman Empires had all ceased to exist. As part of the settlement at Versailles, Britain gained control of new territories in Africa and the Middle East, while the Dominions of Australia,

New Zealand and South Africa grew with the additions of New Guinea, Western Samoa and South West Africa respectively. The Empire was now at its greatest-ever extent, covering 24 per cent of the land on earth, the king-emperor reigning over a similar proportion of the global population, more than 450 million people.

Yet there was nervousness. The spectre of Russian communism stalked Europe, and many feared that war-weakened Britain might not be immune to the Bolshevik contagion. Uneasy glances were thrown towards those outside the established political system. In May 1919 Winston Churchill warned that there were groups who wished 'to provoke an outbreak in the form of a mutiny or general strike, or preferably both together, in the hope that a general smash and overthrow of society may result'. Such people, he said, sought to forge links between soldiers, ex-servicemen and workers, 'to weld them altogether, to rouse them altogether, to make a general overthrow on the Russian model'.[22] That anxiety was felt acutely in the first years of peace.

The Peace Day disturbances in Luton and elsewhere were part of a wider pattern of disorder in 1919. At the beginning of the year, a strike in Glasgow, calling for the working week to be reduced to forty hours, attracted national attention when a public rally descended into fighting between the police and twenty thousand or so demonstrators. The Battle of George Square, it was called, but it was the sequel that really mattered. Detecting the whiff of insurrection in the air, the Sheriff of Lanarkshire called in military assistance, and the following day tanks appeared on the streets, snipers on roofs. By the time the troops were deployed, the crowd had long since dispersed; there were no confrontations between soldiers and strikers, but the army continued to occupy the city for two weeks, by which time the dispute was over. Several of the strike leaders were also arrested.

The sheriff's response was an overreaction. Manny Shinwell, local secretary of the British Seafarers' Union, was found guilty of incitement to riot and jailed for five months, but he insisted that there had never been any revolutionary intent, just a simple attempt 'to draw attention to the need for shortening the hours of labour in order to absorb the unemployed'.[23] But this was precisely the mistake, argued William Gallacher of the Clyde Workers' Committee, who was also jailed; the strikers should have encouraged troops to join the action: 'We were carrying on a strike when we ought to have been making a revolution.'[24]

Tensions stemming from unemployment took a different form in areas where there was a substantial black population. During the war, there had been a rise in immigration from the Caribbean colonies, with workers filling the jobs left by military recruitment, and their numbers were then augmented by demobilised soldiers and sailors from the West Indies, mostly grouped in ports. In June 1919 an altercation in Cardiff between two groups, one white, the other black, escalated into rioting that left two dead, fifteen hospitalised with bullet and knife wounds, and several houses destroyed by fire. Several more nights of unrest followed. 'Why should these coloured men be able to get work when it is refused to us?' demanded one white resident, though his assessment was inaccurate; far from taking jobs, there were around 1,200 unemployed black men in the city.[25] There were further race riots elsewhere that year, mostly targeting the homes and businesses of black and Chinese people, in Barry, Glasgow, London, Newport and South Shields. 'Racial riots in Liverpool are stated to be of almost hourly occurrence,' exaggerated the press.[26]

It was Liverpool too, where a police strike during the August bank holiday weekend of 1919 provoked a wave of rioting and plundering so extensive that it became known as the Loot. Troops were sent in, a battleship arrived in the docks, and *The Times* was horrified: 'London Road is the Ypres of Liverpool.'[27] Elsewhere, a riot that June in Epsom, Surrey saw hundreds of Canadian soldiers, still not repatriated, attack the local police station; one police officer, Sergeant Thomas Green, was killed.

British ex-servicemen were at the heart of much of the dissent, as seen in May 1919 when the National Federation of Discharged Sailors and Soldiers demonstrated in Hyde Park against unemployment and then attempted to march on Parliament, only to be stopped by the police with batons and horses. The fighting wasn't sustained or particularly serious on this occasion, but it did prove potentially significant: the suppression of the protest convinced some that there was no future in seeking accommodation within the existing system.

The result was the creation of the National Union of Ex-Service Men (NUX), a radical organisation which, as its general secretary Ernest Mander explained, 'stood for the abolition of existing conditions of wage slavery and capitalist exploitation'. It sought 'the establishment of a social system which should no longer be based upon privileges of property, but upon plain and simple rights of common people'.[28] Unlike other veterans' groups, the NUX was avowedly political, allying itself to the Labour Party and to the trade unions. As another of its founders pointed out, there were six million ex-servicemen in the country, and 'if they got together with organised labour there was no government in power, or ever likely to be, who could stop their demands'.[29] The NUX had nowhere near those numbers, but at its peak in 1920 it claimed a membership of 300,000, and that was sufficient to scare some in authority, raising the prospect of the Labour movement acquiring its own workers' militias. These were, after all, men who had only recently been trained in the use of firearms. Indeed, many of them still possessed weapons, the demobilisation process having been far from tidy.

The Labour Party welcomed the affiliation of local NUX branches, since 'the general interests of the ex-service man are identical with those of his fellow-workers'.[30] The union's policy positions, however, were not always in tune with the party leadership. In addition to better pensions and backdated pay for ex-soldiers, the NUX called for the nationalisation of land; it stood against Britain's military involvement in the Russian civil war; and it opposed militarism in all its forms, including the Boy Scouts. It also supported the Irish independence struggle, and that was the most controversial element of all at a time when the long-running saga of Britain's relationship with Ireland was entering a pivotal phase.

Before the war, the Irish Parliamentary Party (IPP) had been the third largest grouping in Westminster, and had supported the Government of Ireland Act, which received royal assent in September 1914, providing for a devolved parliament to sit in Dublin. This was the first Home Rule legislation to be passed, and the determined opposition it faced – complete with dire and believable talk of civil war – meant it was a very limited settlement: powers were only partially devolved and, in deference to the wishes of Protestant communities in the industrial north-east of Ireland, six counties in Ulster were to be 'temporarily' excluded from the process. Further, implementation of the act was to be deferred until the end of hostilities in Europe.

The plan was never realised, because the political mood was transformed during the course of the war. The suppression of the 1916 Easter Rising in Dublin – a bid at armed revolution by nationalists – together with an attempt to introduce conscription in Ireland in April 1918, turned public opinion against the government and against the pre-war agreement.* A string of by-elections in 1917–18 saw six seats fall to Sinn Féin, a party that rejected the compromise of Home Rule and instead demanded full independence. In the 1918 general election the IPP was reduced to just seven MPs, while Sinn Féin took seventy-three constituencies on a manifesto that promised to use 'any and every means available' to establish an independent Irish republic.†

Having secured this mandate, Sinn Féin refused to take its seats

---

* Opposition to conscription ensured that it was not introduced in Ireland and, although 200,000 Irishmen served in uniform, the level of volunteering outside Ulster was far below that in the rest of the United Kingdom.

† Among the Sinn Féin victors was Countess Markievicz, the first woman elected to Parliament. The general election also saw sixteen unsuccessful female candidates, with the highest vote among them being the 8,600 cast for Christabel Pankhurst of the Women's Party, running a close second to Labour in Smethwick, Staffordshire.

in Westminster and instead convened its own parliament, the Dáil Éireann, in Dublin, which unilaterally declared independence in January 1919. Courts, police, tax-collectors were established in a parallel state, and the Irish Republican Army (IRA) was formed, starting a guerilla campaign of attacks on the vestiges of UK rule. The coalition responded by declaring Sinn Féin illegal, and by reinforcing the Royal Irish Constabulary with English recruits: the Special Emergency Gendarmerie, as Winston Churchill named them; the Black and Tans, as everyone else knew them.

Thus began the Irish War of Independence. The IRA was small but had wide public support, and by the spring of 1920 the *Irish Times* was reporting that 'the King's government has virtually ceased to exist south of the Boyne and west of the Shannon'.[31] Much of Ireland effectively became ungovernable, and more than two thousand lives were lost in the conflict before a ceasefire was agreed in July 1921. That December the Anglo-Irish Treaty formally brought the war to an end, paving the way for the creation of the Irish Free State, still part of the Empire, still under the Crown, but in every other respect an independent nation. The six Ulster counties, however, would not join the new country, remaining in the now shrunken United Kingdom of Great Britain and Northern Ireland.

The partition of Ireland was pragmatic as well as democratic: the strength of Protestant feeling in Ulster was so intense that any attempt to impose a united Ireland under Dublin would have resulted in a bloodbath. As it was, the proposal split the independence forces, and upwards of another two thousand lives were lost in the ten-month Irish Civil War, fought between those who supported the treaty – thereby accepting partition – and those who were opposed, the latter now adopting the name of the IRA. The pro-treaty forces were victorious, and the Irish Free State was founded in 1922, extending to just the twenty-six counties.

There was no such dispute in what remained of the UK. The Ulster Unionists, who took forty of the fifty-two seats in the newly formed Parliament of Northern Ireland, objected vociferously to having been excluded from the negotiations, but the treaty was ratified with huge majorities in both Houses in Westminster. 'No agreement ever arrived at between two peoples has been received with so enthusiastic and so universal a welcome,' trumpeted David Lloyd George.[32]

That was overstating the case, but there was at least a general feeling of relief at a solution that allowed Britain to withdraw without too much humiliation, that preserved the status of Ulster, and that ended a dispute which had periodically disrupted the peace of the nation for centuries. There was no economic loss as a result of Irish independence – the south was much poorer than the north – and the resolution of the issue allowed the government to focus on growing nationalist movements in India and Egypt, which posed far greater threats to the Empire. Further, there had been public disquiet over British troops fighting in Ireland at a time of supposed peace, and uneasiness over accounts of brutality: nearly 300 members of the British forces were dismissed for misconduct. So there was almost universal approval in Britain for a treaty whose defining characteristic, said Labour leader Arthur Henderson, was 'that it means peace. That is a consideration beyond measure.'[33] The Conservative Party, once so hostile to Home Rule, tended to agree, an early indication that Tories would now opt for a quiet life over ideological conflict.

The war in Ireland, the ramifications of the Russian Revolution, the fear of insurrectionary mobs, race riots, recession, a rise in strikes – these first years of peace bubbled with discontent. Which was why the growing militancy of ex-servicemen, most notably the NUX, was taken seriously. One response to the situation was the passing of the Firearms Act of 1920, which removed the old legal freedom to bear arms, as enshrined in the 1688 Bill of Rights; henceforth, ownership of a gun required a licence issued by a chief constable. A longer-term solution was the founding of the British Legion, which Douglas Haig, its creator, intended as a way of depoliticising veterans' grievances. Some of the groups absorbed into the Legion 'were Bolshevist in intention', Haig said later. 'They had machine-guns, arms and munitions.' As he saw it, 'the Legion saved this country from bloodshed during the critical years after the Armistice', by ensuring that 'the Bolshevist organisations were broken up'.[34]

The British Legion offered an alternative path to political and cultural influence, using its connections to lobby for ex-servicemen in the corridors of power, and launching the poppy as a fundraiser and symbol of 'remembrance and reverence to the many thousands of our heroes who rest beneath this flower in Flanders fields'.[35] Just as important were the social clubs that were formed across the country, which became a bulwark of consensus, an embodiment of conservative values. The organisation, said Lieutenant-Colonel R. W. Lees, chairman of the 14,000-strong Southampton branch, was 'democratic, non-sectarian, not affiliated or connected directly or indirectly with any political party'; it was, however, based on 'loyalty to the Crown, community, state and nation'.[36]

The launch of the Legion spelled the end for the NUX. The union sent delegates to the 1920 meeting that approved the creation of the new body, but they abstained in the final vote and never participated. They were rapidly marginalised, and in November that year Ernest Mander recommended that members focus their activities within political parties. By 1922 the NUX had ceased to exist. Though Haig's fear of bloodshed was probably exaggerated, nothing had been certain in 1919. But the storm had passed, and henceforth the waters would be calmer.

iv

Stanley Baldwin was no one's idea of an assassin. His father, Alfred, had been an iron and steel manufacturer in Bewdley, Worcestershire, and, as a Conservative MP, had represented the town in Parliament (as had his cousin, Enoch Baldwin, before him, though he'd been a Liberal). Stanley followed a predestined path: after Harrow and Cambridge, he worked in the family business and then inherited the parliamentary seat, elected unopposed when his father died in 1908. He became a minister in the wartime coalition, and in 1921 he joined the cabinet.

His image was one of studied normality. He 'cultivated the character of an amateur in politics', said *The Times*.[37] He noted that 'politicians have always been despised for hypocrisy and dishonesty',[38] and distanced himself as much as possible. 'I had many ambitions as a child', he would say. 'One was to be a blacksmith.'[39] Alternatively, he'd claim that his aspirations were simply to 'read, live decently and keep pigs'.[40] The adoption of this homely, pastoral image was a bold choice for someone who'd been a senior manager in a manufacturing firm with 4,000 employees, but he carried it off. He took care to dress carelessly. 'Mr Baldwin is unfortunate with his raiment', fretted the editor of the *Tailor and Cutter*. 'No matter how well fitted out, his clothes are doomed so soon as he wears them.'[41] And he was studiously non-intellectual. When asked which political thinker had most influenced him, he cited the Whig historian Henry Maine. 'Rousseau argued that all human progress was from contract to status', he explained, 'but Maine made it clear once and for all that the real movement was from status to contract.' Then he paused, apparently confused. 'Or was it the other way round?'[42]

'I am not a clever man', he told the Conservative conference in 1923. 'I know nothing of political tactics.'[43] This was disingenuous. Lloyd George later said Baldwin was 'the most formidable antagonist whom I ever encountered'.[44] And Lloyd George knew, for it was he that Baldwin assassinated.

By 1922 the coalition was fraying. An election was due shortly, and a decision had to be made as to whether the Conservatives and Lloyd George's Liberals should enter it together, as they had last time, or as rivals. Some Tories saw the alliance as a proven vote-winner, but there were others who resented the presence of Liberals in cabinet – hindering their prospects of promotion – and the policy initiatives that had resulted. Having survived the first test of the new franchise in the 1918 election, these latter argued, it was time for the Conservative Party to go it alone.

There was also concern over Lloyd George selling honours to

raise money for party funds. This was not illegal at the time and was by no means a new development, but it had never been practised so widely nor quite so openly. The prime minister had appointed an agent, a failed actor named Maundy Gregory, who approached potential recipients directly. 'There are only five knighthoods left for the June list,' he would urge; the time to buy was now.[45] As a broad rule, a knighthood came in at around £10,000, a baronetcy at £30,000, a peerage at £50,000. Exciting new products were also available, with the creation in 1917 of the Order of the British Empire. ('The Order of the Bad Egg,' said Labour MP William Anderson; 'Our Bloody Enemy,' according to his colleague, James C. Welsh.[46]) Some of those honoured were less than suitable: Sir John Drughorn, for example, bought a baronetcy even though he'd been convicted in 1915 of trading with the enemy, while Sir Rowland Hodge was similarly honoured despite his conviction for wartime food-hoarding.

Little of this made the newspapers, largely because the press barons of the day didn't wish to draw attention to the matter, but it was an open secret nonetheless. In P. G. Wodehouse's story 'Comrade Bingo' in *The Inimitable Jeeves* (1922), the recently ennobled Lord Bittlesham cuts off his nephew's allowance, and the impoverished young man understands the need to reduce expenditure. 'That peerage cost the old devil the deuce of a sum,' he reflects. 'Even baronetcies have gone up frightfully nowadays, I'm told.' Two months after that tale was published, the story broke and the Commons debated the issue. Lloyd George was at his brass-necked best; the system of selling honours, he said, 'should never have existed. If it does exist, it ought to be terminated.'[47] And in due course, the Honours (Prevention of Abuses) Act of 1925 made the selling of titles illegal.*

The prime minister survived the scandal, but it was another

---

* Only one person was ever to be convicted under the legislation. Maundy Gregory was still trying to ply his trade in 1933, when he was caught and sentenced to two months in jail.

item to be added to the charge sheet. His actions were resented by the Conservatives as immoral, but also because they brought the honours – and possibly themselves – into disrepute. There was further irritation that much of the money raised was being syphoned off to fund Lloyd George's Liberals.

In October 1922 a meeting of Tory MPs was held in the Carlton Club to resolve the question of the coalition. The party's leader, Austen Chamberlain, spoke in favour of continuing the arrangement, as did the last Conservative prime minister, Arthur Balfour, but the party's previous leader, Andrew Bonar Law, was against. So, most significantly, was Baldwin, who quietly identified the problem at the core of the coalition: Lloyd George himself. 'He is a dynamic force,' said Baldwin, unsheathing his assassin's dagger. 'A dynamic force is a very terrible thing; it may crush you but it is not necessarily right.' And he pointed out, reasonably enough, that Lloyd George had already 'smashed to pieces' the Liberal Party and might yet do the same to the Tories.[48]

Baldwin himself was never to be described as 'a dynamic force', but his understated passion was devastatingly effective. The proposal put to the meeting, that the Conservatives should contest the next general election as an independent party, was approved by 185 votes to 88. Chamberlain resigned as leader, replaced by the returning Bonar Law; the coalition was dissolved, and a general election called for the following month.

Bonar Law's campaign in November 1922 was characterised by precisely the opposite of Lloyd George's dynamism. His election address promised 'tranquillity and stability both at home and abroad', and the nation responded by giving him a substantial majority in a reduced Commons (with the loss of Ireland, the number of MPs had been cut from 707 to 615). The most impressive performance was that of Labour, increasing its share by nine percentage points from the last election, with a net gain of eighty-five seats, to become the main opposition. Lloyd George and Asquith had not reconciled, and both their parties suffered accordingly at the polls.

There was something of a changing of the guard. The leading coalition Liberals were out – including Lloyd George and Winston Churchill – and so were some of those Tories who had wished to maintain the coalition, most notably Austen Chamberlain and Lord Birkenhead, the former lord chancellor. Baldwin reaped his reward, appointed chancellor of the exchequer. Above all, it was the first Conservative government to be elected since 1900.

It was not, though, a government of any consequence. In May 1923 Bonar Law was diagnosed with terminal cancer and resigned as prime minister. He died in October. His successor, appointed by the king after taking advice from senior figures in the party, was Stanley Baldwin, a man even more committed to tranquillity and stability. 'I am myself of that somewhat flabby nature that always prefers agreement to disagreement,' he told the House,[49] and indeed, when he wasn't destroying Lloyd George's career, he was a very conciliatory man.

The foreign secretary, the patrician Lord Curzon, believed that the job should have been his, and was said to have wept on discovering that, of all people, he had lost out to Baldwin. 'Not even a public figure,' he sobbed, 'a man of no experience and of the utmost insignificance, of the utmost insignificance.'[50]

v

The Communist Party of Great Britain (CPGB) was formed in 1920 by the merger of several small Marxist groups, most notably the British Socialist Party, formerly the Social Democratic Federation. 'It is not a new split,' marvelled the *Daily Herald*, as it welcomed the initiative. 'It is indeed a fusion.'[51] This was a rare thing on the Left, but it didn't end the traditional factionalism: that summer also saw the launches of the Communist Party (British Section of the Third International) and of the Communist Labour Party. All the above were condemned by the long-established Socialist Labour Party as bourgeois reformists. Despite rival claims, however, the CPGB was the real deal, backed with money from Moscow, and the recipient of fraternal greetings from Vladimir Lenin himself.*

The party even had an MP, in the unlikely shape of Colonel Cecil L'Estrange Malone. He'd been elected to the Essex seat of Leyton East in 1918 as a coalition Liberal, but a visit to Russia in 1919 so impressed him that he converted to communism, joining the British Socialist Party and then the CPGB. 'I was one of those people who were fooled into fighting the war to make the world safe for democracy,' he explained. 'I now see that it was fought to make the world safe for the imperialists, oil-kings and stockjobbers.'[52] Some comrades doubted his revolutionary commitment, but he talked a good fight. 'What are a few Churchills or Curzons on lampposts compared with the massacre of thousands of Indians at Amritsar?' he asked a 'Hands Off Russia' rally at the Royal Albert Hall in 1920.† 'What are a few Churchills or Curzons against the wall compared with the bombing of harmless Egyptians in Egypt or reprisals in Ireland?'[53] Those words were enough to get him prosecuted for sedition and sentenced to six months in jail. 'I shall propagate Communism fearless of consequences,' he defiantly declared from the dock,[54] but his resolution was not to last. He left Parliament in 1922, reappearing as the Labour MP for Northampton in 1928.

Even with Colonel Malone in its ranks, the CPGB was not a substantial organisation, with a fluctuating membership that probably didn't reach much more than 5,000 at any stage in the first half of the 1920s.[55] Nonetheless, in these febrile times, the party's very existence caused conservative newspapers around the country to issue dire warnings about the threat posed by communism: 'the

---

* The CP (BSTI) and the CLP later saw the error of their ways and dissolved themselves into the CPGB. The SLP, which had split from the SDF in 1903, survived as an independent group until 1980.
† In April 1919 a peaceful, pro-independence gathering in the Punjabi city of Amritsar had been fired upon by troops of the British Indian Army, killing around a thousand people.

agents and sympathisers of Lenin and Trotsky in this country are seeking to organise the unemployed into a striking force for the red revolution', the consequence of which would be 'the forcible establishment of Bolshevist minority tyranny'.[56] The American president, Theodore Roosevelt, had recently popularised the political use of the phrase 'lunatic fringe' (originally coined in the 1870s to describe a New York fashion for a hairstyle), and it crept increasingly into the coverage of communism. The *Scotsman* was not alone in warning about 'seditionists and those of "the lunatic fringe" of the community who are out for purely subversive work, and who are clever enough to seize every possible pretext for fanning class war'.[57] In Lloyd George's definition, the lunatic fringe comprised those who are 'always crying for the moon and will take nothing terrestrial in its place'.[58]

At the meeting that launched the CPGB, delegates voted in favour of affiliating to the Labour Party (this 'may cause a split',[59] warned the *Workers' Dreadnaught*),* but the enthusiasm was not reciprocated; Labour's 1922 conference rejected the application to affiliate by 3.86 million votes to 0.26 million. Nonetheless, there were many on the Right who believed that the two parties were as one, at least in spirit, and that the CPGB tail might be wagging the Labour dog.

This idea became commonplace in the popular fiction of the time. In Agatha Christie's thriller *The Secret Adversary* (1922), a senior figure in the secret service spells out the threat to the nation. 'A Labour government at this juncture would, in my opinion, be a grave disability for British trade, but that is a mere nothing to the *real* danger.' Because the country is being undermined. 'Bolshevist gold is pouring into this country for the specific purpose of procuring a Revolution,' with decent working-class folk being cynically exploited by political subversives. There are 'subtle, insistent forces at work, urging the memories of old wrongs, deprecating the

---

* A newspaper launched by Sylvia Pankhurst in 1914 that at this stage was the official voice of the Communist Party (British Section of the Third International).

weakness of half-and-half measures, fomenting misunderstandings'.

The Secret Adversary was very much in the mould set by Sapper's *Bulldog Drummond* (1920).* Here the eponymous hero is a simple fellow, boisterous and full of back-slapping bonhomie, a man of action, not thought. 'Of brain he apparently possessed a minimum: of muscle he possessed about five ordinary men's share.' Drummond had been a law unto himself in the trenches, roaming no man's land alone at night, seeking out Germans whom he would kill with his bare hands. He won the MC and DSO, but never made it beyond the rank of captain. After the war, struggling with the mundane reality of civilian life, he puts an advert in the paper, looking for excitement – hence the novel's subtitle: *The Adventures of a Demobilized Officer Who Found Peace Dull.* In his adventures, he finds the thrills he needs, leaping from one implausible scenario to another: an encounter with an acid bath, a deadly tarantula, a hooded python, even a gorilla loose in a country garden in Godalming. (He kills the latter with his bare hands, just like he used to kill those Germans.) The book was a tremendous success. Within a couple of months of publication, Drummond was on the London stage, played by Gerald du Maurier, and on his way to becoming the most popular thriller character of the age, with a long sequence of novels and even more movies.[†]

In the second book in the series, *The Black Gang* (1922), Drummond and his cronies take on far-left types who are 'secretly engaged in red-hot Communist work', manipulating the working class. 'Ever since the war you poisonous reptiles have been at work stirring up internal trouble in this country,' Drummond says to a fellow-travelling Labour MP. 'Not one in ten of you believe what you preach: your driving force is money and your own advancement.'

---

* Sapper was the penname of Herman McNeile who joined the army in 1907 and retired in the rank of major in 1919.

† Sapper wrote a total of ten Bulldog Drummond books, and there were seventeen movies, both British and American, in the 1920s and 30s with the character played by Jack Buchanan, Ronald Colman, Ray Milland and Ralph Richardson among others.

Drummond's justice is uncompromising: he inflicts such severe mental torture on the MP that the man is driven insane. Other enemies of society get shot, stabbed to death or flogged, sometimes with a cat o' nine tails, sometimes a rhinoceros-hide whip. Others still get abducted and taken to a remote island in Scotland, where the gang have established a secret labour camp.

If this treatment of left-wingers seemed a little strong, there was the alternative course of gentle mockery. John Buchan's *Huntingtower* (1922) features an earnest young poet with a slim volume titled *Whorls* to his name (he wanted to call it *Drains*, but even publishers of slim volumes have some standards). He has served in the war and wishes to build a new society on the ruins. 'We've got to finish the destruction before we can build,' he urges. 'It is the same with literature and religion, and society and politics. At them with the axe, say I.' His sympathies lie with the Bolsheviks. 'They are doing a great work in their own fashion. We needn't imitate all their methods – they're a trifle crude and have too many Jews among them – but they've got hold of the right end of the stick.'

Similarly, Dorothy L. Sayers presented in *Clouds of Witness* (1926) the Soviet Club in London, a place 'full of Russians and sucking Socialists taking themselves seriously', where the men don't even wear evening dress, 'only Soviet jumpers and side-whiskers'. The amateur detective Lord Peter Wimsey is taken there by a friend of his sister, 'a cheerful young woman with bobbed red hair, dressed in a short checked skirt, brilliant jumper, corduroy jacket, and a rakish green velvet tam-o'-shanter'. These were the outfits of radical young bohemians.

Again there's the assumption that there is common cause between all those on the Left; the club is to be graced by the presence of the Labour leader, Mr Coke, who 'is going to make a speech about converting the Army and Navy to communism'. And again there is the association of communism and modernist high culture. 'Joyce has freed us from the superstition of syntax,' argues one of the gathered socialists, and another asks: 'Have you heard

Robert Snoates recite his own verse to the tom-tom and the penny whistle?'

vi

The policy question that caused greatest controversy in these years was that of tariff reform. In the straitened economic circumstances of the early 1920s, many in the Conservative Party believed that Britain should turn away from free trade and adopt a protectionist approach, imposing tariffs on imports in an attempt to boost domestic industry, while making allowance for goods to pass freely within the Empire. This had been a divisive issue in the party since the days of Joseph Chamberlain (Austen's father) twenty years earlier, and had never been resolved. Tariff reformers were in a minority in Parliament, but they were persistent and hard to ignore.

In the 1922 election campaign, Bonar Law sought to silence disagreement by promising that tariffs would not be introduced without a further election. When Stanley Baldwin was appointed prime minister the following year and became persuaded of the need for reform, he felt duty-bound to honour this pledge. So he called a general election for December 1923, campaigning on a commitment 'to impose duties on imported manufactured goods'.

Another election coming so soon after the last was not the 'tranquillity and stability' that the government had promised. Nor was tariff reform a popular cause, with its threat of higher food prices and a return to the Corn Laws, which still loomed large in folk memory. (In actual memory, too: one of the proposers of the Liberal candidate in Melton, Leicestershire was 100-year-old George Cart, who remembered those days without affection.) Not for the first time, a noisy Tory faction found itself out of step with the country.

The outcome was a hung Parliament. The Conservatives were reduced from 344 MPs to just 258, while the Liberals, with Asquith and Lloyd George having patched up their differences in the interests of defending free trade, won 158 seats. Between them came the Labour Party. Baldwin's obvious course of action was to form a coalition with the Liberals, but having turfed Lloyd George out of office once, he had no intention of inviting him back in. Anyway, his strategic goal was to realign the parties, with Labour replacing the Liberals. So the Tories proposed to continue in office as a minority administration, effectively inviting a challenge from the opposition. And in January 1924 Labour responded by tabling a motion of no confidence.

It was supported by the Liberals, even though the outcome could only be the first-ever Labour government, a prospect that terrified many. Asquith said he'd been deluged with fearful letters, but he put them down to 'an epidemic of political hysteria'. Would Labour really destroy Britain? Could it? He reminded the Commons of Adam Smith's remark 150 years earlier: 'There is a great deal of ruin in a nation.'[60] Thus, Baldwin was brought down and replaced by Ramsay MacDonald, the fourth premier in twenty-seven months.

MacDonald, the illegitimate son of a housemaid and a farm labourer, was the great hero of the Left. A serious thinker and gifted public speaker, he'd been one of the founders of the Labour Party back in 1900, had been elected to Parliament in 1906, and become leader in 1911. He'd had to stand down on the outbreak of war – he opposed Britain's involvement, while the party did not – and lost his seat, largely on that issue, in 1918. But he returned to the House and to the party leadership in November 1922, and within fourteen months, much to his own surprise, found himself prime minister. 'When our time comes we shall be ready,' he'd told the press, as the general election result became clear, but he hadn't meant *this* time.[61] Labour had achieved barely 30 per cent of the vote in the election and had just 191 MPs; it was far from ready.

The composition of the cabinet reflected the party's weak position in Parliament. The longstanding figures were present – William Adamson, J. R. Clynes, Arthur Henderson, Fred Jowett, Philip Snowden and J. H. Thomas had all been Labour MPs before the war – but a number of senior figures had come in from other parties. The lord chancellor was Lord Haldane, who, as a Liberal, had held the same post in Asquith's government. He was joined by Lord Parmoor, first elected as a Unionist MP in 1895 and subsequently given a peerage by the Liberals, and by Lord Chelmsford, formerly the Viceroy of India. There was also Charles Trevelyan, Noel Buxton and Josiah Wedgwood, all first elected as Liberals. As Manny Shinwell, veteran of the Battle of George Square and now secretary for mines, reflected: 'In effect, the cabinet consisted of a coalition.'[62] There was a lot of coalition, as well as splintering, in these years, as the parties – and the country – adjusted to the new electoral conditions.*

MacDonald was 'in office but not in power', wrote Herbert Thomas, editor of the *Cornishman*.[63] Consequently, this was not a radical government. A small package of public works was announced to reduce unemployment, but when strikes continued – in the docks and on the trams – the government threatened to use the Emergency Powers Act, just as its Conservative predecessor had. The one significant piece of legislation was the Housing Act of 1924, introduced by health minister John Wheatley, which increased government subsidies to local authorities for new-build council housing; during the ten years that the act was in force, around half a million homes were built.

The conduct of government would have been even more difficult if Baldwin, as leader of the opposition, had fought hard, but he did not; he wanted to encourage Labour, for he was still seeking realignment at the expense of the Liberal Party. Ramsay MacDonald noted who he could work with. 'The Liberals get meaner and meaner,' he wrote in his diary in March 1924, 'and we respect the Conservatives more and more.'[64] Even so, such a small

---

* Below cabinet rank, there were also ministerial appointments for others who'd once been Liberal MPs, including Sydney Arnold, Fred Hall and Arthur Ponsonby, a former page to Queen Victoria. George Bernard Shaw was offered a peerage and a government job, but refused.

administration was fundamentally unstable, clearly not destined to last. And, as so often in such circumstances, the end was triggered by a trivial matter that played to an existing narrative, in this case those allegations of backstage Bolshevism.

In July 1924, an article in the CPGB newspaper *Workers Weekly* called on servicemen to turn from war to class war. 'Refuse to shoot down your fellow workers! Refuse to fight for profits!' it urged. 'Turn your weapons upon your oppressors!'[65] The editor, J. R. Campbell, was charged with incitement to mutiny, and a number of left-wing Labour MPs were outraged, seeing this as an example of Ramsay MacDonald's hostility towards communism and the Soviet Union. When the charges against Campbell were subsequently dropped, there were further complaints, this time from Conservatives and Liberals, who believed that – to the contrary – it showed Labour's sympathy for communism and the Soviet Union. Tory MP William Joynson-Hicks denounced 'a government which at the dictation of a Communist party has joined hands with the most blood-stained tyrants of modern history'.[66]

The Commons resolved to appoint a select committee to investigate the affair, and MacDonald took this as a vote of no confidence in his government. 'I shall have no more of it,' he declared. 'I shall resign.'[67] And so he did. Parliament was dissolved in October 1924 and, for the third year in a row, a general election was called.

During the 1923 campaign, there had been charges of a lack of patriotism. 'The British Labour Party, as it impudently calls itself, is not British at all,' scorned a *Daily Mail* leader column.[68] That had been in reference to the formation of the Labour and Socialist International (LSI), a loose grouping of left-wing parties from various countries, with Labour's Arthur Henderson and Harry Gosling elected onto the executive committee of the new movement. There was no indication that the *Mail*'s attack had made any difference, though, and in 1924 the paper went in harder.

It was towards the end of the campaign that the *Mail* revealed a letter supposedly sent to the CPGB by Grigori Zinoviev, Russian head of the Communist International, instructing it 'to stir up the masses of the British proletariat'. The Labour Party was not part of the Communist International – indeed, its intention with the LSI was to create a rival organisation to the Soviet-dominated Comintern – but, as the Campbell case had shown, the relationship with Russia was a sore point. 'Moscow issues orders to the British Communists,' claimed the *Mail*, 'the British Communists in turn give orders to the Socialist government, which it tamely and humbly obeys.'[69] It was hardly a fair description of a cabinet pieced together with such an eye to respectability, but the suspicion that there was some kind of Bolshevik influence was well established by now.*

Again, there was no discernible impact on MacDonald's party itself, which increased its share of the vote, but the fear of communism was seen in the big swing from Liberal to Conservative, consolidating the anti-Labour bloc. As a result, Labour's number of MPs fell, while the Liberals were almost wiped out. Asquith again lost his seat, this time taking an earldom, which left Lloyd George as the de facto leader of the handful of remaining Liberal MPs. And Stanley Baldwin, with a massive 209-seat majority, returned in triumph as prime minister, sufficiently secure that he could afford to bring some coalitionists back into the fold: Austen Chamberlain, Lord Birkenhead, even Winston Churchill, the former Tory who'd defected to the Liberals twenty years earlier and who now defected back again.

The first Labour government had lasted just over nine months. By any conventional measure, its achievements had been negligible, yet the experience had brought what D. D. Sheehan (formerly an Irish Party MP, now Labour) called 'the sobering influence induced by the acceptance of power and responsibility'.[70] Ramsay MacDonald professed himself pleased with what he and his colleagues had achieved. 'They have shown the country that they have the capacity to govern in an equal degree with the other parties,'

---

* The Zinoviev letter later turned out to be a forgery, though the identity of the forger – probably an anti-Bolshevik Russian – remains unresolved.

he told the king. They had 'done much to dispel the fantastic and extravagant belief which at one time found expression that they were nothing but a band of irresponsible revolutionaries intent on wreckage and destruction'. And they had acted in the interests of the nation, demonstrating that 'patriotism is not a monopoly of any single class or party'.[71]

The rise of Labour also encouraged the reshaping of Tory thinking. Speaking at a victory rally in the Royal Albert Hall, Baldwin referred to his predecessor Benjamin Disraeli's claim that there were 'two nations' in Britain – 'the rich and the poor' – and declared his ambition to heal the division. 'We stand for the union of those two nations,' he said: 'union among our own people to make one nation of our own people at home which, if secured, nothing else matters in the world.'[72] This one-nation Conservatism was a recognition of the new political landscape.

Or as a major landowner in Oxfordshire said: 'Well, we have been through a revolution, and our throats are still intact.'[73]

3

SOUND AND VISION

I care not what the experts may say, I say it is flying in the
face of experience, it is making nonsense of the very word
'education' to suggest that boys and girls can regularly
witness films that depict glorified prostitution, drunkenness
and adultery; films that often, indeed, are only a veiled form
of pornography.

Reverend H. Ingli Jones, Baptist Union Annual Assembly, 1932[1]

Broadcasting now has a hold on every one of the social
planes. A few days ago even the Queen was saying how
much she enjoyed listening in.

Holyhead Mail and Llandudno & Colwyn Bay Herald, 1925[2]

Sir John Reith, director general of the BBC, leaning on Broadcasting House

MARIE LLOYD WAS NOT AN OLD WOMAN – she turned fifty in February 1920 – but life had taken its toll. For three decades she'd been 'the Queen of the Music Halls',[3] maintaining her position with hundreds of performances a year, extensive international tours and the assistance of alcohol – though not as much as any of her three husbands, all of them abusive, tending to drink. She looked and sounded older than her years.

Having first made her name as a cheeky and flirtatious cockney girl who sang risqué songs like 'What's That For, Eh?' (1895) and 'Among My Knick-Knacks' (1896), she now reinvented herself with new material that reflected her age. In 'I Can't Forget the Days When I Was Young' (1919) she conceded that 'I'm not the flapper now that I used to be,' while insisting she wasn't quite finished yet: 'There's many a bit of frozen mutton tastes as good as lamb.'[4] Her most famous song of all came in this period: 'Don't Dilly Dally on the Way' (1919) – sometimes known as 'My Old Man (Said Follow the Van)' – about a moonlit flit to escape the rent collector, in which she loses her husband, loses her way and goes to the pub instead. To her public, Lloyd was still standing, if a little more careworn and weary than she had been.

In private, she was not well, with serious heart and kidney conditions, and in the summer of 1921 her doctor gave her just three months to live. She took some time away from performing but returned in early 1922, only to break down in tears while on stage in Cardiff. A few months later she was back again, playing shorter sets, though her stage time wasn't much reduced; when she was announced, she'd be greeted with such sustained applause and cheering that it would be several minutes before she could begin. And at the end, she'd be presented with a huge bouquet, and there would be requests for one of the old favourites: 'Oh, Mr Porter' or 'When I Take My Morning Promenade'. The audiences knew, even if no one was prepared to say it aloud, that this might be the last time they ever got to see her perform, and there was a world of affection for her. Despite her health, she gave a good show. 'She is still the greatest comedienne this country has ever seen,' declared one critic in September 1922.[5]

Three weeks after that notice, she was dead. Her final performance was a rendition of another recent hit, 'One of the Ruins that Cromwell Knocked About a Bit' (1920), in which she gets drunk in a pub called the Cromwell Arms and has a fight with the potman. When she began swaying back and forth, slurring her words, the audience took it as part of the act and cheered loudly. As the song finished, however, she collapsed and never recovered, dying a couple of days later. She was fifty-two and, despite earning several fortunes, virtually penniless. Her last words were said to have been: 'I shall work again soon, but I want to rest now.'[6]

Her funeral was spectacular. It took an hour to lay out the hundreds of wreaths, the most striking of them an empty birdcage with the door open, evoking the cock linnet of 'My Old Man'. Fifty thousand people lined the streets for the two-mile procession – 'city men mixed with costermongers, the West End mingled freely with the East End'[7] – and some five thousand members of the public managed to crowd into Hampstead Cemetery before the police had to close the gates. Among the mourners was Old Kate, a race-card seller who'd walked from Newmarket to be there, a distance of sixty miles. The following weekend, an estimated 120,000 people made a pilgrimage to her grave; the crowds were so great that on both Saturday and Sunday, thousands had to be turned away when the cemetery closed. The queues continued through the week, and one in four brought with them a fresh floral tribute – some of them formal arrangements, most homegrown – to add to the sea of flowers.

The newspapers tried to articulate what it was that had made Lloyd so special. To start with, she was of the people and for the people. 'Marie was a democrat, a maker of democrats,' read one obituary. 'No one who had ever heard her could glance at one of the old flower-sellers at Piccadilly Circus or an old apple woman and feel the same way as before.'[8] There was also her non-censorious tolerance: 'the target of all her mischievous fun was our common humanity and its most familiar frailties'.[9] And then there was something else, something hard to define. 'She was more than a favourite, she was an institution.'[10]

The most insightful account came, a little surprisingly, from a thirty-four-year-old expatriate American poet. 'No other comedian succeeded so well in giving expression to the life of that audience, in raising it to a kind of art,' wrote T. S. Eliot, for the New York literary magazine, the *Dial*. 'It was, I think, this capacity for expressing the soul of the people that made Marie Lloyd unique and that made her audiences, even when they joined in the chorus, not so much hilarious as happy.'[11] The joining-in was important in music hall. Lloyd belonged to a time when entertainment was about participation; the audience was part of the act, and she their representative and leader. Although she recorded a few songs in her last decade, she didn't fit the pre-packaged world of gramophone and cinema.

'Her death is itself a significant moment in English history,' wrote Eliot. Others agreed. AN EPOCH PASSES, read the headlines;[12] THE CLOSE OF AN ERA.[13] It was impossible not to look back. As the *Birmingham Gazette* remarked, her death prompted memories which, though happy, were 'touched with melancholy' since they were of 'the years before that great dividing line of war'.[14]

ii

Marie Lloyd was one of the last stars of the Edwardian music hall to leave the stage. Gus Elen and Eugene Stratton had retired in 1914, George Chirgwin in 1919 and Vesta Tilley in 1920; the latter's husband, Sir Walter de Frece – knighted for his fundraising efforts during the war – had been elected as a Conservative MP in a by-election, and she felt her career as a male impersonator was inappropriate for her new station in life.*

---

* Stratton died in 1918, and Chirgwin in November 1922, a month after Lloyd, but

There were others, of course, slightly smaller names, who were still performing, but music hall as a form of entertainment was in decline. Indeed, it wasn't even called music hall any more, that term seeming to denote a bygone world; now it was known as 'variety'. It was the same mixed bill of comedy, music, acrobats, dancers and animal acts, but it was smarter, more respectable, with less vulgarity and crudity. Variety was centred on London's West End, staged in large, conventional theatres, and the audiences contained a greater number of women than had music hall, partly because the balance of the sexes had been skewed by war. That helped to clean up the material, too. 'It is conceivable that as women go into the music hall, humour goes out of it,' wrote critic St John Ervine. 'Women do not so readily abandon themselves to hearty enjoyment as men do, and when they go to a music hall they go in the belief that it is all very silly.'[15] By comparison, the older, smaller venues that were still open were beginning to look tired and a bit seedy. 'You know the sort of place,' said comic Doris Waters, 'knee-deep in peanuts and the smell of last week's tigers.'[16]

The biggest difference was that variety didn't rule the roost as music hall once had. There were other forms of entertainment now, rivals for the attention of both artists and audience. During the war, George Robey ('the Prime Minister of Mirth') had left the music hall to play in the West End revue *The Bing Boys Are Here* (1916), with its hit song 'If You Were the Only Girl in the World'.* That had opened a new career for him, and helped create a public appetite for more of the same. Revue became highly popular through the 1920s, offering a themed evening of music, comedy and dance, a series of elaborately staged and loosely connected items. 'All legs and tomfoolery,' snorted George Bernard Shaw,[17] but the format had the virtue of being up to date. As the double

---

Tilley – now Lady de Frece – enjoyed a long retirement, latterly in Monte Carlo, living until 1952.

* The song was adapted by soldiers: 'If you were the only Boche in the trench, and I had the only bomb.'

act Mr Flotsam and Mr Jetsam sang in 'Only a Few of Us Left' (1928):

> These times aren't like the past,
> For they want foreign stuff and they want it fast.
> You must play jazz and you must sing blues
> Or you won't get a job in the new revues.[18]

Revue was killing off comedy, warned Harry Lauder, still playing the variety theatres and now being referred to as 'the World's Jester', so international was his appeal.[19] It was all about the show and not the star. 'With its sudden rise to public favour,' he wrote, 'revue delivered a stunning blow at the individual performer'; there was now no one to compare with Dan Leno or Tom Costello in their Edwardian pomp.[20]

The border between revue and variety was porous, with performers able to move between them. And then into and out of other formats: concert parties, seaside Pierrot troupes, pantomime, cabaret and beyond. 'The music hall, having ceased to exist as a separate art or entertainment', noted playwright Ashley Dukes,* spilled into other realms, including theatre, with 'not so much plays as inventions of clever music-hall comedians who understand the changing times'.[21] Dukes was talking of shows such as the farce *Tons of Money* (1921), which reached the West End the following year and ran for over 700 performances, written by music-hall comic Will Evans and Arthur Valentine.† Meanwhile, Albert Chevalier ('the Costers' Laureate') was enjoying a last hurrah in *My Old Dutch* (1920), a play he based on his 1892 music-hall song of the same name.

---

* In 1920 Dukes's younger brother, Sir Paul Dukes ('the Man of a Hundred Faces') became the first and only person to be knighted for his work as a spy, having infiltrated the Russian Communist Party.

† Valentine's real name was Archibald Pechey. He was the father of television chef Fanny Cradock.

Then there was the cinema, and that too attracted performers who would previously have been confined to the music-hall stage. George Robey made his first full-length comedy with *The Rest Cure* (1923) and played Sancho Panza in that year's *Don Quixote* (for which he was paid £600 a week), while Harry Lauder starred in an adaptation of John Buchan's *Huntingtower* (1928).

More striking than this crossover of stars, though, some venues offered both live and filmed entertainment. In the Edwardian music hall, short films had been shown between the acts as a novelty. Then, as movies got longer, some cinemas found that their primitive projectors were in danger of overheating; the answer was to employ a 'lantern cooler', a comedian who did a turn halfway through the bill. It was an uninspiring job, noted the press: three ten-minute performances over an eight-hour shift, 'very often in a picture-house where the dressing accommodation is appalling, and where there are no others on the bill to talk to'.[22]

Out of this practice, there emerged in 1928 what the papers called the 'cine-variety vogue',[23] a hybrid entertainment that featured several variety acts interspersed within a full programme of films. The Holloway Empire in north London, for example, offered the German drama *The Crisis** and the Hollywood spectacle of King Vidor's *Show People*, together with a live comedy sketch by Byron & Byron and music by Bobby Howell and his Band. Or there were the Six Roses dance troupe at the Central Cinema in Bury St Edmunds, or Wynette & Roberts ('England's Leading Character Dancers') at the Abbeydale in Sheffield. It still wasn't an easy booking for performers. At the Troxy in east London, there was a local convention that mothers with babies would sit in the

---

* Directed by G. W. Pabst, it was originally titled *Abwege* and became more commonly known in English as *The Devious Path*. It starred Jack Trevor, a British army officer who'd been jailed for fraud during the war, went on to make a career in the German film industry, and appeared in several Nazi propaganda pieces, for which he was subsequently charged with treason. He was convicted, though the verdict was quashed on appeal.

front row to allow room for their prams; coming on stage to the sight of a line of women breastfeeding could be unsettling for some acts.

In the cine-variety coalition, cinema was clearly the senior partner, but some felt it was being downgraded as an art form in its own right. 'Will cine-variety take the place of the ordinary cinematograph programme?' fretted the trade press,[24] before reassuring itself with a defiant declaration: 'The film is not dead! Long live the film!'[25]

The confidence was justified. Cinema grew and grew in the 1920s, becoming bigger and more popular than its rivals. By the end of the decade, inner London had 268,000 cinema seats, one for every twenty residents and more than twice the number of seats in theatres and music hall put together.[26] Movies could reach numbers undreamed of by live acts. The Empire Theatre of Varieties in Leicester Square – one of the most famous of the old music halls – was rebuilt as a cinema in 1927, with a capacity of over 3,000; it screened *The Broadway Melody* (1929) for nine weeks to a cumulative audience of a million. When the Tivoli, on the Strand, showed *Ben Hur* (1925), it was seen by 1.2 million. Even outside the West End, some of the venues were huge. The Premier Electric Theatre in East Ham opened in 1912 with 800 seats; in 1921 it was rebranded as the Premier Super Cinema, with the old premises turned into a foyer and café in front of a new auditorium that could seat 2,400. Biggest of all was Green's Playhouse in Glasgow, which opened in 1927 with a 4,200-seat auditorium at the heart of a complex that also included a 3,000-capacity ballroom and cafes that could take a further 1,200.*

At the other end of the market were small independent picture houses, fleapits as they were known, that survived by undercutting the competition, charging as little as 3*d* or even 2*d* for admission. They didn't have cafes attached to them, couldn't afford to stage

---

* In 1973 Green's closed as a cinema, and re-opened as the Apollo, which for twelve years was Scotland's leading venue for rock concerts.

cine-variety, and the accompanying music – for the movies were still silent at this point – ran to just a single pianist, as opposed to the sixteen-piece orchestra employed by the Stoll Picture Theatre on Kingsway in London. Nationally, there were around 3,000 cinemas, found particularly in industrial areas with high population-densities and in the rapidly expanding suburbs, where there was land for development. The audiences were disproportionately young, female and working class.

That appeal to women and the young ensured that the cinema also assumed the place of music hall as an object of moral indignation. The early signs were already evident before the war. Children were being presented with 'terrific massacres, horrible catastrophes, motor-car smashes, public hangings, lynchings', thundered *The Times* in 1913. 'All who care for the moral well-being and education of the child will set their faces like flint against this new form of excitement.'[27] A 1916 report by London headteachers identified particular 'scenes of crime and horror such as a woman going mad; a woman in drunken madness killing her own child; a mad woman in a padded room; a woman being chloroformed.'[28] There were regular calls for the government to replace the industry's own body, the British Board of Film Censors, with statutory censorship – preferably, said the National Council of Women in 1919, with an equal balance of men and women.[29]

Governments showed no inclination to get involved, but there were plenty of political voices to be heard. Isaac Foot, Liberal MP and Methodist lay preacher, condemned the cinema as 'largely a mixture of strong pornography and weak sentiment produced by people who must have had their apprenticeship in Sodom and Gomorrah.'[30] Even worse, thought Labour MP Arthur Greenwood, films threatened to undermine Britain's moral authority in the world. Movies depicting the less reputable aspects of society might 'bring into contempt Western civilisation'; they could be 'doing incalculable harm in Asia and the East generally.'[31] And the British Socialist Party was angry about films that depicted wicked Bolsheviks deceiving honest workers; this might mislead 'ignorant people, especially women', who 'generally know nothing of political matters'.[32]

Against all the criticism, some argued that cinema kept people, particularly the young, out of the pubs, helping create a more sober nation. Convictions for drunkenness were lower in the 1920s than they had been pre-war, and in 1928 it was reported that the number of public houses had fallen by a third in twenty-five years.[33] As the chief constable of Edinburgh pointed out, 'the picture houses have been instrumental in reducing intemperance in the city'.[34]

iii

Most of the films being made in Britain were cheap, rapidly produced and soon forgotten. Even the better pictures often gave the impression of being poor relations of stage drama. Creatively and technically, the industry was some way behind Germany and France; commercially, it was nowhere near America. It was striking that the two greatest screen actors to come out of the British music hall – Charlie Chaplin and Stan Laurel – were both working in Hollywood. Chaplin was acclaimed as 'the most famous man on earth',[35] which left Walter Forde to be billed as 'Britain's Foremost Screen Comedian',[36] but only after he'd failed to make it in the States.*

There were, though, some trying to explore the possibilities of the new medium. Prompted by the death of Marie Lloyd, director George Pearson made *Love, Life and Laughter* (1923), with Betty Balfour as a working-class girl who becomes a star. The story was hackneyed, but the structure was original; it was, he claimed, the first film to open with the final scene and proceed to tell the story in flashback. The domestic critics loved it: 'his masterpiece';[37] 'coloured with genius in every detail';[38] 'surpasses even the genius

---

* Forde later turned to directing films that starred the leading comedians of the 1930s and 40s: Arthur Askey, Sid Field, Tommy Handley, Will Hay, Jack Hulbert, George Robey and Tommy Trinder.

of D. W. Griffith.'[39] That last was an exaggeration – no British film of the silent era could match the scale of Griffith's work* – but there were a lot of such claims, predictions that Britain was on the cusp of rivalling Hollywood, without it ever quite happening.

The Rat (1925), directed by Graham Cutts, came close, cinematic rather than stagey, with mobile camerawork, including a tracking shot through a crowded dance floor at the White Coffin club, a low-life Parisian dive frequented by knife-wielding petty thief, the Rat, played by Ivor Novello: passionate, tempestuous and dangerously glamorous, all darkened eyes and pallid cheekbones. 'What a fine film face!' D. W. Griffith had exclaimed, as he signed Novello up to a three-year, seven-picture deal.[40] That, at any rate, was the story put out by the publicity boys. In fact Novello made only one film with Griffith – *The White Rose* (1923) – before returning to Britain, where his vulnerable passivity captured some of the spiritual unease of the times. 'I'm going to make you the most attractive man in Paris,' a wealthy courtesan tells the Rat, as he sits submissively at her feet.

In Adrian Brunel's strange, beautiful *The Man without Desire* (1923) Novello played an eighteenth-century Venetian count who, distraught at the death of his lover, has himself hypnotised into suspended animation by an English scientist. Awoken 200 years later, he's baffled by telephones, motorboats and modern dress, to say nothing of modern women. He has remained a young man and is overjoyed to find the descendant of his love, but his prolonged sleep has left him listless and impotent. As the scientist warns him: 'You may even start to find yourself utterly without desire of any kind.' Stranded helplessly out of time, he is lost, 'a man without a heart', and the only option seems to be suicide.

Novello also starred in *The Lodger: A Story of the London Fog* (1927), adapted from the 1913 novel by Mary Belloc Lowndes. It was directed by Alfred Hitchcock, who'd recently returned from

---

* Griffith was the director most famously of *Birth of a Nation* (1915), *Intolerance* (1916), *Broken Blossoms* (1919) and *Orphans of the Storm* (1921).

Berlin, full of new ideas about camera angles and menacing close-ups, dramatic lighting and special effects, as when the ceiling of a room becomes transparent and the viewer can see the man upstairs, nervously pacing. There's a serial killer on the loose and Novello plays the lead suspect, an outsider in the community who's hunted down and beaten by a mob. Again he is a curiously detached figure, someone to whom things happen.

These were impressive and successful films, with substantial budgets, as Novello was quick to acknowledge: 'I made as much in a week as I would have done with two successful musical comedies in London.'[41] Making still more was Dorothy Gish – younger sister of Hollywood star Lilian – tempted across the Atlantic by producer/director Herbert Wilcox, with the offer of a thousand pounds a week for seven weeks' filming. The result was *Nell Gwyn* (1926), in which Gish gave a captivating, flirtatious performance in what the *Daily Express* called 'the sauciest and merriest film ever produced'.[42] It also had a contemporary resonance. Having fallen in love with Nell, Charles II promises to build her a palace at Chelsea, until she persuades him to give it instead to 'the aged and broken men who have fought in his wars'.

The problem was that such big-budget productions were in short supply in Britain, and even the cheap and cheerful pictures were getting thin on the ground. In 1923, only one in every ten films screened in the country's cinemas was British made, and the proportion was falling, down to one in twenty just three years later. This was not merely a concern for the domestic industry, but possibly a threat to British culture, British identity. 'The bulk of our picturegoers are Americanised,' said the *Daily Express* in 1927. 'They talk America, think America and dream America. We have several million people, mostly women, who, to all intent and purposes, are temporary American citizens.'[43] Young people, added A. J. Cummings, political editor of the *News Chronicle*, were becoming 'imperceptibly Americanised in manners and customs, habits and methods, speech and ideas. One day this American-ising influence, if not checked and countered, will constitute a direct menace to British prestige.'[44] Even language was in jeopardy, according to some commentators. 'The printed sub-titles of the silent film have already taught the youth of Britain to bestrew its speech with the racy phrases of the Bowery and the ranch.'[45]

Stanley Baldwin's government, which was not averse to protectionism, responded with the Cinematograph Films Act of 1927, requiring a certain percentage of the material screened by cinemas to be either British or from the Empire. The initial quota was set at 7.5 per cent, rising over the course of the ten years that the act was scheduled to operate. The regulation came into effect in April 1928, and the urgency of the situation was clear in the pages of the trade journal *Kinematograph Weekly*; that month it reviewed forty-seven new full-length films, of which thirty-eight were American, five German and one each from France and Italy – only two were British.

The passing of the act prompted a gold rush of new production companies, fifty-nine being set up in 1929 alone. The films that resulted, however, were uninspiring: not-quite-full-length pictures intended to be shown as a supporting feature to a proper American movie. By 1930 *Kinematograph Weekly* was complaining of 'these Quota Quickies'[46] and the term stuck. The audiences were unimpressed, and it was said that some cinemas heeded only the letter, not the spirit, of the law, screening these titles in the morning when they were seen only by the cleaners.

It took no more than a fortnight to make a quota quickie, often with two shooting in the same studio, one by day and the other at night; producer/director George King, described by *Picturegoer* magazine as the King of the Quickies,[47] boasted that he'd turned out five films in eight weeks. Back in the early 1920s, George Pearson had been making films for £10,000, and he knew even then that his budgets were a fraction of those in America and Germany; a decade later, he was reduced to making quickies – 'the only field open to the few pioneers remaining from the silent film days'[48] – for just £6,000 per title. Despite the limitations, his work gave opportunities to emerging stars; Jack Hawkins, Vivienne

Leigh and Wilfred Hyde White appeared in *A Shot in the Dark* (1933), *Gentlemen's Agreement* (1935) and *Murder by Rope* (1936) respectively.

By then, the world of cinema had been revolutionised by the advent of movies with soundtracks – talkies, as they were known – starting with Al Jolson in *The Jazz Singer* (1927). With the release of Alfred Hitchcock's *Blackmail* (1929), Britain's first talkie, the *Stage* was convinced that the country's moment had arrived: 'It proves without doubt that to whatever extent England has failed with silent films, she can more than hold her own when it comes to the new departure.'[49] Again, the optimism was misplaced; however good Hitchcock's movies were, Hollywood remained the dominant force.

At a time when few British people had met an American, far less visited the States, the talkies were a revelation; it turned out that the stars of Hollywood movies – familiar faces, many of them – sounded very peculiar indeed. 'Nothing can ever persuade British film-goers to take this accent seriously,' wrote the *Daily Chronicle*'s cinema correspondent. 'Over and over again I have heard audiences rock with laughter at the most intense moments of American pictures, just because an actor has been unable to conquer his American accent.'[50] Movies weren't always easy to follow either, due to 'the difficulty of understanding rapidly spoken dialogue in the language of the Bowery or Middle West'.[51] The same was true in reverse. When the British film *The Middle Watch* (1930) was screened in New York City, 'the "quaint English accent" was greeted with many chuckles'.[52]

Nonetheless, the dawn of the talkies ushered in a golden age of cinema in Britain, with ticket sales rising steadily to reach nearly a billion a year by the end of the 1930s. New picture houses were built, reflecting the glory of the time. They were cathedrals of entertainment, built in styles that ranged from the clean elegance of art-deco design to ever more elaborate fantasies.

The suburbs of west London could boast the Palace in Southall (opened 1929), based on a Chinese temple, and the Avenue in

Northfields (1932), with an auditorium recreating a Spanish court-yard, complete with corbelled turrets, Moorish arches and draped tapestries to create a tented ceiling. Elsewhere, the Pyramid in Sale, Cheshire (1934) was Egyptian, and the Beaufort in Meriden, Warwickshire (1929) was Tudor, with an oak staircase and stained-glass windows depicting the kings and queens of England. When the Central Cinema in Yeovil burned down in 1930, it was replaced by a new building with an art-deco exterior 'in Persian style', while the interior was 'the last word in comfort', the 'attractive Oriental setting' complemented by a lighting system that morphed through sixty colours. Its slogan, said proprietor Archie Thring, was: 'Talkies as They Should Talk'.[53] The first presentation was Charlie Chaplin's latest, *City Lights*, which was silent.

The lavish decor reflected how much money there now was in the exhibition of movies. The films themselves might be, for the most part, imported, but Britain knew how to put on a show, and the audiences embraced the fantasy. Regrettably, their behaviour did not always live up to the grandeur of the surroundings. The Trocadero in Elephant and Castle, south London, had a Renaissance theme, full of marble columns, rose-coloured mirrors and Roman eagles in gilt. It seated 3,500 patrons and, remembered a young management trainee, Denis Norden, it was also home – when she managed to get past the cashier – to '"Tossoff Kate", a mild-mannered, middle-aged lady with a greasy black fringe', who used to work her way round the auditorium, offering her services to male customers. Doing her bit to reduce wealth inequality, she had a sliding-scale fee structure that varied according to the price of the seat occupied by her client.[54]

iv

John Reith was a model of late-Victorian rectitude: devout, driven, serious to the point of severity. The *Daily News* summed up his attributes: 'Business ability, austerity, imagination, reticence, aloofness, modesty.'[55] He was also, in many ways, an appalling man, self-absorbed, obsessed with titles and money, often petty and spiteful, even childish. He was deeply sentimental and a domestic tyrant. And in the 1920s and 30s, he exercised a level of cultural power in Britain that was without precedent.

Reith was the fifth son of a Presbyterian minister, born in north-east Scotland in 1889. (His daughter said the sternness of his face gave the impression that he'd 'had bad news in 1889 and had not got over it'.[56]) His schooldays were not successful – he was expelled at fifteen for bullying – and, much to his chagrin, he was not allowed to progess to university, becoming instead an engineer. But even then he knew, deep in his Calvinist core, that he was predestined for greatness. During the war, he served in France, and his trust in God and Destiny was such that he displayed an absurd level of personal courage, until finally he was felled by a sniper's bullet in August 1915. He was spared, though left with a scar on his cheek which, with his six-feet-six-inch frame and glowering countenance, made him an intimidating figure. 'Reith not only towered, but intended to tower,' one of his underlings said.[57] Winston Churchill referred to him as the 'Wuthering Height'.[58]

He had no problem finding work as a civilian, but managing an engineering firm wasn't what he was made for. 'I still believe there is some great work for me to do in this world,' he wrote in his diary in October 1922.[59] The following month he replied to a job advert in the *Morning Post* and was appointed general manager of a new enterprise, the British Broadcasting Company.

He knew nothing of broadcasting, but nor did anyone else; this was entirely uncharted territory. Radio – or the wireless, as it was more commonly called – was new and, the technology having been developed, there had arisen the question of what to do with it. Who was going to transmit material of sufficient interest to warrant buying a receiver? The answer that the six largest manufacturers of radio sets came up with was the BBC, a joint-venture company awarded the exclusive broadcast rights in Britain for four years. In exchange, the government expected to raise revenue from this new medium; it put a sales tax on radios and took a cut of the ten-shilling licence fee that was to be paid annually by those households that wished to listen in.* The rest of the licence went to the company as its sole income – there would be no advertising, no sponsorship.[†]

The primary interest of the shareholders, therefore, was the sale of sets, not the content of the material broadcast, and the obvious approach to programming was to pursue popular taste. In America, where commercial stations had been operating for a couple of years, it had become clear that this was all about keeping the customer entertained. Reith, having been appointed to run the company, was not of that mind. The point was not 'to give the public what it wants', he declared, but 'what you believe they should like'.[60] He had a unique opportunity to shape an entirely new world, and his was a moral mission.

Radio should be a force for good, he insisted. The task of the BBC was to inform, to educate and to entertain, though the last of those three needed a little gloss. Entertainment was not to be seen as simply 'the broadcasting of jazz bands and popular music, or of sketches by humourists'; it should be 'part of a systematic and sustained endeavour to recreate, to build up knowledge, experience and character'.[61] If radio aimed for entertainment alone, it would be 'a prostitution of its powers and an insult to the character and intelligence of the people'.[62] Nonetheless, some concession to the public was required. 'The BBC must lead, not follow, its listeners, but it must not lead at so great a distance as to shake off pursuit.'[63]

At the centre of Reith's work at the BBC was his faith. Do you, he would ask job applicants, 'accept the fundamental teachings of Jesus Christ?'[64] The most obvious manifestation of this drive to godliness was the BBC Sabbath. Reith's first instruction to the

---

* 'Listening in' was the approved phrase, and those who used the radio became known as listeners-in, to the annoyance of Reith, who thought the word should be in-listeners.

† The price of the radio licence remained at ten shillings until after the Second World War.

director of programmes was to 'observe Sundays'.[65] The old Victorian Sabbath, that high-minded day of devotion, had come 'to be regarded as an archaic absurdity', he wrote, and the BBC's task was to bring it back.[66] Only the most serious music was broadcast on Sundays, and a church service was transmitted in the evening. Many would have preferred dance music and comedy to liven up their day of leisure, but with no alternatives available, the dissatisfied could only grumble in the letters pages of the newspapers, as did William Sheppard of Plumstead: 'You plunge the whole country into gloom every Sunday.'[67]

Consumed by self-confidence, Reith had no time for audience research and surveys, no wish to know how many people were listening, or what they thought. In vain did *Punch* magazine mock him for wanting 'to supply the British public with mental uplift', while the British public 'refuses to be mentally uplifted'.[68] Equally fruitless were the complaints of all those others who wished to shape what was to be broadcast: press barons, bishops, trade organisations from other sectors of entertainment. Even with politicians, Reith paid no more attention than was strictly necessary. In return, many held him in less than high esteem. 'We English should have learned by now,' fumed Labour MP Ellen Wilkinson, 'that it is unsafe to give a Scotsman any opportunity for indulging his national passion of directing other people for their own good.'[69]

Yet, for all his arrogance and self-regard, there was something impressive about Reith's single-minded invention of the BBC. He recognised that while this was a business operation, it was unlike other ventures, requiring the continued approval of the establishment if it were to maintain its monopoly position. There was a perilous passage to navigate, with threats and challenges on all sides, and yet he kept a true course, inventing a form of public-service broadcasting that – with rare exceptions – avoided being a propaganda mouthpiece for the government, and that remained above mere commercialism.

The moment Reith knew that he and his company had arrived

came in April 1923, when the king spoke in Wembley Stadium, to open the Empire Exhibition, and was broadcast on the BBC. Many of the leading London shops and theatres had installed speakers to relay his words, and there were further speakers along Oxford Street and in many other public places around the country, often set up by local radio dealers with an eye to advertising their wares. The BBC estimated that five to six million in Britain listened to the king, with many more around the Empire. For the vast majority this was the first time they had heard a sovereign speak, and it was a significant moment not merely in broadcasting, but in monarchy. It was 'one of the greatest ceremonials in Empire history', wrote Reith. 'One can hear little children in far distant villages saying, "I have heard the King".'[70]

v

John Reith would sometimes compare himself to William Caxton; it was a fair likeness, for radio was the biggest technological revolution in culture since the printing press. The growth was spectacular: there were 35,000 radio licences when the BBC was launched in 1922, three million by the end of the decade, nine million by the end of the next. Addressing a banquet at the 1927 Radio Exhibition in London, cabinet minister Lord Birkenhead hailed 'the greatest and most amazing development of modern time' and calculated that one in three households now listened in, compared to one in seven in America.[71]

But it was more just than the numbers. Radio was an entirely new concept. The silent cinema had been startling enough, but at least mime provided a cultural precedent for vision without words; sound without vision, on the other hand, had no such forebears. And the physical structure and experience of cinema was not dissimilar to theatre; the connection between actors and audience was lost, but the communal experience of a roomful of people was familiar. With radio, millions could hear the same thing, but all them isolated in their own homes. It was a revolutionary mix of public and private spheres utterly unlike any previous form of communication, and it presented new demands.

In the 1924 general election, for example, the major party leaders were each invited to make a broadcast on the radio. On the first night came prime minister Ramsay MacDonald, a fine orator with a powerful onstage presence, and a delivery that could hit the thundering heights of passion and then abruptly drop to a whisper. Playing to his strengths, he chose to have the radio microphone attend a public meeting in Glasgow. It was not a success. 'He strode up and down the platform and was at varying distances from the microphone,' one commentator complained. 'This is extremely effective for those who are present in the hall, but very detrimental for broadcasting.'[72] It was, said the *Scotsman*, 'little short of a failure', not for technical reasons, but because of MacDonald's inability 'to adapt himself to the new medium'.[73]

The next night, Stanley Baldwin went to the BBC studios at Savoy Hill in the West End, and spoke directly into a microphone, using what the papers called 'an admirably "wireless" voice'. 'Last night you listened to an orator,' he began, in a conversational tone. 'I am no orator.' Some regretted an absence of drama in his address, and the *Liverpool Echo* gently teased him for his persona: 'a good fellow, a pleasant man, a man about his business, saying plain things in a plain way'.[74] It worked, though. For the estimated three to four million listening in, there was no doubt who had communicated their message the more effectively.*

These broadcasts were unusual, for politics was not much heard on the wireless. The government, explained Reith, had given 'an explicit instruction to avoid anything in the nature of religious, political or industrial controversy'.[75] He said he regretted this, though it was appropriate for the times; the BBC was incorporated on 18 October 1922, the day before the Carlton Club meeting that brought down Lloyd George's coalition, and

---

* The third night it was H. H. Asquith's turn, again addressing a public meeting rather than a radio audience, though he did at least stay still.

the BBC seemed sometimes to believe that it had taken on the mantle of consensus.

Certainly, common ground was the keynote of the radio; inevitable, perhaps, given the sheer size and diversity of the audience. Reith's requirement of religious broadcasts was that they should present 'a non-sectarian Christianity, confined, in respect of doctrine, to those simplest essentials to which all Christians of the West can adhere'.[76] The aim, despite his own Presbyterian principles, was to find a shared culture. Even if some on the fringes might be excluded, he believed there was a substantial centre ground where most of the nation was located. The approach to politics was similarly ecumenical, and similarly mainstream. The BBC's bias was towards parliamentary democracy, which meant that communist and fascist voices were seldom heard. Beyond that, however, the company sought to report events in a neutral and even-handed manner.

Cultural broadcasting was likewise averse to ruffling feathers. The first novel to be serialised was Charles Kingsley's *Westward Ho!* (1855), a longstanding staple of children's literature, and the first theatrical performance was some scenes from Shakespeare. Adaptations of existing works were preferred to new commissions, though there were some premieres, including the world's first-ever radio drama, Richard Hughes's *A Comedy of Danger* (1924), billed as 'a play for the ear only'. How to make drama without vision? Hughes' solution was to set the action in the pitch blackness of a coal mine where the lights have gone out. ('This seems very simple,' he acknowledged,[77] 'but for a first experiment one has to be simple.')* The kind of contemporary writers that the BBC liked were Arnold Bennett and J. B. Priestley – intelligent but popular and familiar.

There was a good deal of music too, most of it serious, though

---

* Hughes became best known for his novel *A High Wind in Jamaica* (1929) about children kidnapped by pirates, a more disturbing vision of childhood than any other in the period.

dance bands were soon elbowing their way in. And there was variety, although it was difficult, since so many acts – juggling, ventriloquism, animals – didn't make sense without visuals. That didn't stop the BBC having a radio dance team, the Eight Step Sisters, or from broadcasting the card tricks of magician Sirdani.*

All of this came cheerfully jumbled up together, with programmes appearing at random rather than regular times, and with little apparent logic or structure. That was intentional. Reith wanted people to find new things, as if by serendipity, though this annoyed some. In the film *Squibs* (1935), a young woman is listening to the wireless as a dance-band number comes to an end. 'That concludes this part of the programme,' says the announcer. 'We are now taking you over for a talk on vegetables and their diseases.' She turns the set off.

Consensus broadcasting also meant no offensive material from comedians and variety singers. Performers were given a card instructing that there were to be 'No gags on Scotsmen, Welshmen, clergymen, drink or medical matters'. Just as importantly, 'Do not sneeze at the microphone.'[78] Reith boasted that in four years there had been only one complaint about vulgarity, 'and that was from a listener whose mental stability was apparently in question'.[79] In fact, the BBC was adept at self-policing. Comedian Claude Dampier was banned for three months after a joke about helping his bedridden friend who'd been put on a fruit diet; he'd 'promised to squeeze Mrs Gibson's oranges'.[80]

The restrictions themselves became the subject of comedy. Regular broadcaster Norman Long ('A Song, a Joke, a Piano') recorded 'We Can't Let You Broadcast That!' (1933), a skit on censorship, in which his entire repertoire is deemed inappropriate; he offers, for example, 'The Song of the Volga Boatmen':

They hated vulgar boatmen,

---

* Despite his Egyptian robes and mangled English ('Don't be fright,' was his catchphrase), Sirdani was born Sid Daniels in the East End of London.

And discouraged vulgar chat;
And songs about rude sailors are barred –
We can't let you broadcast that![81]

The record was, predictably, banned by the BBC.

In short, complained novelist Virginia Woolf, it was all too appallingly middlebrow; she nicknamed the broadcaster the Betwixt and Between Company.[82] She herself made only three broadcasts, but there was room for her had she so wished, just as there was for other highbrow writers, including E. M. Forster and Vita Sackville-West. There was room, too, for intellectuals. Asked in 1933 who their favourite broadcasters were, a group of East End factory girls included scientist Oliver Lodge in their list; they didn't always understand him, they said, but 'he makes us think of queer things we hadn't thought of before'.[83]

Presiding over the output were the announcers who, initially at least, were anonymous; the BBC and not individual broadcasters was the brand. They wore evening dress, in order that they might greet any visiting guests with appropriate formality, and they were held to the highest of standards. It was reported that one announcer was sacked for reading election results with too much feeling; 'his intonation persuaded the public that he was out of sympathy'.[84]

Intonation mattered, and so did pronunciation. In a country famed for its abundance of accents, it was felt necessary to set up an advisory committee that would inform presenters how to pronounce particular words. The committee comprised three writers, two professors of phonetics and an actor (or, looked at another way, two Englishmen, a Scot, an Irishman, a Welshman and an American), and it met three times a year, finding plenty to argue about. As George Bernard Shaw, one of their number, pointed out: 'No two members of the committee pronounce "Yes" and "No" exactly alike.'[85]

Nonetheless, from time to time, edicts were issued covering how specific words should sound. 'Laboratory, usually now spoken with the accent on the first syllable, is to have the accent on the second, in order not to confuse the word with lavatory,' reported the *Stage*, which had an interest in such matters.[86] For the sake of clarity on radio, 'pri-vacy' was preferred to 'priv-acy'. England should be pronounced 'Ing-gland'. When referring to donkeys, the word ass should have a short 'a'.

Some welcomed the prospect of standardisation. 'How pleasant it will be for Londoners to converse with magnates of the great industrial north in a language that both can understand,' dreamed the *Bystander*. 'Fancy going to Glasgow without a glossary!'[87] There was also some anger, though, at the perceived loss of local identity. Alternatives were permitted for some place names – Shrewsbury could be given as Shrowzbury or Shroozbury, and Newcastle upon Tyne as either Néwcastle or Newcássle – but there were directives for other places, and not always to the satisfaction of locals. Despite the BBC's logical pronunciation of Slaithewaite in Yorkshire, the residents of the village stuck with Slowit, as they had done for longer than anyone could remember. Likewise, those who lived in Daventry, Northamptonshire and called it Daintry. 'We hardy recognise Castleford when the BBC say it,' protested the *Yorkshire Evening Post*; 'why should we abandon our way for theirs?'[88] North of the border, there was even more hostility: 'Is it the policy of the BBC to Anglicise all Scottish names?' demanded the *Scotsman*.[89]

The committee did not say that they were providing instruction to the nation, merely that this was guidance for its presenters. As the press noted, however: 'The BBC is the most powerful influence of all in this matter of pronunciation.'[90] Not all usages took off, and not all lasted. The public was not persuaded that calibre should sound as caleeber, bulletin as boolletin, or culinary as kewlinary, nor that the first letter in Celtic was an s-sound (except in Wales, where it was to be k). On the other hand, the rejection of the 'k' for cinema and the Cenotaph was accepted. And the hard 'g' in margarine – which reflected its shared root with the name Margaret – disappeared. The BBC changed the way the nation spoke. 'How cleverly it taught us how to pronounce "Eritrea"!'

wrote essayist Robert Lynd: 'And most of us have learned from it by this time to speak the name of Mr Roosevelt in the American fashion.'[91]

The voice delivering the words became known as BBC English,[92] essentially a middle-class accent from south-east England. Not upper class, though, because if it got too posh, it alienated the audience: envelope was not pronounced 'on-velope', and the 'h' was not dropped from hotel. Still, it was posh enough by most people's standards. 'Those blokes at the BBC 'ave all got such a saloon-bar voice,' complained a public-bar character in a *Punch* cartoon.[93] The standard sign-off at the end of a day's broadcasting was much mocked: 'Good-naight, everybody; good-naight.'[94]

Nonetheless, said Arthur Lloyd James of the advisory committee, talk of standardisation was absurdly overstated. 'There is no "BBC English",' he insisted, 'and nor could there be when the backgrounds of the announcers were so very diverse. 'Their schools range from Weymouth, Radley and Ampleforth to Uppingham and Wimbledon.'[95]

vi

The BBC rapidly became an institution, part of the fabric of society, adding new quirks and customs to the nation. The first weather forecast came in 1923, as did the first coverage of a general election campaign and the chimes of Big Ben, followed by the Greenwich pips and schools broadcasting the next year. The danger that radio might flatten regional diversity was balanced by the fact that it brought the country together. Devout families who were geographically separated took comfort in knowing that they were all worshipping at the same service, and religious broadcasts were seen as a godsend by many who were housebound.

That was the argument that Reith put to the government in 1924, when requesting permission to broadcast the Armistice Day ceremony at the Cenotaph. 'There are hundreds of thousands of people who, however much minded, are prevented from participating in a local service, on considerations of time, infirmity, age, ill health or simple distance,' he wrote.[96] His application was unsuccessful, however, and it was not until 1928 that the government bowed to what the home secretary, William Joynson-Hicks, called 'the public demand for the broadcasting of the service'.[97]

That reluctance to accommodate the BBC was not unusual. There was much suspicion of this interloper within existing institutions, a wish to clip its wings. The press, fearful of being made redundant, successfully lobbied the government to ensure that the first news bulletin of the day was not until 7 p.m., so it wouldn't harm sales of morning or evening titles. This was of particular significance on Saturdays, when football results were not permitted to be broadcast before seven, giving a clear field to the sporting editions of local papers.

There was a further battle over radio schedules, which the newspapers were initially happy to print on a daily basis, before deciding that this constituted advertising and should be paid for. When the BBC refused, there was a press boycott. It only lasted a single day, because Selfridges department store – whose owner Gordon Selfridge was a devotee of radio – took out a paid advert in the *Pall Mall Gazette* containing the schedule, and the jump in sales for that title convinced the proprietors to cave in. 'They had made proper fools of themselves,' gloated Reith in his diary.[98] The episode had, though, exposed a potential weakness, to which the BBC responded by launching the *Radio Times*, a magazine that provided a week's worth of listings, together with related features. The publication added a valuable stream of revenue and became the country's biggest-selling title; by 1937 it had a circulation of 3.5 million, which it boasted was 'the largest ever recorded by a weekly magazine in any country'.[99]

Those who controlled the theatres and concert halls of London were concerned that their audiences might be tempted away by the prospect of listening in at home. William Boosey, who ran music publisher Chappell & Co. as well as the Queen's Hall, home of Henry Wood's Promenade Concerts, ruled that any musician who had broadcast would not be allowed to perform at his venue. The musicians themselves, however, were less enthusiastic about turning down paid work, and Boosey couldn't hold the line. In 1927 the BBC took over the Proms, and in 1930 the 114-piece BBC Symphony Orchestra, under Adrian Boult, played its debut concert at the Queen's Hall.

Similarly, the variety theatres, now dominated by big chains, drew up contracts forbidding the stars that they booked from appearing on radio. They too had to concede defeat, as did the world of sport. Novelist Edgar Wallace was able to broadcast 'My Impressions of the Derby' in 1923, but it was an evening talk, not a commentary. And when the BBC was allowed to broadcast live from Epsom on Derby Day in 1925, it wasn't the race itself, just the atmosphere: 'the bookies' shouts, the cries of the hawkers, the buzz of the expectant crowd, and the cheers for the leading horses as they round the famous Corner'.[100] Or rather, that's what listeners would have heard had there not been a fault on the line that prevented transmission. The BBC blamed 'incessant rain',[101] or a short circuit caused by 'boys climbing the telephone posts to obtain a view of the race'.[102] The experiment was repeated, more successfully, the following year, and in 1927 there was an account of the race itself.

Earlier that year had come the first live sports commentary, with England beating Wales 11–9 in a rugby international from Twickenham, after which the BBC broadcast the Grand National, the Oxford–Cambridge Boat Race and the FA Cup final. This last was a one-off, though, with the Football Association refusing to authorise further live broadcasts. Instead, the 1929 final saw a team of BBC men on the terraces, with one leaving every ten minutes to go to a transmitter installed in a nearby house, relaying what he'd just seen. It wasn't satisfactory, but it did help persuade the FA to accept the inevitable.

It turned out that, far from driving away audiences, the radio drew them in. One exception to the early boycotts was the British National Opera Company; founded the same year as the BBC and yet to establish itself, it happily broadcast extracts from Mozart's *The Magic Flute* (in English) in 1923, and enjoyed an increase in ticket sales. Sporting events discovered that radio brought not only publicity but status; events that weren't broadcast self-evidently weren't as important as those that were.

Those most fearful of radio were the established comedians. On the live circuit, visiting each town maybe just once a year, it was possible to keep much the same act for decades. But once a routine had been broadcast, it was assumed, it would be played out. Here, too, the qualms were unnecessary. Broadcasting changed the delivery of comedy, allowing for subtler styles, but audiences weren't alienated by repetition; precisely the opposite, as the Yorkshire comedian Sandy Powell discovered. He performed his sketch 'The Lost Policeman' on radio, and in 1929 was asked if he'd do a version for release on an 8-inch record. There wasn't much of a market for spoken comedy on record, and he was offered just a £30 fee plus 1½d per sale, but the record sold in the hundreds of thousands and he ended up making around £3,000. There followed dozens of releases, inoffensive little sketches casting him as anything from dentist to dirt track racer, mountaineer to magistrate, in all of which he was a simple-minded soul, bemused by the foolishness of the world. 'We churned them out like sausages,' he recalled, and he found himself earning up to £12,000 a year as the first gramophone comedy star.[103] He was also a regular on the BBC, which did sales no harm.*

The most positive view of the medium was that of Hamilton Fyfe, editor of the *Daily Herald*, who believed that radio might refine the quality of the press. 'Within a short time, we shall all carry earphones about with us and be able to pick up messages wherever we may happen to be,' he told a House of Lords committee in 1926. This instant, disposable medium would meet the needs of those who didn't really care about news, culture and finance,

---

* In June 1933 Sandy Powell appeared in *Televariety*, the first variety show on British television.

so that they would no longer need to buy newspapers; the result would be leaner, more highbrow publications for those with more sophisticated tastes. 'Journalism will become once more a serious profession,' he argued. 'Things that are important will not be sacrificed to snappy or spicy items.'[104] This did not come to pass.

On 1 January 1927, the British Broadcasting Company was wound up, and its assets transferred to the British Broadcasting Corporation, instituted by royal charter as a non-commercial organisation. For listeners, there was little discernible change: the same voices, the same illogical schedules; there was still no advertising, the licence fee still needed to be paid.*

John Reith remained as well, with a new title as director general. For him, this was a personal triumph, the fulfilment of his destiny. The company that he had built from virtually nothing – he had been one of just four employees at the start – had launched him into the establishment. He was now the head of a Crown-chartered corporation, an esteemed figure whose counsel was sought in affairs of state, the recipient of a knighthood (he'd hoped for a peerage). Lord Birkenhead was only half-joking when he said: 'Neither Mussolini nor myself can boast the power and autocratic authority of Sir John Reith.'[105]

---

* Wireless detection vans were introduced in 1932 to catch listeners who hadn't paid up.

4

HIGHS AND HANGOVERS

Not that the crowd who usually foregathered at the
Centurions were much in his line – bright young things
with few morals and less sense might be amusing enough
to read about in the pages of a novel, but they were pretty
punk to meet in the flesh.

Sydney Horler, *Tiger Standish Comes Back*, 1934[1]

Sir or Madam?
Guess if you can.
Aren't you longing to know?

Cambridge Footlights Club revue, *Sir or Madam*, 1934[2]

Novelist Radclyffe Hall

IN EARLY 1919, BRITAIN BECAME AWARE OF STRANGE SOUNDS EMANATING from the United States of America. The country that had, before the war, given the world the ragtime craze appeared to have evolved another form of music, still based on syncopation – the offbeat heart of rag – but somehow even wilder. Publishers Herman Darewski of Charing Cross Road in London began advertising the sheet music of songs with names like 'Buzz-Buzz Jazz', 'Jazzin' Around', 'Hawaiian Jazz' and 'Hong Kong Jazz', and, as those titles indicated, this so-called jazz was seen as a novelty.

The opportunity to hear the music in the flesh was not long in coming. In March 1919, the Original Dixieland Jazz Band were brought over from America to appear at the London Hippodrome in *Joy Bells*, the latest revue to star George Robey. They lasted just one night, removed at Robey's insistence; he'd taken a dislike to what he saw as the low moral tone of jazz, and was further displeased that the band had upstaged him.* Instead the Hippodrome management took over a premises in Bond Street, renamed it the Dixie Club, and installed the ODJB as the resident act.

The instrumentation was odd, a front line of cornet, clarinet and trombone, with piano and drums behind. The combination of brass, woodwind and percussion was derived from the military band but transformed into a chamber version, and singularly lacking in martial discipline. The music was loud and chaotic, starting fast before speeding up, with the instruments seemingly fighting each other in a free-for-all, as though making it up as they went along, storming through pieces whose titles suggested an animalistic lack of restraint: 'Tiger Rag', 'Barnyard Blues', 'Livery Stable Blues' and 'Ostrich Walk'. The band's debut record had been advertised in America under the slogan 'A brass band gone crazy!' and madness was certainly one interpretation. Another was to see jazz, in the words of the *Birmingham Daily Post*, as 'the wild

---

* *Joy Bells* was another hit for Robey, running for over 700 performances.

Bolshevik outlaw in the music world'.[3] It sounded frightfully dangerous, and the band's cornetist Nick LaRocca bragged, 'I am the assassinator of syncopation.'[4]

Despite the threatened disorder, jazz was still regarded as a novelty, and the ODJB kept it so, sweetening the anarchy with silliness. Drum solos were played on saucepan lids, the trombone played with the feet, a bowler hat placed on the end of the cornet and blasted off with the power of the blowing. This was showbusiness. It also helped that, although jazz had been born in the black bars of Storyville in New Orleans, the band themselves were white; what might have been seen as savagery could instead be presented as fun. 'Everybody is going to be "Jazzing" this winter,' promised the adverts for Columbia Records, who released the work of the ODJB in Britain.[5] 'It is the jolliest music imaginable – the real Jazz. It sets the feet a-tingling and is as good as a tonic.'[6] By then, the band had royal backing; they'd played at Buckingham Palace, where George V applauded approvingly and the Prince of Wales was very enthusiastic.

Jazz remained a little jokey for years. At Christmas 1920 the Arding & Hobbs department store in Battersea, south London invited you to 'bring all the family to see the screamingly funny performance of the Arthur Breton Troupe of Performing Animals, including the Animal Jazz Band'.[7] In America, the first half of the 1920s saw the likes of Jelly Roll Morton, King Oliver, Kid Ory and Fats Waller making records that broke new ground and were sometimes very successful, but for the vast majority of Britons, such artists meant nothing. When Lancashire comedian George Formby sang 'John Willie's Jazz Band' in 1926 (claiming to come 'from the tripe plantations down in Wigan land'),[8] it was a parody of Irving Berlin's now-ancient 'Alexander's Ragtime Band' (1911). The public image of jazz was stuck in the past.

There were, though, some fans of contemporary music, particularly among the young and educated, who took it all very seriously. Eventually there were even British bands playing jazz in the New Orleans tradition; hot jazz, as it was called, to distinguish it from commercial, corrupted versions. Spike Hughes, son of the *Daily Telegraph*'s music critic, played hot jazz with his band, the Decca-Dents, and he was definitely serious; he'd studied composition in Vienna and wrote a cello sonata, published in 1928. The members of the ODJB – to say nothing of the new wave of American instrumentalists, led by Louis Armstrong and Bix Beiderbecke – had had no formal education in music.

Equally serious was Fred Elizalde. Born in the Philippines to a Spanish sugar magnate, he was a classically trained pianist who'd disappointed his parents by starting a jazz band while studying law at Stamford University in America. To remove him from such temptation, he was sent to Cambridge in 1927, and within weeks he was again playing in an undergraduate band. By the end of the year he'd secured a residency at the Savoy Hotel in London, putting together a new band that was streets ahead of anyone else in the country. They could play hot jazz to rival the Americans, but there was also a sophistication to the arrangements that hinted at European influences. It was too much for the Savoy, who wanted something sweeter; they let him go in 1929.*

Elizalde's lasting contribution to Britain was the career of Al Bowlly, a singer of mixed Greek and Lebanese parentage who'd been born in Mozambique and brought up in South Africa, before moving to Germany, where he made his first gramophone record. Alerted by a friend to what Elizalde was doing, Bowlly sent a copy of the record as an audition and, after a little haggling, received a £20 advance so he could travel to London to join the band. Being a committed gambler, he promptly blew the money on the horses, but managed to borrow some more and made it to the Savoy, where he was soon acclaimed as the best singer in the field. 'Al Bowlly is a real find,' enthused the *Melody Maker*, a newly launched music paper,

---

* He didn't stay in Britain much longer, or indeed stay with jazz, going on to compose and conduct concert music in France, Spain and the Philippines. He returned to London in the late 1940s to perform his piano concerto and to oversee the recording of his violin concerto.

of his first recording with Elizalde's band;[9] by 1932 he was being promoted by Decca Records as 'England's Bing Crosby'.[10] Just as the British film industry was always measuring itself against Hollywood, so too did popular music look to America to set the standard.

ii

If jazz in its purest form had only limited appeal, it did spark a passion for dancing that swept across all sections of society. Homegrown dance bands sprang up that kept the syncopation of jazz while softening the rougher edges. Tempos were tighter, strings were added, orchestration replaced improvisation, and a smooth-voiced singer was often featured. Mostly, they were not hot. 'Jazz music is essentially erratic; it gets the weirdest possible effects by breaking all the rules,' explained Debroy Somers disapprovingly. He'd served with the band of the Royal Irish Regiment, and now led the Savoy Orpheans, who, he said, were 'a self-respecting syncopated orchestra' which did 'at least pay attention to the rules of music'.[11] Novelist Arnold Bennett liked them, despite himself: 'They play bad music well,' he conceded.[12]

As their name made clear, the Orpheans, formed in 1923, had a residency at the Savoy Hotel, alongside the Savoy Havana Band, who'd started the previous year. Both bands played music for dancing and attracted sufficient customers that other hotels followed the example. Soon, any hotel with aspirations to chic was putting on tea dances in the afternoon, plus music to accompany dinner in the evening, and then dancing after dinner: six hours a day of live performance. Initially, the dancing was modern but modest – foxtrots, one-steps, waltzes, the occasional tango – and the music was often shaded with escapist, exotic themes. At London's Metropole Hotel, the Midnight Follies Orchestra was led by Bert Firman, the youngest bandleader in the world at just sixteen; its repertoire in 1924 included 'Eastern Love', 'Honolulu', 'Nighttime in Italy', 'Pasadena' and 'Riviera Rose'.

Firman was born Herbert Feuerman, the son of Jewish

immigrants from Poland and Austria-Hungary, and in the world of music his ethnicity was not unusual. Most notably there was Benjamin Baruch Ambrose, a Polish Jew who'd come to Britain as a child. Generally known by just his surname, or sometimes as Bert Ambrose, he and his band had a residency at the fashionable Embassy Club in Bond Street, before moving in 1927 to the newly opened May Fair Hotel, lured by the beautiful dining room with its gently domed ceiling, its powder-blue glass pillars and the furniture of polished sycamore. What really swayed him, though, was a contract worth £10,000 a year, in addition to what he could earn from record sales, radio and variety performances. 'The offer was too good to be refused,' he said. 'I am now the highest paid dance-band conductor in the world.'[13] His band was generally reckoned to be the best for dancing, and he was revered by both his musicians and audiences, despite his rudeness to all of them. It was said that when a young aristocrat slipped him ten shillings with a request, he screwed up the note and threw it away – he wouldn't play requests for that kind of money.

Others were less disdainful. Billy Cotton, a veteran of Gallipoli and a Royal Air Force pilot by the age of nineteen, played amateur football for Brentford and Wimbledon after the war, as well as working as a bus conductor. He was also a drummer, and was sacked from the buses after his boss saw him playing with the San Prado Band in the Palace of Dancing at the Empire Festival when he was supposed to be on shift. So he focused on music, and in 1925 got his big break when he was asked to form the London Savannah Band as the resident orchestra at the Palais de Danse in Southport, Lancashire, a new venue that claimed the largest parquet dance floor in the world, capable of accommodating a thousand couples. He didn't stay long, though, because successful bandleaders were regularly poached by other venues; Cotton was soon playing in London at Ciro's Club. Coming out from behind his drums to be the frontman, he decided that he was there to entertain, not to push boundaries. 'If you want to be a pioneer,' he concluded, 'you find yourself having trouble with the bank balance.'[14]

The spread of dance music around the country was largely driven by the BBC, which transmitted its first dance-band programme in April 1923. The Savoy Havana Band were already being promoted as 'the world's greatest exponents of syncopated music',[15] but their real advantage was that they were based just round the corner from the BBC's studios in Savoy Hill. Thereafter, dance bands became a mainstay of broadcasting; live relays reached all corners of the land, and young people danced along in their own homes. When newspapers – the *Daily Mail* in 1927, the *Daily Herald* in 1931 – polled their readers over what they wanted to hear on the radio, dance bands regularly featured in the top five, along with variety, news, light orchestral music and military bands.

They weren't everyone's cup of tea. Labour leader Ramsay Mac-Donald complained to his friend John Reith that there was too much 'rumpety-trumpety kind of stuff' on the BBC,[16] but there was support for dance music in even higher quarters. 'The Prince of Wales has sometimes asked me to play certain tunes,' wrote bandleader Jack Payne in his 1932 autobiography, remembering his time at London's Hotel Cecil. 'When "Two Little Words" was popular, he would sometimes like to have it played seven or eight times in an evening.'[17] The fact that Payne was publishing an autobiography at the tender age of thirty-three reflected the star status of bandleaders. He, in particular, was a household name, having just left his job as the BBC's director of dance music. (He departed, said the *Western Mail*, 'in a perfect orgy of 6/8 time syncopation with moaning saxophones'.)[18]

As the dance craze heated up, foxtrots and one-steps proved insufficient. Novelty was needed and found in a seemingly endless succession of steps coming across the Atlantic: from the Big Apple and the Banana Slide to the Black Bottom and the Dirty Dick, taking in the Conga, the Rumba, the Shag, the Shimmy and the Suzie Q. Biggest of all was the Charleston, introduced to London in 1925. WILL THE 'CHARLESTON' BECOME 'ALL THE RAGE'? asked a newspaper headline,[19] and the answer was a breathless affirmative, as fashionable folk threw themselves into an athletic display of waving their arms and kicking their legs forward and back to a stuttering, syncopated beat. It was 'a muscle-grinding dance with an almost impossible rhythm', complained Major Cecil Taylor, president of the Imperial Society of Dance Teachers,[20] and others disapproved of the ensuing spectacle. 'The couples look like a lot of monkeys licking hot chestnuts,' shuddered the Reverend E. W. Rodgers, vicar of St Aidan's in Bristol. 'It is neurotic. It is rotten. It stinks.'[21] But the Prince of Wales took it up, and its popularity was assured.*

Even more popular – and much less exhausting – was watching other people dance the Charleston – people like Lev Winogradsky, who was just six years old when his Ukrainian family came to London, fleeing a pogrom. Changing his name to Louis Grad, he started entering dance competitions, making his mark by adding a couple of Cossack steps to his routine. In 1926 he won an event billed as the Charleston Championship of the World at the Royal Albert Hall, London, with judges including promoter Charles B. Cochran and the American dancer Fred Astaire, then appearing in the musical *Lady Be Good* at the Empire in Leicester Square.

Grad turned professional, dancing on stage as a solo act and as part of a duo. Meanwhile, his younger brother Boris, now known as Bernard, formed his own double act, acclaimed by the press as 'the cleverest Charleston dancers in the world'.[22] Making the most of the moment, both brothers performed at clubs, cinemas and variety theatres across Britain and Europe, finding regular work without ever becoming stars, though Bernard did join Jack Payne's band for a while, doing a routine where he would pretend to play a saxophone solo before breaking out into a crazed dance.†

---

* British dances were far less successful: the Chestnut Tree never really caught on. Nor did the Twist, a French contribution described in 1928 as 'a gliding, graceful gavotte'; Stanley Baldwin witnessed the Twist at Aix-les-Bains and said he was delighted with the experience.

† Both Lew Grade and Bernard Delfont – as they became known – later moved from performance into management, and were given peerages in 1976.

The fact that dance bands were employing specialist dancers, even comedians, was final confirmation that this was pure entertainment, just another branch of variety. Certainly, it was a long way removed from its roots. 'Jazz was a ghastly banging of drums and tin cans principally practised by negroes,' wrote Jack Payne in 1932. 'It went out years ago – and a good thing too. The kind of music one hears from a good dance orchestra nowadays bears no resemblance to it whatever.'[23]

iii

'Youth is regarded as the one asset worth pursuing,' wrote Patrick Balfour, known professionally as Mr Gossip of the *Daily Sketch*. (He was the inspiration for Simon Balcairn, Mr Chatterbox, in Evelyn Waugh's novel *Vile Bodies*.) And he was clear who symbolised this trend: 'The post-war boom in youth, headed by the Prince of Wales, has brought a profound change.'[24] Like his grandfather, the man who had become Edward VII, the current Prince of Wales was seen to embody a generational shift in British life.

Born in 1894, this Prince Edward – known to friends and family as David – had been the right age to serve in the war, and had done so, though he wasn't allowed to fight in the front line. After the war he was a very public, visible figure, both at home and abroad. He travelled widely across the Empire, visiting Canada in 1919, Australia in 1920, India in 1921, west and South Africa in 1925, east Africa in 1928, and making several trips to America, once with a stopover in Hawaii, where he took surfing lessons.* Wherever he went, he was feted, not just as the future King-Emperor, but for his charming informality. He 'smiled away the difference which Australians believed lay between royalty and the common people', frothed the Sydney *Sun*.[25] 'Tolerant, sport-worshipping, handsome,' wrote British journalist Gordon Beckles, 'he is sincerely democratic, finding relaxation in easily assimilated pleasures.'[26]

---

* The surviving photographs are the earliest known pictures of a British surfer.

Others called him the 'Ambassador of Empire' and 'the most popular young man of his day'.[27]

If the Prince of Wales was treated like a Hollywood star, it was partly because he was seen as being so very modern. He frequented nightclubs, and even if his royal presence sometimes dampened the atmosphere ('When he came in, he put the mockers on, and nobody let their hair down at all,' complained Billy Cotton),[28] just his being there was sufficient for those reading the newspapers. 'I've Danced with a Man Who's Danced with a Girl Who's Danced with the Prince of Wales,' sang cabaret artist Elsa Lanchester, and it didn't seem implausible.

He was also celebrated for his fashion sense, popularising new items of male attire: the Fair Isle sweater, the double-breasted dinner jacket, shirts with a cutaway collar that might accommodate a necktie with a broad knot. He wore a felt hat with a turned-down brim, and plus fours – breeches that extended four inches below the knee – which he helped bring off the golf course and into real life.*

As the heir to the throne, he was able to get away with such sartorial indulgence, but more generally this dandy-ish attention to fashion was viewed with suspicion. The fact that young men cared about clothes was a growing source of concern. 'My son is a good lad,' said one father, 'but wastes his money on Oxford trousers and jazz sweaters.'[29] The trousers in question, commonly known as Oxford bags, appeared in early 1925, bell-bottoms with a twenty-six-inch knee, flaring to thirty-two inches at the ankle. They came in unexpected colours as well: blue, mauve, sage, toffee. In Bradford that spring, there was a sighting of 'a young man in a blue blazer and a wonderful pair of pink trousers'.[30]

Some saw this sort of thing as 'a sad sign of masculine decadence',[31] and perhaps they were right. It was surely no coincidence that as men's clothing was becoming more voluminous, women's fashion was busily flattening curves, emphasising narrowness.

---

* By contrast, his father popularised the wearing of horn-rimmed glasses.

'The boys and girls seem to be engaged in a game of topsy-turvy,' observed one columnist; 'if things go on like this, a couple of weeks will find the women in trousers and the men in skirts.'[32] The same trend was seen in young men having their hair not just cut but styled, while women were taking to the short, severe lines of the bob cut, followed by the shingle bob (with the hairline showing on the back of the neck), styles that were suitable for the cloche hats that were all the rage. In 1924 came a still more sensational development. 'The shingle is being followed by the Eton crop, which shows the ear,' marvelled the *Daily Mirror*; 'exactly like a schoolboy's style of haircut.'[33] As a cartoon in *Punch* had it: 'Grow your hair, man, you look like a girl!'[34] It was very confusing; irreverent somehow, and yet exciting.

These strange developments were particularly noted in students, and they attracted growing hostility. In October 1925, under the headline THE GIRL MEN OF CAMBRIDGE, the *Daily Sketch* attacked the 'soft, effeminate, painted, be-rouged youths' found at that university, adding that Oxford and London were similarly infested.[35] The piece sparked a debate that raged across the nation for weeks.

The rugged explorer F. A. Mitchell-Hedges ('pipe between his teeth, he looks one squarely in the eye', gushed an interviewer)[36] was revolted by those who frequented fashionable West End hotels: 'young fellows with immaculate Marcel-waved hair and heavily powdered faces, and close-cropped, bull-necked girls.'[37] Liliane Faithfull, the former principal of Cheltenham Ladies' College, blamed parents who pursued the cult of youth, who were 'so eager to avoid growing old that they encourage their boys and girls to call them by their Christian names, and to treat them with a familiarity which bordered on contempt'.[38] And in local debating societies – including those in Portsmouth, Hampshire and Nuneaton, Warwickshire[39] – speakers had a variety of explanations: young men nowadays were only concerned with 'money, sport and pleasure', though even there they didn't 'play the manly sports of yesterday', they just wanted to watch and to gamble; they lacked the ability to concentrate; they were without 'feeling for country and empire'; they hadn't been taught the three R's in school.*

This was the new generation, the post-war generation who said they didn't care about the conflict. 'We haven't exactly forgotten it, but it was never anything to do with us,' a foppish young chap tells an ex-serviceman in Nancy Mitford's novel *Highland Fling* (1931). 'It was your war and I hope you enjoyed it.' Mitford herself was one of the cream of this crop, the Bright Young People as they were dubbed, a coterie of London high society whose doings were, for a short while, a source of newspaper fascination. The Bright Young People were dedicated to hedonism, according to the gossip columns; they threw extravagantly themed parties, they engaged in madcap escapades across the city, they had a casual attitude towards sexual morality and intoxicants.

If the disproportionate attention accorded to such a small circle infuriated many – Labour MP Neil Maclean denounced the 'midnight exhibitions of smart-set imbecility'[40] – it reflected a public longing for new pleasures. A young suburban couple from outside the gilded circles might never get to drink cocktails in one of the new American bars that were opening in London hotels, but they could read about them and fantasise. It was possible to listen to dance bands at home on the radio or the gramophone, and to mix one's own drinks: J. C. Vickery of Regent Street offered a basic cocktail shaker for a guinea.[†]

'These are essentially the days of the young,' reflected the press.[41]

---

* Debating societies were another manifestation of the trend for social clubs. To take a snapshot: in the same month as these comments (October 1925), a group in Berwick, Northumberland was debating subsidies to the coal industry, while at the other end of the county, in North Shields, it was 'Should the harbour boroughs be linked by means of a bridge?' In Prestatyn, Flintshire the subject was heredity versus environment, and in Motherwell, Lanarkshire: 'Is suicide cowardly?'

† Popular cocktails in the late 1920s included Bridegroom's Bouquet, Bronx, Clover Club, Cooperstown, Gin Fizz, Gloom Raiser, Horse's Neck, Houla-houla, Love and Hate, Manhattan, Martini, Monkey Gland, Orange Blossom, the Pink 'Un, Prairie Oyster, Pussyfoot (non-alcoholic), Rose, Sidecar, White Lady and Yellow Rattler.

'Nobody admits to being old nowadays.'[42] In this new, unstuffy world, it was important to try to be up to the minute, even if one ran the risk of appearing a little foolish, as when a Tory election agent in south London claimed that 'the young Conservatives were becoming known as the Bright Young People of Streatham.'[43] Commerce was similarly infected. In 1925, Jaeger advertised tweed coats in appropriately sober terms: 'They are correctly cut, well-tailored and finished with every attention to those details which make all the difference in the appearance of a coat.'[44] Five years later, the same garments were being sold in Bright Young Slang: 'I mean, unless it is perfectly sinless in cut and design, nothing can look more bogus. Too completely pseudo, don't you agree – or don't you?'[45]

iv

T. S. Eliot's obituary of Marie Lloyd ended with an apology that her death in November 1922 'has had a depressing effect, and that I am quite incapable of taking any interest in any literary events in England in the last two months, if any have taken place'.[46] He was being overly modest; the previous month had seen the publication of the first issue of literary magazine the *Criterion*, edited by Eliot himself, and to which he contributed his own poem *The Waste Land*. That piece, together with James Joyce's novel *Ulysses*, published earlier in the same year, would prove the most influential modernist works in the language, opening up new paths for poetry and fiction.

Neither attracted much public interest, though. More than a decade on, the annual report of Southampton's public libraries regretted that there had been not a single borrowing of a book by Eliot.[47] But then they were never likely to be popular. Both works employed constantly shifting styles and viewpoints, with dense webs of cultural allusions and a rejection of conventional narrative; this was the epitome of highbrow literature, and such intellectual delights were not intended for a wide readership. When they were noticed at all, they prompted confusion as much as admiration. Eliot had a tendency to 'eccentricity for eccentricity's sake', said one critic,[48] while *Ulysses* was – according to the *Gentlewoman* – 'revolting but original'.[49]

Both writers were essentially internationalist. Eliot was an American living in London – he became a British subject in 1927 – and the *Criterion* was rooted in a shared European culture. And although Dublin-born Joyce remained British all his life, choosing not to take Irish citizenship, he had long since lived abroad: *Ulysses* was written in Zurich and Paris, and wasn't published in Britain until 1936. These two at least escaped the charge of parochial isolationism that was levelled at much of British culture.

Beyond them, there was truth in the accusation, not just in literature but across the arts. Futurism, Dada, Purism, constructivism, surrealism, socialist realism – there seemed no end of radical new movements coming off the cultural conveyor belt, mostly trying to find a way to express the world of mass production and the machine age and, in some cases, deliberately seeking to shock by cocking a snook at convention. But they were all decidedly European, foreign. The closest Britain came was the short-lived Vorticism, from 1914 to 1915, and its even shorter-lived successor, Group X in 1920, after which the entire movement became painter Wyndham Lewis, a one-man avant-garde. Elsewhere in the 1920s, there were painters associated with the highbrow social circle that centred on Bloomsbury – Vanessa Bell, Roger Fry, Duncan Grant – artists who were undeniably modern but didn't cock much of a snook; their work included a good deal of recognisable portraiture, often of themselves and their friends.

When there was the occasional shock, it was hurriedly covered up. The crowd-drawing sensation of the Royal Academy's 1926 Summer Exhibition was John Souter's *The Breakdown*, a painting of a black saxophonist in evening dress, sitting on the head of a toppled statue, while a naked white woman with shingled hair dances, her eyes closed in apparent ecstasy. There was some doubt as to whether the statue was supposed to be of Britannia or of Minerva, Roman goddess of wisdom, but in either case the message was clear enough to the *Devon and Exeter Gazette*: 'Obviously it is the artist's indictment of our hectic, feverish post-war life, with reckless abandonment of old-fashioned conventions, now dubbed "Victorian".'[50] *The Times* understood the point, but didn't agree with it: 'It is not true that any civilisation worth a cent has succumbed to the saxophone, and if it were it would not be a pictorial subject.'[51]

As a 'synthesis of the jazz obsession,' wrote the *Sphere*'s critic, *The Breakdown* was inferior to another exhibit, Laura Knight's *The Saxophone Player*: 'a girl with straight-combed hair and hard, restless eyes, evidently competent with the instrument she holds.'[52] But the greatest outrage of all was voiced by the *Melody Maker*. 'We jazz musicians protest against, and repudiate the juxtaposition of an undraped white woman with a black man,' fumed editor Edgar Jackson. 'We demand that the habit of associating our music with the primitive and barbarous negro deviation shall cease forthwith.'[53]

The Times argued that 'the Academy should not encourage pictures like *The Breakdown*',[54] and Jackson said it should be burned. Both were granted their wish. Within a week, the painting had been replaced by a portrait of Lady Diana Duff Cooper as a child, with a notice saying that the original exhibit had been withdrawn at the request of the Colonial Office. Nonetheless, crowds continued to flock to the exhibition, making their way to where it had once hung. Meanwhile, Souter destroyed his own work. The Royal Academy later explained that the picture had been 'considered to be obnoxious to British subjects living abroad in daily contact with a coloured population'.[55] It was the same argument as Arthur Greenwood's fear of movies that could 'bring into contempt Western civilisation'.[56] It might impugn the purity of white women.*

Also seeking to capture the spirit of the times was Noël

---

* In 1962 Souter reconstructed *The Breakdown* from his original sketches.

Coward's play *The Vortex* (1924). Portraying the moral insecurity at the heart of the Bright Young People, it was the story of an effeminate, cocaine-addicted musician (played by Coward himself on stage, and by Ivor Novello in the 1928 film adaptation) and his mother, who desperately clings on to the tattered shreds of her youth, cuckolding her husband with a string of young lovers. '*The Vortex* is one of the first plays that is completely typical of this age of nervous distraction,'[57] declared the *Weekly Dispatch*, and many were shocked, some pleasantly. 'People were getting tired of insipid drawing-room scenes,' said actress Kate Cutler, who played the female lead in the touring production. 'There is so much more in these modern plays.'[58]

Others denied it was anything new at all. 'Just now there is a fashion for plays which deal with the alleged vices and weaknesses of smart society,' wrote veteran journalist Sir Sidney Low (he'd edited the *St James's Gazette* back in the 1890s), but he claimed that this was simply a modern incarnation of a venerable tradition that went back at least to Restoration comedy.[59] Still, *The Vortex* made Coward 'the most talked-of playwright of the moment,'[60] and he went on to a string of hits with witty dissections of modern life, including *Hay Fever* (1924), *Semi-Monde* (1926) and *Private Lives* (1929).

The musical equivalent came from William Walton, who set Edith Sitwell's eccentric cycle of poems *Façade* (1923) to a score that threw together jazz, classical and music-hall traditions, quoting liberally from other works and taking nothing seriously. At the public premiere in 1923, Sitwell declaimed her nonsense verse via a megaphone poking through theatrical curtains, behind which the twenty-one-year-old Walton conducted a six-piece ensemble. It caused a gratifying scandal. The press denounced it as an insult, decent society was outraged, and even Noël Coward walked out.

All this was wilfully outside Britain's musical mainstream, still dominated by composers who'd made their name before the war. Edward Elgar, in his sixties at the time of the Armistice, was writing little – he'd 'gone off the boil' in his own account[61] – but Arnold

Bax, Frank Bridge, Gustav Holst, John Ireland and Ralph Vaughan Williams were still active.* They wrote within recognisable conventions, a long way removed from the musical experiments on the Continent, of Arnold Schoenberg in Vienna, Kurt Weill in Berlin, Erik Satie in Paris.

The single most popular contemporary composer in Britain was Albert Ketèlbey, whose light orchestral works took an adoring public to exotic locations. His *In a Monastery Garden* (1915) was said to have been the first British piece to sell a million copies, and it was followed by *In a Persian Market* (1920), *In a Chinese Temple Garden* (1923), *By the Blue Hawaiian Waters* (1927), *In the Mystic Land of Egypt* (1931) and *From a Japanese Screen* (1934). Such sweet, melodic pieces – like the repertoire of Bert Firman and the Midnight Follies Orchestra – were as close to foreign lands as most people were going to get.

v

In 1931 the *Daily Express* drama critic, Hannen Swaffer, lamented the death of working-class comedy on stage, and its replacement by 'over-priced cabaret where vulgarities that would not be tolerated by decent costermongers were committed by semi-effeminates in evening dress'.[62] He was thinking, perhaps, of the likes of Douglas Byng, who dressed 'in pink stays, glittering tights, false fronts and pince-nez',[63] and specialised in camp innuendo. In 'I'm One of the Queens of England' (1930), he claimed to be the reincarnation of a former monarch, although he was uncertain which one:

> I don't know who the hell I was,
> or what I may have been,

---

* The most significant name missing from this list is George Butterworth, one of the most talented composers of the new generation. He was killed in 1916, aged thirty-one, in the Battle of the Somme, a fortnight after an action that won him the Military Cross.

But one thing's very certain:
I was not the Virgin Queen.[64]

Also popular in cabaret, and in revue, was Gwen Farrar, daughter of a South African mining magnate. She formed a double act with Norah Blaney, who played piano and sang in a conventional trill, underpinned by Farrar's rather gruffer voice, as they tracked youth culture in a series of topical songs: 'Percy's Posh Plus Fours Are Priceless' (1923), 'Shall I Have It Bobbed or Shingled?' (1924) and 'We Don't Want to Get Married' (1925). There was the added attraction, according to one producer, that 'Norah fills the stalls with all the young men, and Gwen has all the lesbians in London to see her.'[65]

After the act split up, Farrar found a new partner in Billy Mayerl, formerly of the Savoy Havana Band, and a new hit song: 'Masculine Women! Feminine Men!' (1926). When the duo appeared at the Alhambra in Leicester Square, they shared a bill with the veteran music-hall star Hetty King, billed as 'the greatest male impersonator'; to which, suggested the *Era*, 'it would be safer nowadays to add "on the stage"'.[66] In real life, one of Farrar's lovers was Dolly Wilde, niece of Oscar, who'd driven ambulances in France during the war, and was now a socialite with addictions to alcohol and heroin.

Unlike homosexual acts between men, there were no laws against lesbian sex, though an attempt was made. In 1921, a Criminal Law Amendment Bill had a clause added in the Commons: 'Any act of gross indecency between female persons shall be a misdemeanour.' When it reached the Lords, however, the clause was savaged. Arguments were made that it would encourage blackmail, cast suspicion on perfectly healthy relationships, be impossible to prove, and – worst of all – put ideas into women's heads. If a case were brought, said the Earl of Desart, a former director of public prosecutions, 'it would be made public to thousands of people that there was this offence; that there was such a horror'. Lord Birkenhead, the lord chancellor, agreed that ignorance was bliss: 'Of every thousand women, taken as a whole, 999 have never even heard a whisper of these practices.'[67] No one spoke in favour, and the clause was dropped. Lesbianism continued to be legal.

In elevated society at least, male and female homosexuality was open in a way that it had not been before, depicted in skimpy disguise in novels by those who knew: Michael Arlen's *The Green Hat* (1924), Rosamund Lehmann's *Dusty Answer* (1927) and E. F. Benson's *The Inheritor* (1930). Most celebrated in highbrow quarters was Virginia Woolf's *Orlando: A Biography* (1928), in which the eponymous hero changes sex and sexuality, the influence of Woolf's relationship with writer Vita Sackville-West everywhere apparent.

At the centre of another social circle was Evelyn Spottiswoode, whose great wealth came from the family firm, Dewar's whisky. She threw celebrated dinner parties at her country house, Rooksnest near Hungerford in Berkshire, at the end of which the proper conventions were observed: those in women's clothes would retire to the drawing room, while Spottiswoode and others in male attire would remain for port and cigars. One of her resident lovers was Dorothea Macnee, the alcoholic granddaughter of an earl, who had her first child with her own husband (an equally alcoholic racehorse trainer) and her second with someone else's; she continued seeing both men – the latter in his matrimonial home – even after she moved into Rooksnest, taking her older son, Patrick, with her. Spottiswoode insisted that Patrick call her Uncle and wanted him to wear skirts, but settled for a kilt as a compromise. 'Given time, we'll make a good woman of him,' she promised.[68] She also paid for him to go to Eton, though the morality he'd learned at home conflicted with the school's ethos: he was expelled for running a book on Royal Ascot and for selling pornographic magazines to other boys.*

---

* Patrick Macnee would become famous for the twinkling irony he brought to the role of John Steed in the 1960s TV series *The Avengers*, an impeccably courteous, upper-middle-class Englishman.

Most open of all was the novelist Radclyffe Hall, with 'her flaxen Eton crop, her monocle and her masculine style of dress'.[69] She lived with her lover, Una, Lady Troubridge, and she liked to be called John. She was also a much admired writer, whose novel *Adam's Breed* (1926) won both the James Tait Black Memorial Prize and the Prix Femina–Vie Heureuse,* without her ever having become widely known. That changed with her fifth novel, *The Well of Loneliness* (1928), the story of an upper-class woman named Stephen Gordon (her parents had wanted a boy) and her love for Mary Llewellyn, a younger woman she meets when they're driving ambulances in the war.

It was a controversial subject, Hall's first lesbian storyline, 'an accurate psychological study' as she said, 'calculated to encourage mutual understanding between normal persons and the inverted'.[70] Her existing publisher, Cassell, turned the book down and it was published instead by Jonathan Cape, priced at fifteen shillings – twice the price of their other novels – in order to dissuade prurient thrill-seekers. Not that there were any thrills to be found. 'Those with a taste for pornography,' warned Cape, 'will be greatly disappointed.'[71] The closest it came to describing a sexual act was the single line: 'that night they were not divided'. It was a serious work, insisted its defenders, without any of 'the lustful sheikhs and cavemen and vamps of popular fiction'.[72] And the reviews, for the most part, were good. It was 'sincere, courageous, high-minded and often beautifully expressed' in the words of the *Times Literary Supplement*;[73] 'a work of considerable art', said *Tatler*;[74] full of 'great power and pathos', thought *Truth*,[75] and Arnold Bennett agreed: 'great force and beauty'.[76]

Dissenting from this view was James Douglas, editor of the *Sunday Express*, who took grave exception to the book. 'I would rather give a healthy boy or a healthy girl a phial of prussic acid than this novel,' he thundered. 'Poison kills the body, but moral

---

* The only other book to win both prizes had been E. M. Forster's *A Passage to India* (1924).

poison kills the soul.'* His condemnatory article was trailed with billboard posters: A BOOK THAT SHOULD BE SUPPRESSED.[77]

Stung by the attack, Cape sent copies of the novel to the director of public prosecutions and to the home secretary. The latter, William Joynson-Hicks, was notoriously prudish, seeing decadence and debauchery wherever he looked, a man who – said a moral campaigner, approvingly – was 'greatly concerned with the Bolshevik element in literary and artistic circles'.[78] His campaigns against nightclubs had earned him the sarcastic nickname High Kicks Hicks in London's demi-monde.[79] Now, having taken soundings, he told Cape that the novel was undoubtedly obscene and that publication should cease. In response, Cape moved production to Paris and began importing copies, a transparent ploy that didn't work; a shipment was seized under the Obscene Publications Act.

The subsequent trial and appeal became a literary *cause célèbre*. Dozens of leading writers – including John Buchan, T. S. Eliot, E. M. Forster, George Bernard Shaw and Virginia Woolf – signed a letter supporting the suppression of 'obscene photographs and the rest of the trash sold by dealers in vulgar pornography' while asking for serious artists and writers to be treated with more respect.[80] Many of the signatories were recruited as witnesses to testify to the book's merits, but the magistrate refused to hear their evidence. Indeed, the quality of the writing was part of the problem. 'The book is a very subtle book,' ruled the appeal judge, 'and probably more dangerous because of that fact.'[81] The novel was deemed to be obscene, the seized copies were destroyed, and bookshops ceased selling it.

Published the same month as *The Well of Loneliness* was D. H. Lawrence's *Lady Chatterley's Lover* (1928). He'd long been a controversial writer – his novel *The Rainbow* (1915) had been banned

---

* This imagery was long established. When Lord Campbell, the lord chief justice, introduced the Obscene Publications Act 1857, he had talked of obscene literature as a 'poison more deadly than prussic acid'.

– and the new book was the most shocking yet. To start with, the story was deeply immoral: a disabled war veteran is cuckolded as his wife finds sexual fulfilment with his gamekeeper. And then, unlike Hall, Lawrence insisted on describing the sexual encounters in great detail, made immeasurably worse by the language he employed, words previously confined to pornography.*

There was no question of a British publication – it would have been instantly and successfully prosecuted – so the first edition was printed privately in Italy, where Lawrence now lived. Nonetheless, the British papers gave it extensive coverage. Under the headline A LANDMARK IN EVIL, *John Bull* professed itself disgusted by the 'bearded satyr' Lawrence and by 'the fetid masterpiece of this sex-sodden genius'.[82] The controversy ensured that copies were smuggled into the country, changing hands for up to £25. Alternatively, it was sold in the bookstalls of Paris hotels, along with *The Well of Loneliness* and *Ulysses*.†

It was now open season on Lawrence. A film script of *Lady Chatterley's Lover* was submitted to the British Board of Film Censors, and rejected instantly. When he sent a manuscript of new verse from Italy to his London publishers, it was seized by the Post Office, and a dozen or so pieces were excluded from the subsequent volume, *Pansies* (1929). ('A book of savage indignation,' wrote critic Geoffrey Grigson, which 'must be labelled poetry for lack of a better name.'[83])

Also in 1929, the Warren Gallery in London staged the first-ever exhibition of Lawrence's oil paintings and watercolours, most of them nudes; it was raided by the police, and fifteen of the

---

* When the book was charged in 1960 under a new Obscene Publications Act, prosecuting counsel Mervyn Griffith-Jones famously itemised the offence: 'The word "fuck" or "fucking" occurs no less than thirty times. I have added them up, but I do not guarantee that I have added them all up. "Cunt" fourteen times; "balls" thirteen times; "shit" and "arse" six times apiece; "cock" four times; "piss" three times, and so on.' His figures were inaccurate.

† Imported copies of *Ulysses* had been confiscated and destroyed.

twenty-five works were seized under the Obscene Publications Act. The paintings, said the *Bystander*, 'were quite on a par with the less restrained portions of *Lady Chatterley's Lover*', save that, while Lawrence was a gifted writer, 'as an artist he can do rather less with a paint brush than a child of seven without any natural flair'.[84] Nonetheless, a host of artists and critics were again ready to testify to the works' quality; and again none was heard, though the police brief did give his own opinion: the paintings were 'gross, coarse, hideous and unlovely, from any aesthetic or artistic point of view'. The gallery's lawyer protested that there was no precedent for serious art being brought up in a magistrate's court. And, he observed drily, this 'new form of censorship' came under 'a so-called advanced government'; Joynson-Hicks was gone now, replaced by Labour's J. R. Clynes, but there was no change in attitude.[85] A compromise was reached: the gallery agreed to close the show, and the paintings were returned, undestroyed.

Lawrence died of tuberculosis in 1930, aged just forty-four. He'd left England more than a decade before, and he'd always been an isolated figure in British cultural life; too earthy for the Edwardians, too earnest for the 1920s. Perhaps, though, he was ahead of his time. As the mood of the nation turned with the decade, his passionate intensity, his absence of wit, made him ever more relevant and popular. 'No writer has had a greater influence on the younger generation than that great Midland genius, D. H. Lawrence,' wrote Godfrey Sloane, columnist on Birmingham's *Evening Despatch*, in 1937.[86]

After Lawrence's death, there was published a heavily expurgated version of *Lady Chatterley's Lover* that he would surely not have approved. The sex and the coarse language were integral to his search for authenticity; without them the piece was neutered, stripped of its power. 'It is a strange and beautiful book, but inexpressibly sad,' wrote his friend Aldous Huxley, of the uncensored original. 'So at bottom was its author's life.'[87]

vi

November 1928 saw the tenth anniversary of the Armistice. This was the year that the BBC was finally allowed to broadcast the Cenotaph service, with churches across the country installing loudspeakers to transmit the programme. It was also the year that the cultural silence about the experience of the war was finally broken.

In December, Edmund Blunden, a prolific if not best-selling poet, published *Undertones of War*, a memoir of his time in the trenches, and although it was not the first such book, it caught the public imagination like none had before; the first edition sold out in twenty-four hours, the second within a week. The reviews were ecstatic. 'I have read most of the war books,' said Oliver Way of the *Graphic*; 'this is the greatest of them.' It was 'wonderful' (*Daily Mirror*); 'a great book' (*Sphere*), 'beyond shadow of doubt, the war-book for which we in England have been waiting' (*Birmingham Daily Post*). Arnold Bennett was clear: 'This book will be a classic. It cannot *not* be a classic.'[88]

The same month saw the first production of R. C. Sherriff's play *Journey's End*, set in an officers' dugout on the Western Front in 1918. Turned down by several theatres – partly because the idea of an all-male cast was deemed uncommercial – it was eventually put on by the Stage Society, who specialised in difficult new work. The director was James Whale, a former cobbler who had become interested in theatre while in a German prisoner-of-war camp, and it starred an unknown twenty-one-year-old actor called Laurence Olivier (he 'bears a strong facial resemblance to Mr Ronald Colman', observed one critic[89]).* It was a surprise hit and within a year there were dozens of productions around the world, in several languages.

Though *Undertones of War* and *Journey's End* were both remarkable pieces, their impact was largely due to timing. A decade

---

* Olivier was replaced by Colin Clive, who went on to star in James Whale's 1930 film of the play, produced by George Pearson.

on from the war, it seemed the country had suddenly woken from a cultural coma, ready now not merely to mourn the dead, but to listen to the living, to hear the soldiers' experiences. The wall of silence having been breached, a host of ex-servicemen poured through. 'The Great War, as a general interest, has come into its own again,' observed the *Illustrated London News* in 1929,[90] the year that saw the premiere in London of Sean O'Casey's play *The Silver Tassie,** and the publication of Compton Mackenzie's *Gallipoli Memories*, Robert Aldington's semi-autobiographical novel *Death of a Hero* and Robert Graves's memoir *Good-Bye to All That*. There was also Henry Williamson's *The Wet Flanders Plain*, which was followed by *The Patriot's Progress* in 1930, along with Siegfried Sassoon's *Memoirs of an Infantry Officer*.

Not all were received as well as Blunden and Sherriff's work had been. Graves's father was a poet and the harshest review of *Good-Bye to All That* drew attention to this lineage. 'Mr Graves comes of a family with a remarkable record for producing second-rate men of letters; we should say from this volume that its reputation will be maintained.'[91] Nonetheless, the book sold thirty thousand copies in its first few weeks, and there seemed no limit to the wish to examine the war.†

Hubert Griffiths' play *Tunnel Trench*, untouched since its single performance in 1924, was revived, the first offering at the new Duchess Theatre in the West End. R. C. Sherriff attended the first night, and said the piece caught 'the maddening futility of fighting and killing men who were really of my own race'.[92] Another drama, *Who Goes Next?* (1931) by James Wedgewood Drawbell and Reginald Simpson – respectively editor and drama critic of the *Sunday Chronicle* – saw six British officers digging an escape tunnel from a hut in a prisoner-of-war camp. Like *Journey's End*, this was another 'no-woman play',[93] an idea inverted by L. du Garde Peach in his

---

* It had been rejected by W. B. Yeats at the Abbey Theatre, Dublin.

† The father in question, A. P. Graves, took exception to his son's depiction of the family, and responded with his own autobiography, *A Return to All That* (1930).

all-female *Home Fires* (1930), depicting the impact of the conflict on a group of women, including a German governess, in an English country house.

There were also contributions from abroad: Ernest Hemingway's *A Farewell to Arms* (1929), Jaroslav Hašek's *The Good Soldier Schweik* (1923, translated 1930), and two German novels, Arnold Zweig's *The Case of Sergeant Grischa* (1927, translated 1928) and Erich Maria Remarque's *All Quiet on the Western Front* (1929). The latter was the biggest sensation of all; it sold 100,000 copies in the space of weeks, and didn't stop. 'Probably there has never been a publishing success quite like it,' marvelled a Liverpool librarian, noting that demand was strong months after publication.[94] It was also deeply controversial, partly because of its horrific descriptions and its uncompromising anti-war stance, and partly because it invited sympathy for the enemy. So although one public library in London bought 110 copies to cope with the demand, many others – from Bournemouth to Glasgow, Port Sunlight to Romford – refused to stock it at all.

The new mood also saw the republication of some books that had been lost in the silent years. Among them was *Combed Out* (1920) by F. A. Voigt, who'd been conscripted in 1916 and went on to become a journalist on the *Manchester Guardian* after the war. Drawing on his diaries and letters, he caught the confusing, exhausting tedium of army life, in which random cruelties and kindnesses loom larger than victories or defeats. Soldiers admit to being 'thoroughly scared' and throw scorn at politicians: 'If I had Lloyd George here, I'd shoot the blighter.' The most powerful passage is an account of a field hospital, the bloody shambles of a 'butcher's shop'.

Structurally, Voigt's book was a mix of reportage and fictionalised incidents in disjointed episodes, depicting a world without apparent logic or narrative, and this became the standard approach to the subject. Also to become familiar was Voigt's insistence that British and German soldiers had more in common with each other than either had with their own political leaders ('Jerry wants ter get 'ome to 'is missis an' kiddies just as much as what we do!'), and the anti-war sentiments that stem from that realisation.

As ever with such cultural moments, the fashion passed. Subsequent works yielded diminishing returns, and the style became ossified. A. G. Macdonell served two years on the Western Front before being invalided out with shellshock, and opened his humorous travelogue *England, Their England* (1933) with a bleakly ironic account of his experience. But that's just the first chapter; thereafter, he promises: 'There will be no streams of consciousness, chapters long, in the best style of Bloomsbury, describing minutely the sensations of a man who has been caught in a heavy-howitzer barrage while taking a nap in the local mortuary.'

Despite the mockery, the deluge of war literature had made an impact on public attitudes. It seemed to signal a shift in the cultural tone, blowing away the frivolous froth of the Bright Young People. By 1933 the previous decade was looking remote. Gossip columnist Patrick Balfour wrote *Society Racket: A Cultural Study of Modern Social Life* that year, attempting to take stock of what he referred to as 'the Roaring Twenties' in the light of the 'Hungry Thirties'. Neither phrase was yet common currency, though they would become so. And even if they weren't entirely accurate, they did delineate a discernible swing in mood.

The literature also had a political impact. 'The general opinion,' said the *Graphic* in 1929, 'seems to be that this appetite for so much that is terrible, horrible and loathsome will leave all classes and all generations with little stomach for a future affair of the same kind.'[95] There was a rise of pacifism, of anti-militarism – as a political creed and, more importantly, as a sentiment. That year, Labour MPs reported demands from party members that at the Cenotaph service 'the troops should be unarmed as a symbol of the nation's will to peace.'[96]

Back in 1920, Ernest Mander of the National Union of Ex-Servicemen had urged veterans to talk about 'the horrible, sordid, revolting realities of the most degrading and bestial business in the world. If every ex-soldier would tell his own children the truth, the whole truth, about war, the war-spirit would be stamped out for ever.'[97] Now they were doing so. It remained to be seen whether he was right.

5

CONFRONTATION AND COALITION

'There's nothing gross and material about stockbroking. It's like pure mathematics. You're dealing in abstractions, ideal values, all the time. You calculate – in curves.' His hand, holding the unlit cigar, drew a curve, a long graceful one, in mid-air. 'You know what's going to happen all the time.'

May Sinclair, *Life and Death of Harriett Frean*, 1922[1]

During a conversation I had with one of our blood– er, budding politicians, he told me, very aptly, that the large percentage of unemployed in this country was largely due to the number of *people* out of work. And, I don't know, there's an awful lot in that, you know.

Comedian Oliver Wakefield, 'The Voice of Inexperience', 1936[2]

Workers in the north-east during the General Strike, 1926

O N THE EVENING OF SATURDAY, 16 JANUARY 1926, those listening in to the radio were alarmed when the broadcast of
dance music from the Savoy Hotel was interrupted for some breaking news. And was then interrupted again, and again. As the story
emerged, it seemed that a violent mob was rampaging through the
London streets, killing passers-by, looting the National Gallery
and mortar-bombing the Houses of Parliament. Was this just a disturbance that had got out of hand, or might it be the revolution so
many had so long feared? Either way, the fate of the nation seemed
to be at stake.

'I looked across at my daughter,' said a listener in south
London, 'and saw that she had turned deathly pale.'[3] In Berwick,
listeners 'left their sets and spread the news through the town.'[4] At
St Edmund's College in Ware, the butler's wife was said to have
fainted on hearing the news, and at least one Fleet Street hack
raced from his home in the suburbs to his paper's office, ready to
report the historic events. There was 'considerable alarm and consternation,'[5] and newspapers and press agencies were deluged with
anxious callers, demanding more information.

As it turned out, the whole thing was simply a practical joke,
a programme titled *Broadcasting the Barricades*, devised by the
Catholic priest and writer Father Ronald Knox, who was known
in the press as 'the wittiest man in England'.[6] The intention was to
parody the BBC; it was 'a skit on broadcasting', as a subsequent
announcement said, 'a burlesque'.[7] And there were plenty of jokes
scattered through the piece. If you were a reasonably sophisticated
individual who understood modern humour, then the fact that
the mob was headed by someone with the implausible name and
position of Mr Popplebury, Secretary of the National Movement
for Abolishing Theatre Queues, would alert you to the possibility
of a prank; if you were not so sophisticated, it was easy to miss the
humour, and many were duped, hearing the tone more than the
individual words. It didn't help that there was heavy snow the next

day, which hit the distribution of Sunday papers in some areas; their absence seemed to confirm that something had gone badly wrong. It was 'the biggest scare in the history of wireless', said the *Daily News* with relish.[8]

The newspapers, resentful of their young rival, leaped at the opportunity to attack the BBC for irresponsibility, and for lacking the professionalism of the press. In future, said the *Sketch*, people 'will know better than to assume that anything is "news" until they see it in print'.[9] The *Daily Graphic* deplored the 'bulletin of faked news',[10] while the *Western Morning News* called it 'false news', and suggested that the BBC 'will have to learn from the newspapers not to sacrifice truth to picturesqueness'.[11] There seemed little chance of that. 'We regret any alarm that may have been unintentionally caused', said a straight-faced BBC official, before adding smugly: 'I think we are entitled to regard the whole thing as a compliment to ourselves.'[12] Some 2,500 people wrote to the BBC, of whom 90 per cent were said to have appreciated the show. John Reith, not normally noted for his sense of humour, was nonetheless pleased that the episode showed that the wireless mattered.

The primary reason that some people fell for Knox's hoax was because there was no reason not to. There were many things to complain about with the BBC, but no one had ever suggested that it would play tricks on the public. 'We have heard it on the wireless', said the callers to newspaper offices. 'We have even heard the explosions!'[13] Beyond that was the fact that such social unrest didn't seem entirely fantastical, for the country seemed once again to be a little unstable.

'Everywhere there is terrible unrest, crimes of violence, murder and suicide, dishonesty and immorality', wrote veteran suffrage campaigner Margaret Nevinson that year, 'a general loss of honour and self-control and a callousness produced by the long spectacle of pain and suffering.'[14] More specifically, the economy was floundering, and discontent was growing. At the conference of the Trades Union Congress in September 1925, the *Daily Herald*, the TUC's own paper, had reported that 'Congress affirmed that its aim, in conjunction with the party of the workers, was to work for the overthrow of capitalism.'[15] There was talk again of coordinated strike action.

Two months after that, twelve leading members of the Communist Party of Great Britain stood in the dock at the Old Bailey, charged with sedition and incitement to mutiny. Among them was J. R. Campbell, whose article in *Workers Weekly* had precipitated the fall of the Labour government the previous year. The prosecution case was that the creed of communism was in itself seditious, since it sought to overthrow the government by force, to incite the armed forces to mutiny, and to pursue class war; therefore the publication or circulation of any communist literature was a seditious act. The defence counsel demurred, warning that this was 'going a long way towards destroying liberty or opinion', but his objections were to no avail.[16]

The eight-day trial ended with guilty verdicts. Five of the defendants were given twelve-month jail sentences, the other seven were offered the chance to be bound over, if they 'would promise that they would have nothing more to do with the Communist Party and its doctrines'; they declined the judge's invitation and received six-month sentences.[17] In these overheated times, *Broadcasting the Barricades* did little to reassure.*

ii

Stanley Baldwin's second administration, taking office in November 1924, was the most substantial government since the war, with major achievements to its credit. It saw the creation of the Central Electricity Board, charged with building the National Grid and

---

* Among those convicted at the Old Bailey was thirty-four-year-old boilermaker Harry Pollitt, who would later serve as general secretary of the CPGB for twenty-five years. It is said that he spent his sentence in Wandsworth Prison learning how to fart the Internationale.

rationalising what had been a chaotic system of power generation.*
Health minister Neville Chamberlain – younger half-brother
of the former leader, Austen – introduced a substantial body of
reform to local government, including the abolition of the old
Poor Law boards. And the Representation of the People (Equal
Franchise) Act of 1928 finally extended voting to women on the
same basis as men. Millicent Fawcett, founder of the National
Union of Women's Suffrage Societies and now aged eighty-one,
was in the gallery when that legislation was passed. 'It is almost
exactly sixty-one years ago since I heard John Stuart Mill introduce his suffrage amendment to the Reform Bill on 20 May 1867,'
she wrote in her diary. 'So I have had extraordinary good luck in
having seen the struggle from the beginning.'[18]

Meanwhile, Winston Churchill, now the Conservative chancellor of the exchequer, was showing that he hadn't entirely lost
his pre-war Liberal instincts: he reduced the pension age from
seventy to sixty-five, introduced a contributory pension scheme
for widows and orphans, and cut the basic rate of income tax to 4*s*
in the pound (20 per cent). These changes were partially funded by
amending the Ten Year Rule – the assumption that there would be
no war for at least a decade – so that the duration began anew every
day; defence spending could therefore continue to be reduced.

It was also Churchill who took much of the retrospective blame
for the government's monetary policy. The issue was the value of
sterling. Up until the war, the value of the currency had been fixed,
underpinned by gold – the gold standard, as it was known – which
had ensured stability on international exchanges, but Britain had
suspended that system at the start of hostilities. Since then, the
exchange rate of sterling had fluctuated, often influenced by political as much as economic considerations. The installation, and then
removal, of a Labour government in 1924 meant that the value of
the pound varied that year between US $4.20 and $4.74, with an

---

* At the start of the 1920s just one in ten households was wired for electricity; by the
end of the 30s this was two in three.

even bigger range against the French franc. The remedy, agreed the leading experts at the Treasury, the Bank of England and beyond, was for Britain to return to the gold standard. That way lay a fixed exchange rate and economic stability, and although there might be some short-term pain, it would be more than offset by the long-term benefits. So, in his 1925 budget, Churchill did what everyone suggested and reinstated the gold standard.

The problem, as all the same experts were later to agree, was that the exchange rate was set at its pre-war level of US $4.86, but the world was very different. Financially, America had had a good war and the Federal Reserve, created as recently as 1913, had already come to matter more than the Bank of England. The return to the gold standard attempted to set the clock back a decade or so, and it didn't work. Sterling was overvalued, so financial intervention was required to prop it up – which in turn meant that public expenditure was squeezed – ensuring uncompetitive prices for industries that relied on exports.

Among the worst affected was coal, which saw export prices fall by a quarter. The mine owners proposed a package of longer hours and reduced wages, and A. J. Cook, general secretary of the Miners' Federation, responded with a defiant slogan: 'Not a penny off the pay, not a minute on the day.'[19] A national strike seemed inevitable, and was narrowly averted in July 1925, but only by the government offering a ten-month subsidy for the industry. (Labour leader Ramsay Macdonald saw this as capitulation to the militant Left, furious that Baldwin had 'sided with the wildest Bolshevik'.)[20] The impasse remained, however, and the miners had growing support from the union movement. On 2 May 1926 there began the first fully coordinated action to be authorised by the TUC: railwaymen, dockers and transport workers all came out on strike in support of the miners, together with printers and those working in iron and steel.

It was billed as a general strike, and nearly three million workers were involved. (The national workforce was around fifteen million, just over a third of them union members.) This time, some believed, it really was British Bolshevism. The nation had 'been plunged into an upheaval unprecedented in its history,' said the press,[21] and there was talk of 'a situation in many ways reminiscent of that in August 1914, except that, unhappily, this time the menace is not from outside, but from within'.[22] Conservative minister Ronald McNeill warned that the country was nearer 'to actual civil war than it has been for centuries'.[23]

The public's response, said the *Daily Express*, must be to 'Keep calm and support the government,'[24] while Baldwin's message on the radio was much the same: 'Keep steady. Remember that peace on earth comes to men of goodwill.'[25] He once said that his greatest political ambition was 'to prevent the class war from becoming a reality,'[26] and this was his big test. The union leaders, for their part, were equally anxious to distance themselves from extremism. It was reported that a 'a cheque for some thousands of pounds' sent to the TUC from Moscow was returned uncashed,[27] and the emphasis was placed on bread-and-butter solidarity. 'The railwayman, who loves his country just as much as you do, does not want a revolution,' said J. H. Thomas, leader of the National Union of Railwaymen, 'but he stops work tonight because it is his duty to stand by the miners.'[28]

The government took emergency measures that proved to be effective. Factories were put on short hours to conserve coal, Hyde Park was turned into a supply depot, troops were mobilised, special constables sworn in, motorists recruited. Some 300,000 people – about a tenth of the number of strikers – came forward to help keep essential services running, many of them students and from the higher reaches of society. 'They turned out in plus fours and jazz jerseys,' mocked the anarchist paper, *Freedom*, 'and drove – and ruined – trains and trams and buses and lorries, and had a very exciting time.'[29] There were geographical variations: over a third of the volunteers were in London – many more than were needed – and while southern England and the Midlands were also oversubscribed, there was a shortage in Wales and in the north of England.

There was a remarkable lack of violence. Although troops

replaced dockers, unloading food shipments, and supplies were distributed in armed convoys, it was done without provocation. The soldiers were accompanied by a Guards band playing selections from *HMS Pinafore*. There were instances of disorder – strike-breaking buses and vans came under attack from crowds who threw stones, the *Flying Scotsman* train was derailed by miners at Cramlington in Northumberland – but there were no sustained battles with police or troops.* For most people, normal life was largely unaffected. Food supplies were not interrupted, public transport – though disrupted – improved each day, the stock exchange remained open, cricket continued to be played. Midway through the strike, Christ Church School in Macclesfield, Cheshire went ahead with its scheduled jumble sale, raising £7, while the great Czech composer Leoš Janáček, now seventy-two, made his first visit to Britain, for a concert of his chamber music at the Wigmore Hall in London.

Newspaper production was hit, however, so the government responded with its own title, the *British Gazette* – printed on the *Morning Post* presses – which achieved a circulation of over two million, the first British title ever to do so. (The TUC's rival publication, the *British Worker*, managed just a fiftieth of that.) The paper was run by Churchill, already hated by many in the Labour movement for his strike-breaking use of troops at Tonypandy in 1910; he incensed still more with the uncompromising tone of the *Gazette*. 'The strike is intended as a direct hold-up of the nation to ransom,' it said.[30]

The absence of the national press allowed the BBC to fill the gap, with a rise in sales of radio sets; by the end of the year, there were half a million more licences than at the start, up by a third. Even those households without a set could hear broadcasts on speakers set up in public places. More news bulletins were added to the schedules, starting at 10 a.m. – the old 7 p.m. curfew was

---

* In Plymouth, striking workers played a football match against the police, winning 2–1.

broken, never to return – and the public perception of the wireless was transformed: no longer just a novelty entertainment, it was now an integral part of public and private life.

The government had the power to commandeer the BBC in times of national emergency and there were some in the cabinet who wished to exercise this – most notably Churchill – but Baldwin overruled them. Pressure was brought to bear behind the scenes, though, as John Reith complained to his diary: 'I do not think they treat me altogether fairly.'[31] The result was that, without descending to overt propaganda, the BBC was clearly more favourable to the government than to the strikers. Nonetheless, the strike was good for the BBC; at a time of inflated rhetoric and wild rumour, it retained a calm, detached tone.

Baldwin too was calm. When he went on the radio to address the nation, a week into the strike, he started the broadcast with the homely, perhaps hammy, gesture of striking a match to light his pipe. 'I am a man of peace. I am longing and looking and praying for peace,' he said, using words written by Reith. 'Cannot you trust me to ensure a square deal and to ensure even justice between man and man?'[32] An estimated eight million were listening.

Reith's view was that the BBC 'could act as a link to draw together the contending parties by creating an atmosphere of goodwill towards its service on both sides'.[33] This was very much where the churches would have liked to have been, and the Archbishop of Canterbury, together with other religious leaders, put his name to an appeal for peace. He wanted also to broadcast the message, but the government instructed Reith to refuse the request, and instead it was read out during church services that Sunday and published in the *British Worker*. It felt like a defining moment in the passing of cultural power from the church to the media.*

---

* Not all church leaders were conciliatory. The strike was 'a sin against the obedience which we owe to God', said Francis Bourne, the Catholic Archbishop of Westminster. 'All are bound to uphold and assist the government, which is the lawfully constituted authority of the country.'

On 12 May 1926, after nine days of action and threatened with the confiscation of union funds, the TUC abruptly called off the General Strike, having failed to impose its will on the government. 'Our first feelings must be of profound thankfulness to Almighty God,' said Reith, announcing the news on radio,[34] and the Labour-supporting *Daily Herald* said there was 'a feeling of intense relief everywhere'.[35]

The miners, abandoned as in 1921, stayed on strike and remained out for months, largely unnoticed by the national media. There was great hardship and a devastating impact on local economies. The proprietor of a clothes shop in a Yorkshire mining town said it was scarcely worth opening; worse yet, the cinemas were suffering, and he saw them as a barometer: 'When working-class people can't afford to find fourpence for a visit to a picture show, then there's nothing left in the family stocking.'[36] The miners finally conceded in late autumn, and longer hours and lower pay were duly introduced.

The whole episode had been a devastating defeat, and in the recriminations that followed, many activists blamed the leadership of the unions and the party for a lack of commitment. 'In its hour of trial the Labour movement was deserted by those in whom it had placed its greatest trust,' said left-wing MP John Wheatley.[37] Certainly there was no great support at the top of the parliamentary party. Ramsay MacDonald had always denied the morality of a general strike, arguing in his book *Syndicalism* (1912) that 'it hits the poorer people heaviest, the middle classes next, and the rich least of all'.[38] Former leader J. R. Clynes had no faith in the efficacy of the tactic, either; the unions couldn't win 'a fight between masses of men and a government claiming to act for the nation and backed by unlimited resources'.[39] Others criticised the TUC leadership for its lack of strategic thinking. Labour MP Manny Shinwell asked 'whether it was wise to engage in a general strike without adequate preparation, considering the consequences either of defeat or victory'.[40]

Lloyd George's challenge to the Triple Alliance of rail, coal mining and transport unions in 1919 – were they really prepared to take over the running of the state? – had been answered. The unions were clearly not revolutionary organisations, and henceforth there was far less talk of 'the overthrow of capitalism', much more of constructive cooperation. In 1928 the general council of the TUC resolved that the unions' role was to have 'a voice in the way industry is carried on'; they should 'use their power to promote and guide the scientific reorganisation of industry'.[41] When this was debated at that year's TUC conference, the most notable voice in opposition was that of miners' leader A. J. Cook; he spoke for forty-five minutes, declaring that there was 'irreconcilable antagonism' between the unions and employers, and at the end he fainted from his exertions.[42] He was followed by the president of his own union, announcing that, despite Cook, the federation would be backing the general council. The resolution was carried by a majority of nearly four to one, and the dreams of political action were over. That same year, the number of trade unionists fell below five million for the first time since the war, and the prospect of there ever being another general strike receded over the horizon.

The unions were cowed by the defeat. A record 162 million work days were lost to industrial action in 1926, nearly twice as many as in any previous year, but in 1927 the number fell to barely a million, the lowest peacetime level of the century. Meanwhile, the Conservative government introduced the Trade Disputes and Trade Union Act, which rolled back what were seen as key union rights. Sympathetic strikes and mass picketing were outlawed; civil service unions were banned from affiliating to either the Labour Party or the TUC; union members now had to opt into contributing to a political party, rather than have the union leadership do it on their behalf (the Labour Party saw its finances hit hard by this). There were also calls for compulsory secret ballots before a strike, though this was not included in the legislation.

'Something had happened, something whose ultimate significance had yet to be reckoned,' concluded the septuagenarian schoolmaster in James Hilton's novel *Goodbye Mr Chips* (1934).

Yet he felt reason to be hopeful: there had been 'not a life lost, not a shot fired'. The same feeling was voiced by the king. 'Our old country will be proud of itself,' he observed; 'not a shot has been fired and no one killed; it shows what a wonderful people we are.'[43] In private, he was far more blunt. 'That was a rotten way to run a revolution,' he told the Dean of Windsor. 'I could have done it better myself.'[44]

iii

'Lord Northcliffe's health is understood to have been causing uneasiness to his friends for some time,' the British press had reported in June 1922,[45] though the American papers were less respectful and more accurate: 'They say that Lord Northcliffe has become insane.'[46] He had, and the greatest press baron of his era – the man who'd virtually invented the role in the first place – ended his days paranoid and raving, isolated even from his own newspapers; his direct telephone lines were cut off, telegrams were intercepted, and *The Times* put guards on its doors to keep him out. He died that August in a wooden hut, built on the roof of the Duke of Devonshire's London house, with a loaded revolver under his pillow.*

The payment of death duties meant that *The Times* had to be sold off, bought by American-born John Jacob Astor, but the most important title stayed in the family. The *Daily Mail*, founded in 1896, still had the largest circulation in Britain – in the world, it claimed – with an average daily sale of 1.75 million copies; it was now taken over by Northcliffe's younger brother, Harold, Lord Rothermere, to whom he had already sold the *Daily Mirror* ('my bastard offspring').[47] Rothermere was the financial brains behind the brothers' business, but he lacked Northcliffe's journalistic gifts.

---

* After his death, Northcliffe appeared in spirit form at various seances, as witnessed by his former secretary, Louise Owen, and by one of his editors, Hannen Swaffer. The latter wrote a book detailing these appearances, *Northcliffe's Return* (1925), a title that was suggested by the dead man himself.

'Harold will ruin my paper,' said the latter on his deathbed. 'He thinks too much of money.'[48] And under Rothermere, the *Mail* duly lost much of its vitality and vision, though it remained a significant voice in public debate.

Far more plausible as Northcliffe's spiritual heir was Lord Beaverbrook. Born Max Aitken, he was a Canadian businessman who had come to Britain in 1910 and been elected as a Conservative MP the same year. In 1916 he left the Commons to exercise real power, having bought both a peerage from Lloyd George and a controlling stake in the *Daily Express*.

The *Express* had been launched in 1900 with a promise to 'please, amuse and interest', and it continued in the same vein, though now with the addition of Beaverbrook's rugged colonial individualism. 'It will uphold the right of people to advance their own interests and shape their own lives,' he announced, 'and will oppose all attempts to interfere with the simple and healthy pleasures of the nation.'[49] It was also disruptive and disrespectful. 'Max always wants to cut the heads off the tall poppies,' said Lloyd George. 'That is his whole psychology.'[50] Beaverbrook's stewardship was a triumph, mounting the first serious challenge to the *Daily Mail's* long domination of the market, largely because he stamped his personality on the paper, and his instincts were in tune with his times, as Northcliffe's had been with his.

Unlike Rothermere, Beaverbrook was highly regarded in the trade, even among those newspapermen who didn't share his politics. He was 'a journalist among journalists', said Hugh Cudlipp, editor of the *Sunday Pictorial*,[51] an 'intuitive impresario', according to Tom Driberg, a public-school-educated gossip columnist who was a member of the Communist Party.[52] *Express* correspondent Harry J. Greenwall tried to capture the core of Beaverbrook's faith: 'He believes in three things: himself, the Presbyterian Church and the *Daily Express*.'[53] As a character in Michael Powell's film *The Night of the Party* (1934) exclaims of her press-baron father: 'He's a beast! The only thing he cares for is his newspapers. Not because they're something he created, but because of the power they give him.'

Rothermere and Beaverbrook were business rivals and utterly different characters. What they shared was a great dislike for Stanley Baldwin, enraged by the quiet reassurance that was going down so well with the electorate. As *John Bull* put it, there was an 'incompatibility of temperament' between the prime minister and the two leading press barons. 'They represent everything he despises. He represents everything they despise.'[54] The antipathy was mutual. 'I do not care what they say or think,' Baldwin said in 1924. 'They are both men that I would not have in my house. I do not respect them.'[55] People were starting to ask, said the *Spectator* in 1925, 'Can a political party possibly survive when the most popular newspapers, which normally support it, are engaged, day and night, in ridiculing its leader?'[56]

Baldwin's government did survive, but the constant drip of hostility in the *Mail* and the *Express* had an effect, eating away at Conservative support. So too did the worsening economic situation, and when a general election came due in May 1929, the outcome was far from certain.

It was the first contest fought under universal adult suffrage, and therefore the first in which women formed the majority of the electorate, with 14.5 million women and 12.25 million men eligible to vote.* The Conservative campaign centred on the prime minister as a figure of experience and reliability. One poster showed him wearing oilcloths at the wheel of a ship ('Trust Baldwin. He will steer you to safety!'), another as a brand of pipe tobacco: 'Smoke Baldwin's Security Mixture.'[57] His slogan was 'Safety First'. On this occasion, though, it wasn't sufficient: the Conservative vote and number of seats fell substantially.

The victors were the Labour Party. Its share of the vote had been rising in every election, and now reached a peak of 37.1 per

---

* The imbalance was particularly noted in seaside towns: in Bournemouth and in Hastings over 60 per cent of the electoral rolls were female, with Southport and Weston-super-Mare not far behind, far in excess of the national average of 54 per cent; in the City of London, on the other hand, male dominance remained.

cent, just one point behind the Conservatives. More importantly, it was, for the first time, the largest party in the Commons, with 287 MPs against 260 Tories, not enough for a majority, but still a momentous result for Labour and its leader, Ramsay MacDonald.

One option was to form a coalition with the Liberals, the addition of whose fifty-nine MPs would be enough to control the Commons. Lloyd George offered support in exchange for the introduction of proportional representation, but there were many in his own party unwilling to work with Labour, and many in Labour who saw the pitfalls of electoral reform. 'PR would be the devil,' advised Labour minister F. W. Pethick-Lawrence, a former Liberal. 'It would destroy our constitution and substitute the folly of continental politics.'[58] Indeed Lloyd George himself had described proportional representation as a 'device for defeating democracy' that would bring 'faddists of all kinds into Parliament'.[59] That, though, had been in 1917, when he was still prime minister, and the Liberals had yet to be eclipsed by Labour; he had something to lose. In any event, MacDonald turned down the offer, and instead formed his second minority government.

Baldwin's defeat at the polls convinced the press barons that they'd been right about him all along, and that it was time for them to intervene directly in the political process. In the summer of 1929, Lord Beaverbrook launched the Empire Free Trade Crusade, calling for protectionism, tariff reform and imperial preference.* When advocated by Joseph Chamberlain in the early years of the century, this programme had split the Tories, and Beaverbrook was asked if it might again mean 'a war in the Conservative Party'. 'Yes,' he replied.[60]

Emboldened by the reported 200,000 who had signed up, Beaverbrook turned his crusade into the United Empire Party the following year, calling for radical, modern politics. 'Not only have free imports let us down,' he declared, 'the old political parties, slaves of tradition, impervious to new ideas, have let us down too.'[61]

---

* The logo of the Crusader on the *Express* masthead was launched at this time.

He was backed in this endeavour by Lord Rothermere, who joined the executive committee of the new party and pledged 'to fight fifty selected constituencies in London and the south of England'.[62] Those numbers never materialised, but the idea of a new force to the right of the Tories, advocating a change to Britain's trading relationships, seemed briefly as though it might be significant. Certainly it was a serious threat to Baldwin's authority. In October 1930, the Paddington South by-election saw a Conservative constituency fall to an Empire Crusade candidate, Vice-Admiral Ernest Taylor; three months later, Brigadier-General Alfred Critchley, formerly of the Royal Air Force, came second in the Islington East by-election, splitting the Tory vote to allow a Labour victory.*

This wasn't really a party, more a pressure group. The most that could be hoped for from the campaign was to change Conservative policy, and – maybe – to change leader. Because this was personal, Baldwin vs the Barons. It was also politicians vs the press, democrats vs plutocrats. The showdown came in March 1931, in Westminster St George's, where a by-election was fought between just two candidates: the official Conservative, Duff Cooper, and a self-declared Independent Conservative with the backing of Beaverbrook and Rothermere.

Two days before polling, Baldwin delivered a speech that began by praising the 'fairness' of the British press, 'the high principles of journalism to which it adheres'. But, he said, there were exceptions to this rule: the titles owned by Beaverbrook and Rothermere. These were not 'newspapers in the ordinary acceptance of the term' but 'engines of propaganda' that used 'direct falsehood, misrepresentation, half-truths, the alteration of a speaker's meaning by putting sentences apart from the context, suppression, and editorial criticism of speeches which are not reported'.[63] This was a new, combative Baldwin – 'Baldwin Berserker' in one account[64] – engaging in a 'vicious and personal attack',[65] a man who 'returned

---

* Both Taylor and Critchley – the latter Beaverbrook's cousin by marriage – were later elected as Conservative MPs.

with interest seven years of personal attacks', giving 'taunt for taunt, sneer for sneer, blow for blow'.[66] The most contemptuous line in his speech was his description of the press barons as men seeking 'power without responsibility – the prerogative of the harlot throughout the ages'.[67] That phrasing had been supplied by his cousin, Rudyard Kipling; as if to prove the truth of Baldwin's charges, it wasn't reported in the *Daily Express*.

The press barons wanted him out of office? he challenged. 'Let them throw me out if they can.'[68] They could not. The Tory candidate, Duff Cooper, won the election convincingly with 60 per cent of the votes, and Beaverbrook and Rothermere retreated in disarray from the electoral battlefield, routed by a man they disliked and had underestimated. The Conservative Party survived the hostile takeover bid by external forces, and Baldwin remained leader of the opposition.

iv

On 24 October 1929, as trading opened on the New York Stock Exchange, shares were sold in such quantities that 11 per cent of the market's value was instantly wiped out. This was Black Thursday, the start of the Wall Street Crash. By mid-November, the Dow Jones Industrial Average stood at barely half its September peak, and the shock waves were being felt around the world. Over the next two years, the value of British exports fell by nearly half and unemployment more than doubled; in 1931, consumer spending fell for the first time since the war.*

Black Thursday, just five months after the general election, fell on Ramsay MacDonald's watch. He was not well suited to such a sustained national crisis, combining age with inexperience. His

---

* In response to the crisis of consumer confidence, retailers began slashing prices. 'Values Which Put the Clock Back Seventeen Years – to the Levels of 1914!' proclaimed Pontings department store on Kensington High Street in London as it launched a spring sale.

time in government was limited to those nine months as prime minister in 1924 – while doubling up as foreign secretary, which divided his attention – yet he was now sixty-three years old, having spent his entire adult life in politics: he'd joined the Social Democratic Federation in 1885.

MacDonald had been around so long, wrote Egon Wertheimer, London correspondent of German socialist paper *Vorwärts*, that he had 'become a legendary being – the personification of all that thousands of downtrodden men and women hope and dream and desire'. He was still capable of delivering a powerful speech, and he retained the affections of many Labour voters, but he looked increasingly remote, not least because of his embrace of – and by – the establishment. He 'enjoys the glory of richly embroidered uniform and white knee-breeches', as one commentator put it.[69] Temperamentally, added Wertheimer, he was a Conservative,* and he was becoming isolated at the top of the party: 'He moves today in a personal vacuum that is almost painful to behold.'[70] Winston Churchill said he could 'cram the minimum amount of thought into the maximum amount of words'.[71]

Sitting alongside him was Philip Snowden, the chancellor of the exchequer, even older than MacDonald and with the same scant knowledge of office: he'd been chancellor in the short-lived 1924 government. He too had become thoroughly respectable, no longer 'a fervent apostle of Utopian Socialism', noted sociologist Beatrice Webb, sadly,[72] cleaving instead to principles of sound finances and free trade. He presented no challenge to prevailing orthodoxy at a time when it had clearly been found wanting. As Churchill put it: 'The Treasury mind and the Snowden mind embraced each other with the fervour of two long-separated kindred lizards.'[73]

With MacDonald and Snowden at the helm, the government looked helpless in the face of the economic storms, while

---

* Similarly, Wertheimer said, the other leaders had characters out of kilter with their politics: Stanley Baldwin was 'essentially a Liberal' and Lloyd George 'a typical Socialist'.

their shortcomings were thrown into stark relief by the opposition leaders they faced in the Commons – Stanley Baldwin and Lloyd George – who had each spent years as prime minister and as chancellor.

The one serious alternative came from an unlikely Labour figure. Sir Oswald Mosley, a sixth baronet, was educated at Winchester and Sandhurst, then served in a good cavalry regiment during the war, before becoming an RAF pilot. In 1920 he married the daughter of Lord Curzon, former Viceroy of India. By then he was a Conservative MP, elected in 1918 having been the youngest candidate in England at the age of just twenty-two. Soon after, he crossed the floor to become an independent, retaining his seat in the next two elections despite an official Conservative challenge. Then he decided to join the Labour Party, causing, teased the *Clarion*, 'much consternation in the purlieus of Belgravia and Mayfair'.[74] In 1924 he failed to unseat Neville Chamberlain in Birmingham Ladywood by just seventy-seven votes, but in 1926 he returned to Parliament after a by-election in Smethwick, Staffordshire.

Glamorous, wealthy, bursting with youth and energy, a good speaker in Parliament and on a platform, Mosley stood out in the 1920s Labour Party. He wasn't much liked by his colleagues, though, being seen as aloof and full of himself. Even Clement Attlee, himself an ex-public schoolboy, said he had the air of 'a feudal landlord abusing tenants who were in arrears with their rent'.[75]

Unusually for a Labour MP, he took economics seriously, and in 1930 he presented his plan for dealing with the crisis: a programme centred on the reduction of unemployment, calling for long-term economic planning, regional investment, industrial subsidies and public works, all backed by the nationalisation of the Bank of England and government control of the financial sector, and by high tariffs on imports. Much of this was heretical at the time, as was his suggestion that it should be financed by higher taxes on the wealthy and by borrowing; industrial recovery, he insisted, was more important than balancing the budget.

The Mosley Manifesto, as it was called, divided opinion.

MacDonald and Snowden weren't convinced, and Lloyd George said it was 'an injudicious mixture of Karl Marx and Lord Rothermere'.[76] The latter rejection was short-sighted, for much of Mosley's thinking derived from that of economist John Maynard Keynes, whose ideas were already shaping Liberal policy, as seen in the party's pre-election pamphlet, *We Can Conquer Unemployment.* Keynes himself approved, and said that at the very least, the 'manifesto offers us a starting point for thought and action'.[77] Mosley also attracted support from a few Labour MPs, including some of the most notable of the new intake: Eton- and Oxford-educated John Strachey; former miner Aneurin Bevan; even Oliver Baldwin, socialist son of the Tory leader. And beyond Parliament, wrote Ian Mikardo, a twenty-two-year-old contributor to Mosley's magazine *Action*, he inspired 'many of the younger members of the party at the grass roots'.[78]

The manifesto was rejected first by the cabinet and then by the parliamentary party. In October 1930, Mosley took it to the Labour Party conference, where his speech was wildly popular in the hall. The leadership, however, remained adamantly opposed – he was 'calling for the moon', was cabinet minister George Lansbury's verdict – and the block vote of the trade unions saw his proposals rejected by 1.25 million votes to 1.05 million. It was a narrow margin, though, and not necessarily the end of the story. 'Mosley is a coming man,' they said in the bars that evening, and some saw a parallel with a dynamic German politician who, only the previous month, had seen his party come from nowhere to gain ninety-five seats in the federal elections and become the second-largest group in the Reichstag. 'You are the English Hitler,' called out one delegate enthusiastically during the speech, and a visiting German pressman agreed: 'He may yet be a British Hitler.'[79]

v

By the summer of 1931, there was a run on sterling, industry was starved of credit, bankruptcies were mounting, foreign investment

– fearful of a banking crash – was fleeing the country, and the budget was in serious deficit. Attempting to manage this was a minority government with limited experience riven by irreconcilable forces: the Treasury's determination that sterling remain on the gold standard; a commitment to free trade; a massive increase in benefits spending as a result of rising unemployment.

Having rejected Oswald Mosley – who as a result left Labour to found a new party (called the New Party) – the only proposal left on the cabinet table was the Treasury's programme of substantial public-spending cuts, including a 10 per cent reduction in unemployment benefit. Ramsay MacDonald and Philip Snowden argued in favour, most other ministers were against, and the trade unions were in absolute opposition. In August 1931, unable to agree among themselves, the entire cabinet resigned, and the second Labour government fell. It had lasted twenty-six months.

The obvious next step was the formation of a Conservative–Liberal administration able to command a Commons majority. Instead, the king – supported by key figures from the other parties – urged MacDonald to stay on as prime minister, heading a coalition. MacDonald went to Buckingham Palace, looking, said the king's secretary, 'scared and unbalanced',[80] and allowed himself to be persuaded. He was now sixty-four years old, and feeling it. 'I'm old. My friends are dead. I feel solitary,' he'd written in his diary in March. 'A "national government" is attractive.'[81]

The National Government was indeed what it was called, not formally a coalition, but a grouping of individuals led by MacDonald, Stanley Baldwin and – representing the Liberals – Herbert Samuel. There was a ten-man cabinet, four each from Labour and the Conservatives, with two Liberals. It was only temporary, they agreed, a short-term mechanism. 'When the emergency is dealt with, the government's work will have finished,' Samuel wrote in a memorandum approved by the three men; future elections 'will not be fought by the government but by the parties'.[82]

Baldwin, much strengthened by his defeat of the press barons five months earlier, took the Conservatives along with him in this arrangement, though there was some dissent among Liberals, since Lloyd George – absent through illness at the critical moment – never approved. The real controversy was in Labour ranks, where there was outright fury. MacDonald and Snowden remained as prime minister and chancellor, with J. H. Thomas as colonial secretary, and a handful of other MPs signed up to the National Government, but the vast majority of the parliamentary party wanted nothing to do with the project. In the wider movement, no constituency branch supported working with the Tories, nor did any trade union. MacDonald was seen as a traitor, collaborating with the class enemy and abandoning the party he'd helped to create. A trade union branch which had a banner depicting MacDonald plucked out its eyes, and activists sang of vengeance:

We'll hang Ramsay Mac on a sour apple tree,
We'll hang Snowden and Thomas to keep him company;
For that's the place where traitors ought to be.[83]

The first ever Labour prime minister was expelled from the party via a pro forma letter. 'Dear Sir,' it opened, and it closed not with a signature but a rubber stamp. 'They wanted to insult me,' he concluded, accurately.[84]

Despite the acrimonious nature of his departure, and despite the failure of both the governments he led, MacDonald had made significant gains for Labour. Above all, it was now established as the second party, and if that owed something to the extension of the franchise, something to the Liberals' self-destruction (with Baldwin's assistance) and much to the trade union movement, MacDonald's cautious constitutionalism also played its part, allaying fears that Labour would usher in a Bolshevik revolution.

In the National Government's budget of September 1931, Snowden implemented the policy at which Labour had baulked: taxes were raised and there were cuts in public spending, including unemployment benefit and the pay of state employees.* Barely a week later, with the pound still under massive pressure, Churchill's 1925 decision was finally reversed, and sterling came off the gold standard again. The pound was devalued from US $4.86 to $3.80, subsequently falling still further.

Having now taken decisive action – and despite its earlier resolve not to fight elections as a joint enterprise – the National Government went to the country in October 1931, seeking an endorsement of the coalition. It was a confusing election. There were three separate Liberal groupings, two of them part of the National Government (differing over tariff reform), the other led by Lloyd George in opposition. There were two Labour parties – MacDonald's National Labour and the official party, with Arthur Henderson back as leader – as well as the Independent Labour Party. There was also Mosley's New Party, though it did not replicate Adolf Hitler's 1930 success: its twenty-four candidates averaged just 1,500 votes each. And, as ever, there was just one Conservative Party.

The result was an even greater endorsement of the incumbent coalition than the election in 1918 had been. Between them, the National parties won 67 per cent of the vote, with 554 MPs, nine out of every ten members. Labour collapsed spectacularly, from 287 MPs in 1929 to just 46, shedding all the gains made since 1918. Seen more positively, the party's share of the vote was still over 30 per cent, a fall certainly, but only to the level it had been in 1923, when Labour first took office.

MacDonald remained prime minister, though with noticeably less authority, an exhausted man whose decline was all too visible; what energy he had was directed towards international conferences. 'He has lost power of moving crowds, or even of expressing himself intelligibly,'[85] said Labour peer Lord Ponsonby.†

---

* The king and Prince of Wales took cuts of £50,000 and £100,000 respectively. MPs' salaries were cut from £400 to £360, though they were restored in 1934.

† Even the heavens gave up on MacDonald, according to astrologer Edward Lyndoe

Snowden didn't stand in the election, replaced as chancellor by Conservative Neville Chamberlain, and went on to criticise Mac-Donald's decision to stay in office. The prime minister would become 'an exhibition on Tory platforms in Tory chains, as a one-time socialist who has seen the error of his ways and who has found salvation', Snowden predicted. 'He will be used for the same purpose as the reformed drunkard is used at temperance meetings.'[86] Perhaps, though, there was a genuine convergence. John Buchan – now a Tory MP – got to know MacDonald in these years and concluded that 'he tended towards a creed scarcely distinguishable from left-centre conservatism'.[87] Meanwhile, the *Manchester Guardian*'s parliamentary correspondent said of Baldwin: 'He got the Tory party to pass Liberal measures entirely repugnant to its ideas.'[88]

The abandonment of the gold standard was accompanied by a cut in the bank rate and a fall in long-term interest rates, allowing the start of an economic recovery. Further action was taken. Food imports were restricted to protect British agriculture, and there was government intervention to support textiles, iron and steel. For shipbuilding, there was a subsidy to encourage owners of tramp steamers to scrap their vessels and buy new ones. The Import Duties Act 1932 introduced some tariffs, and an Imperial Economic Conference in Ottawa strengthened the principle of preference for goods traded within the Empire. In response there was a rise in inward investment, as overseas manufacturers sought to beat the tariffs. Of the 1,500 new factories opened in 1932–4, some 12 per cent were set up by firms from abroad, ranging from food, perfume and tobacco to textiles, chemicals and steel. A good deal of manufacturing that was now seen as integral to British industry was foreign-owned, most visibly with large employers on the fringes of London: the Ford Motor Company in Dagenham, Heinz in Harlesden, Hoover in Perivale, Nestlé in Hayes.

---

of the *People*: 'He has so flouted all the good offered him in his birth horoscope that he can hope for little mercy from the planets.'

Most significantly, there was a huge rise in housebuilding, with 2.5 million homes built in the 1930s.

The recovery was driven by domestic spending, and the economy looked different as a result: one in eight workers was employed in export industries, down by a half from the pre-war years. Britain could no longer boast of being the workshop of the world. Different, too, was the attitude towards defence spending, which had, as a proportion of GDP, sunk to pre-war levels. In 1932–3 the defence budget was £100 million, 14 per cent below where it had been six years before. That was the lowest point, for in 1932 the government finally abandoned the Ten Year Rule introduced by the coalition in 1919. As expenditure gradually increased, however, the Royal Air Force took priority, leaving the Royal Navy and, particularly, the army woefully underfunded and the country ill-prepared should there be another conflict.

Nonetheless, Baldwin – the most high-profile member of the government – was still exuding reassurance. 'We can take comfort,' he said in 1932, 'that in the very heart of this economic blizzard this old country is holding its own.'[89]

vi

John Ellis was fifty-one years old when he retired from his post as a hangman in 1924. By his calculation, he'd executed over two hundred people, including some big names: wife-killer Henry Crippen, George Smith (the Brides in the Bath murderer) and Roger Casement, the Irishman who'd collaborated with Germany and been convicted of treason in 1916. For a part-time job, the pay was adequate – £10 per hanging, plus expenses – but it was ruinous to one's social life. 'When I walk into a drawing room, it is quite a common experience for other people to get up and walk out,' he said. 'I can feel people eying me, as if I am some exhibit in a chamber of horrors. Then they will avoid shaking hands with me when they are introduced.'[90] There were also the nightmares that haunted his sleep.

Shortly after his retirement, Ellis was in court himself, pleading guilty to having attempted suicide. He'd been drinking heavily and had shot himself, but he promised he wouldn't do it again and would 'lead a useful life as an atonement', so the magistrate let him walk free.[91] His problems continued, though. His business, as a hairdresser in Rochdale, Lancashire, was affected by the worsening economy, and without the extra income from executions, he was forced to trade on his celebrity. In 1927 he formed a theatre company, staging a melodrama about one of the most notorious nineteenth-century murderers, *The Life and Adventures of Charles Peace.** It wasn't much of a play, but it did end with the onstage execution of Peace, conducted by Ellis himself, which drew in the crowds for a while, until the novelty wore off and the company collapsed.

By the start of the 1930s, Ellis was touring fairgrounds, using the gallows from *Charles Peace* to demonstrate how a hanging worked. He was accompanied in this macabre entertainment by an assistant, who was tied, hooded and dropped through the trapdoors (he landed on a bag of straw), and who later claimed he'd been 'hanged' 12,000 times over his two years with Ellis, his record being seventy-four executions on a single August bank holiday. Offstage, life was even more difficult, travelling with the morose, increasingly depressed ex-hangman who was drinking himself into oblivion. In September 1932, after a drunken and violent altercation with his wife and daughter, Ellis broke his promise to the magistrate and slit his own throat with a razor.

Such events were not uncommon. The male suicide rate continued to rise, peaking at just over 30 deaths per 100,000 in 1934. Now it was older men who were most prone to killing themselves; for those aged fifty-five to sixty-four, the rate was 57 per 100,000.

---

* Peace was sufficiently remembered to warrant him being the subject of a novel by best-selling author Edgar Wallace, *The Devil Man* (1931). And 'Mr Ellis, the eminent hangman' was famous enough to be mentioned in another Wallace novel, *Jack O' Judgment* (1920).

(The female rate remained much lower, at around a third of the male level.)[92] It was the most extreme indicator of the desperation felt in much of the country.

Because, despite the economic recovery, and despite Baldwin's optimism, times were still hard. For many, the Great Slump, as it was known – later, the Great Depression – had not gone away. Unemployment had been stubbornly high since 1921, hovering around 12 per cent, then rose rapidly after the Wall Street Crash, peaking at 23 per cent in 1933, with nearly three million out of work; that meant, allowing for dependants, that some six to seven million people were living on the dole. Thereafter, the numbers began a steady decline, finally returning to pre-Depression levels by 1937.

The misery was amplified when benefits began to be means-tested in August 1931. In an attempt to bring down the money spent on welfare payments to the unemployed, the government decreed that households, rather than individuals, be assessed; a man who was out of work might not be paid the dole if other family members had an income. The policy was successful in reducing public spending – by the end of the year, some 700,000 households had had their benefits either cut or withdrawn – but it split up families, left some in desperate deprivation, and attracted a hatred and a resentment previously reserved for the workhouse.

There were also fears that this slump might not be temporary. Because even when the jobless figures began to fall, the improvement was patchy. In Wales, northern England and Scotland, unemployment remained between 20 and 30 per cent, three times higher than in the south and Midlands. There was much talk of what were called 'the distressed areas', places where industry had died and unemployment seemed to have become entrenched as a permanent fact of life. 'It is a deadly thing to see a skilled man running to seed, year after year, in utter, hopeless idleness,' wrote George Orwell in his travelogue *The Road to Wigan Pier* (1937).[93] Lord Mottistone, who had been war secretary in Asquith's cabinet, and had served in the Boer War and on the Western Front,* was similarly despairing: 'I have seen nothing more terrible in war than is to be seen in the real depressed areas, and no suffering and hardship met with more tremendous courage by the people.'[94]

With the National Government now in complete control at Westminster, and the unions still crushed by the defeat of the General Strike, little could be expected via conventional politics. Instead, a tactic from more than a century earlier was adopted: marches from the afflicted areas to London, to force national attention towards the suffering of the unemployed. These Hunger Marches were substantial affairs – 150,000 turned out to welcome a group of marchers to Hyde Park in 1931 – and were mostly organised by the National Unemployed Workers' Movement. They received, however, no official support from the leaders of the Labour movement, since the NUWM was led by Wal Hannington, a communist; the organisation was 'a subsidiary of the Communist Party', said Walter Citrine, general secretary of the TUC (knighted in 1935).[95] The view from the Right was much the same. Many of the marchers were 'young men and women, many of them still students at the Universities, union officials and healthy-looking sympathisers waving red banners, shouting slogans and singing the Internationale', wrote journalist W. F. Deedes in 1936. The unemployed were being 'exploited'.[96] He was, certainly on this occasion, incorrect.† The Jarrow Crusade, as it was billed, was not organised by the NUWM, and the 200 men who had walked 275 miles from Jarrow in County Durham over 26 days had genuine grievances.

In 1932, the destroyer HMS *Duchess* had been launched, the 109th and final warship built by Palmer's Shipbuilding and Iron Company in Jarrow. The following year, with an empty order book, the firm went out of business and closed the shipyard,

---

* Mottistone led the cavalry charge at the Battle of Moreuil Wood in March 1918.
† In his memoirs, *Dear Bill* (1997), Deedes acknowledged that he'd been wrong. 'I was reflecting the sympathies of the *Morning Post*, for which all left-wing activity bore sinister implications.'

leaving around three in four men in the town unemployed. This was the very epitome of the distressed areas. 'There seems to be nothing before Jarrow but a slow process of decay,' said the local paper. 'That has already started as the empty shops and the declining population indicate.'[97] The infant mortality rate was twice the national average. 'We dread the winter,' said the town's medical officer in 1936; 'after fifteen years of privation and want, this one if going to be worse than ever.'[98] A couple of miles to the north was a district described by J. B. Priestley in his *English Journey* (1935): 'If T. S. Eliot ever wants to write a poem about a real wasteland instead of a metaphysical one, he should come here.'[99]

Consequently, the Jarrow Crusade attracted much public sympathy, while media coverage was aided by the profile of the town's MP, Ellen Wilkinson ('fearless, red-headed, short in stature and sharp of tongue', as the *Daily Mirror* described her, 'Westminster's Mighty Atom', in the words of the *Daily Herald*), who accompanied the marchers.[100] Wilkinson was a veteran of the anti-war movement and of campaigns for women's suffrage and equal pay. She'd been a founder member of the Communist Party but left in 1924, the year she was elected as Labour MP for Middlesbrough East; having lost that seat in the 1931 wipeout, she returned to Parliament to represent Jarrow in 1935. She never quite gave up her early loyalties, though – she always kept a portrait of Lenin over her bed – nor her commitment to the working-class cause. 'I've often thought that one of these days I really must find time to be a wife and mother just once,' she reflected, before dismissing the idea. 'There isn't really anything I care as much about as politics, and there's no use pretending there is.'[101]

As with losses during the war, the objective facts of the Depression were not as bad in Britain as elsewhere. Partly this was because there wasn't so far to fall; the economy had been so sluggish for most of the 1920s that the downturn was shallower and shorter than in competitor nations. At its lowest point, the UK's gross domestic product was 95 per cent of what it had been in 1929; in America the bottom was 73 per cent and in Germany 75 per cent. Similarly, the low point on the London stock market was 60 per cent of its 1929 level, 31 per cent in America, 38 per cent in Germany.[102] In the decade from 1929, industrial production grew faster in Britain than in Germany or America – and in France, it declined. No one on Tyneside was going to take any comfort from such international comparisons, but the government could reasonably claim some success. Even if, at the depth of the Depression, six million people were directly affected by unemployment, that still left forty million who were not. The pain was localised, and outside the distressed areas there was a more positive mood.

In 1936, as the Jarrow Crusaders were making their way to London, the Hollywood film star Edward G. Robinson was already there, filming a new movie, *Thunder in the City*. He played Dan Armstrong, an American salesman who learns that the British approach to business is both more civilised and, ultimately, more effective. 'We Americans are mighty good on the short sprints, but you English seem to be better over the distance,' he concedes. A colleague of his asks rhetorically: 'What was the first country to come out of the Depression? England. Why? Dignity.' This was what the government, and most of the country, wanted to hear – a message of hope that things were getting better and would continue to do so. 'Goodbye England,' says Armstrong, as he boards a plane at the end of the picture. 'It's a wonderful place. I love it. It's a country with a future.'

6

PEACE AND COMFORT

There is a new spirit in the world. Oxford will no longer
fight for its King and Country. And yet ...

Francis Beeding, The One Sane Man, 1934[1]

Films have made millions realise that all forms of war
constitute a colossal and ghastly human mistake. It has
educated millions to hate war and love peace.

Gertrude Lawrence, actress, 1929[2]

Gracie Fields with Douglas Wakesfield in the film *Look Up and Laugh*, 1935

THE THEATRICAL HIT OF 1931 was Noël Coward's musical drama *Cavalcade*, the story of an upper-middle-class household – family and servants – over the first three decades of the century, 'from jingoism to jazz-mania', as the papers said.[3] It was intended as an epic, a pageant of modern British history that required twenty-two sets and a cast and crew of some 400 people, including forty-three speaking roles. Not so much a play as a spectacle, a theatrical experience to stir the emotions. And what a spectacle! exclaimed the critics. 'A wonderful, breathtaking show';[4] 'heady and exciting';[5] 'a veritable triumph of stagecraft'.[6]

The play ended with a depiction of the present, a noisy chaos of simultaneous images. 'Here on the same stage are the communist, the religious fanatic, the wireless announcer, the foxtrotting dancer – a bewildering number of spotlights move about, darting from one to another.'[7] Then, abruptly, blackness and silence, before the lights rose on the Union flag and the National Anthem was sung.

Behind the scale and splendour, the running theme was one of loss and the terrible price of war, combined with national pride and faith. The message was to be found in a toast in the final scene: 'Let's drink to the hope that one day this country of ours, which we love so much, will find dignity and greatness and peace again.' The production was balm 'for the nation's disturbed soul', concluded the *Hull Daily Mail*.[8] Opening two weeks before the general election, it was, said the *Sphere*, 'a tremendous plea for sanity, stability and patriotism, which may be interpreted as propaganda for the National government or even for the Conservative Party'.[9]

There was some surprise that this had come from Coward, a writer primarily associated with 'post-war disillusionment and cynicism',[10] but he felt he was moving with the times. The seriousness that had been heralded by the war literature and strengthened by the Depression had, he said, resulted in 'a rapid swing, especially among young people, away from the tired cynicism of the last decade, which could see little use in ideals and treated love of country as something rather out of date'.[11] The young people to whom he referred were predominantly those of the educated classes, and he was right about the change – though perhaps not about the patriotism.

'Oxford looks more cosmopolitan than ever before; there are men and women here from all parts of the world,' wrote John Brown, a student at Ruskin College, in 1933. And yet the university was also detached from the country beyond. 'There are few signs of the world depression outside to be seen within these grey walls. Unemployment is comparatively low, and the desperate struggle that is life in the industrial town today for so many is undreamed of.'[12] Brown was an atypical student – the son of a South Shields fisherman, he'd experienced years of unemployment before going to Oxford in his mid-twenties – but his political awareness was not unusual.*

Just a few years earlier, students had rushed to volunteer during the General Strike, but that seemed a long time ago now. 'Oxford politics in the last few years has taken a decidedly radical turn,' noted another left-wing student, Michael Foot, son of Liberal MP Isaac.[13] 'There has been a decided swing from the right to the left,' agreed the *Cambridge Review* in 1934, 'an increase in political consciousness amongst the undergraduates of Oxford and Cambridge, and also in provincial universities.'[14] And the mood did indeed spread. 'Everything was in the melting pot,' Huw Wheldon, a young student at the London School of Economics, later remembered: 'anarchists and communists and fascists.'[15]

The development came to wider public attention in 1933, when

---

* Brown wrote an account of his early years in *I Was a Tramp* (Selwyn & Blount, 1934), the first of several books of reportage. He also stood as the Labour candidate in the Liberal constituency of Plymouth Devonport in 1935, and as an independent in the Labour constituency of Forest of Dean in 1945, being unsuccessful on both occasions.

the Oxford Union voted in favour of a motion that 'This House will under no circumstances fight for its King and country.' It being a thinnish week for news, the vote attracted a good deal of condemnation, particularly in the *Daily Express*. The philosopher C. E. M. Joad, who had proposed the motion, received dozens of letters, 'ranging from a detailed and unfavourable analysis of my present character, my past life, my views and my appearance, to a postcard which abruptly announced, "You ought to be shot."' Meanwhile, boxes of white feathers were sent to the Union, some of which were worn proudly by the recipients in their buttonholes, and the students were denounced as 'yellow cowards', 'sexual indeterminates', 'hermaphroditic traitors', 'cowardly scum' and 'moral perverts'. They were 'effete, effeminate, side-whiskered, no good to God nor man', spluttered Colonel B. B. Oreton, formerly of the Devonshire Regiment. 'We have thousands of girls in Devonshire who, if you put them in trousers, would make much better men.'[16]

Much of this was the same abuse that had been directed at students in the days of 'The Girl Men of Cambridge', and it perhaps missed the point that there was a political dimension to youth now that had been lacking then. John Brown voted for the motion and insisted that it hadn't been intended as 'a schoolboyish piece of disloyal bravado', but as a wake-up call to a sleeping nation, an attempt at 'drawing the attention of the public to the existing apathy with regard to war'.[17] Despite which, the whole affair was, for many noisier students, a very pleasing controversy, even if it came at a cost to the union, with benefactors announcing they would withdraw financial support. There was also a law of diminishing returns; in May 1936, when the union voted 'that this House recognises no flag but the Red Flag', barely anyone noticed.

ii

When the handful of Labour MPs assembled after the defeat in the general election of 1931, their first task – in the absence of Arthur

Henderson, who'd lost his seat – was to select a new leader.* There wasn't a great deal of choice, since all but one of the former cabinet ministers had fallen; by default, the baton passed to that one survivor, seventy-three-year-old George Lansbury. He'd never sought the leadership, didn't even feel comfortable with the title – preferring to call himself the 'spokesman of my colleagues in the House of Commons'[18] – but at a time when the party felt betrayed by the turncoat Ramsay MacDonald, he was a reassuring presence, the living soul of Labour.

Born in 1859, seven years before MacDonald, Lansbury had grown up in the East End of London, remaining there his entire working and political life. Elected as Labour MP for Bow and Bromley in 1910, he resigned two years later to force a by-election, which he fought on the issue of votes for women, seeking to attract attention to the cause. He lost and didn't return to Parliament until 1922. In the interim, he became the founding editor of left-wing newspaper the *Daily Herald*, campaigned for peace during the war, and spoke in favour of the revolution in Russia. Then, in 1919, he was elected mayor of Poplar, which was where he really made his name.

At the time, local authorities were financially responsible – via the rates, the property tax levied by each council – for the poor in their area. This meant that the heaviest burden fell on those boroughs least able to bear it; a rise of a penny in the pound would yield £29,000 in wealthy Westminster, but just £3,200 in Poplar and, since the latter's need was far greater, its rates ended up being twice as high as the former. Under Lansbury, Poplar Council took a stand against what it saw as an unfair system, refusing to make its statutory contributions to the London County Council and to the Metropolitan Police, voting to use the money instead for poor relief. Lansbury and twenty-nine other councillors were jailed for

---

* This was the fourth time Henderson had been defeated as a sitting MP, having lost in Barnard Castle in 1918, Widnes in 1922, Newcastle upon Tyne East in 1923, and now Burnley.

contempt of court, but they were released after six weeks, and the law was changed.* 'Labour councillors must be different from those we replace, or why replace them?' asked Lansbury.[19]

In MacDonald's second government, he had been commissioner of works, and had focused on recreation facilities, responsible, in the words of the *Daily Express*, for 'almost the only monuments for which that Socialist government will be remembered – the Lansbury Lido for sun-bathing by the Serpentine in Hyde Park, and countless ponds, sandpits, swings and chutes in all the parks under Office of Works control'.[20] The press called him 'Lido Lansbury',[21] though he was 'Good Old George' to his constituents.[22] 'I like the kids to be 'appy,' he said. 'I'm all for abolishing schools.'[23] In the cabinet split of 1931, he had stood solidly against benefit cuts.

A campaigner for women, peace and the working class, his socialist credentials were impeccable, and his advanced age had conferred upon him something approaching sainthood. He was a teetotal non-smoker, and said that it was 'part of my religion' not to swear – though he admitted that the House of Commons tried even his patience: 'The exasperations and frustrations of that place would drive an angel to profanity – and I'm no angel.'[24] Some thought he wasn't far off. He had 'the moral earnestness of the Victorians', said his colleague, Clement Attlee,[25] and looked, according to Oswald Mosley, like a cross between an Old Testament prophet and a dairy farmer: 'As he came rolling in with his mutton-chop whiskers, you would say, "Here's a man up from the country who has just milked the cows."'[26]

He wasn't much one for detail. 'Don't let us worry our minds with difficulties,' he'd say, encouragingly. 'If we know the end, we shall devise the means.'[27] But, even if no one believed he was ever going to be prime minister, he proved to be the ideal leader for the circumstances. 'I think that the Labour Party will be a very strong,

---

* Also jailed were Edgar and Minnie Lansbury, George's son and daughter-in-law. As a result of her imprisonment, Minnie contracted pneumonia and died. Edgar later remarried and fathered the actress Angela Lansbury.

compact little party, and will put up a real good opposition,' he said,[28] and he kept his word; a Conservative whip called him 'the ablest leader of the opposition I've ever seen'.[29] At the very least, he kept the party together at a time when Labour was severely weakened by the decline of the unions and the defections to the National Government. More than that, his task was to restore faith in a party that had been found wanting. Labour was in office when the Wall Street Crash produced the capitalist crisis that the Left had long predicted, and yet it had had no answers to offer, let alone socialist ones. It was reasonable to ask what the point of Labour was.

There was also a danger of serious fragmentation. Smaller parties saw opportunities to exploit the 1931 split. The Independent Labour Party, which had always taken the Labour whip, now disaffiliated itself, arguing that the last government had been, in the words of party chairman Fenner Brockway, 'disloyal to the working class'.[30] This provoked its own split; two of the ILP's five MPs were expelled and remained attached to Labour, while membership numbers fell dramatically. There was also the left-of-centre National Party of Scotland, founded in 1928, which fielded five candidates in 1931, averaging over 4,000 votes each.* And then there was the irritant of the Communist Party of Great Britain, which had taken to standing candidates in Labour seats, in the hope that this would assist a Conservative victory, thereby shattering the illusion that Labour could deliver socialism. The numbers were small – twenty-six candidates in 1931 – and so were the votes, averaging around 2,300 per constituency, with no MPs returned. Damage could be done, though; in Sheffield Attercliffe, for example, the Labour MP Cecil Wilson lost his seat to the Tories by just 165

---

* In 1934 the NPS merged with the right-of-centre Scottish Party to form the Scottish National Party. The cause of devolution was, however, not yet taken very seriously outside these small groups. 'Scotland for the Scottish!' a nationalist newspaper publisher declares in the film *Storm in a Teacup* (1937), and an English reporter is mildly surprised: 'Oh, does somebody else want it?'

votes, while the Communist candidate picked up 2,790. Unsurprisingly, Labour had no affection or respect for the CPGB. 'That lot run a revolution?' scoffed George Lansbury. 'They couldn't run a whelk-stall.'[31]

Under Lansbury's collegiate leadership, Labour involved the trade unions in decision-making and continued to insist on the primacy of parliamentary politics. It was rewarded with a string of by-election victories, retaking Wakefield, Wednesbury, Rotherham, Hammersmith North, Upton, Swindon and Liverpool West Toxteth from the Conservatives, and Lambeth North from the Liberals. There were also Fulham East in 1933 and Liverpool Wavertree in 1935, seats never previously held by Labour but now taken from the Tories on massive swings (29.2 and 30 per cent respectively). The wounds of 1931 had, it turned out, not been fatal.

Lansbury missed some of this. In December 1933 he fell over while opening a bazaar in Gainsborough, Lincolnshire and fractured his thigh. 'Tell everyone I'm very cheerful and very comfortable,' he said as he was wheeled into the hospital where he'd spend the next seven months, fearing at times that he might never walk again.[32] While bedbound, he wrote a series of articles for the *Clarion* newspaper, and then turned them into a book, *My England* (1934), which he said was a 'partly utopian and partly practical suggestion of what I should like to see'.[33]

On the practical side were proposals for 'a full state medical service', for planning controls to restrict ribbon developments on arterial roads, and for the banning of coal fires 'in the interest of clean air, health and sunshine'.[34] On the utopian was his proposal that, after having their guns removed, the ships of the Royal Navy should be used for international cruises 'so as to enable the children of this country to see the world'.[35] Such pacifist fantasies were a large part of Lansbury's appeal, offering comfort and political escapism. 'I would close every recruiting station, disband the army, dismantle the navy, dismiss the air force,' he said in a 1933 speech. 'I would abolish the whole dreadful equipment of war and say to the world, "Do your worst."[36] Some said of him: 'Heart of gold, head of feathers.'[37]

iii

George Lansbury's uncompromising pacifism was not widely shared, but it was part of a wider current on the Left. In 1933, the year that the Oxford Union voted against fighting for King and country, the Labour Party conference passed a resolution calling for 'the total disarmament of all nations throughout the world and the creation of an international police force'.[38]

This was also the year that the Co-operative Women's Guild introduced, as an alternative to the blood-red Flanders poppy of the British Legion, a white poppy, intended to symbolise peace as well as remembrance. The symbol was subsequently adopted by the Peace Pledge Union, founded in 1936, which called on people to support a simple statement: 'We renounce war and never again directly or indirectly will we support or sanction another.'[39] Over 100,000 signed up, including writers Vera Brittain, Aldous Huxley and Siegfried Sassoon. Meanwhile, A. A. Milne put away childish things to write a pacifist book, *Peace with Honour* (1934).

For those unwilling to go so far, hopes for peace were pinned on the League of Nations, the organisation created in 1920 in pursuit of collective security: the principle that aggression against a member state was to be considered aggression against all. The league was intended to provide a forum for resolving international disputes, for promoting disarmament, and – even more ambitiously – for addressing social questions, from labour conditions to drug smuggling; in 1923 it announced that it was going to fight the trade in obscene publications. Dozens of countries joined, including Germany in 1926 and the Soviet Union in 1934, though the US did not, an absence that restricted the authority of the enterprise. Nor did the organisation have any independent means of enforcing its resolutions.

Even before it was officially launched, the league was portrayed as the political embodiment of remembrance. Many of the

Armistice Day services in 1919 included prayers for the venture, and the London County Council instructed its schools to teach children about this hope for humanity immediately after the Silence. Lloyd George suggested that Armistice Day be known as League of Nations Day; that didn't take off, but enthusiasm for the league became an article of faith in liberal, socialist and Christian circles. At an Armistice service in 1924, Edmund Pearce, Bishop of Derby, urged his congregation, 'as Britishers and Christians', to support the organisation, which 'stood for a nobler conception of life between nation and nation'.[40]

The League of Nations Union spread the good word through local meetings and national rallies; by 1927 it was claiming 2,000 branches and half a million members in Britain. There were similar organisations in forty or so other countries, though none so large. The union's early chairman was classicist Gilbert Murray (one of the few Oxford academics who was Liberal rather than Conservative); his secretary was A. G. Macdonell, whose experience of conflict made him a passionate advocate for the organisation. 'There is only one way of averting another world war and that is by supporting the League of Nations,' he told an election meeting in Lincoln, where he was standing as the Liberal candidate, in 1923.[41] It was 'the only hope of a better world, a better Europe and a better England.'*

Macdonell wrote detailed accounts for the newspapers of the league's deliberations on diverse subjects, from the status of the former German colonies to the silk trade, but even his enthusiasm waned in the Tower of Babel that was the league's unfinished headquarters in Geneva.† His satirical account of proceedings in *England, Their England* (1933) depicted East Europeans unwilling to let go of historical disputes, South Americans obsessed with pornography, and Britain ensuring that nothing happens. 'I'm all

---

* Macdonell came third in Lincoln in 1923, and did so again in 1924.
† The Palace of Nations in Geneva, a vast complex built to house the league, was completed in 1938, by which time the organisation had outlived its usefulness. It was later taken over by the United Nations.

in favour of peace myself,' says Sir Henry Wooton, a Tory delegate, 'but I've got a sort of notion that the best way to keep the peace is the good old British way of building a thumping great fleet and letting the dagoes do what they damned well like, eh?'

John Buchan's *The House of the Four Winds* (1935) displayed an even more jaded weariness. An MP sent to Geneva for 'the usual Disarmament Conference',* detests the city, 'full of the ghosts of mouldy old jurisconsults, and the living presence of cosmopolitan bores'. In real life, Buchan was slightly more sympathetic, having chaired the editorial committee of the League of Nations Union. Before the war, he wrote later, he had 'believed profoundly in the possibilities of the Empire as a guardian of world peace'; now he hoped that the league could take that role, though he was doubtful there was sufficient international will.[42]

Even in popular fiction, the dream of progress remained alive. Among those with permanent jobs in Geneva were Hilary St George Saunders and John Palmer, who wrote thrillers together under the name Francis Beeding. In *One Sane Man* (1934), a mysterious financier has acquired the power to control the weather ('the greatest discovery since Prometheus'), and threatens the league unless it meets his demands. Unusually for a thriller, the financier is not an evil mastermind seeking global domination, but a would-be benefactor to humanity; he has a World Reconstruction Plan that seeks to accelerate the more hopeful end of league thinking. 'The nations must get together,' is the essence of his proposal. 'An international currency. No more wars. Complete disarmament. Transport to be organised on a world basis. States to settle their disputes, like private citizens, in a court of law.'†

---

* The reference is to the League of Nations Disarmament Conference for the Reduction and Limitation of Armaments, which sat 1931–4 and ended in failure. It was chaired by former Labour Party leader Arthur Henderson, who was awarded the Nobel Peace Prize 'for his untiring struggle and his courageous efforts'.

† The best-known Francis Beeding novel was *The House of Dr Edwardes* (1927), filmed by Alfred Hitchcock as *Spellbound* (1945).

Another of those who worked in Geneva was Lionel Fielden, a veteran of Gallipoli, who later became a radio producer. He said he found at the BBC's offices in Savoy Hill 'the same feeling of dedication and hope which had characterised the League of Nations in its earliest days'.[43] Some saw an extension of John Reith's moral purpose into a more secular evangelism, attracting criticism that – in the words of Conservative peer Lord Radnor – there was a concerted attempt 'to educate the people of this country towards socialism, and even communism'.[44] Certainly, there was a spirit of internationalism, encapsulated in the BBC's new motto: 'Nation Shall Speak Peace Unto Nation'. That wording had been suggested by Ethel Snowden, appointed a BBC governor by Stanley Baldwin, even though she was a pacifist and socialist, married to Labour's once and future chancellor Philip Snowden. 'We want, through broadcasting, to make the nations of the world known to each other,' she explained.[45] 'We want to spread among all nations a wish to establish in the world a real brotherhood and a substantial peace based upon understanding.'*

The cause of peace and internationalism seemed ever more pressing. 'It is an age of dictators,' said the *Yorkshire Post* as early as 1923, pointing to Benito Mussolini in Italy, Miguel Primo de Rivera in Spain and Mustafa Kemal Atatürk in Turkey. There was much coverage too that year of Bavaria, where, said the *Manchester Guardian*, 'one Adolf Hitler, a house painter by trade, has found a large and dangerous following'.[46] The *Daily Express* mistakenly called him 'Dr Adolf Hitler, the "Bavarian Mussolini"'.[47] Eight years later, following the spectacular rise of the Nazi Party in the Reichstag elections, the latter paper ran what it claimed was the first piece by a foreign journalist allowed into the party's headquarters in Munich. Four officers were glimpsed studying maps, and the reporter asked what they were doing. 'They are discussing the war,' replied his guide. 'The next war.'[48]

---

* Reith did not approve of Snowden, referring to her in his diaries as 'the Whore of Babylon' and the 'Mother of Harlots and Abominations'.

Hitler was appointed German chancellor in January 1933, initially heading a coalition that was swiftly dispensed with. By then he had become part of the vocabulary of British politics. Oswald Mosley might have been the first to be associated with his name, but he was far from alone. In 1930 Labour minister Arthur Greenwood called Winston Churchill an 'English Hitler',[49] and in a 1934 debate at the Oxford Union, student Michael Foot made the same comparison: 'If the day ever comes when the fascists attain power in this land, you may (I pray not) see Mr Churchill as the British Hitler of that revolution.'[50] At the 1933 Labour Party conference, Reginald Sorenson, a Unitarian minister who had been MP for Leyton West (and would be again), broadened the field of fire: 'The operation of imperialism in India is in essence no different from the operation of Hitlerism. We are appalled by what is happening to the Jews in Germany, but what has been happening in India is just as bad.'[51]

From the other side, the *Scotsman* suggested that Fenner Brockway of the Independent Labour Party 'would like to achieve power in the same way as Herr Hitler',[52] and Lance Mallalieu, a National Liberal MP, attacked a leading Labour left-winger: 'Stafford Cripps and his socialist friends' were trying to do in Britain what Hitler had done in Germany.[53] The insult passed rapidly through society. At a stormy public meeting in Desford, Lincolnshire in September 1933, the parish council's proposal to spend £120 on extending the water and sewer system to the outskirts of the village was fiercely attacked. 'You are a gang of Nazis under a British Hitler,' exclaimed a protestor, to 'loud applause from other parishioners'.[54]

There was a bewildered fascination in Britain. The words 'an English Hitler', reflected novelist Louis Golding in 1931, were 'comically contradictory of each other'.[55] The man seemed so very alien to the British mind. Why, wondered one profile in 1933, did he have such a mesmerising influence over his audiences? The conclusion: 'He is utterly without humour. Hence his power.' The same piece also noted his anti-Semitism, a prejudice common enough in Britain, but not like this, not as a political creed: 'He hates the

Jews with a fanaticism an Anglo-Saxon can scarcely understand.'[56] To confirm his complete foreignness, there was even a story, told by Conservative MP Oliver Locker-Lampson, that during the war Corporal Hitler had approached some British prisoners of war, with a view to learning how to play cricket; having studied the laws of the game, however, he concluded that the ball should be harder and that the use of pads was 'unmanly and unGerman'.[57]

Then there was the strange use of arcane symbols. 'The whole heathen business of the swastika is utterly tenth-rate,' snorted novelist G. K. Chesterton, suggesting that Hitler was 'the sort of man who deals in tarot cards and talismans and shabby occultism'.[58] The Nazis said they were Christian, but the British press saw the party as 'a self-imposed cult'[59] with 'a primitive worship of Hitler',[60] 'a new religious movement with an all-German deity'.[61] This echoed the reports from Russia, a decade earlier, of 'the cult of Lenin', with images of the Soviet leader accorded almost holy status; 'his portraits and photographs are requisites of all official and public buildings', while 'private individuals are more apt to decorate their houses with his likeness than they were to set up the Tsar's pictures before'.[62] In this age of dictators, the decline of religion, it seemed, was being addressed by an authoritarian creed of leader-worship.

Above all, there was the totalitarian nature of the Nazi state, the intrusion of politics into everyday life. 'No position is too insignificant for a Nazi to fill,' noted the *News Chronicle* in 1933. 'Wherever Germans gather in an organised group – for prayer, on the tennis courts, at chess tournaments, as hikers – there will be the watchful and attentive Nazi.'[63] Fascism, said the *Daily Herald*, involved 'control not only over the policy of the government, but over the everyday lives of all the citizens'.[64] A cartoon by Will Dyson in the *Daily Express* showed a Nazi wedding: 'We swear to love, honour and obey Adolf Hitler ...'[65] Britons were both captivated and repulsed by this incomprehensible spectacle. 'Autocracy is abhorrent to the British mind,' wrote John Playfair of the *West Sussex Gazette*, 'and the kind we see in operation in Germany seems to us almost incredible.'[66]

Some saw danger in the clash of political cultures. 'After all, we stand for something in this country,' former Foreign Secretary Austen Chamberlain admonished the Commons ten weeks after Hitler became German chancellor. 'Europe is menaced and Germany is afflicted by this narrow, exclusive, aggressive spirit, by which it is a crime to be in favour of peace and a crime to be a Jew. That is not a Germany to which we can afford to make concessions.'[67]

There were few such voices. The paramount wish was for peace. George Lansbury's talk of disarming and challenging the world to 'Do your worst' was escapist make-believe, a retreat into utopia, but less starry-eyed statesmen also had their judgement impaired, perhaps by the sheer implausibility of anyone misguided enough to seek another conflict. Anthony Eden, the minister for League of Nations affairs, met Hitler in February 1934, and reported back to Baldwin: 'I find it very hard to believe that the man himself wants war.'[68]

There was similar cheerfulness elsewhere, a determination to see and hear no evil. British bandleader Jack Hylton was on a fifteen-city German tour when Hitler took power; on the band's return home, saxophonist Dave Shand reassured the press: 'We gathered the impression while we were over there that war was not such an imminent event as some people fear.'[69] The fact that he needed to say so told its own story.

iv

If today was starting to feel unsettling, there was always yesterday. In the mid-1920s, the capital's theatrical community began to notice that something was stirring beyond the usual West End beat. Down at the Theatre Royal, on the New Kent Road in south London, a repertory company was reviving old plays that had long ceased to be fashionable – if ever they had been – blood-and-thunder melodramas awash with sentimentality: *Dick Turpin, East Lynne, Jack Sheppard, The Silver King, Spring-Heeled Jack.* This was, said the *Daily Mirror*, 'lowbrow theatre' and it turned out to be very popular.[70]

The biggest draw was *Maria Marten, or the Murder in the Red Barn*, a Victorian piece based on a real-life 1827 murder in Polstead, Suffolk. It had been a mainstay of English drama for over a century without ever, as far as anyone could remember, having reached London. Now it did, and by the time it got to its fiftieth performance, a century after the crime it depicted, it was reported that 'The play has attracted a large number of West End playgoers, and the stalls and private boxes nightly hold many prominent members of society.'[71]

It was all deliberately old-fashioned, a lost world preserved in limelight. Innocent maidens were menaced by villainous squires in scenes thick with fog, frock coats and churchwarden pipes, with Bow Street Runners and Gypsy women who would tell the fortune of anyone who crossed their palms with silver. *Maria Marten* even ended with a hanging. And it was delivered in suitably dated style, with exaggerated gestures and gloating laughter, by characters who were either good or bad or comic, and in all cases easily identified, unafraid to reveal their innermost thoughts in soliloquy. The villain wore disguises – whether physical or social – and the audience saw through them in an instant. There was no room for moral ambiguity.

Presiding over this unlikely revival of melodrama was actor-manager Tod Slaughter. That wasn't his real name. He was born Norman Slaughter in 1885, into a Tyneside family that claimed descent from Captain James Cook – Slaughter said he owned Cook's waistcoat and dagger – and his acting career had been interrupted by the war, when he served in the Royal Flying Corps. He specialised in seductively suave villains, though he didn't really have the physique for it, with a barrel torso supported by slightly bowed, spindly legs, and a big, gormless face. But there was no faulting the relish with which he attacked his roles.

When the Theatre Royal closed at the end of 1927,* Slaughter

---

* It reopened in 1932 as a cinema.

took his company, now known as the Barnstormers, on a nation-
wide tour. Then he expanded into radio, starting with *Sweeney
Todd* in 1934 (he prided himself on not using a script when broadcasting), and then into movies the following year with *Maria
Marten*. He was successful in both media. The films were quota
quickies – made by George 'King of the Quickies' King – but they
were popular enough to be the main attraction in some cinemas
well into the next decade. Indeed, the small budgets merely height-
ened the pleasure of the artificiality. *Maria Marten* opened with
the principal characters coming out from behind a stage curtain
to be introduced by a master of ceremonies, from 'Poor Maria –
how little she dreams of the awful fate that awaits her,' to Squire
William Corder, 'a villain whose blood may be blue, but whose
heart is as black as night'. ('That's Tod Slaughter himself,' said the
MC, as if there could be any doubt.)

'I am not quite sure whether I liked it because its melodramatic
simplicity made me rock with laughter or because its murders and
effects chilled my blood,' puzzled one critic, and the truth was
that both responses were appropriate.[72] 'Thrills–Tears–Laughs,'
promised the adverts;[73] or else they advised: 'Cheer the Hero.
Hiss the Villain.'[74] Slaughter's audiences responded appropriately,
marvelled the press, loving 'him best when he is rolling his eyes
with diabolical wickedness and chuckling with evil laughter as he
throws the hero, bound and gagged, into the river. The wickeder
he is, the more they laugh.'[75] They understood melodrama, a genre
that was both ridiculous and honest. 'This is no laugh up the sleeve
for the highbrows, but a straight production of a really popular old
drama,' wrote a critic,[76] and Graham Greene, film reviewer for the
Spectator, said that Slaughter was 'certainly one of our finest living
actors'.[77] The man himself respected the conventions of these old
dramas more than anyone. 'I always play them straight,' he said 'I
have never burlesqued them. That would be madness.'[78]

His popularity, some concluded, was proof that the cultural
tide had turned. 'The public are now wearying (not without some
cause) of what has passed for sophisticated sentiment, preferring

something more unashamedly sentimental.'[79] There was a wish for simpler, pre-war times, and Tod Slaughter's revival of melodrama provided a warmth that seemed lacking in much contemporary entertainment.

In 1934, the Barnstormers appeared at the Garrick Theatre with a short piece 'The Ghost of Jerry Bundler' (1902), adapted from a story by W. W. Jacobs. It was part of an evening titled *Then and Now*, in which a first half of contemporary acts was followed by old-time entertainment. As well as Slaughter, this included some survivors of the music hall, with Tom Costello and Tom Leamore singing their hits from yesterday – 'The Ship I Love' (1893), 'Percy from Pimlico' (1898) – to an appreciative crowd. 'Complete with paper hats, and replete with hot saveloys and fish and chips, the audience join in with gusto.'[80]

That self-aware nostalgia for entertainment past was increasingly common. As Bobbie Comber sang in his hit 'Let's All Go to the Music Hall' (1934):

There's no entertainment like the good old Music Hall,
That's the place to go to when the evening shadows fall.[81]

In 1933 *The Sporty Nineties*, billed as 'a burlesque of an old-time music hall',[82] opened at the Palace Theatre in Southampton: 'We invite you to dance the polka! Hear the songs your parents sang! See the old-time comics!'[83] It was still touring nearly two years later. Meanwhile, the Coventry Hippodrome was putting on a programme of old-time music hall ('The kind of show that Father talks about!'),[84] and the 1935 Royal Command Variety Performance celebrated George V's Silver Jubilee with some veterans of the pre-war stage: Kate Carney, Harry Champion, Florrie Forde and Arthur Reece. Regal Records did well with two 12-inch records of 'An Old Time Music Hall', including songs such as 'Daisy Bell', 'Beer, Glorious Beer' and 'Two Lovely Black Eyes', the latter performed by Charles Coburn, who'd popularised it more than forty years earlier.

There were also movies that rode the revivalist wave. *Elstree Calling* (1930), *Say It with Flowers* (1934), *Music Hall* (1934) and *Variety* (1935) were little more than a series of music-hall turns,* while *Evergreen* (1934) and *Road House* (1934) were musical dramas that recreated the old halls. Alfred Hitchcock's film of *The 39 Steps* (1935) added a music-hall setting that hadn't been present in John Buchan's novel, hingeing the denouement on an act called Mr Memory, based on the real-life Datas, 'The animated encyclopaedia, who holds the history of the world in his brain'.[85] In 1931, Albert Chevalier's play *My Old Dutch* was revived at the Royal Court Theatre in Liverpool, before being filmed in a version starring Betty Balfour and Gordon Harker. Even the BBC joined in with the long-running variety series *Music Hall*, which debuted in 1932; the bill-topper for the first episode was Gus Elen, now in his sixties and tempted out of retirement. Other BBC shows gave a similarly dated impression of an Edwardian end-of-pier: the *White Coons' Concert Party* (1932)[†] and *The Kentucky Minstrels* (1933).

Like Tod Slaughter, this was a cultural retreat, a sloughing off of the modern world. And, as with melodrama, a large part of the appeal was the return to audience participation, an assertion of community spirit. When the London County Council built the vast Downham Estate (over 6,000 dwellings) in Lewisham to rehouse people from the East End slums, the Downham Tavern kept the old traditions alive with a weekly music-hall night. In the years of the Depression and the age of dictators, these revivals were a chance to find solace, if only for an evening, in older, more enduring values. There was comfort in an inherited, shared culture. And if there were no great depths to the characters of melodrama, there were perhaps psychological truths in the wish to see decency and virtue triumph – and evil men punished.

---

* *Say It with Flowers* also includes a scene with a street flower-seller seeing a masculine woman and an effeminate man, and shrugging: 'Oh well, boys will be girls and girls will be boys.'
† 'Come on and listen to the Gay White Coons,' ran the theme song.

V

In America, cultural depictions of the Great Depression defined the era, with novels such as John Steinbeck's *The Grapes of Wrath*, films – *Mr Deeds Goes to Town, Hallelujah, I'm a Bum* – and hit songs: 'Buddy Can You Spare a Dime?' 'Remember My Forgotten Man'. It was not really the same in Britain. The good reviews for George Orwell's reportage in *Down and Out in Paris and London* (1933) were unmatched by sales, and although Walter Greenwood's novel *Love on the Dole* (1933) and its spin-off stage play did well, its reach was limited; it never made it to the screen because the British Board of Film Censors rejected a proposed movie version in 1936. It had 'too much of the tragic and sordid side of poverty',[86] and particular objection was taken to 'the final incident of Sally selling herself'. The British film industry struggled with anything that smacked of social realism.*

Nor would such a movie have necessarily found much of an audience. 'I know far more about my own problems than film producers do or ever will,' said a cinemagoer in Bolton, Lancashire. 'I go to be entertained.'[87] It was all about escapism, according to a cinema owner from the same town. 'They're working all day and they come up here at night all dressed like dandies,' he said. 'They feel like they're on top of the earth; you've got to make them think they are.'[88] That feeling could be sustained even beyond the cinema. 'You may have three halfpence in your pocket and not a prospect in the world,' wrote Orwell, but 'you can stand on the street corner, indulging in a private daydream of yourself as Clark Gable or Greta Garbo.'[89]

The British film industry struggled to compete with that kind of glamorous fantasy, but it could continue the music-hall tradition of laughing at hardship. So instead of *Love on the Dole*, there was comedian George Formby in the film *Off the Dole* (1935),

---

* *Love on the Dole* was eventually filmed in 1941, by which time conditions had been transformed, and it looked like a historical curio. It was still a bit too sordid for some, though. 'I can't say I enjoyed it,' wrote fifteen-year-old schoolgirl, Margaret Hilda Roberts, from Grantham in Lincolnshire.

playing the gormless Lancastrian layabout John Willie, 'sacked' by the Labour Exchange after four years of not working. It was not a very good film, despite the occasional line ('A Member of Parliament is a man who gives your life for his country'), but it was a hit in northern England and very profitable; made by the Mancunian Film Company for £8,000, it took £40,000 at the box office. It did so well that it won Formby a contract with a major London company, Associated Talking Pictures. The first product was *No Limit* (1935), with a budget of £30,000 and a comedy script by Walter Greenwood, author of *Love on the Dole*.

Formby's father, who originated the stage name George Formby, had been a music-hall star, billed as the Wigan Nightingale with a mournfully optimistic persona, but he was dead now, having collapsed on stage in 1921 – the year before Marie Lloyd – his already damaged lungs weakened further by the Spanish flu. On his death, Formby Junior, then a jockey (he claimed to have ridden 2,000 races, winning none), took to the stage, borrowing heavily from his father's act, including many of his songs and the character of John Willie. At the time of *No Limit*, he was still being talked about as George Formby the Second,[90] but the film was big enough that he stepped out of the paternal shadow and swiftly eclipsed the memory of the original.*

It was the movies that made him; he was the first British comedian to become a major star through the cinema rather than the stage. Like his father, he was helpless and hapless, bashful in the presence of women, but he replaced John Willie's air of resignation with an irrepressible cheerfulness that compensated for his deficiencies as an actor. And if he wasn't much of a comedian or a singer either, with his thin, high-pitched voice, the songs were insistently catchy and his banjolele playing impressive. The films cast him as the plucky underdog who triumphs in physical challenges – motorcycle racing in *No Limit*, boxing in *Keep Fit* (1937),

---

* In a parallel case, Marie Lloyd Junior had a moderately successful career recreating the act of her mother, but never really established her own persona.

ice skating in *I See Ice* (1938) – and ultimately wins the girl, while singing ditties that are laced with double entendres.

As the song titles show, however, his imagery wasn't exactly priapic: 'With My Little Ukelele in My Hand' (1933), 'With My Little Stick of Blackpool Rock' (1937), 'I Blew a Little Blast on My Whistle' (1938). Even in his best-known number 'When I'm Cleaning Windows' (1936) – banned by the BBC, but said to be a big favourite of Queen Mary – he was cast as voyeur and not protagonist of the implied naughtiness. He was cheeky but unthreatening. 'English humour a long way from its best, but by no means at its worst,' said the *Bystander* of *Come On, George* (1939).[91] 'An ounce of joke to a pound of dialect,' said the *Daily Mirror*.[92]

There was a charm to this, and in 1938 Formby was named the biggest homegrown star in the *Motion Picture Herald*'s annual poll of British film exhibitors, triumphing over fellow comics Will Hay and Sandy Powell, as well as serious actors Charles Laughton and George Arliss. More impressive yet, he knocked into second place the previous chart-topper, and (briefly) his stablemate at Associated Talking Pictures, Gracie Fields.[93]

Like Formby, Fields was from Lancashire – born above her grandmother's fish-and-chip shop in Rochdale – and never shed her accent; unlike him, she was a gifted actor and singer. She made her stage debut at the age of seven in 1905, and her breakthrough twenty years later as a singer and comedian in the revue *Mr Tower of London*. The show had opened in the last weeks of the war and toured the country for years, with over 4,000 performances, before reaching the Alhambra in Leicester Square in 1925 – when the industry woke up to the star potential of its leading lady.

There followed another revue, *By Request*, and variety bills, but she was capable of more. In 1928 she stepped effortlessly into straight drama, appearing with actor-manager Gerald du Maurier in Walter Ellis's play *S.O.S.* at St James's Theatre, where she got 'an enthusiastic reception, the audience applauding for fully a minute when she came on.'[94] The same year, she began releasing records, with a version of the American song 'My Blue Heaven' that sold half a million copies; the other side was a jokey send-up of ballad singers: 'Because I Love You'. She was also broadcasting on radio, and when the London Palladium reopened as a variety theatre that September – it had been struggling with cine-variety until impresario George Black took over its management – it was Gracie Fields who headlined the first show, along with Ivor Novello.

'She breaks all the rules and can never do a thing wrong,'[95] Black said, and that was as close as anyone got to identifying Fields' extraordinary talent. She was quick-tongued, assertive and irreverent, but, unusually for a young woman in variety, she could also play physical comedy, immune to the indignity of slapstick. She had a voice of operatic range, power and subtlety, but was happy to twist it into a harsh screech for comic effect on 'Walter, Walter' (1938), and to sing absurd nonsense like Leslie Sarony's 'I Lift My Finger and Say "Tweet Tweet"' (1929). On more serious material, she couldn't resist pulling faces and sticking her tongue out, as though to deny any artistic affectations.

Indeed, a lack of pretension was integral to her appeal. 'Let's forget we're in the Holborn Empire,' she told a London audience. 'Let's imagine we're in our front room and we're having a bit of a do. We've had a nice tea – some boiled ham and lettuce and a tin of salmon – and we're all right now.'[96] Every year she went back to Rochdale for a week, playing benefit shows for local charities, and she gave financial support to the town's football club. She also founded an orphanage for the children of actors. By 1930 she was being referred to familiarly as Our Gracie, and the name stuck. When she came on stage, the cheers were mixed with cries of 'Good old Gracie,'[97] in the same way that George Lansbury's audiences acclaimed him as 'Good old George'.

Having made her screen debut in *Sally in Our Alley* (1931), she went on to prove a charismatic presence in a sequence of films that were resolutely upbeat: *Looking on the Bright Side* (1932), *Love, Life and Laughter* (1934),* *Sing as We Go* (1934), *Look Up and Laugh*

---

* Not to be confused with George Pearson's *Love, Life and Laughter* (1923).

(1935). Time and again, she took arms against a sea of troubles, and was rewarded for her resourcefulness, determination and service to the community. When *Britannia and Eve* magazine identified 'Europe's "Number One" Women' in 1937,[98] it concluded that in Britain 'the liveliest, most typical, best known spark in the place is probably Gracie Fields', and the following year she became the first female variety star to be awarded the CBE.*

She was happier playing to an audience than making movies, but she was good enough on screen that she was courted by Hollywood. In 1937, Twentieth Century Fox signed her on a contract worth £50,000 for each of four films ('reliably said to be the highest salary ever paid to any woman star', recorded the British press, wrongly)[99] and accepted her demand that the movies be made in Britain. The first release, *We're Going to Be Rich* (1938), had a budget of US $500,000 and won over the American critics. 'Miss Fields, who is neither young nor glamorous is a born entertainer,' said the *New York Daily News*; 'the more you see of her, the better you like her.'[100] Others were more effusive still: 'One can readily understand why the British public is so mad about her' (*World Telegram*); 'Let's have more and more and more of her' (*New York Post*); 'She not only brought the house down but had the ruins chuckling' (*New York Times*).[101]

Despite the international acclaim, she remained, said the *Observer*'s film critic C. A. Lejeune, 'as much part of English life as tea and football pools, our green hedge fields and Nelson's Column',[102] and she was held in enormous affection. When she had a hysterectomy in 1939, an operation that left her unconscious for three days, half a million letters and cards were sent to the hospital. She 'has a stronger hold on the public affection than anyone

---

* Other British women mentioned by *Britannia and Eve* were artist Laura Knight, composer Ethel Smyth, tennis player Dorothy Round, actresses Sybil Thorndike and Jessie Matthews, writers Edith Sitwell and Virginia Woolf, politicians Ellen Wilkinson and Margery Corbett Ashby, and the 'somewhat faded out' aviator Amy Johnson.

since the days of Marie Lloyd', observed the *Western Daily Press*,[103] and the comparison was made elsewhere, as in M. Willson Disher's book *Winkles and Champagne* (1938), an illustrated celebration of the great music-hall acts that placed Fields alongside the greats: Marie Lloyd, Vesta Tilley, Dan Leno.

She didn't have Lloyd's earthy embrace of sex, as was apparent when she occasionally sang something saucy. In 'What Can You Give a Nudist on His Birthday?' (1934), she observes of her brother John Willie, 'A watchchain would look silly, draped across the front of Willie,' before giggling to ensure that no offence is taken.[104] 'Full of talent and virtues though Miss Fields is,' noted film critic George Campbell, 'beauty and sex appeal are not the first of them.'[105] As with George Formby, there was innocence rather than knowingness. That was perhaps inevitable in an entertainment industry dominated by the all-encompassing demographics of radio and cinema, where there was less freedom than there had been in the narrower world of the music hall. But Fields did share with Lloyd a connection to her audience that became something more, something that made her a symbol of the nation. Eliot's comment could still apply: 'she represented and expressed that part of the English nation which has perhaps the greatest vitality and interest' – and if the expression had changed a little, the essence remained.

It was surely no coincidence that – after decades of popular culture being dominated by London – the two biggest British movie stars of the 1930s were Gracie Fields of Rochdale and, from twenty miles to the west, George Formby of Wigan, places particularly scarred by the Depression. Both performers offered resilience in the face of adversity, faith that the human spirit might yet triumph, and, with their evocations of the old music hall, they were surely part of the growing turn to nostalgia as a refuge.

They also found that box-office returns were greater in the provinces than in London, in parts of the country where the need for hope was greatest. Fields, said the *Birmingham Mail* in 1934, 'captures the spirit of good humour and optimism which alone has prevented the legions of the depressed and dispossessed in smitten industrial areas from succumbing to the tragedy surrounding them.'[106] As she sang: 'I'm looking on the bright side, though I'm walking through the shade.'[107]

vi

In 1932 the BBC moved from its home in Savoy Hill to the newly constructed Broadcasting House, just up from Oxford Circus in London's West End. The first words to be transmitted came from Studio 8A, spoken by the man who would become the country's best-known bandleader. 'Hello everyone, this is Henry Hall speaking.' And then the band broke into 'It's Just the Time for Dancing'.

Born in 1898, Henry Hall came from a Salvation Army family and received a catholic musical education; apart from the brass bands of his childhood, he studied classical piano at the Guildhall School of Music, and after the war – he served in the Royal Field Artillery – he played the concertina on the variety stage and accompanied silent movies on piano. In 1922 he joined the six-piece band at the Midland Hotel in Manchester as pianist, and soon became its leader, before adding the Adelphi Hotel in Liverpool to his responsibilities and then, in 1924, moving to the newly built Gleneagles Hotel in Perthshire. This presented an unexpected challenge as Scotland strictly prohibited the playing of dance music on the Sabbath. Hall got round the regulation by having Sunday-evening band practice, running through the full set onstage but behind drawn curtains; if people chose to dance on the other side, he argued, that was not his business.

Hall's opening night at Gleneagles was transmitted by the BBC, and he soon became a regular on the radio, sufficiently popular that in 1932 he was invited to take over the BBC Dance Orchestra from Jack Payne. Now he was on air several times a week, calculating in 1937 that he'd made 2,000 broadcasts and played 3,000 different tunes. To fill that amount of airtime, and to do so while satisfying a diverse audience, required versatility, variety and a lot of musicians.

By 1936 the orchestra boasted a seven-piece string section, six brass, five saxophones, piano, guitar and drums, plus singers; the instrumentation included oboe, xylophone and sousaphone. Even though this was radio, they wore uniforms – Hall believed it aided cohesion – and they played with impeccable precision.

At the time, interest in American jazz was spreading through so-called rhythm clubs, circles of enthusiasts that consisted 'practically entirely of young people who make an ardent study of jazz, however much the highbrows may scorn such a possibility'.[108] In 1933 Mathison Brooks, editor of the *Melody Maker*, went along to one such group, meeting in a room off Regent Street in London, where some sixty young people sat facing three young men with a gramophone. 'They bring along their own favourite records and lecture about them,' Brooks reported, his account hinting at the social milieu of young club members: 'This, mark you, after a hard day's work in city offices and with sacrifice of tennis and other outdoor pursuits.'[109]

The sensation of the rhythm clubs in the mid-1930s was the music of Americans like Jimmy Lunceford, Don Redman and, most revered of all, Duke Ellington, 'who is considered in Europe to have the finest band in the world'. These were bigger orchestras than the early jazz bands; Ellington had six brass players, four wind, four rhythm, with himself on piano. That meant they required full arrangements and big dance halls, but the solos and the heavy stress on the backbeat ensured that it was still hot. 'All this is known as "swing" music, and is considered the prerogative of the Negroes,' explained Brooks.[110]

Some British bandleaders, such as Ambrose and Lew Stone, took to swing with enthusiasm. Not Henry Hall of the BBC, however. His audience was the listener-in at home, not the rhythm-club aficionado, and he was the epitome of the bandleader as entertainer. He could play swing and he could play hot, but he preferred sweet numbers and novelties. He revived music-hall songs from the last century, such as 'The Daring Young Man on the Flying Trapeze', and he made records with comedians, including

Bud Flanagan and Chesney Allen ('Underneath the Arches') and Leslie Sarony ('Wheezy Anna'). His first big hit was Jimmy Kennedy's charming – if vaguely sinister – children's song 'The Teddy Bears' Picnic' (1932), which captivated the Christopher Robin generation and sold a million copies.

Hall was also quick to cover the more sophisticated American songwriters: Irving Berlin, Jerome Kern, Cole Porter. 'We have given the public something rather different,' he said, 'something more refined.'[111] Had he been allowed, he would have refined still further; on a trip to America, he picked up an arrangement of Sibelius's *Finlandia* made for Fred Waring and his Pennsylvanians, but a BBC regulation against 'jazzing the classics'[112] prevented him from broadcasting it.

Backed by the cultural power of the BBC, Hall was a huge star. He appeared at the London Palladium and the Royal Command Performance, signed a profitable record deal with Columbia, made a movie – *Music Hath Charms* (1935) – and conducted the ship's orchestra on the 1936 maiden voyage of Cunard's ocean liner, the *Queen Mary*. He was everywhere, the public face of British dance bands, and he rather enjoyed the role.

He had rivals, of course. Some bandleaders made better records, some were more colourful. Men like Harry Roy, who introduced scat singing to Britain, in imitation of another American swing star, Cab Calloway, and who had a line in suggestive songs: 'My Girl's Pussy' (1931), 'Lucy's Lips' (1934), 'She Had to Go and Lose It at the Astor' (1939). Or the expatriate American Roy Fox, who cultivated an image of Hollywood glamour and bought himself a new Rolls-Royce every year. Or Jack Hylton, who had the most extravagant lifestyle of them all. He was 'the centre of Angmering scandal', it was said in the small Sussex village where he lived; 'baffled whispers and head shakings usually accompanied the mention of his name'.[113] His motto was 'If you think champagne, you'll drink champagne,' and he had multiple horses, cars and mistresses. 'He lived like Nero,' noted his friend, comedian Arthur Askey, 'and was, naturally, a good socialist!'[114]

None of them could match the size of Hall's audience, though, and he was a perfect fit for a BBC that didn't really approve of jazz. 'The family man and his wife think of Henry Hall as the man who has given them hours of pleasant melody,'[115] said the critics, and pleasant was the right word. He was as far removed from a wild jazz man as could be. He wore double-breasted suits that sagged on his slight frame, and with his round, metal-framed glasses, studious expression and hesitant speaking voice, he resembled an earnest young curate on his way to a meeting of the League of Nations Union. He was a very British bandleader.

Hall used his prominence to promote homegrown talent: he had a rule that half the material he broadcast should be British-written, thereby helping to raise the standard of songwriting. As with movies, British popular music was always outgunned by America, but it was beginning to produce songs that became international standards: 'Among My Souvenirs' (1927), 'By a Sleepy Lagoon' (1930),* 'Jolly Good Company' (1931), 'These Foolish Things (Remind Me of You)' (1935), 'A Nightingale Sang in Berkeley Square' (1939). The most consistent hitmaker was bandleader Ray Noble, who recorded 'Goodnight Sweetheart' (1931), 'Try a Little Tenderness' (1932), 'Love Is the Sweetest Thing' (1932) and 'The Very Thought of You' (1934); the latter two each spent five weeks at number one in the American charts, and were popular enough for Noble and his vocalist Al Bowlly to relocate to the States.[†] Then there was lyricist Jimmy Kennedy from Omagh in County Tyrone, who wrote 'Teddy Bears' Picnic' and had an extraordinary strike rate: 'Isle of Capri' (1934), 'Red Sails in the Sunset' (1935), 'Harbour Lights' (1937), 'South of the Border' (1939), 'My Prayer' (1939).

---

* Eric Coates's 'Sleepy Lagoon' became best known as the theme tune to the long-running BBC radio series *Desert Island Discs*, starting in 1942, the same year that trumpeter Harry James took a version to number one in America.

† Noble stayed but Bowlly, after a successful stint that included his own show on NBC radio, returned to Britain in 1937. He was killed in a German air raid on London in 1941.

Hall played his part in encouraging homegrown writers, but he was chiefly notable for perfecting a specifically British take – full of discipline and restraint – on an American art form. He brought about 'the healthiest musical revolution that this country has ever known', approved entertainment paper the *Era*, and it was 'long overdue. Many of our present troubles began when we allowed so much of popular entertainment and recreation to be corrupted by the jungle imbecilities and frenzied barbarisms that pass under the general name of "jazz".'[116]

Yet still there were complaints from all sides. Some felt the music hadn't been anglicised enough. '"British Broadcasting" and "Henry Hall" suggest something very native', a *Daily Mirror* reader wrote to the paper, 'yet all we get are those transatlantic and negroid noises.'[117] On the other hand, Ronald D. B. Crisp, secretary of the West Midlands Rhythm Club, said the real problem was that the low pay offered by the BBC failed to attract the best musicians; consequently, 'the standard of playing of this band is very low'.[118]

Hall could be seen as another manifestation of the nostalgia boom, bringing comfort to the nation. The music was certainly modern, but the sensibility was that of old-fashioned variety, mixing together nonsense, singalongs and sentimentality on the same programme, keeping it light and taking none of it too seriously. 'I am one of those Englishmen whose real theatre is the music hall', he said, and it showed.[119]

In September 1937 Hall broadcast for the last time as a BBC employee, leaving to take up lucrative offers of work in variety theatres. He was joined for his final show by Gracie Fields, who welcomed him into his new career. 'Variety is a wonderful British institution', she said, 'and, far from being dead, is very much alive.'[120] And then – instead of his usual sign-off song, 'Here's to the Next Time' – she sang the big hit from her latest film *The Show Goes On*, in which she played a northern mill worker who becomes a star. It was a characteristically uplifting number:

You've got to smile when you say 'Goodbye',
You've got to smile till the clouds roll by.[121]

Hall had every reason to smile. His star name meant he had a year's worth of bookings lined up, starting two days later at the Birmingham Hippodrome, where, emerging from a dress rehearsal, he was mobbed by fans and required police assistance to get to his car. Exploiting John Reith's 'natural aversion to dance band leaders' and consequent reluctance to negotiate, he had secured very favourable terms for his departure, taking his band with him, together with its entire library of arrangements, worth around £40,000.[122] He was not replaced at the BBC, but the following weekend he was back on the air as a freelancer, which paid better. When it came to business, Henry Hall wasn't as meek as he looked.

7

LEISURE AND LIBRARIES

'It is never wrong to be in love,' said Mr J. G. Reeder soberly. 'Love is a very beautiful experience – I have frequently read about it.'

Edgar Wallace, The Mind of Mr J. G. Reeder, 1925[1]

Ursula: You've been reading too many detective stories.
Huey: Yes, but so do lots of intelligent people.

Trunk Crime, 1939[2]

Butlin's magazine advert, 1938

EMILIO SCALA WAS BORN IN NAPLES IN 1886, one of twelve children in a desperately poor family. At the age of fifteen, he moved to London, starting up in business with an ice-cream barrow. Later, he bought a little café next to Battersea Park station in London, but it wasn't easy; his wife became an invalid, and he later said he had 'been struggling for forty years to make ends meet'.[3] Then, in 1931, everything changed when he won a ticket in the Irish Free State Hospitals' Sweepstake for the forthcoming Grand National.

The Irish Sweepstake was popular in Britain, where gambling laws made it illegal to run such competitions but not to participate. It cost ten shillings to enter, and there were two phases. In the first, a draw was made from a giant revolving drum, several days before the race; more than three million entrants were whittled down to, in this instance, forty-three, each of which was allocated at random a ticket bearing the name of one of the horses entered in the Grand National. Then, come the actual race, those who held a ticket for one of the top three finishers would win a proportionate share of the very substantial prize money. The names of those who had been successful in the draw were publicised, and anyone with a favoured horse would be approached by rich gamblers and consortiums, offering to buy a share of their ticket.

Each ticket holder therefore had to calculate how much of their potential winnings they were prepared to sacrifice in exchange for a guaranteed sum. In that 1931 Grand National draw, for example, the sixty-year-old colliery worker from County Durham who drew the favourite, Easter Hero, sold all but one fifteenth of his ticket for £17,000, and then counted himself fortunate when the horse fell at Becher's Brook. Similarly, when Emilio Scala drew Grakle, not one of the most fancied runners at odds of 100/6, he decided to sell a share to a group of executives from the bookmaking firm Ladbrokes for £10,500. However, he still made over £100,000 in prize money when the horse came home a length and a half clear of the field.

The win was not an unalloyed benefit. Scala's mother died of shock on hearing the news, and he had to fight off a legal challenge from two Italian hairdressers in London, who claimed they were part of a three-man syndicate with him. That issue resolved, he gave £5,000 to each of his four brothers, sent money to family in Italy, and bought a twenty-two-room mansion in Forest Hill, south-east London. But he soon found himself deluged with phone calls, letters and callers, asking for handouts or offering investment opportunities. It was overwhelming. 'We have our own folk to think of first,' said his wife. 'Mr Scala's family in Italy are poor; I have a poor sister with nine children, and a brother with four – he is out of work.'[4] Disillusioned by his experiences, Emilio went back to work, investing the remainder of his winnings.*

His was the largest-ever win, for the sweepstake thereafter limited its top prize to £30,000. Moreover the British government concluded that the enterprise was not good for the country; at a time when money was scarce, large sums were being sent to Ireland. So the Betting and Lotteries Act of 1934 banned the British from participating in such competitions.

Those who disapproved of gambling on moral grounds were much cheered. Small-scale local lotteries were still permitted, and continued to be used for charitable fundraising, though objections were raised even here; the 1932 Methodist Conference denounced such events as 'the degradation of the Christian virtue of charity', confirming a long-standing religious objection.[5] Back in 1923, the London Diocesan Conference had passed a resolution that, 'in view of the increasing spread of the spirit of gambling among all classes', churches should no longer organise raffles.[6]

It was also in 1923 that John Moores – a young would-be entrepreneur in Liverpool – set up the first football pools, under the

---

* Still an Italian national, Scala was to be interned in 1940 on the Isle of Man, even as his sons, both British subjects, were waiting to be called up. He died at the age of seventy-three while on holiday in Italy in 1959, leaving an estate valued at over £100,000.

company name Littlewoods, a competition that proved more durable than the Irish Sweepstake. For a small entry fee, customers were asked to identify a number of forthcoming football matches that would end in a scoring draw. The winnings weren't as spectacular as Emilio Scala was to enjoy, but they were sufficient to tempt an estimated million punters by 1929 – and to make Moores a millionaire. Sufficient too to provide the plot of several British movies: *The Last Coupon* (1932), *Lancashire Luck* (1937), *The Penny Pool* (1937), *Penny Paradise* (1938). Similarly *The Lucky Number* (1933), directed by Anthony Asquith (son of the former prime minister), centred on the winner of the French lottery. These were all comedies, though generally there was a moral lesson in there too – that unearned wealth brought disruption and difficulty to the lives of decent folk.

The film *Love from a Stranger* (1937), adapted from a stage play of Agatha Christie's short story 'Philomel Cottage' (1924), also began in a light tone. 'I'm fed up with routine and drabness; daily life all cut out of the same pattern,' says the heroine. 'I want something exciting, something new and interesting and romantic.' She then wins the French lottery and falls for a man who gives every appearance of being a gold-digging gigolo. The reality, however, is much worse; traumatised by his experience of the war, he's a deranged psychopath, and what starts as comedy turns to tense thriller. The message, though, is the same as the other screen stories of windfall winnings: gambling is no short cut to happiness.*

Despite the cautionary tales, betting was on the rise – and some blamed the government. As chancellor of the exchequer, Winston Churchill had sought to combat illegal bookmakers by creating the Horse Betting Control Board in 1929, a state-owned

---

* The lottery element was not in Christie's story (there was an inheritance instead), but the theme turned up in other detective novels of the time, including J. J. Connington's *The Sweepstake Murders* (1934) and Francis Beeding's *The Norwich Victims* (1935). The latter was adapted for cinema as *Dead Men Tell No Tales* (1938).

enterprise that had exclusive rights to betting at racecourses.* Such government approval of vice, admonished the Reverend Frederick Watson of the Scottish National League Against Gambling, 'would open the sluice gates of betting which would overwhelm the nation'.[7] Racecourses also attracted a spectrum of criminality, from pickpocketing to protection rackets.

It wasn't just the horses. There was the new excitement of greyhound racing, which emerged from the old blood sport of hare coursing once the electric hare had been invented. The first purpose-built track, at Belle Vue Stadium in Manchester, opened in 1926, and the next year, in London alone, the first races were run at Clapton, Harringay and Wembley, followed by Wimbledon (1928) and Catford (1932). Scores followed, in big cities like Liverpool – which had four tracks – down to the small Staffordshire town of Willenhall. The success of the sport made a star of Irish-born dog Mick the Miller, who won the English Greyhound Derby, at White City Stadium in London in 1929, and again the following year.[†] He was a big enough name that, after his retirement from the track, he appeared in the title role of the film *Wild Boy* (1934), alongside Sonnie Hale and comedy double act Bud Flanagan and Chesney Allen. He 'plays his part with intelligent imperturbability',[8] said the critics, 'revealing an inborn sagacity'.[9] Mostly, though, greyhound racing was about gambling.

So it too came within the purview of the Betting and Lotteries Act of 1934, which limited the number of days on which racecourses and dog tracks were allowed to operate; previously there had been no restriction, now it was a maximum of 104 days each year. That did little to hinder the public enthusiasm for having a flutter. In 1936 the Reverend Watson argued that his sluice-gate

---

* The organisation was later renamed the Horserace Totalisator Board, commonly known as the Tote, and was finally privatised in 2011, sold by the coalition government of that time to the bookmakers Betfred.
† This feat was not equalled until 1973, when Patricias Hope [*sic*] won the Derby for the second time.

prophecy had come true; some four to five hundred million pounds was being spent on gambling every year, considerably more than the government was spending on rearmament – which revealed a lack not only of principle and priorities, but of national backbone. 'Many people are rather disgusted at the way the British government toadies to Hitler and Mussolini,' he said. 'One cannot be surprised, however, in view of the fact that they truckled to the pools promoters.'[10]

Meanwhile, the churches were counting a financial as well as a moral cost. In 1939 the vicar of Old Windsor in Berkshire complained that the collection plate was noticeably lighter during the football season, the result, he concluded, of people spending their money on the pools.

ii

The growth of gambling was driven by two opposing factors. On the one hand, there was the quiet desperation engendered by the Depression, the straw-clutching hope of salvation from wretched poverty. On the other, a lot of people were doing rather well; the proportion of the average household income that went on food and rent declined in the 1920s and 30s, leaving greater scope for spending – and dog tracks, racecourses and football pools were among the beneficiaries. Just like the cinema, betting was a feature of a consumer boom.

So too was the inexorable rise of the motorcar. At the beginning of the 1920s there were around a million drivers in Britain; by the end of the following decade that had tripled, and there were some two million private cars on the road, and around half a million motorcycles, many with sidecars. This growth was assisted by falling prices. The Austin Seven, launched in 1922, cost £165, which made it cheaper than the Model T Ford and the first domestic challenger to American dominance of the lower end of the market; by the end of the 1920s a Morris Minor cost just £125, and within a few years a Ford Saloon could be bought for £100. In the process, the British industry became more professional and more concentrated; the number of car makers declined dramatically, and the rich diversity of marques was lost.*

To cater for cars, road signs and markings began to be more regulated, the Ministry of Transport issuing official guidelines in 1926 to standardise white lines in the middle of the road.† At the same time, the first accident statistics were compiled, showing that just under 5,000 people were killed on British roads that year, most of them pedestrians. The annual toll rose to 7,000 by the end of the decade, with a further 178,000 injured, and there was much talk as to whether there should be some sort of aptitude test before a driving licence was issued. The other area of controversy was the speed limit, which had stood at 20 miles per hour since 1903, and was now being widely flouted, with cars advertised as having a top speed of 70 mph.

In 1930 Labour transport minister Herbert Morrison introduced the Road Traffic Act, which created offences of reckless, dangerous and careless driving, and of driving under the influence of drink or drugs. It also created the Highway Code, made third-party insurance compulsory, and banned those under the age of sixteen from driving a motor vehicle. No driving test materialised, however; there was just a requirement that those acquiring a licence

---

* British makes of cars in the inter-war years included: Abingdon, Albatross, Albert, Angus-Sanderson, Arrol-Johnston, Ascot, Aston Martin, Astral, Austin, Bean, Baylis-Thomas, Belsize-Bradshaw, Bentley, Brough, Burney, Calthorpe, Chambers, Cluley, Clyno, Crossley, Crouch, Cubitt, Daimler, Dawson, Frazer Nash, Galloway, Gibbons, Gnome, Godfrey-Proctor, Gwynne, Hampton, Hillman, Humber, Iris, Invicta, Jaguar, Jensen, Jowett, Lagonda, Lammas-Graham, Lanchester, Lea-Francis, Leyland, Little Midland, Marlborough, Maudslay, MG, Moon, Morgan, Morris, Napier, Nomad, Ogston, Palladium, Palmerston, Phoenix, Railton, Reliant, Rhode, Riley, Rolls-Royce, Rootes, Rover, Ruston-Hornsby, Siddeley-Deasey, Singer, Standard, Straker-Squire, Sunbeam, Swift, Talbot, Tamplin, Trojan, Triumph, Vauxhall, Waverley, Whitlock, Windsor, Wolseley.
† White lines to mark the sides of the road followed in the 1940s, and no-parking yellow lines in the 1950s.

declared they had no 'disease or physical disability' that would make them 'a source of danger to the public'. As for increasing the speed limit, Morrison instead abolished it altogether, arguing (to the cheers of MPs) that 'the fixing of an arbitrary speed limit for light motor-cars to be observed in all circumstances is unreasonable and indefensible'.[11]

That freedom did not survive for long. Under the National Government, the 1934 Road Traffic Act made driving tests compulsory and reinstated speed limits, that for built-up areas were set at 30 miles per hour. Warning lights were also introduced for pedestrian crossings, known as Belisha beacons after the new transport minister, Leslie Hore-Belisha of the National Liberals. It was striking, though, that neither the 1930 nor the 1934 act made any difference to the continuing rise in road fatalities.*

Britain was becoming a more mobile, more connected nation. For the majority who couldn't afford a car, motorised buses and coaches linked cities and towns in a way that even the railways had not achieved. In 1932, around 34 million long-distance coach journeys were made, and there were over five billion bus journeys.[12] That mobility, in turn, sparked a golden age of holidaymaking: fifteen million people had a holiday away from home in 1939,[13] most of them benefiting from the Holidays with Pay Act passed the previous year. The pre-war seaside resorts, from Blackpool to Margate, saw a surge in trade, new caravan and camping sites sprang up, and in 1936 Billy Butlin opened his first holiday camp in Skegness, Lincolnshire.

This last was a true revolution. Born in South Africa in 1899, Butlin had spent much of his childhood travelling around England with his grandmother's fair, before joining his mother in Canada. After war service, he returned to Britain and to the family trade, renting a fairground hoopla stall. He was ambitious and expanded his operations until, within a decade, he had the noisiest, most

---

* The figures reached a record high of nearly 8,000 deaths in 1941, before starting to fall.

garish amusement arcade in Skegness, where he ran the country's first-ever dodgem cars.

His holiday camp, though, was a much larger proposition: a leisure complex that had access to the sea and to the surrounding countryside, but was intended to be self-contained. It had gardens, a swimming pool, boating lake, a putting green, a bowls lawn, a skating rink, dozens of tennis courts, facilities for billiards, netball and table tennis, and several bars and dance halls, including the Viennese Ballroom, where the orchestra of Italian-born bandleader Mantovani held sway. Church services were offered, and there was a resident doctor and nursing staff. Visitors were housed in residential huts – known as Elizabethan chalets – and, with 'sixty modern deluxe bathrooms, marble tiled and with porcelain baths',[14] there was capacity for 2,000 campers, soon increased to 5,000. The campers were divided into four 'houses' on the public-school model, which meant that competitions could be staged: sporting and dancing tournaments, beauty parades, talent shows, knobbly-knees contests. Waking moments were expected to be spent in a programmed whirl of activity and entertainment.

In addition, there were one-off events – brass-band contests, boxing tournaments – and celebrity endorsements. The camp was opened by aviator Amy Johnson, still famous for her 1930 solo flight from Britain to Australia, and there were visits by a succession of stars, from radio comedian Stainless Stephen to footballer Cliff Bastin, who'd won five league titles and two FA Cups with Arsenal. In 1938, cricketer Len Hutton scored 364 runs in a single innings against Australia, beating the test record set by Australian Don Bradman against England eight years earlier; Butlin immediately invited him to appear at Skegness, offering him £100 to face the bowling of Gracie Fields and actress Florence Desmond – George Formby's co-star in *No Limit*.

It cost £3 3s for a week at Butlin's in early summer, rising to £3 13s 6d at the height of the season and falling to £3 in autumn, inclusive of all amusements and four meals a day in the two large dining halls. 'Clearly,' wrote J. B. Priestley, 'if this is the kind of holiday you want, it is a bargain.' It wasn't to his taste – 'its atmosphere was so obviously American' – but he saw it as a harbinger of a future in which living would be more communal. 'It belongs to the same new world of mass-produced bargains as the cheap chain-store, the inexpensive motor-car, the movie theatre.'[15]

If Billy Butlin revolutionised British holidaymaking, a man born Benjamin Cohen in 1878 did the same for home furnishing. He started as an office boy in the City at fourteen, assiduously saved his money and, still in his teens, spent £12 to buy a draper's shop in Rotherhithe, south London. The area was so impoverished that he struggled to attract customers, until he found the solution. 'I let them have it on credit,' he recalled. 'That gave me the first insight into the possibilities of the easy-payment system.'[16] He continued the practice when, now known as Benjamin Drage, he opened a furniture shop in Holborn in 1908. 'Credit for the ordinary workman was practically unheard of,' he said, but by the mid-1920s, hire purchase schemes were widely available.[17]

Mr Drage – as he became famous, through extensive newspaper advertising – offered four-year payment plans. 'A small first payment and small monthly payments will enable men and women of moderate means to gain pleasant homes easily and safely,'[18] said the adverts. One pound a month bought you £50 worth of furniture. The tone was one of friendly trust, and there was no need for references or guarantors: 'I shouldn't like to be asked for a reference myself, and my motto is "Do as you would be done by."'[19] The occasional defaulter, he calculated, was far outweighed by the additional custom generated.

Mr Drage's advertising was boosted by a steady stream of positive news stories. In 1928, he funded Christmas dinner for the 6,000 inhabitants of two Welsh mining villages – Abersychan in Monmouthshire and Mardy in Glamorganshire – and for 10,000 homeless and destitute people in London. In 1929, he celebrated twenty-one years of his Holborn shop by having a four-ton birthday cake made and distributing a slice to each of 60,000 customers, as well as every London policeman and fireman. And in 1930 he hosted a series of parties over five consecutive Saturdays for a total of 50,000 children in London Zoo, with his friend George Lansbury as guest of honour. ('He is too good for these days,' he said of the future Labour leader. 'He is living a hundred years before his time.')[20]

Knighted in 1932 for services to the Empire Marketing Board, Drage was successful because the aspirations of the nation were changing. An extensive programme of house-building brought falling property prices, and by the end of the 1930s around a third of the population lived in owner-occupied homes, more than three times the pre-war figure. Those new homes needed to be furnished, and often there wasn't enough ready cash to do so.

Hire purchase still wasn't quite the done thing, though. In 1925, rising young comedian Arthur Askey and his wife moved into their first home. 'The furniture was on the "never-never",' he said, 'but after paying one instalment I felt it was a stigma and went and settled for the full account.'[21] For precisely this reason, Mr Drage delivered his goods in plain vans, so that nosy neighbours need never know.

iii

When Neville Chamberlain, the chancellor of the exchequer, presented his budget in 1934, he told the House there was cause to feel optimistic that the worst of times were over. 'We have now finished the story of *Bleak House*,' he promised, 'and are sitting down this afternoon to enjoy the first chapter of *Great Expectations*.'[22] These were literary references he could confidently expect the country to understand, for Charles Dickens was enjoying a popular renaissance, having – thanks to the unlikely intervention of Fleet Street – become part of the home-furnishing boom.

As the Depression settled in, the big national newspapers opened a new front in their perpetual circulation wars. Medical and accident insurance had already been offered to loyal readers, now there were material gifts as well, redeemed for a certain number of cut-out coupons. There ensued what the *Economist* called a fit of 'competitive insanity', with 50,000 canvassers roaming the land, promising new subscribers a host of consumer goods – 'toys, cutlery, cameras, hosiery, underwear and finally even mangles and complete tea-sets'.[23] One analysis at the time concluded that 'a whole Welsh family could be clothed, from head to foot, for the price of eight weeks reading of the *Daily Express*'.[24]

The conflict became ruinous. Advertisers of other products were annoyed, profits were hit, and the cut-throat competition did little for the public standing of journalism. Early in 1932, the Newspaper Publishers' Association agreed a ceasefire, banning free gifts. The truce did not last, however, broken by an unexpected contender in the field, the *Daily Herald*.

Launched in 1912, and growing out of a bulletin produced by striking printers, the *Herald* was closely associated with the trade unions, and had been owned by the TUC since 1922. It was not profitable, though, and the Labour Party was repeatedly called upon to bail it out; a quarter of a million pounds went from party to paper in the 1920s. In an attempt to salvage the title, a majority stake was sold in 1930 to Odhams Press, one of the biggest publishing houses, then run by Julius Elias, who already owned the weekly *John Bull*.* After Elias introduced a new business ethic, the paper was relaunched and circulation quadrupled to over a million. Unfortunately, that was still some way behind the sales of the *Daily Mail* (1.85 million), *Daily Express* (1.69 million) and *News Chronicle* (1.45 million) – and a long way behind in terms of advertising revenue, since the *Herald*'s readership was too poor to have much discretionary spending power. Elias calculated that he would need a two-million circulation to compensate for the imbalance, so he found a loophole in the marketing peace treaty.

---

* *John Bull* had been founded in 1906 by Liberal MP and crooked financier Horatio Bottomley, with Elias as business manager. Bottomley was bought out in 1921, just before his downfall; in 1922 he was sentenced to seven years in jail for fraud involving the sale of government Victory War Bonds.

The *Herald* began to offer, not free gifts but heavily discounted books, all of which were printed in-house by Odhams. Initially these were too dull for anyone to worry about – popular reference books on medicine, gardening, handicrafts and the like – but then, in March 1933, came a much more spectacular offer: the works of Charles Dickens, in sixteen volumes.

'A Complete Set of Dickens is the rightful heritage of every English home,' trumpeted the adverts. 'To possess these works is to have one's humanity quickened, one's mind enlarged, and one's whole life enriched.' Anyway, never mind the quality, feel the width: 'over 12,000 pages – over five million words – it weighs 19 lb and it measures 26 in. long by 7 in. high by 4¾ in. deep'. The books were bound in 'lustrous red silk-grained cloth, tooled and decorated in real 22-ct. gold', each one 'wrapped in a protective covering of cellophane'. The set was worth £4 4*s*, but it was available for just sixteen weeks' worth of coupons from the *Herald*, plus eleven shillings for delivery, a total outlay of £1 7*s*. This was 'the greatest publishing enterprise in history', said the *Herald*. 'Magnificent, unique, stupendous,' agreed its Sunday sister, the *People*; 'nothing like it has ever been attempted in the whole history of journalism.' Personal testimonies were solicited from writers and politicians. 'You have performed a miracle,' enthused George Lansbury, himself a former editor of the *Daily Herald*.[25]

Beneath the hyperbole, it was a genuinely good offer, and a good product: the books looked well in a suburban living room, better still in the front parlour of a respectable working-class terrace. The other proprietors fought back. 'This is war, war to the death,' Lord Beaverbrook told Elias, drawing an imaginary sword. 'I shall fight you to the bitter end.'[26] Books were the new battleground. Within a week, the *Daily Mail*, *Daily Express* and *News Chronicle* were also offering sets of Dickens, the latter plaintively reminding readers that it was 'Charles Dickens's own paper'.[27] By the end of the year, *John Bull* had joined the crowd, making up for lost time by throwing in 'A Magnificent Solid Oak Bookcase Free',[28] but Dickens was becoming a little passé. The *Chronicle* was instead urging readers to 'Make it a Gilbert and Sullivan Christmas', with a four-volume set of the operas.[29]

Local papers tried to find their own angle. The *Daily Independent* in Sheffield had *The Children's Shakespeare*, and the *North Mail* in Newcastle had *Lamb's Tales from Shakespeare*, together with five other randomly selected children's books, from *Gulliver's Travels* to *Black Beauty*. Various local titles pooled their resources to offer a ten-volume set that contained a thousand short stories (because even 'the keenest booklover simply cannot devote endless hours to reading vast works').[30] Less cheerfully, *Answers* had *A Popular History of the Great War* in six volumes, and most misguidedly, the *Aberdeen Press and Journal* went with the works of Shakespeare in forty miniature volumes, 'the smallest books published with readable type'.[31]

In this frenzy of cultural consumerism, the *Herald* finally achieved its objective of a two-million sale, but at a price; the *Economist* calculated that its new readers had cost a pound each. And still the advertising that Julius Elias sought did not materialise, because his readership remained short of funds. Research commissioned by the Incorporated Society of British Advertisers in 1936 showed that just 5 per cent of *Herald* readers had an income above £250 per annum. This compared to 25 per cent for the *Express* (which also reached sales of two million, becoming the country's most popular paper), while the *Mail* was even more attractive, with 43 per cent of readers earning above that threshold.

At least the *Daily Herald* survived, though.* Many others did not. In a parallel with the car industry, dozens of daily and Sunday papers closed, there was a decline in sales of local titles, and the circulation controlled by the five largest companies mushroomed from 15 to 43 per cent.[32] Over the course of the 1930s, the *Express, Herald, Mail, Mirror* and *News Chronicle* increased their combined daily sale from seven to nine million.[33]

---

* Sales declined in later years, and in 1964 the *Herald* was relaunched as the *Sun*.

iv

The fact that newspapers wished, as trade journal the *Bookseller* put it, to 'dabble in bookselling at cut-throat prices,'[34] reflected not only people's need to furnish their home, but the buoyant state of publishing. The production of fiction books doubled in the 1920s to reach record levels, and then continued to rise, aided by new commercial practices. The sixpenny paperback, for example, previously a lowbrow format considered appropriate only for thrillers and boys' adventure stories, was reinvented by Allen Lane with the launch of Penguin Books in 1935; middlebrow fiction and non-fiction was reissued in respectably dull livery, and a million books were sold in the first ten months.

In 1939, the *Bookseller* celebrated 'a wider and progressive recognition of the place of books in the life of the people', citing as causes for this happy state of affairs a rise in media coverage, manifest in 'the BBC's gradual extension of book talks', and the spreading of review pages from the serious papers to popular titles like the *Daily Mirror* and the *Daily Sketch*.[35] It also mentioned the Sunday Times Book Exhibition (later the Sunday Times National Book Fair), which was first staged in London in 1933 and ran annually, inspiring similar trade shows in New York and Toronto.

There were also book tokens, introduced for Christmas in 1932, following a similar system in Sweden. A customer bought a voucher, sent it to another as a gift, and the beneficiary redeemed it for books to that value in one of the shops participating in the scheme. The intention was to spread the love of reading by experience; rather than simply being given a book, 'the recipient shall be led into a bookshop and thus brought more effectively into the atmosphere of books'.[36] The tokens came in the form of stamps, ranging in price from 3*s* 6*d* up to a guinea, and were put inside an attractive Christmas card. It was 'really an ornamental voucher', wrote J. B. Priestley, who did a good deal to publicise the scheme.[37] That first year, though, the packaging confused some recipients; unaware that such tokens existed, they threw away what they believed were merely cards when the decorations came down on

Twelfth Night. Nonetheless, the National Book Council, which administered the tokens, reported that more than 1.25 million were sold in the first six years, with a face value of £400,000 – an average of 6*s* 5*d* per gift – enough for a dozen Penguin paperbacks.

Most importantly, the reading boom was driven by libraries, of which there were several varieties. At the worthier end of the market were the public libraries administered by local councils, of which there were already around 5,000 by 1920, with the numbers still growing. By the mid-1930s there were some seven million borrowers, each taking out an average of thirty books a year. In 1934, George V opened the Manchester Central Library – an impressive, classical rotunda with domed roof and columns – saying that, 'to our urban populations, libraries are as essential to health of mind as open spaces to health of body'.[38]

Since these public libraries offered free loans, they hit the profitability of the old nineteenth-century model, the commercial circulating libraries that charged a monthly or annual subscription, aimed at middle-class readers. In 1937, Mudie's, once the biggest of all the circulating libraries, closed its doors for the last time. Those of W. H. Smith's and Boots survived, though, the latter with a third of a million subscribers borrowing an average of eighteen titles a year.* The market was declining, but there were still genteel readers to please. The title character in May Sinclair's *Life and Death of Harriett Frean* (1922) has always seen herself as something of an intellectual, but in her lonely, fading years, she relaxes her standards. 'Her serious reading, her Dante, her Browning, her Great Man, lay always on the table ready to her hand,' but she's actually reading novels from the circulating libraries: 'She was

---

* As a snapshot of the material stocked, the Boots' Booklovers' Library compiled a list of its ten most-borrowed books of 1930: Vicki Baum, *Grand Hotel*; Arnold Bennett, *Imperial Palace*; O. Douglas, *The Day of Small Things*; Gilbert Frankau, *Martin Make Believe*; A. P. Herbert, *Water Gipsies*; Ethel Mannin, *Confessions and Impressions*; H. V. Morton, *In Search of Scotland*; J. B. Priestley, *Angel Pavement*; Ernest Raymond, *Jesting Army*; E. H. Young, *Miss Mole*.

satisfied with anything that ended happily and had nothing in it that was unpleasant, or difficult, demanding thought.'*

Also surviving, indeed flourishing, were the 'evil little libraries' attacked in George Orwell's novel *Keep the Aspidistra Flying* (1936). He depicts a single-room premises in the working-class district of Lambeth in south London, located 'between a flyblown ham-and-beef shop and a smartish undertaker'. These were places that required no subscription or deposit, that charged per loan, and that stocked the lowest form of genre fiction, the stuff that council libraries – with their keen sense of civic responsibility – would not touch. 'The books are published by special low-class firms and turned out by wretched hacks at the rate of four a year, as mechanically as sausages and with much less skill,' wrote Orwell. 'Nothing has ever been devised that puts less strain on the intelligence.' These tuppenny libraries, as they were known – 'tuppenny dram shops' as academic Q. D. Leavis called them, equating them with the societal evil of alcohol[39] – had the great advantage of being cheap and conveniently local, often located in the back of a shop.

By the mid-1930s there were several thousand tuppennies, and authors and publishers were complaining – just as they had once complained of Mudie's – that these places were 'dragging down the standard of fiction', particularly with their insistence on stories having a happy ending, as demanded by the real-life Harriett Freans.[40] On the other hand, they provided a refuge for those whose lives were lacking in glamour and excitement. 'I yearned for adventure, for love, for romance, and I seemed condemned to an existence of drab utility,' reflects the heroine of Agatha Christie's *The Man in the Brown Suit* (1924), and she escapes into not just movies but books. 'The village possessed a lending library, full of tattered works of fiction, and I enjoyed perils and love-making at second hand.'

The number of libraries, and the social breadth of their readers,

---

* W. H. Smith closed its library in 1961, and Boots' Booklovers' Library ended in 1966.

transformed publishing, pushing genre fiction to the fore. Some firms, in the hope of finding sales across the spectrum, reshaped their entire business model. Most notable was a publisher founded before the war by Gerald Mills and Charles Boon, and initially producing general fiction and non-fiction. Among the early titles published by Mills & Boon was the first British edition of Gaston Leroux's *The Phantom of the Opera* (1910), together with work by Hugh Walpole, E. F. Benson and Jack London. Into the 1920s it was still responsible for a wide range of titles, from an early Georgette Heyer novel to the reactionary political essays of Harold Begbie, writing under the name A Gentleman with a Duster.[41]

Early in the following decade, however, the imprint began to concentrate on its romance list – and on standardisation. Novels now came in uniform packaging, and were turned out in large numbers; the first six months of 1938 saw forty-seven new titles and thirty-seven reprints. They had small print runs – between 3,000 and 8,000 – they didn't come in paperback, and they weren't cheap, costing 7s 6d. Consequently, sales were not great, but the readership was very substantial indeed, for these were aimed squarely at libraries, where their sturdy covers ensured they were a sound investment; they could survive hundreds of borrowings.

This was fiction for the assembly-line age. The sales point was Mills & Boon itself, not individual titles or even writers. If you liked one book, you would like the next, because the storylines were also becoming standardised, based on a familiar nineteenth-century template: a sexually inexperienced young woman, an older, emotionally taciturn man, an explosion of passion that ends not in sex but in marriage. Although there are hurdles along the way – temptations, gossip and misunderstandings – heartache is invariably followed by happiness.

To reflect the new, democratic world, the heroine tends to come from a humble (but decent) background, while the man is several rungs higher up the social ladder, though steadfastness and integrity matter more than riches. Indeed, if poverty is unattractive, so too is extreme wealth. In Constance M. Evans's *Fortune's Wing*

Feather (1933), our heroine wins a vast sum in a lottery and learns that it doesn't bring happiness; she enters high society, before realising its futility and returning to a simpler life with her first love. Similarly the title character in the same author's 1936 contribution *Janna, the Actress* ('a delightful romance of the stage', said the *Daily Mirror*)[42] turns down a millionaire for the love of a better man. It's different, naturally, when the rich man is initially unrecognised: in Jean S. MacLeod's *Mist Across the Hills* (1938), the heroine falls for a deck hand on an expensive yacht, only discovering later that he's actually the son of the boat's owner.

The Queen of Mills & Boon was Sophie Cole, whose debut, *Arrows from the Dark*, had been the first-ever title from the publisher, back in 1908. ('A strong piece of work', judged the *Daily Telegraph*, while the *Morning Post* invoked the hallowed name of Jane Austen.)[43] Most of the sixty-odd novels that followed from her pen were also published by the firm, spinning out a very female line in fantasy and aspiration; 'Sophie Cole makes shopping a delight to read about', said a reviewer.[44] She was a stalwart of the public and circulating libraries: in the mid-1930s, Mudie's had thirty-eight of her books in stock, including such recent titles as *Truant Memory* (1931), *Sixpence in Her Shoe* (1932), *Obituary to Love* (1934) and *The Unexpected Gift* (1935). There was also *Secret Joy* (1934), in which the heroine writes a romantic novel, published by the familiar sounding Spencer & Trant. So committed to the firm was Cole that, when Gerald Mills died suddenly in 1928, she bought 10 per cent of his shareholding. There was money to be made from books, even if not by writers.*

---

* Cole eventually left Mills & Boon, selling her shares, a few years before her death in 1947. The break was seemingly in protest at an affair between Boon's sister, who worked for the firm, and the husband of Cole's own sister. Love, it transpired, wasn't everything.

v

The male equivalent of the romance was the thriller, which meant, above all others, Edgar Wallace, the most newsworthy and self-advertising writer in the country. He'd made his name with his first novel *The Four Just Men* (1905), though it drove him to bankruptcy. Since then, he'd written relentlessly as a novelist and as a star journalist, and frittered away most of his earnings on theatre ventures that seldom paid off. What was left went on the horses, where he was spectacularly unsuccessful, which didn't stop him getting a job as a racing tipster on Lord Beaverbrook's *Evening Standard*. So attached was he to lost causes that in the 1931 general election he stood in Blackpool for Lloyd George's version of the Liberals; the previous MP had been Walter de Frece, husband of Vesta Tilley, so the town was accustomed to showbiz, but Wallace still polled badly.

The only sure winners in Wallace's life were his facility for storytelling and his extraordinary work rate. Between the end of the war and his death in 1932, he published around a hundred books, as well as writing twenty-one plays and a handful of films, including an adaptation of *The Hound of the Baskervilles* (1932). Most of his books were thrillers and crime stories, though he also wrote colonial novels, science fiction and adventure tales, and one horror classic: he died in Hollywood, where he had just written a screenplay, *The Beast*, that would prove his best-known creation when it emerged as *King Kong* a year later.

'Seen the midday Wallace, Sir?' a bookstall attendant asked a commuter in a *Punch* cartoon,[45] and he dominated the railways and the libraries; it was said that one in every four books read in Britain was written by him. His readership, acknowledged the press, was wider than many would admit: 'Members of the "intelligentsia" are inclined to sneer at Edgar Wallace because of his tremendous output, but they read him in secret just the same.'[46] As *The Times* observed on his death, 'Edgar Wallace became a habit.'[47]

Beyond Wallace, Sapper's Bulldog Drummond was still keeping the country safe for rowdy, right-thinking chaps, and he was joined by others of his ilk, such as Sydney Horler's creation, the Honourable Timothy Overbury Standish, son of Lord Quorn, in *Tiger Standish* (1932). He had 'once been the most famous centre-forward in English football' and now worked for a secret government department known as Q.I. Like Drummond, he had 'attractively ugly features' and a penchant for 'cracking jokes of the worst description', and he survived into further volumes.*

There was a more modern model, though, in the shape of Simon Templar, who was introduced in Leslie Charteris's *Meet the Tiger* (1928) and went on to appear in twenty-one volumes in the 1930s.† He was another upper-class adventurer from Mayfair, a freelance campaigner for justice, a latter-day Robin Hood, who was prepared to go where the police would not, often in defiance of their instructions. He was 'a terror to the underworld and a thorn in the side of Scotland Yard, a gay crusader in modern dress'. But he was more sophisticated than Drummond, wittier and more imaginative, replacing the rollicking camaraderie of the rugger player with the sarcastic superiority of the fencer. And there was a less celebratory tone; the carefree nonchalance felt more world-weary, even nihilistic. In the underworld, there were 'legends that told of a slim bantering outlaw whose smile was more deadly than any other man's anger, who faced death with a jest and sent men into eternity with his flippant farewell ringing in their ears'. Templar operated under the name of the Saint, and he had a calling card bearing his logo: a stick man with a halo.

Among the many imitators of Charteris, the best was John Creasey, who wrote *Meet the Baron* (1935), about another gentleman adventurer, this one with an alter ego as a jewel thief. Creasey completed the 75,000-word novel in just six days to meet the deadline for a 'Cracksman Competition' being run by the publisher George G. Harrap, and took the £1,500 first prize. It may

---

* There were a dozen Tiger Standish novels, through to *The House of Jackals* (1951).
† Over the course of the twentieth century, Simon Templar was the hero of fifty books, fourteen movies, eight television films and two major TV series.

have given him a false impression of the financial rewards available from writing. A standard contract for a thriller was a flat fee of £50, with no royalties; the only way to make a living was to be prolific and to establish recurring characters. In 1939 alone, Creasey published twenty-three books under eight different pseudonyms: there were two Barons, and two apiece for his other creations, Patrick Dawlish, Department Z, Bruce Murdoch and the Toff, together with a Sexton Blake, five romances, four westerns and three stand-alone novels. (So much for George Orwell's 'wretched hacks' writing books 'at the rate of four a year'.) He claimed that his record was writing two novels in a week, 'and on the Saturday afternoon, I played cricket'.[48]

Of those characters, the most popular was the Honourable Richard Rollison, alias the Toff. 'He came down from Cambridge worth half a million of money and with a hatred of dullness,' explains *Introducing the Toff* (1938). So he travels the world and 'from the dope-dens of Shanghai, the dives of San Francisco and the cesspools of Marseilles trickled fantastic stories of his speed on the draw, his uncanny accuracy with a knife, the punch like the kick of a mule which he carried in both hands'.* He has his logo printed on calling cards as well: 'a top hat set at a rakish angle and beneath it a monocle, cigarette in a jaunty holder and bow tie'. The Toff worked alone, but would cooperate with the police on 'the suppression of crime, particularly crime with violence or drug trafficking or blackmail and that vilest trade of all, white slavery'.

This was the biggest difference with the new breed of thriller. Bulldog Drummond's obsession with international conspiracies and Bolshevik plots was starting to look decidedly out of date. The Saint, the Toff and a host of others tended to battle economic, rather than ideological, foes: racecourse touts, crooked coppers,

---

* Throwing a knife was acceptable in British fiction, stabbing was not, as a woman makes clear in Alfred Hitchcock's *Blackmail*: 'A good, clean, honest whack over the head with a brick is one thing. There's something British about that. But knives? No, knives is not right.' This did not reflect reality.

domestic tyrants, drug dealers and conmen. These Depression-era heroes lived in a smaller world than their 20s forebears, but one riddled with vicious exploiters of decent folk, where financiers and businessmen are seldom virtuous. In 'The Smart Detective' (1933), the Saint is visited by a woman who works for 'Oppenheim who owns the sweat shops'. She explains the system: 'I work with fifty other girls in an attic in the East End. We work ten hours a day, six days a week, sewing. If you're clever and fast you can make two pieces a day. They pay you one shilling a piece.' Oppenheim, by contrast, has just bought a collection of emeralds for a quarter of a million pounds. 'It's just one of those things that makes you feel like turning communist sometimes.'

These were heroes who cared for the underdog. In W. B. M. Ferguson's *Crackerjack* (1936), Drexel Drake is a genial, middle-aged man who gives vast sums to children's hospitals and other charities, but it turns out to be money that he's stolen, under his alias, Crackerjack (whose logo is a masked face inside the curve of a large question mark).* Likewise, the burglar hero of Bruce Graeme's million-selling *Blackshirt* (1925) makes a large donation to a charitable school. Even the Baron in his early days, when he was a jewel thief, 'used the profit more for other people than himself'.

Breaking the law in this unjust world is sometimes necessary, so long as a higher moral code is observed – and so long as there are sufficient thrills and exotic excitements, observing the conventions of the genre. One of these, curiously, is that a gentleman adventurer should have the hands-on approach to deadly animals pioneered by Bulldog Drummond. Cornered by a pair of savage Alsatian guard dogs, the Baron punches them unconscious. Meanwhile, the Toff is sent a package containing 'a blood-lusting tarantula', but as an experienced thriller hero, he's well used to such dangers and soaks the box in hot water for an hour before opening it.

---

* Renamed Jack Drake, he was played by Tom Walls in the film *Crackerjack* (1938).

vi

In 1916 Captain Arthur Hastings was invalided home from the front, and chose to spend his sick leave with an old friend in Styles Court, a big house in Essex, as far distant from the trenches as could be imagined. 'I descended from the train at Styles St Mary,' he remembered, 'an absurd little station, with no apparent reason for existence, perched up in the midst of green fields and country lanes.' Also living in the idyllic village were some Belgian refugees from the war, including an acquaintance of Hastings, a retired detective named Hercule Poirot. His presence proved very useful when the owner of Styles Court was found murdered, poisoned with strychnine.

Agatha Christie's first novel, *The Mysterious Affair at Styles* (1920), inaugurated what would become known, following a 1939 essay by John Strachey, as the Golden Age of Detective Fiction, a decidedly British phenomenon. 'The crime novel,' observed German writer Bertolt Brecht, 'like the world itself, is ruled by the English.'[49] There had been detective stories before, and many of the pre-war sleuths were still working – G. K. Chesterton's Father Brown, A. E. W. Mason's Inspector Hanaud, R. Austin Freeman's Dr Thorndyke – while new tales about Sherlock Holmes's old cases continued to appear. But it was in the 1920s and 1930s that the trickle of publications became a torrent. And a blood-flecked one at that, for the old tales of burglars, blackmailers and stolen documents were no longer sufficient; modern detectives dealt almost entirely with murders – and lots of them. 'The reading public nowadays is never satisfied with only one murder,' points out a character in Harriet Rutland's *Knock, Murderer, Knock!* (1938). 'They like plenty of thrills for their money.'

The emphasis on violent death, and on logical deduction rather than emotion, might have suggested that detective fiction was a male art form, but as Christie and Rutland demonstrated, there was scope for female writers, and indeed they came to dominate: Margery Allingham, Josephine Bell, Dorothy Bowers, Mavis Doriel Hay, Georgette Heyer, E. C. R. Lorac, Ngaio Marsh, Gladys

Mitchell, Edith Pargeter, Dorothy L. Sayers, Josephine Tey, Ethel Lina White. Even Labour MP Ellen Wilkinson wrote a murder story, *The Division Bell Mystery* (1932), during her time away from Parliament.

It was also a far more respectable genre than romance or thrillers. In *The Mask of Demetrios* (1939), Eric Ambler teased 'the great army of university professors who write detective stories in their spare time', and plenty of highbrows did enter the field, most notably poet Cecil Day-Lewis, who wrote as Nicholas Blake and based his sleuth, Nigel Strangeways, on W. H. Auden. Also plying their trade were Father Ronald Knox, of *Broadcasting the Barricades* fame, Dr C. P. Snow, Professor J. I. M. Stewart (as Michael Innes), and married couple G. D. H. and M. Cole of the Fabian Society. Their detectives tended to treat murder as a light-hearted game, with wit and a fair bit of intellectual showing off. At a less cerebral level, though, there was no shortage of dull plodders. 'Life's too short to get metaphysical,' says Inspector French in Freeman Wills Croft's *Mystery in the Channel* (1931). 'I've got to go and earn some bread and butter.'

Hanging over the entire field was the memory of the war. Many of the male writers – Anthony Berkeley, Lynn Brock, Henry Wade (the pseudonym of Sir Henry Aubrey-Fletcher) – had served, as had the husbands of Dorothy L. Sayers and Agatha Christie, while Ngaio Marsh's great love was killed in action. Consequently, the world of the detective story, however stable it seemed on the surface, was one of crumbling social structures, full of the products of fractured families: widows, spinsters, divorcees and stepchildren. The most despised characters were those who had profiteered in the war and those who played the system, securing 'a staff appointment of bewildering unimportance' (in a Ngaio Marsh story) or getting through the conflict 'without killing so much as a rabbit' (Margery Allingham).[50]

By contrast, there's a good deal of sympathy for the shellshocked, of whom there are many. 'It was the war that sent him rocky,' says a policeman in John Bude's *The Cornish Coast Murder* (1935). 'He's always talking about the Jerries. Poor devil!' A character in Mavis Doriel Hay's *The Santa Klaus Murder* (1936) is so damaged that he's disturbed by the sound of Christmas crackers being pulled. 'The man's not normal,' someone exclaims, but the more common reaction he provokes is less censorious: 'He's just neurotic, through shellshock. But it's not his fault.' In J. Jefferson Farjeon's *Mystery in White* (1937), the daughter of an afflicted ex-serviceman says he's got ideas fixed in his head that cannot be shaken. What sort of ideas? 'Well, one is that there is going to be another war.' Another character says sadly: 'That fixed idea is not born only of shellshock.'

Most notable of these sufferers was Dorothy L. Sayers's creation, Lord Peter Wimsey, who served four years on the Western Front and was wounded in 1918. 'I was in a nursing home – with shellshock – and other things,' he explains, and it took him two years to come back from 'a bad nervous breakdown'. He's mostly recovered and, having worked in military intelligence, he's now pursuing a civilian life as an amateur detective. But he can never quite shake off the horror. 'At the end of every case we had the old nightmares and shellshock over again.'

In *The Unpleasantness at the Bellona Club* (1928), Wimsey tries to help an old friend who was gassed in the trenches and also suffers from shellshock. His condition manifests in 'queer fits', such as 'the time when he had been found dancing naked in a field among a flock of sheep and singing to them' or when he 'deliberately walked into a bonfire'. Published just before Edmund Blunden kickstarted the war-book boom, *The Bellona Club* has veterans express dissatisfaction with the ritual of remembrance. 'What's the damn good of it, Wimsey? A man goes and fights for his country, gets his insides gassed out, and loses his job, and all they do is give him the privilege of marching past the Cenotaph once a year.' Wimsey agrees: 'It's my belief most of us would be only too pleased to chuck these community hysterics if the beastly newspapers didn't run it for all it's worth.'

Like thrillers, detective fiction had little time for the financier, as the title of Arthur Wynne's *Death of a Banker* (1934) indicated.

Nor was the capitalist popular: in John Rhodes's *Death of the Board* (1937) the directors of a firm are the targets of a killer, while Gathorne Cookson's *Murder Pays No Dividends* (1938) sees the managing director of Cyclone Motors Ltd strangled in his own safe; as ever in such cases, there are plenty of suspects because he's so widely disliked. The same is true of the brewery owner murdered in Nicholas Blake's *There's Trouble Brewing* (1937), the setting of which illustrated another trend. Following *The Mysterious Affair at Styles*, there were plenty of what P. G. Wodehouse called 'gloomy, sombre country-houses which seem to exist only for the purpose of having horrid crimes committed in them',[51] but the constant need for novelty in a crowded marketplace meant that unusual situations and workplaces were at a premium: Gladys Mitchell's *Death at the Opera* (1934), R. C. Woodthorpe's *A Dagger in Fleet Street* (1934), Denzil Batchelor's *The Test Match Murder* (1937), Leonard Gribble's *The Arsenal Stadium Mystery* (1939), Val Gielgud and Holt Marvell's *Death at Broadcasting House* (1934).*

As the fictional crime wave swept on, the BBC joined in with *Inspector Hornleigh Investigates* (1937), created by Hans Wolfgang Priwin and starring S. J. Warmington. The character was successful enough to extend into a stage play, a series of stories in *Leader* magazine and three films, though these latter added a comic element to the radio original, with Gordon Harker taking on the role; he played it as a blunt, bluff cockney detective, accompanied by Alastair Sim as a fool of a sergeant. The first movie, *Inspector Hornleigh* (1938), hinged on the theft of the government's budget two days before it is due to be delivered. 'It seems incredible to me that anybody should be allowed to rob the chancellor of the exchequer with impunity,' exclaims the chancellor. 'Quite so, sir,' replies Hornleigh. 'Generally the other way round.'

That jokey tone was found widely in British crime movies, of

---

* *Death at Broadcasting House* was filmed shortly after publication. ('It's ghastly, Caird! To think that we broadcast a murder, and that millions of people must have heard the man actually being strangled.')

which there were many. Few of these films were of any worth, but there were exceptions to the lightweight froth. A new generation of directors turned the limitations of the quota quickie – a small cast, few sets, a constricted running time – to their advantage, making psychological thrillers rooted in character studies and simple narratives, making up in claustrophobic intensity what they lacked in action. Out of this trend came Brian Desmond Hurst's *The Tell Tale Heart* (1934), a stylised, disturbing and almost silent adaptation of Edgar Allen Poe. And Michael Powell's *Crown v. Stevens* (1936), in which an amoral woman, having killed a moneylender, turns her attention to murdering her husband. And Arthur B. Woods's *They Drive by Night* (1938), where a man wrongly suspected of murder disappears into the shadowy world of long-distance lorry drivers, while the real killer is a studious ex-schoolmaster. Best of all was Roy Boulting's *Trunk Crime* (1939),* a macabre tale of a university student, an intense, studious loner who's bullied by the sporty set, and who takes revenge by drugging his chief tormentor, locking him in a trunk and trying to bury him alive in swampy mud. ('Grim but gripping,' said the *Kinematograph Weekly*.[52])†

Despite all the quickies, British cinema made little use of the leading writers of the time, with the massive exception of Edgar Wallace (over sixty films were made of his work). Many of the best-known fictional sleuths made no appearance at all on screen in the 1930s: Roderick Alleyn, Albert Campion, Inspector French, Colonel Gore, Miss Marple, Inspector Poole, Roger Sheringham, Nigel Strangeways. Alfred Hitchcock bought the rights to Josephine Tey's *A Shilling for Candles* (1937) but then dropped her detective, Inspector Alan Grant, from the ensuing *Young and Innocent* (1937).

When movies were made, they were deeply unsatisfactory.

---

* Based on a play by Reginald Denham and Edward Percy, the latter of whom was elected as a Conservative MP in 1943 under his full name, Edward Percy Smith.

† Hurst, Powell and Boulting went on to great success in later decades, but Arthur B. Woods was killed on active service with the RAF in 1944, his promise unfulfilled.

Peter Haddon played Lord Peter Wimsey in *The Silent Passenger* (1935), but the film was so poor that Dorothy L. Sayers turned down the offer from MGM for the rights to *Murder Must Advertise* (1933). Little better was *Alibi* (1931), adapted from Agatha Christie's masterpiece *The Murder of Roger Ackroyd* (1926).* This came from a 1928 stage version in which Charles Laughton received much praise as the first man to play Hercule Poirot, but for the film the inappropriately lean, clean-shaven Austin Trevor took the role. 'Bad casting,' said *Picturegoer*, though Trevor returned for two more movies.[53]

The problem here was that Poirot – by far the biggest star of the Golden Age – was such a curious kind of a hero. He's endearing rather than daring; 'a funny little man', says his friend Hastings, 'a great dandy, but wonderfully clever'. His first name evokes the greatest hero of Greek mythology, and then undercuts it with an echo of the Pierrot troupes that provided song-and-comedy entertainment in English seaside resorts. Similarly, his intellectual vanity and self-regard are unmistakably male, but are outweighed by his obsession with his physical appearance ('a speck of dust would have caused him more pain than a bullet wound') and by his lack of stature, just five feet four inches in height. He's delicate and precise, he smokes 'tiny Russian cigarettes', and the closest he gets to action is a brisk, waddling walk or the occasional leap of delight. His suspicions are aroused by the most mundane and domestic of clues; in *The Mysterious Affair at Styles*, the ornaments on a mantelpiece have been moved and there's 'a scribbled over old envelope, and a freshly planted bed of begonias'. His method is to exercise consciously what is generally understood to be feminine intuition. 'Women observe subconsciously a thousand little details,' he says in *The Murder of Roger Ackroyd*. 'Their subconscious mind adds

---

* In 1939 novelist Michael Arlen included *Roger Ackroyd* in his choice of 'the five finest detective novels of the last thirty years', along with Bernard Capes's *The Skeleton Key* (1919), American Dashiell Hammett's *The Maltese Falcon* (1930), Eric Ambler's *The Mask of Dimitrios* (1939) and Christie's *Ten Little Niggers* (1939).

these little things together – and they call the result intuition. Me, I am very skilled in psychology. I know these things.'

Christie depicted a world of intricate, interconnected patterns where everything has its place so very precisely that one small detail gone awry is evidence of larger problems. The implication is that, even in the post-war disruption, there is still an underlying and unknowable order – and what is generally understood as mere chance is a manifestation of that order. 'I've often noticed that once coincidences start happening they go on happening in the most extraordinary way,' says Tuppence Cowley in Christie's *The Secret Adversary* (1922). 'I dare say it's some natural law that we haven't found out.'

The same thought recurs throughout the detective fiction of the time, and in the thrillers. John Buchan's hero Richard Hannay talks of 'those trivial things which look like accidents but I believe are part of the reasoned government of the universe'.[54] There is little religious faith on display in either thriller or detective story, but the need remains for some pattern, some meaning to life that might explain the randomness of violent death. So there's a good deal of coincidence, and as Leslie Charteris wrote of Simon Templar: 'Coincidence was a queer thing, but he had ceased to marvel at its complexities.'[55]

There was another article of faith underpinning detective fiction. 'Still got the notion that human life's valuable?' asks a character in J. J. Connington's *The Case with Nine Solutions* (1928). 'The war knocked that on the head. Human life's the cheapest thing there is.'* But the obsessive focus on fictional murder implies precisely the opposite. In a world scarred by industrial, anonymous slaughter, a civilised society needed to restate the idea that individual human life remained sacred. The essential storyline in the books is the eruption of violence into a community more fragile than it realises, a threat to life and morality, and then the resolution

---

* Connington was another intellectual, the nom de plume of chemistry lecturer Alfred Walter Stewart.

of that violence a couple of hundred pages later, the cause of the infection having been diagnosed by the detective.

'In an age when all the deepest emotions can be successfully laughed out of existence by any decently educated person,' wrote Margery Allingham in *Dancers in Mourning* (1937), 'the sanctity and importance of sudden death was a comforting and salutary thing, a last little rock, as it were, in the shifty sands of one's own standards and desires.' On the final page of *The Mysterious Affair at Styles*, Hercule Poirot concludes: 'The happiness of one man and one woman is the greatest thing in all the world.'

8

OUTSIDERS AND INCOMERS

It was surprising to see so many men with thin necks
and large Adam's apples; it had something to do with
Nonconformity, she supposed.

E. H. Young, Miss Mole, 1930[1]

Captain Carruthers: It's the old story of the mad dreamers of
this world who are half-empire-builders and half-gangsters.
If they succeed, the history books call them great.
Mrs Carruthers: And if they don't?
Captain Carruthers: Another gangster sinks into oblivion.

The Drum, 1938[2]

Sir Oswald Mosley, leader of the British Union of Fascists, 1936

CAPTAIN HAROLD HUBERT VINCENT BA BSc WAS ONE OF MANY who felt that society had taken a wrong turn. He wrote poetry bemoaning 'The sex perversions of modernity' and 'This hell-begat curse known as civilisation',[3] and in pursuit of a purer, simpler world, he founded the Sun-Ray New Life Society, dedicated to the promotion of sunbathing. At the end of the 1920s, he and members of the society began to gather on the grassy banks of the Welsh Harp reservoir in Hendon, north London, a popular venue for speedboat races and other leisure activities.

The trouble started when sunbathing turned to nudism. 'Dress or undress is optional with us,' explained Vincent. 'Some of us wear nothing.'[4] Many local residents disapproved. One spoke of his revulsion at 'a movement which allows adult men and women perambulating in full view of the public, particularly children, absolutely nude'.[5] The issue came to a head on a Saturday in June 1930 when some forty society members gathered to watch the display of bombers at the Hendon air pageant, and were attacked by a crowd angered at the wanton exhibition. It didn't help that the sunbathers were not, for the most part, from the area – it was said that two were 'very dark skinned men'[6] – and there were cries of 'Drive them out of Hendon.'[7] There were no serious injuries, but the sunbathers were warned there'd be more trouble if they dared return the next day.

They did dare, and were surrounded by a 300-strong mob, jostling and jeering. 'Hottentots would behave with more decency,' shouted the protestors. 'Even cannibals wear loincloths.' One woman sunbather, stripped to her underwear, retorted, 'To the pure all things are pure,' a sentiment that 'was received with roars of derision'. There were blows and kicks, the police were called, and the crowd was dispersed.[8]

The council threatened to prevent the society from having access to the reservoir, and Vincent concluded that the answer was to buy the land. Unfortunately, its market price was £3,500 and the celebrities he approached for contributions were unwilling to help. 'I am quite in sympathy with any amount of undressing,' replied H. G. Wells, 'but regret I am unable to come to your financial aid.'[9] Nonetheless, the publicity did the society some good. 'The membership has grown steadily,' Vincent told the press in 1932. 'We now have about 400, including young clerks and typists and many married people. No class distinctions are made, and the only qualification for membership is decency.'[10]

That was the same year, however, that Vincent was jailed for three months after an altercation with a policewoman in Hyde Park, which ended when he pushed her into the Serpentine. There was also the incident when a Mrs Virago of Gloucester Place reported him to the police for standing naked in his window with a sign that read, 'Throw away your clothes'. Quite apart from the offence to herself, she protested, her servants could see him as well.[11] The Sun-Ray New Life Society did not survive his imprisonment.

Five miles south of the Welsh Harp, another group was attracting the attention of the law. In 1933 Austin Salmon, a barman aged twenty-three commonly known as Lady Austin, and John Packer, a twenty-two-year-old waiter, were charged with keeping a disorderly house and conspiracy to corrupt public morals, in connection with a property in Holland Park Avenue, west London. Thirty-one other men were charged with aiding and abetting, having been present when a party was raided by police. Most were working class – waiters, shop boys, valets, chefs and porters – and only five were aged thirty or above, one of the outliers being a thirty-seven-year-old art director who'd served as an RAF officer. There were so many defendants in the dock that they were each obliged to wear a large numbered card round their necks to identify them.

The police witnesses said they'd seen men – some wearing make-up, some dressed as women – dancing with each other, embracing and kissing. One man was 'nude except for a small belt round his waist and a small cape hanging from his shoulders'. It was all 'sickening and revolting', shuddered the arresting officer, 'deplorable and horrible'. There was said to have been little contrition on display. 'Isn't it wicked for these boys to interfere with our fun?' said one of the dancers roguishly. 'The cruel things don't understand the way we live.' Another became agitated – 'Oh dear, will we be sent to prison?' – and his companion had to calm him down: 'Don't upset yourself, Clarice.'[12]

All pleaded not guilty, and the defence was that this was no clandestine gathering, but a fancy-dress festival, publicly advertised as such with notices outside, and an admission fee of 1s 6d. No impropriety had taken place. And indeed there was no evidence produced of sexual activity, hence the catch-all conspiracy charge.

The judge, Sir Ernest Wild – he who had earlier complained of the 'spirit of lawlessness in young men nowadays' – said in his summing-up that indecency between men was 'a foul and horrible canker' engaged in by 'sexual perverts' who 'regard any kind of interference as an infringement of individual liberty'. ('Surely it is a free country and we can do as we like?' one had protested to the police.) Wild did add, however, that these general comments should in no way be considered a reflection on the accused.[13] The jurors simply had to consider, 'as men of the world, if these men dressing as women was not merely an additional spur to their unholy appetites'. There were just two options: 'Either the police have trumped up a horrible charge against decent citizens, or these offences, generally speaking, were committed.'[14]

Of the thirty-three defendants, twenty-five were found guilty, and sentenced to between three and twenty months' imprisonment. Some of those sentenced burst into tears, 'crying aloud in effeminate tones', but 'others received their punishment in silence with smirks on their faces'. On arrest, Packer had said, 'This trouble would be avoided if only they would make our love legal,' but Sir Ernest Wild was having none of that nonsense: 'We shall have to wait a long time in this country before that kind of love is made legal.'[15]

For a real disorderly house, though, few could compete with a flat in Carleton Road, Tufnell Park in north-west London, where there lived in 1937 Queenie Day, said by the police to be the 'worst woman in England'. The road backed onto His Majesty's Prison Holloway, the largest women's jail in the country, so it was conveniently located when Day went to see her imprisoned ex-flatmate Elsie Carey on visiting days. It was even possible for Carey to communicate with her friend by shouting out of the window until she got moved to another cell.

Day was the older of the two, a mixed-race 'coffee-coloured beauty'[16] born in 1908, first convicted of theft at the age of nine and sent to a reformatory. There followed a long series of jail sentences, with convictions for housebreaking, shoplifting, larceny and – in May 1927 – assaulting a policeman. This last occasion was said to be 'the first time the woman when arrested had not been in possession of either a razor or a knife'.[17] In another arrest, in 1936, she pulled an automatic pistol on the police officers.

Meanwhile, Elsie Carey had been pursuing her own career in crime. She started by stealing change from tram conductors, before moving on to shop-breaking. In 1934 she was arrested trying to break into a Marks & Spencer store in Upton Park, east London. She had a jemmy and a hacksaw on her, and when her home was searched, substantial quantities of stolen clothes were found. 'It is no good saying I know nothing about it, because I do,' said her forty-six-year-old stepmother wearily, as she was charged with receiving stolen goods. 'I told her before not to bring the stuff here.'[18]

Elsie Carey got a year in jail for that, and then, within four months of her release, another year for further thefts. She expanded her field of activity, getting a series of young male dupes to drive her and an accomplice out of town, so they could rob shops in Bognor, Worthing, Oxford and Slough. She was again caught. In September 1937, as yet another judge handed down yet another sentence, this time for four years, 'a woman at the back of the court moaned, rose to her feet and went hurriedly out'.[19]

This was Queenie Day, with whom Carey was now living, and who had herself only just been released from a twenty-eight-day sentence, after a disturbance at the Dreamland Amusement Park in Margate. Day and her younger sister had been very drunk and took noisy exception to being turned away from a ride. They were further incensed when other fun-seekers joined the fracas. 'I could not stand them calling me a nigger and pulling me about,' said Day in court, and the altercation turned to violence. She punched the ride attendant in the face, and when a park inspector intervened, she drew a knife and slashed his arm. 'Their language was the filthiest I have ever heard,' said the inspector, giving evidence; 'and I have had some experience.'[20]

Queenie Day was portrayed in the press as 'a violent criminal with no respect for the laws of this country',[21] but Elsie Carey was an even more colourful character. Nicknamed Lady Jack, she had an Eton crop, smoked a pipe, spoke in 'a deep, masculine voice'[22] and wore male clothes, 'a dark blue belted overcoat with square shoulders, a dark trilby hat, light fawn jacket, grey flannel trousers and blue and white shoes'.[23] She was a criminal-class version of society lesbians like Evelyn Spottiswoode or Radclyffe Hall, and the newspapers were fascinated. She was also cast as the 'Blonde Bandit',[24] a 'hard-bitten West End woman gangster', and a police detective said she was 'a very clever, determined, cunning and dangerous thief'.[25]

Her number of convictions argued against Day's cleverness and cunning, but the gangster image played well. For years, the British public had been enthralled by the underbelly of America's prohibition of alcohol in 1920, relishing accounts of 'crime-ridden Chicago'[26] and 'lawless America',[27] with their language of speakeasys, hooch and Public Enemy No. 1, where gang violence involved 'armoured cars and exploding machine-guns and hand-automatics'.[28] By comparison, domestic crime seemed very tame, and the likes of Lady Jack were eagerly seized upon by the press to pretend that things were more exciting than they truly were.

Even after Prohibition ended in 1933, envious glances were still thrown across the Atlantic. Some British novelists had hits with violent thrillers set in the American underworld, notably Peter

Cheyney with *This Man Is Dangerous* (1936) and James Hadley Chase with *No Orchids for Miss Blandish* (1939). 'Slim Grisson was a killer,' we learn in the latter. 'He had killed things as a child, not for any reason, but because to kill was in his blood.' His British equivalent was Pinkie in Graham Greene's novel *Brighton Rock* (1938), a sociopathic seventeen-year-old who's a gangster and a murderer. But there's no American glamour here – it's grubby and squalid rather than mythic. 'I have seldom, if ever, met a more detestable creature,' winced one reviewer. 'One feels that a few beefy thrashings in childhood might have knocked some sense and decency into him – despite what the psychologists may have to say on that subject.'[29]

Similarly, British crime movies lacked the thrill of Hollywood gangster movies with James Cagney, Edward G. Robinson and Humphrey Bogart. There were plenty of homegrown pictures, including *Crime over London* (1936), *Wolf's Clothing* (1936), *The Green Cockatoo* (1937), *Wednesday's Luck* (1937) and *Gangsters* (1937), but they simply couldn't compete. Many were comedies, others unintentionally comic. 'I find the very sound of a cultured voice saying "Stick 'em up" extraordinarily funny,' reflected British director James Whale. 'The accent suggests that he should be saying, "Would you mind sticking them up, please?" But then English gangster and crook dramas always affect one that way. I can't take them seriously.'[30]

In 1936 Birmingham's *Sunday Mercury* sensationally revealed that 'The gangsters are already here,'[31] but although there were gangs in Britain – most notoriously in Soho, west London, with its prostitution, gambling dens and semi-legal drinking clubs – they tended to use coshes and knives, not guns, and to avoid killing each other. 'After all, chivving is chivving,' reasoned London gangster Billy Hill, 'but cutting an artery is murder. Only mugs do murder.'[32] These villains clearly weren't in the same league as American criminals like Machine Gun Kelly, Baby Face Nelson or Pretty Boy Floyd, let alone Al Capone, John Dillinger or Ma Baker. Britain remained a remarkably peaceful country. The homicide rate was lower than it had been in Edwardian times, and less than a tenth of that in America.

ii

Rollo Ahmed first attracted press attention in 1930, while living on Jersey. A farmer on the island was struggling to make his business pay and, being of a superstitious inclination, he became convinced that someone had cursed him. So when he heard that Ahmed had occult powers, he asked the supposed magician to come round and drive out the evil spirits. Ahmed agreed to do so for a fee and, dressed in a black gown, red girdle and fez, he performed various rituals, burning incense, striking doors and windows with a knife, all the while mumbling unintelligible incantations. Regrettably, the fortunes of Cemetery Farm – an ill-starred name – did not improve. Indeed, the farmer was now even worse off, having made several payments amounting to over £90.

It was when Ahmed came back for a further £70, issuing dire warnings of what would happen if his demands weren't met, that the farmer went to the police. Ahmed was charged with obtaining money by threats and false pretences, and the case received national coverage, much of it amused at the utter credulity of the farmer. Ahmed was sentenced to nine months' hard labour.

He'd been born at the end of the previous century in Demerara, British Guiana, to an Egyptian father and a mother of West African descent, and had come to Britain after the war. The narrator of his semi-autobiographical novel *I Rise: The Life Story of a Negro* (1937) follows the same path, arriving in Liverpool in 1921, where it doesn't take him long to find that his skin makes him unwelcome. 'I had not expected equality in England, but neither was I prepared for a colour bar,' he reflects. 'If I apply for work, the white man's taken ahead of me. If I manage to secure casual labour, the chances are that the men down tools.' Similarly, he struggles to find accommodation; one bed and breakfast has a sign reading: 'No Jews. No coloured people.' The message everywhere is the same: 'We can't have niggers! We won't work with niggers! Slam! Slam! Slam! went the doors of England.'[33]

The one exception, he discovered, was in the world of entertainment. 'The British public tolerates colour as long as colour contributes to its amusement.'[34] The book was dedicated to Paul Robeson, the greatest exemplar of that rule, a thirty-year-old black American singer and actor who came to London in 1928 with the musical *Show Boat*, singing 'Ol' Man River' in the richest bass-baritone anyone could remember hearing. He was rapidly accorded celebrity status, invited by the Labour Party to the Houses of Parliament and singing at Buckingham Palace. 'London has been captivated,' said the *Liverpool Echo*. 'I challenge the most prejudiced to listen to Paul Robeson's singing and to come away an unchanged man.'[35]

Robeson stayed for some years in Britain, most famously playing the title role in a 1930 production of *Othello*, opposite Peggy Ashcroft as Desdemona. PAUL ROBESON'S TRIUMPH, said the headlines;[36] NEGRO ACTOR'S GREAT SUCCESS.[37] Robeson was 'magnificent, not because he is a man with black skin, but because he is a great actor'.[38] He even managed to shed his American accent. It was 'the theatrical event of the season',[39] though it wasn't a box-office success, the theatres hit that year by talking pictures and economic recession.* He also starred in several British movies, calling cinema 'the most important medium for my work'. He talked of the problems in American film with its 'anti-negro feeling' and its stereotype of 'the conventional, howling-savage conception of the African'; things were better 'here in England, where I don't have to fight against Hollywood attempts to make me another Stepin Fetchit'.[40]

Other black performers were thriving on London stages, many of them expatriate Americans like Robeson, finding a more

---

* Even John Gielgud's rapturously received *Hamlet* struggled when it transferred from the Old Vic to the West End that summer.

tolerant working environment in Britain.* There were sufficient numbers that when the Thames flooded in 1928, 'an all-black matinee'[41] was staged as a benefit for the relief fund, a four-hour show acclaimed as 'the greatest negro jamboree ever held in London'.[42] Most of the artists were resident in Britain, but there were visiting stars, too. Alberta Hunter came from Monte Carlo to sing the blues and stayed to star opposite Paul Robeson in *Show Boat*, while the biggest name was American Josephine Baker, who flew over from Paris in a chartered plane to make her British debut. Wearing a rose-pink dress, she draped herself across a grand piano to sing 'Pretty Little Baby', before changing into a flame-coloured frock with ostrich feathers to dance the Charleston. The press disapproved of her 'wriggling in the more eccentric posture that Parisian audiences are understood to love' (it made her look 'definitively unattractive'),[43] but there was no doubt that she was impressive: 'She can waggle her body until it looks like breaking.'[44]

Also appearing on the bill was singer Leslie Hutchinson, commonly known as Hutch, who'd been born in Grenada in 1900 and had recently arrived in London, via the clubs of New York and Paris. He sang with an agreeable tenor, played a sophisticated jazz piano, and appeared in revue and nightclubs, scoring his biggest hit with 'These Foolish Things (Remind Me of You)'. Inevitably, he was a favourite of the Prince of Wales, and he mingled in rarefied social circles. He adapted his persona accordingly: immaculately tailored (he had twenty-four evening suits), he acquired an English accent, rode to hounds and went to the cricket. Less reputably, he wore Chanel No. 5 scent and had a prodigious number of lovers,

---

* This had long been the case. In 1904 the Jewish American escapologist Harry Houdini wrote home from Britain: 'I have been on the bill with several American colored acts that have "made good" without question. I may mention Brown and Navarro, Grant and Grant, La Belle Morcschania, Johnson and Dean, White and Black, the Four Black Troubadours, Eph Thompson, George Jackson, etc., and all have done well.' (*New York Dramatic Mirror*, 12 November 1904)

from actresses Tallulah Bankhead and Merle Oberon to songwriters Cole Porter and Ivor Novello.

In 1932 the *People* ran a story about rumours of a 'society woman' and a 'coloured man' being 'caught in compromising circumstances'.* It didn't name names, but everyone in the know knew it referred to Edwina, socialite wife of the minor royal Lord Louis Mountbatten. The Mountbattens sued for libel, their counsel insisting that 'Lady Louis has been informed by her friends of the identity of the coloured man' and that 'she has never even met him'.[45] That was just about true, since her friends thought 'the coloured man' referred to Paul Robeson, but her friends were wrong: actually it was Hutch with whom she was indeed having an affair. In the absence of evidence, however, the *People* issued a full apology. That was some comfort, at least, to Lord Louis, who had earlier been overheard by Alf Van Straten – bandleader at Chez Quaglino's restaurant – bemoaning the fact that 'Hutch has a prick like a tree trunk, and he's fucking my wife.'[46]

Meanwhile, Rollo Ahmed was finding his own route into social acceptance via the magical reputation that had landed him in jail in Jersey. Moving to London, his knowledge of occult traditions made him a man of some interest, for he was a genuine scholar, as well as having first-hand experience of the tribal magic that he said was still powerful in British Guiana. He now claimed to come from Egypt, sidestepping much of the prejudice he'd faced, and tapping into the post-Tutankhamun enthusiasm for all things Egyptian. He became acquainted with the more mystically inclined fringe of artistic society, as well as the renegade sex magician Aleister Crowley, and was introduced by journalist Tom Driberg to Dennis Wheatley.

Wheatley drew on Ahmed's knowledge when writing his hit novel, *The Devil Rides Out* (1934), a thriller in which the Duke

---

* One rumour said that the woman in the case had experienced severe muscle spasms during intercourse, and that the conjoined couple had to be taken to hospital to be separated.

De Richleau battles a Satanist super-villain in a chase to find the mummified penis of the Egyptian god Osiris. It was preposterous fun, decked out in occult trimmings – black magic, numerology, Stonehenge, the tarot, vampires – and containing a radical new account of the origins of the war. 'The monk Rasputin was the evil genius behind it all,' explains De Richleau. 'He was the greatest Black Magician that the world has known for centuries. It was he who found one of the gateways through which to let forth the four horsemen that they might wallow in blood and destruction.'*

The success of *The Devil Rides Out* was such that Wheatley was asked to follow it with a non-fiction account of magic, but he declined and instead passed the project on to Ahmed. The resulting book, *The Black Art*, was published in 1936 to good reviews – 'a comprehensive and readable account for the common reader', it was said;[47] 'horribly fascinating'[48] – and sold well, becoming one of the more popular works on the occult.† Now that he had some status in society, Rollo Ahmed could afford to be more sanguine about progress. 'Gradually, racial hatreds are breaking down,' he observed in 1937; 'intelligent and reasonable men are awakening to the fact that spiritually man himself cannot afford to raise artificial barriers.'[49]

iii

For the first decade of his writing career, which began in 1916, Aldous Huxley was well regarded, rather than widely read. Three novels, four volumes of short stories and another four of poetry, together with travel books and collections of essays, had

---

* Rasputin was much in the news. Earlier in 1934, the exiled Prince Yusupov – the man who claimed to have killed the Russian mystic in 1916 – had brought a successful libel case in the English courts against MGM, makers of the film *Rasputin and the Empress* (1932).

† Rediscovered in the 1960s, *The Black Art* was reprinted several times over the remainder of the century.

established him as the cleverest voice of the post-war generation. His fiction was full of fearfully intelligent characters discussing art, science and sex, dissecting modern morals and mores, and was much admired by the critics: 'witty, grotesque, dangerous, brilliant, beautiful'.[50] As J. B. Priestley noted, Huxley enjoyed 'extreme popularity with undergraduates and the more intellectual Americans'.[51] He didn't, however, reach a wider public, his work rather giving the impression, said the *Sketch*, of 'a little group of intelligentsia clinging unhappily together in a grossly hostile world'.[52] He was, in short, a highbrow.

Point Counter Point (1928) was bigger, cleverer and even more rarefied than its predecessors, and yet somehow became his first big commercial success. The novel was a vast panoramic network of interlocking plots and characters, depicting the frustrated sterility of British intellectual and artistic life a decade on from the Armistice. 'He has done for the post-war period what Thackeray, in *Vanity Fair*, did for the early Victorian age,' admired the *Clarion*.[53] It was, his friend D. H. Lawrence told him, 'the truth, perhaps the last truth, about you and your generation'.[54] The most memorable character was the upper-class Everard Webley, fascist leader of the Brotherhood of British Freemen. 'Socialism without political democracy, combined with nationalism without insularity' is Webley's message, and the BFF wear green uniforms echoing the outlaw Robin Hood, 'for outlaws they are in this stupid democratic world'. This doesn't stop others from mocking: the Freemen look 'like the male chorus at a musical comedy', observes one character, and another calls them 'the B—y B—ing F—s'.

'It has been said,' Oswald Mosley later wrote, 'that I was one of the characters in *Point Counter Point*.'[55] If so, Huxley was remarkably prescient, for Webley resembles the Mosley yet to come. At the time the book was being written, Mosley was still a socialist, so far from being a fascist leader that a meeting of his in Cambridge was broken up by 'several hundred undergraduates, carrying Union Jacks and Fascist flags'.[56]

But then came Labour's rejection of the Mosley Manifesto,

followed by the creation of the New Party, and its humiliation at the polls in 1931. Mosley blamed the voters ('the continuing complacency of the electorate defeated the New Party'),[57] but that didn't resolve his problems. He was thirty-six, out of Parliament, all ties with both Conservatives and Labour had been cut, and the experimental political plane he'd launched had crashed a few fields from the end of the runway. Seeking inspiration, he visited Italy, where he got to meet Benito Mussolini, and Germany, where he met some Nazis. Although the *Daily Herald* suggested his Grand Tour was less impressive than he made out – 'The general impression in Fascist quarters in Rome is that Sir Oswald was not taken seriously by Signor Mussolini'[58] – it persuaded him to embrace the cause of fascism.

The economic message was essentially the same, with a slightly greater emphasis on corporatism, but the packaging was very different. The New Party was rebranded the British Union of Fascists (BUF), and Mosley's onstage persona changed to include a more declamatory tone and exaggerated arm gestures. Out went the conventional tweeds and suits that he used to wear; this season's look was black polo-neck sweater tucked into black trousers, held up by a wide black leather belt. He looked as though he'd been studying – in P. G. Wodehouse's words – 'those pictures in the papers of Dictators with tilted chins and blazing eyes, inflaming the populace with fiery words'.[59] His followers took to wearing black shirts, following the monochromatic tailoring that had been popular in Europe ever since Giuseppe Garibaldi's mid-nineteenth-century Redshirts. As one newspaper columnist joked in 1931: 'The number of nations that may be led to salvation, generally an undemocratic salvation, need to be limited only by the number of colours that shirts may be dyed.'[60]*

---

* 'It's funny what a big part fancy haberdashery plays in the world today,' observes a character in John Buchan's *The House of the Four Winds* (1935), a Ruritanian novel that features a youth movement named Juventus who are Green Shirts. There are Greenshirts too in Richmal Compton's *William the Dictator* (1938), battling the

For a moment in 1934, it looked as though Mosley might be a significant figure. Critically, the BUF had support in the press, with the backing of Lord Rothermere, who heard an echo of the United Empire Party that he and Lord Beaverbrook had launched. 'Hurrah for the Blackshirts,' he wrote in a *Daily Mail* editorial; they espoused 'sound, commonsense, Conservative doctrine'.[61] Rothermere had recently disposed of his shares in the *Daily Mirror* to his son, Esmond Harmsworth, but he remained sufficiently influential that that title and its sister paper the *Sunday Pictorial* were also sympathetic: 'The patriotism and discipline of the Blackshirts set a practical example to the young men and women of Britain, who are being defrauded by Old Gang politicians.'[62]

At a time when the National Government enjoyed a near-monopoly of parliamentary politics, Mosley had a certain appeal. Membership of the BUF grew rapidly to 50,000,[63] spanning a wide social range, from Major General J. F. C. 'Boney' Fuller – an influential theoretician of mechanised warfare who had a deep interest in the occult – through to former world welterweight boxing champion Ted 'Kid' Lewis (the Aldgate Sphinx, born Gershon Mendeloff), an East End Jew who'd retired from the ring in 1929, going out on a high at the Pitfield Street Public Baths in Hoxton, east London with the 233rd win of his career.* There were also some high-profile Blackshirt women, including Diana and Unity Mitford (two of the daughters of the 2nd Baron Redesdale; Mosley married the former) and some leading ex-Suffragettes: Mary Sophia Allen, Norah Elam and the notorious Mary Richardson, who, back in 1914, had vandalised the *Rokeby Venus* in pursuit of Votes for Women.

Blueshirts, while Evelyn Waugh's *Scoop* (1938) features the White Shirts, and Agatha Christie's *One, Two, Buckle My Shoe* (1940) has the unspecified Imperial Shirts. Roderick Spode, a parody of Mosley in Wodehouse's *The Code of the Woosters* (1938), however, has to settle for black shorts. 'There were no shirts left,' explains Bertie Wooster's friend, Gussie Fink-Nottle.

* At the time of writing, the website BoxRec.com had Lewis listed as pound-for-pound the second-best British boxer of all time, behind Welshman Joe Calzaghe.

A series of BUF rallies drew large crowds, culminating in June 1934 with the biggest meeting yet, an audience of 15,000 at Olympia in London. As was becoming common, the rally also attracted large numbers of left-wing protestors. Both sides came armed – knuckledusters, rubber truncheons and knives were reported – and there was fighting on a scale not seen at a political meeting for a long time. Newsreel cameras filmed scenes of communist hecklers being assaulted by fascists, and it looked very ugly. In the wake of the Battle of Olympia, as it was dubbed,[64] the BUF's membership collapsed, and the *Daily Mail* and *Daily Mirror* abandoned the cause.

Two years later, in October 1936, came the Battle of Cable Street,[65] when the BUF attempted to march through a part of the East End of London with a large Jewish population. This reflected its increasingly hostile rhetoric against Jews. At the start in 1932, Mosley had been unequivocal: 'Anti-Semitism is no issue of Fascism, and is, therefore, no part of the policy of the British Union of Fascists.'[66] Not all his followers agreed even then, and the *Daily Herald* noted 'the violent antipathy which his young Fascists are working up against the Jews. This is entirely alien to British sentiment, and is a sheer imitation of Hitlerism.'[67] As public support declined, the anti-Semitic note had grown more strident, and Cable Street demonstrated that the *Herald* had been accurate in its assesssment; the Fascists numbered in the low thousands, the anti-fascists in the hundreds of thousands. The numerical imbalance persuaded the police to ban the march, fearing uncontrollable disorder, and Mosley was turned away.

'Under the present government,' thundered the BUF, 'free speech can be prevented by anyone who cares to organise violence against it in defiance of the law. The necessity for fascism could not be more clearly proven.'[68] Most people, however, saw it rather as proving the case *against* fascism, this strange creed that always seemed to result in violence and which looked so outlandish, its members giving stiff-arm salutes and wearing paramilitary uniforms.

It wasn't quite the end of Mosley. As late as the summer of 1939, he could still attract 20,000 people to a meeting in Earl's Court, London. That was close to the total membership of the BUF, though, a long way off its 1934 peak. After that early boom, the party never really amounted to anything. The momentum rapidly dissipated, and no candidates were fielded in the 1935 general election. It wasn't entirely clear what the movement was supposed to do, save to provide a dramatic backdrop to Mosley's speeches, and it failed at that: the thuggery and anti-Semitism ensured that no one paid attention to what its leader was saying.

Mosley himself remained a man without influence, his destiny unfulfilled. In a period dominated by coalition and compromise, he was a lone wolf, walking out of political parties and unable to work with anyone else. He even fell out with his own lieutenants, and a group split from the BUF in 1937 to form the National Socialist League. The problem at root was that he didn't convince. He looked as though he was playing a role, yet couldn't decide whether it was that of intellectual or populist rabble-rouser; in any event, he didn't really suit either. 'There is no place in this country for any sort of National Socialism,' said the *Liverpool Daily Post*,[69] and there was no obvious place for Mosley either.

When *Point Counter Point* was adapted for the stage as *This Way to Paradise* (1930), most of the diversity of the novel was trimmed out, foregrounding the story of the proto-Mosley character Everard Webley, played by Alan Napier.* A programme seller at Daly's Theatre in Leicester Square, where the play was being staged, was asked what it was about. 'Oh, I don't know, dear,' she replied. 'It's a highbrow sort of thing.'[70]

iv

The adverts for the Vidor All-Wave Radio (£8 8s for the battery-operated version, £10 10s for mains) promised that, with its

---

* Napier, a cousin of Austen and Neville Chamberlain, would become best known as Pennyworth, Bruce Wayne's butler, in the 1960s American television series *Batman*.

international reach, it allowed 'the ordinary listener to search the globe for entertainment', and to 'hear Hitler, Stalin, Mussolini on the European Crisis'.[71] However tempting the dictators were, it was the entertainment that most attracted British listeners, particularly on the Sabbath, when John Reith's BBC was a little joyless; in 1931, the *Daily Herald* asked its readers about their experience of radio, and reported that 'Sunday performances were shown to be overwhelmingly the most unpopular part of broadcasting'.[72]

It was also in 1931 that Captain Leonard Plugge, formerly of the RAF and now organising package tours to the Continent, came up with the solution to the nation's frustration: if the BBC wasn't going to give listeners what they wanted, a gap in the market could be filled by stations from outside the country. Setting up the International Broadcasting Company, he bought time on European stations – first on Radio Normandy, then Lyons, Poste Parisien and Toulouse – and began broadcasting in English, aiming the programmes at Britain. In 1933 came the real breakthrough: the launch of Radio Luxembourg, with a 200-kilowatt transmitter that it claimed was 'the most powerful broadcasting station in Europe',[73] and an English-language schedule that was unapologetically lowbrow, centring on dance bands.

The BBC was outraged by this erosion of Reithian standards, Plugge's 'blatant American manner' approach to radio.[74] The real problem, though, was that he was outside British jurisdiction and that his monopoly-busting was very popular. On Sundays, half the audience was listening in to the foreign stations, with Luxembourg the market leader; by 1938 it had four million listeners in Britain.* It also had the most expensive advertising space in the world, selling products that addressed the health worries of listeners – Carter's Little Liver Pills, Owbridge's Lung Tonic, Zam-Buk Ointment – and their dreams of riches: the Irish Sweepstakes, Littlewoods

---

* By that stage, Luxembourg had broken with Leonard Plugge. He had in the meantime been elected as Conservative MP for Chatham in 1935, defeating Labour's Hugh Gaitskell, a young economics lecturer.

Pools, Vernon's Pools. Consequently, the station had the financial resources to tempt all the biggest band leaders. Ambrose and Jack Hilton were sponsored by soap companies (Lifebuoy and Rinso respectively), Billy Cotton by Kraft Cheese, Jack Payne by Beecham's Pills, and Debroy Somers by Horlicks.

It also tempted BBC employees. Christopher Stone had arrived at the corporation in 1927 – via Eton, the Royal Fusiliers and the *Gramophone* magazine – and had become the first person to play records on British radio. In 1934, he began also appearing on Luxembourg, where he was given more licence, and where he introduced the practice of talking over the start of a record. Determined to show that such moonlighting would not be tolerated, the BBC sacked him, but the message didn't seem to get through; acts continued to work for both broadcasters, even, it was suspected, Henry Hall and the BBC Dance Orchestra under an assumed name.

Other obstacles were put in the path of Luxembourg. The newspapers, fearing a rival for advertising revenue, didn't list the foreign schedules, and nor did the *Radio Times*; in response, Plugge launched his own listings magazine, *Radio Pictorial*. The General Post Office (lobbied by the BBC) refused the station a direct line from Britain, so it had to pre-record shows and concerts in London and take the recordings to the Grand Duchy for broadcast. Mostly this was done on large shellac discs – the studios had thirty-inch turntables – but even better was to use the audio track of film, which gave a cleaner sound and didn't require changing so often.

A decade earlier, the BBC had been the upstart, and it had won against theatrical, sporting and other commercial interests that tried to curb its influence. Now it was itself the establishment, trying to smother a rival, and it failed; audiences and artists continued to straddle both domestic and foreign stations, and in 1937 the war with Luxembourg was quietly abandoned. There were, though, no concessions to popular taste. At the end of 1938, an opinion poll asked whether the BBC should broadcast dance music on Sundays. Yes, said 52 per cent, as against 32 per cent rejecting the idea (with opposition more marked among those who were older and wealthier), but still it didn't happen.[75] Although John Reith had stepped down as director general earlier that year, his influence lingered.

If Radio Luxembourg was a British enclave on mainland Europe, the BBC sometimes gave the impression that it wanted to be the reverse, cajoling its audience into being better Europeans. In March 1934 it announced that it would be converting to the twenty-four-hour clock, so that instead of a programme being trailed as, for example, 'tonight at eight o'clock', announcements would say 'tonight at twenty hours'. For the first month, both formats would be used, 'until listeners have become accustomed to the change', when the old system would be discarded.[76] The *Radio Times* set a lead with its programme listings, and gave away a cardboard clock showing how this worked.

The idea had been around for a while; a Home Office committee in 1919 recommended the twenty-four-hour clock be adopted for official use. As its supporters argued, 'during the war our present system was shown to be thoroughly impractical'.[77] The case was perfectly rational, and had support from powerful groups including the Federation of British Industries, yet none of the organisations that were approached – the Post Office, the railways – showed much desire to be the first to try it out, nervous of hostility from the public. 'I can imagine listeners-in who pride themselves on being "typically British" (of the bulldog type) sitting down and penning letters which literally drip with indignation,' wrote one commentator, when eventually it fell to the BBC to test the water. 'Other gallant patriots will be denouncing the 24-hour clock system as a foreign production.'[78]

Some did indeed suspect that British ways were being jettisoned to fit in with Europe. 'The BBC has been asked to make the experiment because practically all Continental countries use that time language,' reported the *Evening Despatch*.[79] 'Hardly anyone favours it, and it serves no useful purpose,' editorialised Newcastle's *Sunday Sun*. 'Perhaps it is just another indication of their foreign complex, so often evidenced in their programmes.'[80]

Some listeners wrote to the papers denouncing 'this new form of modernist plague which the BBC are trying to foist on to our unfortunate population'.[81] We should not have 'to suffer hideous confusion under the "whims" and "fads" of a few', they complained.[82] The people 'who have decreed this change are what we good-humouredly call "cranks", who happen to have the argument of logicality'.[83] There was some support – 'Let us follow it up with a reformed calendar, the decimal system and simplified spelling,' urged one correspondent[84] – but those voices were in a minority. Not that the protestors were particularly numerous, either. The BBC said it received under 200 letters in the first fortnight, far fewer than expected, running four-to-one against the new system. It was noted, though, that sales of the *Radio Times* fell, and that newspapers carried on using the old format in their own listings.

When the twin-timings period came to an end in late May 1934, there was a further bout of complaints, with the BBC's board of governors expressing their nervousness at 'the great and increasing tide of criticism'.[85] The death blow came two months later, when the government decided against the official adoption of the twenty-four-hour clock; left stranded, the BBC finally quit the field in August, after seventeen weeks. UNPOPULAR EXPERIMENT FADES OUT QUIETLY, read the headlines.[86]

If this were indeed part of a 'modernist plague', as alleged, another outbreak was to be found at London Zoo's Penguin Pool, which opened that same year and had, reported the *Daily Mirror*, a printed notice with the feeding times. 'These do not read "Noon and 3 pm". Nothing so old-fashioned! They read: "12 and 15".'[87] It seemed more appropriate here than on the wireless, though, for the Penguin Pool was a startlingly contemporary creation, constructed in reinforced concrete with interlocking ribbon-like ramps that framed a central pool. It was also, unusually for modernist architecture in Britain, popular with the public.*

---

* The Penguin Pool was accorded Grade I listing in 1970. In 2004 the penguins were moved elsewhere.

The creator was Berthold Lubetkin, an expatriate Georgian Jew, one of many European artists and designers finding refuge in Britain. In 1933, the innovative Bauhaus art and design school in Berlin was forced to close – the Nazis having deemed its work to be decadent – and several of its key figures moved to London, including the school's visionary founder, Walter Gropius. The following year, an exhibition of his work was staged, prompting press coverage of 'this great ultra-modernist', though there was a cautionary note: 'the conservative-minded may well boggle over the simple rectangular forms of the furniture, textiles and pottery.'[88] Gropius looked forward to the production of houses by machines, advocated standardisation and argued that this was the spirit of the times. 'The outward forms of modern architecture are not the whims of a few architects hungry for innovation,' he explained, 'but the inevitable consequence of the social and technical conditions of our age. Architecture's new aspect corresponds with our civilisation.'[89] For those suspicious of the direction that civilisation was taking, that was precisely the problem.

Together with another refugee, the Hungarian artist László Moholy-Nagy, Gropius planned to recreate the Bauhaus in London, although this didn't come to pass, partly because Moholy-Nagy didn't find the atmosphere in Britain sympathetic. An exhibition of his paintings in 1937 received poor critical notices. 'Doubtless there are people to whom these works are stirring, but I am not one of them,' sniffed the *Scotsman*.[90] That year he emigrated to America and set up the New Bauhaus, later renamed the Chicago School of Design.*

The gap between British taste and the European prophets of modernism was a source of great sorrow to some; instead of unornamented, geometric blocks with flat roofs, the country was building suburban houses with gables, bay windows and sunburst

---

* Moholy-Nagy was also recruited to work on the design of the British science-fiction movie *Things to Come* (1936), though little of his contribution made the final cut.

fanlights. Designer Noel Carrington* took to the popular press to bemoan the way domestic architects failed to embrace concrete and factory-made components: 'They have become a superior profession, very learned in styles and quite oblivious of their real business.'[91] Possibly, but Britain was hardly short of its own visionaries, from the imperial genius of Edwin Lutyens – designer of the Cenotaph and of New Delhi, who *Country Life* called 'the greatest living English architect, and perhaps the most outstanding since Wren'[92] – through to Giles Gilbert Scott, famed for the Battersea Power Station and the red telephone box. For those with more idiosyncratic tastes, there was Clough Williams Ellis, creating a holiday village for the wealthy at Portmeirion in North Wales, in a fantastical Italianate style.

There was, though, less room for avant-garde innovators. And, perhaps, less need for them, since the old order had not failed as spectacularly as elsewhere. Unlike Germany, Britain had not been defeated; unlike France, the country had not been physically devastated; unlike Italy, it had not been driven to near bankruptcy. As in the 1920s, European modernism was seen as mildly interesting, but mostly irrelevant.

In 1936 a gallery in London's Mayfair staged the International Surrealist Exhibition, a huge show that featured work by Georges de Chirico, Salvador Dalí, Marcel Duchamp, René Magritte, Pablo Picasso and Man Ray, as well as British representatives including Eileen Aga, Henry Moore, Paul Nash and Graham Sutherland. The press predicted that the exhibition would 'create a storm in the art world',[93] that it would 'shock, annoy, cause arguments and hatred'.[94] It didn't live up to its billing, and coverage of the opening recorded no such outrage: 'No sign of a thrill, only a slight titter.'[95] Another journalist reported that 'ripples of happy laughter were ever rising from parts of the galleries'.[96] Surrealism may have been, as the *Bystander* said, 'nearly as incomprehensible to the

---

* Carrington is best remembered as the founder in 1940 of Puffin Books, an imprint of Penguin that specialised in children's books.

uninitiated as Einstein's relativity',[97] but there was no real indignation; more a pleasurable profession of bewilderment.

Even in highbrow circles, there was little enthusiasm for the mass production celebrated by Gropius. Aldous Huxley followed the success of *Point Counter Point* with *Brave New World* (1932), a dystopian satire of a future world state in which industry and totalitarianism have merged. The assembly line has extended into human biology, so that babies are now incubated in state-owned hatcheries as multiple clones, conditioned from conception to their place in a rigorous caste system. Life is comfortable, aided by an agreeable recreational drug called soma. ('All the advantages of Christianity and alcohol; none of their defects'.) Further hedonistic entertainment is provided by the Feelies – a version of cinema that allows viewers to experience physical sensation – and by music from the likes of Calvin Stopes and His Sixteen Sexophonists. The death of more serious culture is regrettable but inevitable. 'That's the price we have to pay for stability,' says Mustapha Mond, Resident World Controller of Western Europe. 'You've got to choose between happiness and what people used to call high art. We've sacrificed the high art.' After all, it's what people want; 'whenever the masses seized political power, then it was happiness rather than truth and beauty that mattered'. History has also been obliterated, because 'most historical facts are unpleasant', though the 1930s roots of this world are indicated in the names of the characters: Bernard Marx, Benito Hoover, Polly Trotsky, Lenina Crowne.

Despite much of this being a defence of the highbrow against the plebian taste of the masses, the masses responded – with wonderful irony – by turning *Brave New World* into Huxley's most popular book, largely attracted by the sexual promiscuity that it described. If it wasn't quite the pornography of *Lady Chatterley's Lover*, there was still controversy. 'It is a highly moral sermon,' claimed a Liverpool librarian,[98] though those who actually preached sermons on the book didn't tend to approve; it was 'an offence to innocent minds', thundered the Reverend A. G. Peaston of the Huddersfield Unitarian Church.[99] A character in Harriet Rutland's *Knock, Murderer,*

Knock! had much the same reaction: 'I don't wonder that the youth of today is corrupt, with that kind of dirt lying on every library shelf.'

v

In June 1935, Ramsay Macdonald stepped down as prime minister on grounds of ill health, and Stanley Baldwin, already the most powerful figure in cabinet, returned for a third premiership. Although it was still officially the National Government, with Labour and Liberal members, it was now a Conservative administration in all but name.

There was more substantial change that year on the opposition benches. In October, the Labour conference debated a policy statement, *War and Peace*, which argued that Britain should reserve the right to oppose fascist aggression with armed force if necessary. As a pacifist, leader George Lansbury was horrified, and appealed to the party's better instincts. 'I cannot believe that the Christ you worship,' he implored, 'would be found pouring bombs and poison gas on women, on children or men for any reason whatsoever.'[100]

Unable to reconcile his personal principles with the requirements of collective responsibility, Lansbury was evidently signalling that he was prepared to quit. Just to ensure that this was the case, he was followed to the podium by Ernest Bevin, general secretary of the Transport & General Workers' Union (TWGU), who delivered a scathing attack on his leader, accusing him of 'taking your conscience around from body to body asking distant people what you ought to do with it'.[101] Lansbury was shaken by the vehemence, and when conference later voted in favour of sanctions against Italy, as punishment for its invasion of Abyssinia, it proved to be the final straw and he resigned as leader.

In the confusion that followed, Stanley Baldwin immediately called a general election. Needing someone to take the reins until a proper contest could be held, Labour installed Clement Attlee as acting leader, a job he'd held when Lansbury was in hospital with a broken leg. He'd also been a minister in the 1929–31 government, without ever being much noticed, highly regarded in Parliament but unimpressive as a platform speaker. 'Never in its history has Labour had a leader more unknown to the rank and file of the movement,' said general election candidate Gilbert McAllister.[102] Attlee wasn't one for the grand gesture either, and Lansbury's pacifism was swiftly discarded. 'We do not stand for unilateral disarmament,' he told the Commons. 'We stand for collective security through the League of Nations.'[103]

The election in November 1935 saw the National Government returned with over half the vote, 429 MPs and another convincing majority. The renewed mandate was a recognition that things were improving and a personal endorsement of Baldwin himself, who remained the master of modern media. 'He alone talked; the others orated,' wrote journalist Hamilton Fyfe of the party broadcasts that year. 'His effort came near being a chat, while the rest were just speeches.'[104] A campaign cinema van was sent round the country, showing films of speeches by Baldwin and MacDonald, interspersed with propaganda and light entertainment. Ventriloquist Arthur Prince was seen persuading his dummy, Sailor Jim, not to vote for socialism, while comedian Stanley Holloway, who specialised in droll monologues for variety and revue, contributed a piece, 'Sam Small at Westminster', to promote the cause:

No government ever was perfect,
But the National's the best in the land.
So let them as thinks they'd do better
Stop grousing and lend them a hand.

Further support came from the *Daily Mirror*'s recently launched comic strip *Ruggles*, published on the leader page of the paper. 'Who reduced unemployment?' asked John Ruggles, the week before the vote. 'Who reduced the price of beer? Stanley!' And his wife agreed: 'I put my trust in Mr Baldwin.'[105]

Elsewhere, the Liberals were still split into three parties – only one of which now supported the National Government – and between them managed just fifty-eight MPs. The following spring saw the publication of George Dangerfield's influential history *The Strange Death of Liberal England*, charting the party's decline since the heady days of its 1906 landslide.

Labour, on the other hand, registered its highest vote share yet (38 per cent) and gained over a hundred seats, looking again like a respectable opposition. The promised leadership election duly followed, and saw Attlee remain at the head of the party, scoring a clear victory over his two opponents, Herbert Morrison and Arthur Greenwood. Of the recent leaders, Ramsay MacDonald lost his seat in Seaham, County Durham, his 6,000 majority turned into a 20,000 Labour majority for his old friend, Manny Shinwell. 'I never mentioned MacDonald's name during the whole of the campaign,' recorded Shinwell sorrowfully, 'nor indulged in any personal vilification or abuse.'[106] George Lansbury was returned as MP for Bow & Bromley, but was an increasingly peripheral figure in Parliament, his idealism out of place in Attlee's hard-headed Labour. He was still revered by activists, though, and rapturously greeted at meetings,[107] where he was introduced as 'Public Pacifist No. 1'.*

Meanwhile, the party's future lay largely in the hands of the man who had stabbed Lansbury in the front. Like MacDonald, Ernest Bevin was the illegitimate child of farm labourers. He was born in Winsford, Somerset in 1881, his father unknown, his mother dead when he was eight.† After no more than a couple of years at school, he started work at eleven, doing a succession of labouring jobs that eventually led him to become active in the dockers' union. He turned out to have a genius for organisation, and in 1922 he forged a single union, the TGWU, from an amalgamation of dozens of groups, some substantial, others with memberships that barely reached the thousands, including the Amalgamated Carters, Lurrymen & Motormen's Union, the North of England Trimmers

---

* Both men died not long after the election; MacDonald in 1937, Lansbury in 1940.
† Nearly a century later, Winsford Village School was attended by future Conservative Prime Minister Boris Johnson.

& Teemers Association, and the National Union of Ships' Clerks, Grain Weighers & Coalmeters. Others were subsequently added until the TGWU was the biggest union in the country, with a presence in scores of industries. Bevin himself was acclaimed 'the most outstanding figure in the British trade union movement'.[108]

His stock rose still higher when the crisis of 1931 tilted the balance of power in the Labour movement towards the unions. There was talk of him as a possible future leader of the party, though he was not even an MP (he had stood unsuccessfully in Gateshead), and he didn't discourage such speculation. 'He likes the feeling of power, and has high belief in his own abilities as a leader of men,' observed the political correspondent of Birmingham's *Sunday Mercury*.[109]

Although a Baptist lay preacher, Bevin was never much of an orator – 'his grammar was improvised', said Attlee[110] – but as his attack on Lansbury showed, his bluntness could be devastating and ruthless. 'Lansbury has been going about dressed in saint's clothes for years, waiting for martyrdom,' he told his friends. 'I set fire to the maggots.'[111] He was a Christian patriot and a pragmatic socialist, convinced that political wisdom resided in the solid common sense of the unions, not among the middle-class graduates increasingly drawn to Labour. He argued against the gold standard and in favour of protectionism and imperial preference, but he had no faith in visionaries and utopians, and it was his opposition that had ensured the rejection of the Mosley Manifesto. (He was 'bitterly against me,' Mosley reflected.)[112] Despite Bevin's own autocratic nature, he was above all a democrat, opposed to dictatorships of Left and Right. 'I stand for a social revolution brought about by a freely elected parliament,' he'd said in a speech back in 1918,[113] and he had no time for those on the Left who celebrated the Russian Revolution: 'fatuous' was his conclusion.[114]

His destruction of Lansbury came from the same grim realism. 'From the day Hitler came to power, I have felt that the democratic countries have to face war,' he told his union colleagues. 'I cannot see any way of stopping Hitler and the other dictators except by force.'[115]

vi

Ernest Bevin was not alone in looking anxiously across the Channel at the European dictatorships, but most Britons wanted little to do with the outside world. 'I see there has been fresh trouble in China,' says elderly Aunt Lilian in Georgette Heyer's novel *Footsteps in the Dark* (1932). 'I feel one has so much to be thankful for in not being Chinese.' The reference was to Japan's invasion of Manchuria in 1931. Both countries were members of the League of Nations, and the organisation's failure to resolve the dispute was an early indication of its limitations. Still, from a British perspective, it was a long way away, and Aunt Lilian was right to be feel thankful. But then the problems started getting closer, and the world outside began to demand more attention.

In 1935, with Italy threatening an invasion of Abyssinia, the foreign secretary, Samuel Hoare, told the League of Nations that Britain stood for 'steady and collective resistance to all acts of unprovoked aggression'.[116] Calling his bluff, Italy went ahead with its invasion, and the implied threat of a British military response failed to materialise.* Nor was there any great appetite for such action. It was all 'a very small matter', said Winston Churchill. 'No one can keep up the pretence that Abyssinia is a fit, worthy and equal member of a League of civilised nations.'[117] Collin Brooks, editor of the *Sunday Dispatch*, quoted approvingly the *Daily Mail*'s call to 'Keep the war in Africa',† and asked rhetorically: 'Because tribesmen are bombed in Africa, are we to have women and children bombed in Britain?'[118]

The league's impotence was seen again the following year, when German troops marched into the Rhineland. This was a deliberate

---

* In December 1935, Hoare resigned as foreign secretary when details of his discussions with the French foreign minister, Pierre Laval, were leaked to the press. The two men had, in essence, agreed to let Italy have most of Abyssinia.
† To aid their readers' understanding, the *Daily Mail* offered a picture map of Abyssinia for just sixpence: 'that whole wild land is spread before you like a vivid aerial scene'.

flouting of the Treaty of Versailles, which had stipulated that there should be no military presence by Germany west of the Rhine. Again, neither France nor Britain was inclined to take a stand, and nor were the press. 'The reoccupation of German territory by German troops is no cause for war,' reasoned the *Spectator*,[119] while the *Daily Mirror* declared, 'It must not be war,'[120] and the *Daily Express* was certain: 'There will be no war.'[121]

Despite the public's aversion to becoming involved in overseas conflicts, it did not go unnoticed that the events in both Abyssinia and the Rhineland had involved aggression by fascist states. Similarly, an attempted military coup in July 1936 against the left-coalition government of Spain precipitated a civil war that ultimately brought the fascist General Francisco Franco to power. The age of dictators was reaching its peak, and abroad – as at home, but more so – fascism seemed inevitably to lead to violence.*

Communism, on the other hand, was no longer the bogeyman it had been during the previous decade. Vladimir Lenin had died in 1924, replaced as Russian leader by Joseph Stalin, whose pursuit of 'socialism in one country' meant there was less emphasis on the exporting of revolution. And anyway, the British Left was a long way from power. By the mid-1930s, communism was seen by Britons as far less of a threat to peace in Europe than fascism. 'If there were a war between Germany and Russia, which side would you rather see win?' asked an opinion poll in January 1939.[122] The Soviet Union, said 59 per cent, while just 10 per cent opted for Nazi Germany, with the rest undecided.†

Some of the changed perception of Russia came as a result of new instructions from Moscow that communists should work with others in the fight against fascism. In conventional political

---

* Other authoritarian regimes in late-1930s Europe included those of Tsar Boris III in Bulgaria, Ioannia Metaxas in Greece, Miklós Horthy in Hungary, Józef Piłsudski and his successors in Poland, António Salazar in Portugal, and King Carol II in Romania.
† A similar poll in America yielded similar results: excluding Don't Knows, it split 85 to 15 per cent in favour of Russia.

terms, this new tactic brought little benefit to the Communist Party of Great Britain, the membership of which reached a high of no more than 16,000 or so by the end of the decade – as Ernest Bevin scorned, it 'failed utterly to get any hold on the minds of the electorate'.[123] Nonetheless, the party did begin to exert some cultural influence, and the second half of the 1930s saw socialism, and even communism itself, become fashionable in educated and self-educated circles.

The most visible manifestation of this was the Left Book Club, launched in 1936. For a monthly fee of 2s 6d, members received a copy of a specially selected book (normal price: 7s 6d), together with the magazine *Left Book News* and access to a wider list of titles. Within a year, the LBC had 40,000 subscribers, and by 1939 that had risen to nearly 60,000, with two and a half million books in circulation.

This was not a CPGB initiative, though it did meet with their approval. The prime mover was publisher Victor Gollancz, under whose imprint the titles appeared, an erstwhile member of the Liberal and Labour Parties and now, in his words, 'as close to the communists as one hair to another'.[124] With his hand on the tiller, the LBC set a course 'to help in the struggle for World Peace and a better social and economic order and against Fascism'.[125] In this endeavour, Russia was understood to be on the side of righteousness, so that when the LBC reissued Sidney and Beatrice Webb's epic *Soviet Communism: A New Civilisation?* (1935), the question mark was omitted.

The club's membership was predominantly middle class, attracted not just by the books but by the social network that rapidly evolved around the LBC. Some 1,200 local groups sprang up, meeting regularly to discuss the monthly selections and to listen to talks. There were other groups organised by trade, from accountancy to taxi driving; the actors' group included such high-brow figures as Michael Redgrave and Dame Sybil Thorndike. Then there was the allied Theatre Guild, founded in 1937, which rapidly grew to over 250 amateur-dramatics groups around the country, putting on left-wing sketches and plays; in 1939, for example, the

Nottingham branch staged a translated version of Friedrich Wolf's German play *Professor Mamlock* (1933) about Nazi anti-Semitism. There were even foreign trips for those who could afford them, visits to Belgium and Sweden, as well as, inevitably, Russia.

Film shows were popular, with LBC branches screening documentaries about unemployment at home or wars abroad, particularly the Japanese invasion of China and the Spanish Civil War. A favourite was *The Spanish Earth* (1937), co-scripted by novelist Ernest Hemingway and narrated by a young American actor, Orson Welles. There was also a vogue for Soviet films – the likes of Grigori Kozintsev's *The New Babylon* (1929), Nikolai Ekk's *The Road to Life* (1931) and Yakov Protazanov's *Marionettes* (1934). Still more adventurous, the branch in Hastings in Sussex acquired a rare print of Robert Weine's classic German horror movie *The Cabinet of Dr Caligari* (1920), screening it as a silent triple bill alongside René Clair's comedy *The Leghorn Hat* (1927) and Hanns Schwarz's *Hungarian Rhapsody* (1928), with 'gramophone accompaniment, selected and played by Mr Frank Bennett'.[126]

Within a couple of years, the LBC had become a missionary movement that carried considerable cultural weight. At its core were the monthly selections, distributed to the subscribers. These were serious works, primarily on political and economic subjects, and were intended to provide people with facts and analysis of current events that could be deployed in argument. Some publications were more popular than others; it was said that large numbers of Clement Attlee's *The Labour Party in Perspective* (1937) went uncollected, but a twopenny pamphlet by John Strachey, 'Why You Should Be a Socialist' (1938), sold over 300,000 copies.*

---

* Strachey had broken with Oswald Mosley over the New Party's turn to fascism, and had instead become a communist. Meanwhile, his older sister Amabel Williams-Ellis – married to Portmeirion architect, Clough, and a secret member of the CPGB – was writing politically conscious mainstream novels aimed at female readers: *The Big Firm* (1938) and *Learn to Love First* (1939), the latter an anti-fascist update of the play *The Maid's Tragedy* (1619) by Francis Beaumont and John Fletcher.

The occasional fictional work was included, and again they were serious: Clifford Odets' play *Waiting for Lefty* (1935) about striking New York cabbies; a translation of André Malraux's *Days of Contempt* (1935), set in a Nazi concentration camp.

The most enduring title of all was George Orwell's *The Road to Wigan Pier* (1937), a documentary of the distressed areas. This was Gollancz's idea, though he was dissatisfied by the result, objecting to Orwell's attacks on middle-class socialists. So he added an unsolicited introduction by himself, explaining where the author had got it wrong. He then rejected outright Orwell's reportage on the Spanish Civil War, *Homage to Catalonia* (1938), unhappy with its criticism of communist policy. He did, however, have a three-novel contract with Orwell and there was still one book to come. That turned out to be *Coming Up for Air* (1939), in which Orwell duly took revenge on Gollancz. In a scathing depiction of a suburban Left Book Club meeting, much of the audience 'sit there like lumps of pudding. They don't know what the meeting's about and they don't care.' The narrator, George Bowling, is deeply sarcastic about proceedings. 'We're the West Bletchley revolutionaries,' he mocks. 'Doesn't look hopeful at first sight.'*

Gollancz tried to interest the Labour Party in the LBC, but its communist connections made many distrustful. The club was 'a political movement with substantial money behind it', said Ernest Bevin, who believed this was an attempt at infiltration, moving 'in the direction of manipulation and controlling local Labour Parties'.[127] An official party version, the Labour Book Service, was set up in March 1939, but it failed to emulate the success of the original.

The Right Book Club, launched in 1937 by booksellers Christina and William Foyle on the same model, also fell short,

---

* Having been rejected by Gollancz, *Homage to Catalonia* was published by Secker & Warburg and sold very poorly. Secker did, however, reap the huge commercial rewards of Orwell's subsequent novels: *Animal Farm* (1945) and *Nineteen Eighty-Four* (1949).

attracting 20,000 members but lacking the social dimension of the LBC. The most notable titles in its first year were by *Daily Mail* journalists: Harold Cardozo's pro-Franco *March of a Nation*, and George Ward Price's *I Know These Dictators*, an enthusiastic account of Hitler and Mussolini that rivalled the Stalin worship seen in some LBC publications. Apparently, Hitler 'never misses an opportunity of declaring his desire for peace', and his consistency demanded 'a certain presumption of sincerity'.[128]

The other rival on the Right was the National Book Association, founded in 1937 by historian Arthur Bryant and publisher Walter Hutchinson, again offering subscribers a book of the month. Stanley Baldwin was persuaded to lend his name to the endeavour as president, and one of the early offerings was a book about him by Bryant. But then the association announced that its choice for January 1939 was a translation of Hitler's *Mein Kampf* ('specially bound in fine quality crash cloth with frontispiece and coloured top'),[129] at which point Baldwin resigned. No further books were published.

9

RESIGNATION AND RESOLVE

Frank Burdon: The people of this country are the most long-suffering on God's Earth. They'll put up with humbug, hypocrisy, shillyshallying and hardship. They'll pull in their belts if they think it's their duty. They'll go to the four corners of the earth and get blown to bits if needs be. But two things they will not stand. Bullying and cruelty.

Storm in a Teacup, 1937[1]

Gilbert Redman: Never climb a fence if you can sit on it – it's an old Foreign Office proverb.

The Lady Vanishes, 1938[2]

Prime minister Neville Chamberlain shakes hands with Adolf Hitler, 1938

BY THE BEGINNING OF 1936, THE CAREER OF GERMAN COMPOSER AND VIOLA PLAYER Paul Hindemith was in a precarious state. A few months earlier, he had been denounced in a speech to the Reich Chamber of Commerce by Nazi propaganda minister Joseph Goebbels as an 'atonal noisemaker', and although his work was not officially banned, it was certainly not being played in the concert halls of the Third Reich.[3]

The charge of atonalism wasn't really accurate, but Hindemith did come out of the melting pot of modernism and the avant-garde. He'd written the music for Hans Richter's Dadaist movie *Vormittagsspuk* (1928); he'd worked with Bertolt Brecht and Kurt Weill on the theatre piece *Der Ozeanflug* (1929), and his opera *Neues vom Tage* (1929) had featured onstage nudity. In Nazi Germany these things smacked of communism, decadence and immorality. Furthermore, his wife, the singer Gertrud Rottenberg, was Jewish.

Despite disapproval at home, however, Hindemith enjoyed an international reputation, and in early 1936 he travelled to London at the invitation of the BBC. On Monday 20 January he gave a half-hour viola recital on the radio – sandwiched in the schedule between Bertram Mill's Circus and Borrah Minevitch and his Harmonica Rascals – but this was merely a warm-up. The main event was scheduled for two days later, when he was to play the British premiere of his viola concerto, *Der Schwanendreher*, in a concert also to include work by Haydn, Beethoven and Schoenberg and to be broadcast live.

The concert never happened. Even as Hindemith was playing his sonata for viola d'amore that Monday night, George V was being pronounced dead by his doctor, Lord Dawson.* The news was announced on radio by John Reith himself, and the schedules

---

* George V's reported last words were 'How's the Empire?', though an alternative story had Lord Dawson telling him that he would soon be well enough to recuperate in Bognor, to which he replied, 'Bugger Bognor.'

were immediately scrapped; virtually all programmes were cancelled until the funeral, with only solemn music being played between the equally solemn news bulletins.

George's death was felt deeply. He had been a conservative and conscientious king, a symbol of continuity and stability during an eventful twenty-six-year reign. There had been moments of national trauma in that time, and he had risen to the occasion: the war, when he'd set a moral tone for the country; the General Strike, when he'd exerted quiet pressure on the government to tone down its wilder members; the economic crisis of 1931, when he brought together the National Government. In his 1934 broadcast to the Empire, he spoke of being 'in some true sense the head of this great and widespread family', and that was how he saw his role.[4] He was a modest monarch, the royal equivalent perhaps of Stanley Baldwin – his father, Edward VII, once observed, 'A fine country squire and his wife were lost in George and Mary'[5] – and he would be remembered, said one obituarist, simply as 'George, the man who was King'.[6] In 1935, during his Silver Jubilee, he'd been astonished by the warm reception he met across the country. 'I'd no idea they felt that about me,' he said. 'I'm beginning to think they must really like me for myself.'[7]

Instead of the scheduled BBC broadcast, Paul Hindemith spent six hours on 21 January writing a beautiful eight-minute elegy, *Trauermusik*, for viola and orchestra. He performed it the next day, with Adrian Boult conducting the BBC Symphony Orchestra, from a studio rather than a concert hall. The piece received rapturous reviews, especially compared with other tributes to the late king; it 'showed a higher level of art than [John Masefield] the Poet Laureate's damp verses', said the *News Chronicle*.[8]

Hindemith was praised too at home, though more for his efficiency than his music. Only a German could have written such a piece in so short a time, enthused *Deutsche Zukunft* magazine,[9] and for a few months he was restored to favour; there were public performances of his work, and he was commissioned to write a piece for the Luftwaffe. The rehabilitation didn't last long. At the

Nuremberg rally later that year, Hitler demanded a renewed puri-
fication of culture, and in October 1936 Hindemith's work was
finally banned. Two years later, he featured in the *Entartete Musik*
(Degenerate Music) exhibition in Düsseldorf, alongside Gustav
Mahler, Arnold Schoenberg, Igor Stravinsky and Kurt Weill.

ii

In preparation for the state funeral, the coffin of George V was
taken to London, where it was placed on a gun carriage and draped
in the Royal Standard, on which lay the Imperial State Crown and
the orb and sceptre, together with a single wreath. This was then
pulled through silent, crowded streets to lie in state in Westminster Hall, the stillness reminiscent, said the papers, of 'the hush of
Armistice Day'.[10]

Towards the end of the journey, there was a minor incident
when the cross on top of the crown – comprising the octagonal
sapphire of Edward the Confessor, set in two hundred diamonds –
fell off, tumbling into the street. A sergeant major from the Brigade
of Guards picked it up without breaking step, and the parade was
not interrupted, but at least one participant saw it as an omen;
the new King, walking behind the coffin, was heard to murmur,
'Christ! What's going to happen next?'[11]

George V hadn't been overly optimistic about his son, seeing
him as self-indulgent. 'After I am dead, the boy will ruin himself
in twelve months,' he told Stanley Baldwin.[12] His foreboding was
not shared by the public. Edward VIII, as he was now known,
had been popular as the glamorous symbol of post-war partying,
and he remained so in his early forties, seen as having grown into
seriousness. In November 1936 he visited South Wales, where the
pain of the Depression was still being felt. THE KING BEHIND
THE DOLE COUNTER was the front-page headline in the *Daily
Mail*.[13] The *Daily Mirror* went with SOMETHING OUGHT TO BE
DONE, reporting that, as he stood by a slag heap in Dowlais, the
king had observed: 'These steelworks brought all these people

here. Something must be done to find them employment.'[14] His 'concern for the Distressed Areas'[15] was appreciated by many; someone was at least speaking for the people.

The story that interested the American press, however, was very different. KING WILL WED WALLY, the *New York Journal* had confidently asserted three weeks earlier.[16]

'Wally' was Wallis Simpson, an American socialite and an intimate friend of Edward, having met him some five years previously. It wasn't exactly love at first sight – they'd discussed central heating – but by the time of his accession they were an established couple. The obstacle to their public union was the fact that she was already married – to her second husband, having already divorced once – and the idea that the monarch, the head of the Church of England, might marry a divorcee was bound to be controversial at the very least. Yet so he intended to do.

As Simpson began the process of extricating herself from her second marriage, Edward asked Lord Beaverbrook to use his influence to suppress any speculation about the divorce suit. The other proprietors dutifully obliged, and there was no mention of the king's affair. There was a territorial limit, though, even to Beaverbrook's authority, as the *New York Journal* demonstrated, and by mid-November 1936 the story was also appearing in the Irish press: 'British newspapers have been so effectively muzzled that scarcely more than a few hundred people have heard anything about the "Yankee at the Court of King Edward".'[17]

Among those few hundred were the people that mattered, and there was near unanimity that this union could not take place. Even a morganatic marriage, with Simpson not being given a royal title or status, would be unacceptable. 'Although it is true that standards are lower since the war,' Baldwin told Edward, 'it only leads people to expect higher standards from their king.'[18] The government shared this view, and so did the opposition, as Clement Attlee later made clear: 'All the Labour Party – with the exception of a few of the intelligentsia who can be expected to take the wrong view on any subject – were in agreement with the cabinet.'[19] Cosmo Gordon Lang, the Archbishop of Canterbury, concurred, as did his secular equivalents, John Reith of the BBC and Geoffrey Dawson, editor of *The Times*. And the Dominions were of the same mind. 'Canada is the most Puritanical part of the Empire and cherishes very much the Victorian standards of private life,' advised John Buchan, now ennobled as Lord Tweedsmuir and serving as Canadian governor general.[20] But the king was not to be persuaded.

The story finally broke in Britain in the first days of December and, once in the public domain, it demanded a swift resolution. The impasse between monarch and establishment ended with the former abdicating the throne, the first time such a thing had happened in all the centuries of English and British monarchy. The crown passed to his younger brother, the Duke of York, now George VI, and when the former king spoke on the radio from Windsor Castle at 10 p.m. on Thursday 10 December 1936, he was introduced by Reith as 'His Royal Highness Prince Edward'.

The BBC made the most of this extraordinary broadcast. In order to set an appropriate mood, the schedules were, again, hastily rewritten. This was no time for Labour MP Philip Noel-Baker's talk about resettling refugees for the League of Nations,* nor for Henry Hall and the BBC Dance Orchestra, certainly not for comedian Sandy Powell's Road Show. All were bumped in favour of sombre orchestral and chamber music. The speech itself went around the world. In Australia and New Zealand, it was heard over breakfast; in Canada and the USA, offices closed early so that employees could listen in. At home, it was the biggest shared moment since the Great Silence. Families gathered round their radio sets; pubs were crowded and hushed; hospitals and boarding schools allowed their inmates to stay up late; theatres and cinemas – even an evening of wrestling in Manchester – interrupted performances

---

* In 1920 Noel-Baker had won an Olympic silver medal in the 1500 metres, and in 1959 was to be awarded the Nobel Peace Prize, the only person ever to achieve the Olympic–Nobel double.

so the speech could be relayed across their public-address systems. The broadcast reached, it was said, 'a larger audience than any other speech in history'.[21]

Edward was dignified, though understandably subdued. He spoke of it being 'impossible to carry the heavy burden of responsibility and to discharge my duties' without 'the help and support of the woman I love', and it was reported from every quarter that listeners wept at his words.[22] The king who gave up his throne for love was the ultimate romance; *Abdication* by Sophie Cole would have made for a Mills & Boon classic. Sympathy did not extend much beyond the broadcast, however, and normal life returned almost immediately. At the Metropolitan Music Hall on the Edgware Road in London, the speech was relayed after comedy double act Lucan and McShane had done their turn;* afterwards, the pit orchestra played 'Land of Hope and Glory' and the National Anthem, 'then a Dutch band came on and threw balloons and streamers across the footlights'.[23]

More generally, the public mood turned against Edward, despite his previous popularity. It was felt that he had let everyone down. According to a reader of the *Grimsby Evening Telegraph*, the attitude of the people was that, 'If he thinks the lady is more important to him than the Empire, then we are well rid of him.'[24] The lady was largely held responsible. Children around the country were heard singing new words to a favourite carol: 'Hark, the herald angels sing: Mrs Simpson's pinched our King.'[25] In his own broadcast, on the following Sunday, the Archbishop of Canterbury regretted that Edward 'should have sought happiness in a manner inconsistent with the Christian principles of marriage, and within a social circle whose standards and ways of life are alien to all the best instincts and traditions of his people'.[26] That suspicion of un-British influence was shared by John Reith. 'Thank God he and

---

* Arthur Lucan was best known as a drag act, with his wife, Kitty McShane, playing his daughter. His *Old Mother Riley* (1937) was the first movie to centre on a female character played by a male actor.

his ways have passed,' he wrote in his diary. 'It seemed as if the old England was back.'[27] On the other hand, his departure was regretted in Germany; it was 'a severe loss to us,' Hitler later reflected.[28]

It had all come at a difficult time for Baldwin, who – despite the international crises in the Rhineland, Abyssinia and Spain – had to ask Foreign Secretary Anthony Eden 'not to trouble me too much with foreign affairs just now'.[29] Further, the press had been reporting for months that there was a 'whispering campaign' against the prime minister: 'Baldwin is going very soon.' As was inevitable with a leader who'd been in office for so long, and with a coalition that had to accommodate other parties, there were many dissatisfied Tories in Parliament: old men who'd been relegated to the back benches, young men who'd been passed over, ambitious men who hadn't been promoted quickly enough. There was a ready-made alternative in the shape of Neville Chamberlain, chancellor of the exchequer, and so the word went round: 'If Neville were prime minister, we could get things done.'[30]

The Abdication put an end to such talk, at least temporarily, and re-established Baldwin's image as a steady captain of the ship of state. In services all over the country that Sunday, sermons were preached in his honour. It was a sign of God's care for the nation, said Canon W. H. Bradley in Bangor parish church, 'that a man of the stamp of Stanley Baldwin – a fine English gentleman whose Christian character and outlook could not be questioned by anyone – should have been the nation's leader when a crisis involving such principles burst upon us'.[31]

The monarchy, of course, marched ever onwards, registering a slight stumble but not breaking step. The coronation scheduled for May 1937 went ahead as planned, the first ever to be broadcast on radio.* The lead role was taken by George VI, a quieter figure than his brother, a diffident man whose reticence and quiet dignity were

---

* There was also television coverage of the royal coach passing out of Hyde Park, the world's first high-definition outside broadcast, though hardly anyone saw it, as there were fewer than two thousand TV sets in the country.

more in tune with the sentiments of the nation. Nonetheless, it had been a difficult, destabilising episode. And one that had, curiously, been foretold. When astrologer R. H. Naylor cast Princess Margaret's horoscope for the *Sunday Express* back in 1930, he'd predicted that 'events of tremendous importance to the Royal Family and the nation will come about near her seventh year'.[32] She had entered her seventh year in August 1936.

iii

One of the few things that Edward VIII achieved in his short reign was to rescind a ban on theatrical portrayals of Queen Victoria. George V had asked the lord chamberlain – the official who controlled censorship of the stage – to forbid such depictions while any of her children remained alive, and the British Board of Film Censors had followed suit. With the ban due to be lifted in June 1937, it was reported in January that 'the race to produce films and plays has started in earnest'.[33] Of the works that emerged, the most celebrated were Laurence Housman's play *Victoria Regina* (1935), which had been a success on Broadway and now came to London, and the film *Victoria the Great* (1937), which saw Anna Neagle add to her repertoire of historical figures.*

As their titles made clear, there was nothing disrespectful about these treatments. In a very timely fashion, *Victoria the Great* presented an ideal royal marriage that combined personal devotion and imperial duty. It made sufficient profit on its £150,000 budget to warrant a sequel, *Sixty Glorious Years* (1938), and was respectful enough that this time Buckingham Palace, Windsor Castle and Balmoral were allowed to be used for location shooting. Neagle became the model for the wax effigy of Victoria at Madame Tussaud's.

---

* Neagle had made her name as *Nell Gwynn* (1934), and went on to play *Nurse Edith Cavell* (1939), Amy Johnson in *They Flew Alone* (1942) and Florence Nightingale in *The Lady with a Lamp* (1951).

The film industry's embrace of Victoria was part of a wider trend for historical movies. In 1932 the Hungarian-born director Alexander Korda had come to Britain, via Hollywood and France, and the following year – inspired, he said, by hearing a taxi driver sing Harry Champion's pre-war music-hall hit, 'I'm Henery the Eighth, I Am' – he made *The Private Life of Henry VIII*. Charles Laughton played Henry without reverence, as a self-indulgent, vain, womanising, yet attractive figure, and the film was essentially a romantic comedy. 'You're the nicest girl I ever married,' he tells Anne of Cleves (played by Laughton's real-life wife, Elsa Lanchester) on their wedding night. He does, though, occasionally find time to comment on contemporary politics. 'If those French and Germans don't stop killing each other, the whole of Europe will be in ruins,' he says, and he worries that England may not be able to keep the peace on its own: 'There's no one in Europe to help me.' The only answer is to rearm, 'to build ships, ships and then more ships'. Told that this will cost money, he retorts, 'To leave it undone will cost us England.'

The film's budget was fifteen times that of a quota quickie, but its success in America – where it was the twelfth-biggest box-office hit of the year – amply repaid the investment; within a couple of years, it was reported that it had earned back more than ten times its costs.[34] It was the first foreign film to be nominated in the Best Picture category at the American Academy Awards, while Laughton became the second Briton to win Best Actor, following George Arliss in the title role of 1929's *Disraeli*.*

The success of the movie sparked a new gold rush, convincing potential investors that there were good returns to be made. Nearly 200 new production companies were set up in 1934–5, and the number of films doubled from the level at the start of the decade.

---

* A third British actor, Robert Donat, would later win for *Goodbye Mr Chips* (1939), beating probably the best-ever slate of nominees: Clark Gable for *Gone with the Wind*, Laurence Olivier for *Wuthering Heights*, Mickey Rooney for *Babes in Arms*, and James Stewart for *Mr Smith Goes to Washington*.

It was not so much a boom as a bubble, though, and it duly burst as the realisation dawned that the likes of *Henry VIII* were rare.

Instead, Britain continued to import American cinema movies and to export actors, lured by the much greater wealth of Hollywood.* British literature and history were also pillaged for source material; films nominated for the Best Picture Oscar in 1935 included adaptations of *David Copperfield* and *A Midsummer Night's Dream*, as well as four movies with a British historical setting: *Mutiny on the Bounty*, *Captain Blood*, *The Informer* and *The Lives of a Bengal Lancer* – all American productions. The last was adapted from a 1930 memoir by retired officer Francis Yeats-Brown, though the Hollywood version looked more like the Wild West than eastern India; indeed, it was to be remade as *Geronimo* (1939).† Also on the list that year were *Ruggles of Red Gap*, about an Englishman in America, and *Top Hat*, about an American in England. Three of the nominated films starred Charles Laughton.

Those British films that could compete internationally tended, like *The Private Life of Henry VIII*, to confirm the image of Britain as being more concerned with its history than present reality, though contemporary concerns would keep intruding. *The Iron Duke* (1934) saw the Duke of Wellington (played by George Arliss) arguing that – with the defeat of Napoleon – the victors should not impose punitive measures on a vanquished nation. 'I don't think we should regard France as our enemy,' he declares. 'If we insist on taking her territory, war is merely deferred until France is once more strong enough to take what she has lost.' The parallel with the Treaty of Versailles was implicit. Wellington refuses financial

---

* Apart from those already mentioned, British actors working in Hollywood in the 1930s included Lionel Atwill, Lionel Belmore, Colin Clive, Ronald Coleman, Errol Flynn, Cary Grant, Leslie Howard, Ian Hunter, Boris Karloff, Elsa Lancaster, Vivien Leigh, Herbert Marshall, Ray Milland, David Niven, Merle Oberon, Claude Rains, Flora Robson, George Sanders, Ernest Thesiger, Hugh Williams and Roland Young.
† The Cambridge University Socialist Society picketed a screening of *The Lives of a Bengal Lancer*, complaining that it was imperialist propaganda. It was one of Hitler's favourite films; he reportedly had it screened three nights in a row in his home cinema.

recompense for Britain in pursuit of greater reward: 'The peace of Europe and the salvation of the world from unexampled tyranny.' Despite which, he's not convinced that it's all been worthwhile. 'I sometimes wonder why we bothered about Europe.'

That feeling of not wanting to be involved was also seen in *The Scarlet Pimpernel* (1934), adapted from Baroness Orczy's tales of the French Revolution. Things are bad in Paris, says Sir Percy Blakeney (Leslie Howard): 'Innocent people, kindly people, herded like sheep, butchered like cattle by men who make high-sounding principles an excuse for the most bestial cruelty.' But there's a limit to how far Britain wishes to intervene. 'The government does everything in its power to save those threatened by death in the prisons of the French Republic,' explains the Prince of Wales (Nigel Bruce), 'but if a country goes mad, it has the right to commit every horror within its own walls.'

The main beneficiary of the success of *Henry VIII* was Alexander Korda himself, who went on to direct more big-budget pictures, and then focused on production, still with a strong leaning towards historical adventure, as in the star-studded *Fire Over England* (1937), about the defeat of the Armada in 1588, when 'Spanish tyranny is challenged by the free people of a little island'. The same conflict had been covered in *Drake of England* (1935), with much the same thinking. '[King] Philip has swallowed the Netherlands,' says Francis Drake. 'Soon he may swallow France. How long do you think England will hold?' Again, the echoes in this age of dictators were unmistakable.

Korda also produced a 1935 version of Edgar Wallace's pre-war *Sanders of the River*, directed by his younger brother Zoltán. Leslie Banks took the title role – a colonial administrator in a remote part of west Africa – and Paul Robeson played Bosambo, an educated tribal chief.* Wallace's novel had been unapologetic about imperial

---

* Among the hundreds of extras was Jomo Kenyatta, who in 1963 would lead Kenya to independence from the British Empire. Robeson was warned by British security agents to be wary of Kenyatta's subversive views during filming.

power. Sanders makes native leaders into kings, it is explained, but only 'little ones – that is the custom of the British-African rule, they break a big king and put many little kings in his place, because it is much safer'. The film jettisoned such cynicism and gave audiences a more agreeable version. 'I have learnt the secret of government from your lordship,' Bosambo tells Sanders. 'A king ought not to be feared but loved by his people.' And Sanders replies complacently, 'That is the secret of the British.' There is an evident need for reassurance, heard too in *Drake of England*: 'Only by fear can the people be made to do their duty,' says the Spanish king, the implication clear that this is not the British way. Yet the very fact that it needed saying hinted at a lack of national self-confidence. There was a sense of whistling as the darkness gathered.

These films were released at a time when the Empire was feeling a little nervous. The concept of Dominion status had been formalised in 1926, providing for self-government under the Crown, and with Australia, Canada, the Irish Free State, New Zealand, Newfoundland and South Africa recognised as Dominions within the British Commonwealth of Nations. There were calls for India to be granted similar status, and in 1930 the Labour government convened what was billed as a Round Table Conference in London to discuss the future of the country. Absent from the talks, however, was the Indian National Congress, the main independence movement; its leaders were in jail.

The most significant figure in the Congress was Mohandas Gandhi, a lawyer who espoused the cause of non-violent resistance and whose campaigns of civil disobedience and non-cooperation proved far harder for Britain to combat than violent rebellion. In 1931, he and other Congress leaders were released so that they could participate in a second Round Table Conference, a move that had the backing of Stanley Baldwin, though not of Winston Churchill, who resigned from the Tory front bench in protest; it was, he said, 'nauseating to see Mr Gandhi, a seditious Middle Temple lawyer, now posing as a fakir of a type well known in the East, striding half-naked up the steps of the Viceregal Palace'.[35] Others were no more impressed. He was 'the fanatic leader of a fanatic Indian horde', said the *Daily Mirror*,[36] and Harry J. Greenwall, veteran foreign correspondent of the *Daily Express*, concluded that, 'Twenty-five years hence, historians writing about India will discard Gandhi almost entirely as a great figure.'[37]

Neither of those conferences, nor the third in late 1932, resolved the question of India's future, but the holding of such talks was an indication of changing times. Some saw the idea of negotiating with Indians as a weakening of racial resolve – 'The Round Table Conference is the biggest tragedy since the Battle of Waterloo', opined Adolf Hitler[38] – but Baldwin was a realist. 'There is a wind of nationalism and freedom blowing around the world and blowing as strongly in Asia as anywhere', he said, as his government passed the Government of India Act 1935, providing a large measure of devolution without quite granting Dominion status.[39]

Paul Robeson later apologised for *Sanders of the River*. He'd originally been 'alight with enthusiasm over the project', but felt betrayed by how it turned out. 'I hate the picture', he concluded. By then, he'd visited Moscow to meet the Soviet Union's most celebrated director, Sergei Eisenstein, and been inspired by what he found. 'Here I am not a negro', he told Eisenstein. 'Here, for the first time in my life, I walk in full human dignity.'[40] Resolving never again to compromise his principles in such a manner, he made some of the more uplifting British films of the time – *Song of Freedom* (1936), *Big Fella* (1937), *Jericho* (1937) – in which he embodied dignity, decency and aspiration.

iv

Despite the lifting of the ban on depictions of Queen Victoria, there was no relaxation of censorship. The Lord Chamberlain's Office still forbade the theatrical representation of living people, so that when the Duke of York's Theatre in London put on *All Wave* (1936), a revue satirising the BBC, it wasn't allowed to depict John Reith. But the stricture was selectively applied; the previous year another revue, *Stop Press* at the Adelphi Theatre, had lampooned George Bernard Shaw and Jacob Epstein – a controversial sculptor who drew on non-European influences for such pieces as *Genesis* (1930) and *Ecce Homo* (1934) – and that had been permitted. Radical figures, it seemed, were considered fair game.

The British Board of Film Censors took its work even more seriously, since, they said, they had to consider 'the impression made on an average audience which includes a not inconsiderable proportion of people of immature judgement'.[41] When it was founded in 1912, the BBFC had had just two rules – no depictions of Christ and no nudity – but in the post-war years, a set of regulations began to develop. In 1920 its annual report said that twenty-eight films had been rejected for various reasons including depictions of drug use, executions and venereal disease. Other things that produced an outright ban were to do with political opinion: the espousal of revolution or free love, the 'insistence on the inferiority of the coloured races' and 'scenes calculated to inflame racial hatred'. There was also disapproval of 'indecorous dancing', of 'references to controversial politics' – including 'relations between capital and labour' – and of anything 'calculated to wound the susceptibilities of foreign people'.[42]

Language was also a source of concern. 'We do allow "damn",' said J. Brooke Wilkinson, secretary of the BBFC, 'but we don't allow "bloody".'[43] Other forbidden words included: anti-Christ, bastard, bawdy, belly, bitch, blasted, bum, gigolo, harlot, lewd, lousy, masochist, nappies, nuts, nymphomania, old cock, privy, prostitute, sex appeal, sexual degenerates and strumpet.[44]

The regulations became sufficiently established that the industry learned to toe the line. The BBFC reported that no films were banned at all in 1935, and that there were 50 per cent fewer cuts than in the previous year. It was also the first time in many years that the censors issued more 'U' certificates – 'Universal', meaning a film was suitable for any age – than it did 'A' certificates ('Advisory', recommending that children under fourteen be accompanied by an adult).

This simple division of films came under stress with the arrival from America of the horror movie *Frankenstein* (1931), starring Boris Karloff and directed by James Whale, who had gone from *Journey's End* to Hollywood. The film had been cut – very clumsily – by the BBFC and given an 'A' certificate, but many local councils disagreed and went their own way. Some, such as Leicester, simply banned it (which meant that the Trocadero in Humberstone, just outside the council boundary, did very good business), while others, including Birmingham, Manchester and Plymouth, ruled that children under fourteen should not be allowed to see the film, even if they were accompanied. Fearing a fragmented marketplace, the BBFC hurriedly restored a national standard with a new certificate, 'H' for 'horrific', which barred under-sixteens – the first age restriction.

If the stage and screen were tightly censored, the same was not quite true of the BBC, which had a greater tolerance for political work, so long as it was progressive without being revolutionary. The dramatist L. du Garde Peach, described by the papers as 'broadcasting's most versatile playwright',[45] was a committed writer – a failed Liberal parliamentary candidate, and a supporter of the League of Nations and the Peace Pledge Union – and some of his BBC work dealt with difficult subjects: the economic exploitation of Africa in *Ingredient X* (1929), rural poverty in *Bread* (1932), the Elizabethan roots of the slave trade in *John Hawkins, Slaver* (1933), local politics in *Our Town* (1935).

In *Patriotism Ltd* (1937), a satirical one-act drama, Peach depicted an arms company deliberately provoking conflict between the invented nations of Andania and Segovia, and selling weapons to both. It was a story, he said, of 'two countries brought to the brink of war by a mixture of buffoonery, self-interest and opportunism which you will find nowhere else in the world, except in most of the Chancelleries of Europe'.[46] Advance notices said it had a 'simple directness that is continually amusing',[47] and talked of the way it exposed 'bland cynicism on the part of the firm and its customers'.[48]

Three days before its scheduled broadcast, however, the government leaned on the BBC and the piece was withdrawn, on the grounds that 'it might be mistaken for a comment on current national affairs'.[49] Which, of course, it was. 'No direct veto has been exercised by the postmaster general,' it was reported, but 'the BBC was given to understand that such a broadcast would be looked upon in an unfavourable light.' Peach, who was not personally told about the ban, was furious: 'I regard the action as just another instance of BBC timidity.'[50] He was probably right. At a time of international tension, there was growing criticism of the corporation – some detected 'a definite bias in the presentation of news items and talks'[51] – and there was a fear that *Patriotism Ltd* would simply give its enemies more ammunition. The play was replaced in the schedules by *Murder with Menaces*, a drama about blackmail, first broadcast a few weeks earlier and written by Patrick Hamilton (who was a Marxist).*

Peach rewrote *Patriotism Ltd* as a full-length stage play, and it received its premiere later in the year in a production by the Great Hucklow Village Players. This was an amateur group he'd founded himself in a Derbyshire village so remote that performances were restricted to nights with a full moon, so that people could find their way home across the moors.† It was staged as part of the Buxton Dramatic Festival, which was being judged by Val Gielgud, the BBC director of drama – he gave second place to *Patriotism Ltd*. The publicity accorded to the banned play ensured a massive demand for tickets, which turned out to be ruinous; the cost of

---

* Hamilton is best known for his stage plays *Rope* (1929), filmed by Alfred Hitchcock, and *Gaslight* (1938), from which the term 'gaslighting' would later be taken. Peach went on to write the children's non-fiction series *Adventures from History*, published by Ladybird Books, 1957–74.

† In 1933 the Great Hucklow Players had scored a major coup, securing the world premiere of *Clive of India*, by W. P. Lipscomb and R. J. Minney, a play which went on to a successful West End run and to be filmed in Hollywood, with Ronald Colman in the title role. Unfortunately, there was a heavy snowfall on the scheduled opening night, which meant a month's postponement till the next full moon.

returning payments to unsuccessful applicants meant that the production lost money.

The cancellation of *Patriotism Ltd* reflected a wider turn against pacifism in culture. 'This damned pacifist rot is collapsing right and left,' says a character in A. G. Macdonell's novel *Lords and Masters* (1936), another satire on the arms trade. 'I mean rearmament is obviously all the thing now.' In the movie *The Four Just Men* (1939), adapted from the Edgar Wallace novel, an MP arguing for disarmament at a public meeting is heckled by a working man: 'These 'ere pacifists never done nobody no good.' In case there's any doubt who's speaking sense, the MP later turns out to be a traitor. As Charters, the archetypal Englishman in Alfred Hitchcock's *The Lady Vanishes* (1938), says: 'Pacifist, eh? Won't work, old boy. Early Christians tried it and got thrown to the lions.'

This sort of commentary on current affairs, like that in the films about Henry VIII, Wellington and the Spanish Armada, was oblique, buried in order to satisfy censors who were looking increasingly out of touch. The BBFC regulation on not offending foreigners was such that the nationality of the villains in *The Lady Vanishes*, and in Hitchcock's other masterpiece *The 39 Steps*, could not be specified, even though they were obviously German. This was a very British take on censorship, quite unlike that of most European countries, for it was not any particular political viewpoint that was banned, but politics itself. 'We may take pride,' said Lord Tyrrell, president of the BBFC, in 1937, 'in observing that there is not a single film in London which deals with any of the burning issues of the day.'[52] He sounded like a pub landlord banning talk of religion and politics in the bar.

Some deplored this situation, but these were the rules that British cinema set itself. For the BBFC had no statutory authority; it was an independent body, created by the industry to regulate its own output. This was, acknowledged Labour politician Herbert Morrison, 'a curious arrangement', but it was surely better than the intense government control seen in Germany under Joseph Goebbels, or in Russia, where the head of the Soviet film industry, Boris

Shumyatsky, was executed as a traitor in 1938 for not doing his job well enough. And, as Morrison went on to say, 'the British have a very great habit of making curious arrangements that work very well'.[53]

In fact, the whole system of determining what was acceptable in art was curious, a patchwork that had evolved over generations without any sense of logic or coherence. Like the BBFC, the BBC was self-regulating, though it was governed by a royal charter and, as the General Strike and *Patriotism Ltd* had shown, was susceptible to political pressure; drama was under the eye of the lord chamberlain, while variety theatres were overseen by local councils; books and exhibitions required no prior approval but were subject to the Obscene Publications Act (as with *The Well of Loneliness*), and the same was assumed to be true of gramophone records, though none were prosecuted.* In addition, the Post Office could intercept mail, and customs officers were empowered to seize material brought into the country, sometimes with comic effect; in 1933, copies of an illustrated book on the Sistine Chapel were confiscated on suspicion of obscenity.[54] And then there was the self-censorship of the press, as during the Abdication crisis.

None of it made sense, and yet somehow Herbert Morrison was right: it did work. The lack of cultural engagement with burning political issues was, no doubt, regrettable, but perhaps too the lack of controversy on stage, screen and radio was part of the reason why the country felt – and was – so much more stable a society in the 1930s than most of Europe. Culture in Britain was far quieter than in its neighbours.

Not that European culture was much seen. In 1930, an application was made to the London County Council for permission to screen some Soviet films that had been refused a certificate by the BBFC, including Sergei Eisenstein's *Battleship Potemkin* (1925)

---

* The risk was demonstrated much later when Manchester police seized copies of the album *The Fucking Cunts Treat Us Like Pricks* (1984) by punk band Flux of Pink Indians, under obscenity legislation.

and Vsevolod Pudovkin's *Mother* (1926). It was unsuccessful. 'I do not think anyone could be more opposed to political censorship of films than I am,' said Rosamund Smith, Conservative chairman of the LCC committee. 'But I think we are up against something quite different in these Russian films.'[55]

v

As the coronation procession of George VI made its way through the streets in May 1937, the biggest cheers, apart from those directed towards the king and queen, were for Stanley Baldwin. Two weeks later, he announced his retirement as prime minister. His last act was to give MPs a 50 per cent pay rise – up to £600 a year – and he went out with great goodwill on all sides. 'He was never superior to anybody,' wrote Hannen Swaffer, former editor of the *People*. 'He did not arouse suspicion. He always looked a decent sort of guy.'[56]

His successor was, as widely expected, the chancellor of the exchequer, Neville Chamberlain. He was the first in his family to be prime minister, though not the first to aspire to the office: his father, Joseph, had been the most significant government figure at the beginning of the century, and his older brother, Austen, had been both chancellor and foreign secretary, but neither had made it to the very top. Neville was a less likely candidate for premier, a latecomer to politics, a businessman who was fifty years old when he became an MP in 1918 (Austen was elected at twenty-eight). He was junior to Baldwin by less than two years and to Ramsay Mac-Donald by less than three. These three men, separated in age by just thirty months, occupied 10 Downing Street for seventeen years.

Chamberlain was not as appealing a figure as Baldwin. 'He always looks like the president of an undertakers' union,' observed the *Daily Herald* in 1932.[57] It was hard to warm to him. 'In public he seems cold and unsympathetic, more like the chairman of a municipal committee anxious to keep the rates down,' said the *Spectator*. 'Even in the House of Commons he appears aloof and slightly magisterial.'[58] Baldwin once warned him that he gave the impression of thinking that the Labour Party were dirt, but Chamberlain didn't mind. 'The fact is,' he noted in his diary, 'that intellectually, with a few exceptions, they *are* dirt.'[59] He wasn't much impressed by his own cabinet either. Above all, he had no time for levity in politics, or humour in his speeches. 'If they want jokes, let them go the pictures,' he declared.[60]

In truth, these weren't the times for levity. The economy was recovering – partly thanks to Chamberlain's work at the exchequer – but the international situation was becoming ever more threatening, and British foreign policy ever less effective. The overriding aim since the Armistice had been to avoid war, for pragmatic as well as moral reasons. 'Our sole objective is to keep what we want and live in peace,' noted a Foreign Office memorandum in 1926; 'whatever else may be the outcome of a disturbance of the peace, we shall be losers.'[61] To this end, Britain sought the rebuilding of Europe, the maintenance of friendly relations with other countries, and the restoration of Germany as an economic power. Officially, the path to this goal lay in collective security and disarmament under the aegis of the League of Nations, though Conservative governments were not wholly committed; it was noted that Baldwin never visited the league's headquarters in Geneva.

The avoidance of war also required the pacifying of those governments that posed a threat to peace, and there was an inclination to conciliate rather than confront. 'My government will continue to do all in their power to further the appeasement of Europe,' said Edward VIII in his first and only King's Speech at the opening of Parliament in November 1936.[62] Increasingly, though, the dictators were not to be appeased, and the situation in 1937 was fraught with danger.

Italy's invasion of Abyssinia had concluded in February with outright victory and the exiling of Emperor Haile Selassie. In July, Japanese forces began a full-scale attack on China, taking Peking and Shanghai later that year. Meanwhile, the Spanish Civil War continued and dragged in external powers, with Germany and Italy backing the fascists, and the Soviet Union the republicans. France and Britain stayed out of the conflict, though some two thousand Britons – nearly half of them Communist Party members – went to serve in Spain on the republican side, including writers W. H. Auden, Laurie Lee, George Orwell and Stephen Spender; around five hundred lost their lives. The political aspects of the conflict were obscure to many in Britain, but the horrors of the war were real enough. In particular, the aerial bombing of the Basque town of Guernica in April 1937 by German and Italian aircraft, resulting in the death of hundreds of civilians, was deeply shocking; it was an 'abominable outrage,' said the *Daily Mirror*,[63] and Foreign Secretary Anthony Eden said it suggested 'a terrible future for Europe'.[64]

Most menacing of all was Adolf Hitler's Germany, rearming, emboldened by its successful reoccupation of the Rhineland and clearly looking for further expansion of its borders. 'The independence of Austria is a key position,' Austen Chamberlain had warned the Commons in April 1936. 'If Austria perishes, Czechoslovakia becomes indefensible; then the whole of the Balkans would be subjected to a gigantic new influence.'[65]

Austria was indeed key. The idea of union with Germany had been around since the nineteenth century, and had acquired new momentum following the rise of Hitler. In 1934, an attempted coup by Austrian Nazis had seen the assassination of Chancellor Engelbert Dollfuss, and was intended to provide an excuse for a German invasion; only the pre-emptive mobilisation of Italian forces prevented this. Once the fuss had died down, the stratagem was repeated with another attempted coup, and this time, in March 1938, German troops crossed the border. In what was termed the *Anschluss* ('joining'), Austria was absorbed into a greater Germany, in direct contravention of the Treaty of Versailles and against the wishes of the Austrian government. 'It deals a blow to the policy of appeasement,' fretted *The Times*,[66] and the *News Chronicle* was clear: 'The time has come to say quite bluntly that this kind of thing must not, shall not, be repeated.'[67] Speaking bluntly, however, was very different to doing something. 'The hard fact is,'

Neville Chamberlain told the Commons, 'that nothing could have arrested what has actually happened unless this country and other countries had been prepared to use force.'[68] The democracies were not so prepared.

And then, as predicted, Hitler's attention turned to Czechoslovakia. The situation here was unstable. The country had been created in the aftermath of the Great War, when the Austro-Hungarian Empire was carved up and new, smaller states brought into being. Just over half the population were ethnically Czech, with the next largest group – around one in five – being German. Mostly, these latter lived in the western part of the country, in areas they referred to as the Sudetenland, and the growing mood there was for separation from Czechoslovakia and possibly union with Germany. In September 1938 German troops began massing on the border, supposedly to protect the Sudeten Germans from the Czech-dominated government. Chamberlain, still in pursuit of appeasement, had two fruitless meetings with Hitler, at which it became clear that Germany's demands were not to be contained.

The British people, who had long wished to ignore such a possibility, now had to contemplate the prospect of war. And a war even more terrible than the last, because – as Guernica had shown – it would also be fought from the air, and British civilians would be in the front line; estimates presented to the cabinet suggested that a sixty-day Luftwaffe bombing campaign could result in a death toll of 600,000.* Preparations began for conflict, and gas masks were issued in anticipation of the dropping of poison-gas bombs. 'How horrible, fantastic, incredible it is,' said the prime minister, in a radio broadcast from Downing Street, 'that we should be digging trenches and trying on gas masks here because of a quarrel in a faraway country between people of whom we know nothing.'[69]

On 28 September, Chamberlain announced to the Commons that he would be flying to Munich the next day to meet Hitler,

----

* British civilian casualties from bombing in the whole of the Second World War were around 60,000, a tenth of that estimate.

Benito Mussolini and French prime minister Édouard Daladier in 'one last effort' to secure peace. His words were greeted with roars of approval and relief in the chamber. Labour leader Clement Attlee welcomed the announcement; Queen Mary, the queen mother, was seen in the Speaker's Gallery 'raising a handkerchief to her eyes'; and in the Peers' Gallery the Archbishop of Canterbury 'beamed like a schoolboy', while Stanley Baldwin – now Lord Baldwin, making his first return to the Commons since he was prime minister – 'appeared to be beating his stick on the floor'.[70]

There was more rejoicing still when the meeting of the four powers reached an agreement, even though it was little more than a capitulation to Hitler: in essence, Germany could have the Sudetenland so long as it didn't go any further. The agreement was presented to the Czechs as a fait accompli; if they chose to resist German aggression, they now knew they would be doing so alone. With great reluctance, they acquiesced to the dismemberment of their country.

In exchange, Chamberlain brought back from Munich a piece of paper, signed by Hitler, that described the agreement as 'symbolic of the desire of our two peoples never to go to war with one another again'. It was 'peace with honour', Chamberlain told the crowds that had gathered in Downing Street, 'peace for our time'. They were rapturous. 'You have saved us!' they shouted, and they sang 'Rule Britannia', 'O God Our Help in Ages Past' and 'He's a Jolly Good Fellow'.[71] Only a curmudgeonly few refused to be swept up in the adulation: 'Silly old bastard,' snorted a newsreel cameraman.[72] Privately, Chamberlain told Lord Dunglass, a young Tory MP who had accompanied him to Munich, that Hitler was 'the most detestable and bigoted man',[73] and that the point of the paper was simply to illustrate the dictator's deceit if he broke the agreement.*

As with the non-response to the *Anschluss*, Munich was an

---

* Lord Dunglass would later succeed to the title Earl of Home, and later still renounce that title to become prime minister as Alec Douglas-Home.

acknowledgement of Britain's impotence. Perhaps if a stand had been taken in 1936 over the Rhineland, Hitler's expansionism could have been curbed, but there was at that point vanishingly little political or public support for confrontation, and Britain was hardly arguing from a position of military strength. Nor was it at Munich. Rearmament was happening, and the defence budget had been increasing since the abandonment of the Ten Year Rule in 1932, but it was only in 1937 that there was any sense of urgency. Britain was not in a state of readiness for war. Further, it was by no means certain that the Dominions – Australia, Canada, New Zealand, South Africa – were willing to join a European conflict, as they had in 1914.

Amid the relief at the Munich Agreement, there was a recognition that it had merely postponed the inevitable. Earlier in 1938, the independent MP Eleanor Rathbone had published *War Can Be Averted*, warning that any concession over Czechoslovakia would not be the end.[74] 'If that price is paid, what will be the next demand? Where is it going to stop?'* Now, an editorial in the *Daily Mirror* celebrated the calming of tensions, but noted that it was just a reprieve: 'We do not ask you to plunge back into gloom, but we ask you to agree that the mood ought to be one of confidence with caution.'[75] Despite which advice, some retained their illusions of safety. As the new year dawned, the *Daily Express* was in optimistic mood: 'There will be no great war in Europe in 1939.'[76]

The person who emerged with the most credit was Chamberlain. ONE MAN SAVED US FROM THE GREATEST WAR OF ALL was the headline to the newsreel shown in cinemas. Reviewing the year that December, journalist Leonard Mosley, who had travelled with Chamberlain, was still enthused. 'All of us waited for

---

* Eleanor's cousin, Basil Rathbone, was one of the more successful British actors in Hollywood, Oscar-nominated for *Romeo and Juliet* (1936) and *If I Were King* (1938). In 1939 he starred in *The Hound of the Baskervilles*, the first of his fourteen movie appearances as Sherlock Holmes.

Armageddon. But instead of that came Munich,' he wrote. 'Peace had been saved by the courage and tenacity of one man.'[77] This 'austere, rather melancholy-looking and mordant-speeched' figure, marvelled the *Belfast Telegraph*, had now won a place 'in the hearts of millions'. He was 'the Umbrella Man of Peace'.[78]

That last reference was to the tightly furled umbrella with which Chamberlain was always pictured, a symbol of Britishness that played into a contemporary cultural image of rainy weather.* Even as the Sudetenland crisis was threatening war in September 1938, the revue *These Foolish Things* opened at the London Palladium, including the hit song 'The Umbrella Man', performed by comedians Bud Flanagan and Chesney Allen. 'Don't mind the rain,' it advised, because the umbrella man will 'patch up your troubles'.

A range of umbrella-decorated merchandise appeared 'in the form of toffee, pens and pencils, paper knives and numerous other things'.[79] The Chamberlain Clock was exhibited at the British Industry Fair at Earl's Court, London in February 1939, an elegant art-deco piece bearing the motto 'Peace in Our Time', with a single umbrella at each hour and with larger umbrellas for hands; it was 'the new symbol of peace and prosperity'. ('Splendid idea!' said Queen Elizabeth when she visited the show.) Abroad, the sobriquet was seen as a little ridiculous, and there was a joke in Europe about how the Pax Britannica had been replaced by a Pax Umbrellica.[80] 'People who carry an umbrella can never found an empire,'[81] said Mussolini contemptuously.†

---

* The best-known songs on this theme came from Depression-era America: 'Singin' in the Rain' (1929), 'The Clouds Will Soon Roll By' (1932), 'Stormy Weather' (1933).
† In an odd postscript, a key figure in the conspiracy theories around the assassination of US President John F. Kennedy in 1963 was the Umbrella Man, a bystander seen acting suspiciously with an umbrella – despite it being a sunny day – just as the presidential motorcade passed him in Dealey Plaza, Dallas. In 1978 the man finally came forward to explain that he'd been protesting against Kennedy's father, who, as American ambassador to London, had supported appeasement. The umbrella was a reference back to Chamberlain.

In March 1939, Hitler duly broke his word that the Sudetenland was the limit of his territorial demands, when German troops took Prague and occupied the remaining parts of Czechoslovakia. So ended the last surviving democracy in central Europe. And so too ended the policy of appeasement, the Pax Umbrellica having failed to contain the Nazi threat. Britain and France now gave assurances that they would not desert Poland as they had deserted Czechoslovakia. 'In the event of any action which clearly threatened Polish independence,' Chamberlain told the Commons, 'His Majesty's government would feel themselves bound at once to lend the Polish government all support in their power.'[82] The following month, Italy invaded Albania. Rearmament stepped up further.

The days of collective security, let alone of pacifism, were long gone. The possibility of another war had hardened into probability, and was beginning to look like certainty. There was a sense of resignation and fatalism, and sometimes of grim humour. In January 1939 comedian Ronald Frankau's 'There's Absolutely Nothing Wrong at All' took a heavily sarcastic line:

> We've known what quaking knees meant,
> But thanks to this appeasement,
> There's absolutely nothing wrong at all.[83]

vi

The fourth of August 1939. Twenty-five years since Britain declared war on Germany. 'The war that was supposed to end all wars,' reflected the *Western Morning News*. 'It was a phrase of sincere hope in those days. Now it is one which rankles with hollow mockery.'[84] The news was becoming steadily worse. The *Liverpool Echo* published a map of Europe, showing the reality of a Germany that included Vienna and Prague; as expected, Hitler was now manoeuvring towards an invasion of Poland.

Meanwhile, the world still turned. 'After a slow start, the holiday season now looks like breaking records,' enthused the press. 'Every aeroplane going to Switzerland and Paris this week will be full to capacity.' The same phenomenon seemed to be true in Europe: 'Incoming steamers and aircraft are nearly as full as the outgoing ones.'[85] As W. H. Auden wrote in a poem published that year, 'The dogs go on with their doggy life.'[86]

In August 1939, it was reported that Britain's favourite pastime was darts; five million people played, and radio broadcasts of matches were attracting big audiences. The Wine, Spirit and Allied Trades Exhibition commissioned a poll that discovered the country's favourite alcoholic drinks were, in order, beer, whisky, port, gin and brandy. 'The slimming craze is on us,' said the papers,[87] and products were being extensively marketed – Natex Slimming Food, Marienbad Anti-Obesity Tablets, Slimming Beans No. 2 – as well as Dr Eustace Chesser's book *Slimming for the Million*. The new edition of *Housewife* magazine carried adverts for Stork margarine, the Ewbank carpet sweeper, Euthymol toothpaste, Dr Oster Mann's Pills, Nestol ('makes baby's hair grow curly'), Su-Can sanitary towels and the newly launched Tampax ('Sanitary protection is now worn internally!'). A survey in Wales found that nine in ten parents of schoolchildren wanted 'sex hygiene lessons at school'.[88] In Weymouth, on the other hand, the Reverend F. E. Coryton, Anglican vicar of St John's, objected to women's holiday wear, on patriotic, as well as biblical grounds.* 'A tendency to wear beach trousers and shorts is not going to produce the best of the nation,' he said, adding: 'I do not approve of bobbed hair or Eton crops either.'[89]

On 19 August, on Coniston Water in the Lake District, Malcolm Campbell broke his own water-speed record, travelling at more than 140 miles per hour in his powerboat *Blue Bird II*. (In 1935, he'd become the first person to drive a car at over 300 miles per hour.) The same day, with a week to go before the start of the new football season, a round of friendly matches was played to

---

* 'The woman shall not wear that which pertaineth unto a man, neither shall a man put on a woman's garment: for all that do so are abomination unto the Lord thy God.' Deuteronomy 20:5.

raise money for George V's Jubilee Fund, set up in 1935 to provide 'facilities for the recreation and guidance of the younger generation'.[90] Tottenham Hotspur hosted the League champions Arsenal in front of 35,000 fans, and there were 20,000-strong crowds at Anfield, Old Trafford and Villa Park.

Band leaders were still celebrities, filling variety theatres and dance halls. Henry Hall was on tour, playing everywhere from Morecambe Winter Gardens to the Plymouth Palace. Jack Hylton was at the South Parade Pier in Portsmouth, with a company whose comedian, the thirteen-year-old Ernest Wise, was getting rave reviews. A new star, Ken 'Snakehips' Johnson, born in British Guiana and leading an all-black ensemble, the Emperors of Swing ('all "hi-de-ho" in the ecstasy of throbbing, whirling, modern syncopation'),[91] was at the Aberdeen Tivoli.*

The need for nostalgic comfort had not faded. The Sheffield Empire offered a bill of eight veterans of the Edwardian music hall, headed by Charles Austin, Ada Reeve and Albert Whelan; all three were also to be heard on the BBC radio show, *These Names Made Variety*, together with Harry Champion and Wilkie Bard. Tod Slaughter's most recent movie, *The Face at the Window*, was doing good business, as were the latest from George Formby (*Trouble Brewing*) and Gracie Fields (*Shipyard Sally*).

The biggest attraction at the pictures was the newly released *The Four Feathers* (1939), another production from Alexander and Zoltán Korda. It came from A. E. W. Mason's 1902 novel, though it shed the psychological and political emphasis of the original in favour of big battle scenes that looked spectacular, having been filmed in Technicolor on location in Sudan. Far more bellicose and patriotic than the novel, it felt consequently a little nervous, as though protesting too much. Mason had been challenging the values of the Empire; now it seemed as though even to ask questions was beyond the pale.

---

* Johnson was killed in 1941, when a German bomb hit the Café de Paris in London, where he was performing. He was twenty-six.

That month, libraries took delivery of new adventures for old heroes: the Saint in Leslie Charteris's *The Happy Highwayman*, John Creasey's *The Toff Goes On*, Gerald Fairlie's *Bulldog Drummond Attacks*.* Detectives continued to solve murders in unexpected situations, in Josephine Bell's *Death at Half Term*, Mavis Doriel Hay's *Murder Underground* and Charles Barry's *The Boat Train Mystery*. Mills & Boon didn't stray from their formula, with titles including Berta Ruck's *Mock Honeymoon* and Linda Muir's *Pathway to Paradise*, as well as a new Sophie Cole, *Beckoning Romance*. Highbrow readers, on the other hand, were still trying to make their way through – and make sense of – James Joyce's *Finnegans Wake*, which had been published in May and was even more impenetrable than *Ulysses*. 'An Irish stew of verbiage,' said the *Daily Herald*, 'with unexpected beauty emerging now and then from the peculiar mixture.'[92]

H. G. Wells published *The Fate of Homo Sapiens*, in which he cast a gloomy eye across the world. Chamberlain was 'ignorant, narrow-minded, subconsciously timid, cunning and inordinately vain', while Hitler 'shows all the symptoms of a recognised form of sex mania, the jealous fear and hate of the great raping black man – who in his case is a Jew'. Not that the Jews, particularly the Zionists, were blameless: 'Why should any country want these inassimilable aliens bent on preserving their distinctness?' Wells had even lost faith in Stalin. 'I thought he was honest and strong and decent,' he lamented, but disillusion had set in with 'those foolish films of personal propaganda he has allowed to be made'.[93] The book went through three printings that August.

This was the last summer of peace, and it was mostly peaceful. Despite the fascination with fictional violence and foreign gangsterism, the streets were by and large safe; the number of murders was lower than it had been in the reign of Queen Victoria, and

---

* Fairlie was a friend of H. C. McNeile (Sapper), creator of Drummond, and was, at least in part, the inspiration for the character. After McNeile's death in 1937, he inherited the right to continue the series.

although the crime rate was higher, offences such as drunken disorder were down, most of the increase accounted for by theft and burglaries, a by-product of improved material conditions. Britain was a country united by a shared culture, comfortable with its history and heroes, Christian in values and morality, if not so much in worship. Disagreements were largely confined to sporting rivalries, leaving serious commentators infuriated by the nation's misguided sense of priorities: 'The English, who can be tolerant about religion and politics, are nearly always intolerant about pastimes,' complained J. B. Priestley that August.[94] But this was an attitude that also produced such a marked disregard for political extremism, so that neither communism nor fascism amounted to much, while the Labour Party and the trade unions remained committed to parliamentary democracy. By historical standards, and by comparison with most of the world, it was a land of liberty and contentment.

But the reports from Europe could not be ignored indefinitely, and Britain was being increasingly drawn into the problems of the Continent. Ever since the rise of the Nazis, there had been a steady stream of Jews and others leaving Germany, and after the *Anschluss* the numbers had risen dramatically. Despite immigration controls, there were by the end of August 1939 some 78,000 refugees from Germany and Austria living in Britain, 90 per cent of whom were Jewish.[95] Others failed to make it. That month, two young Jewish men, having escaped from Germany, tried to row across the English Channel from Ostend in a ten-foot dinghy, but ran into heavy weather and had to be rescued by the Walmer lifeboat; they landed at Deal, and were promptly deported back to Belgium.

On 23 August, the Soviet Union and Germany signed a non-aggression pact that ensured Russia would not protect Poland in the event of an attack, making an invasion even more likely. Parliament was recalled to pass the Emergency Powers (Defence) Act, putting the country on a war footing.

Two days later, a bomb exploded in the centre of Coventry, killing five civilians. This was not German sabotage, though, but part of a campaign by the remnants of the Irish Republican Army that had started back in January, when five bombs exploded in London and three in Manchester. Over the following months, there were some three hundred bombs and acts of sabotage in English cities and towns. Initially the campaign was strategically targeted at the electricity, gas and water systems, before spreading to bridges, railway stations, shops, hotels and cinemas, even Madame Tussaud's waxworks. There was much damage and some injuries, but the deaths in Coventry were on a different level, and the ensuing outrage took much of the impetus from the campaign. Nonetheless, the attacks continued sporadically, through to the early months of 1940.*

In the final week of August, nearly 4,000 campers arrived at Billy Butlin's Skegness camp for a last-chance holiday. Elsewhere, preparations were being made for war and the fearful possibility of aerial bombing. 'Plans for the evacuation of 3,000,000 children, mothers of young children and blind people from London and other big cities are ready to be put into operation at a moment's notice,' reported the press.[96] Museums and galleries in the capital closed their doors, so that treasures could be packed up and removed to places of safety. Drapers experienced a rush on material for blacking out windows, and cellophane was also selling fast – it was used to cover windows to minimise flying glass in an explosion. Trains from London to Liverpool 'were crowded with Americans acting on their embassy's advice to return home'.[97] A planned rail strike was called off. The West Indies cricket team curtailed its English tour after three test matches. Also abandoned incomplete was the Promenade Concert season, the highlight of which had been the British premiere of Arthur Bliss's Piano Concerto.

On 1 September 1939, German troops invaded Poland, and this time Britain and France kept their promises. Shortly after the

* The IRA sought to coordinate their efforts with those of Germany; a series of meetings with military intelligence officers in Berlin aimed to win Nazi support for a united Ireland.

eleventh hour of Sunday 3 September, the nation again fell silent. Nearly nine million homes now had radios and could listen in to Neville Chamberlain broadcasting live from Downing Street. It was a brief address, for there was only one thing that needed saying: 'This country is at war with Germany.'

An hour later – and the sequence was a tacit recognition of the BBC's importance – the House of Commons assembled to hear the same message. The prime minister allowed himself a personal reflection as he stood among the ruins of his attempt to hold the peace in Europe. 'I cannot tell what part I may be allowed to play,' said Chamberlain. 'I trust I may live to see the day when Hitlerism has been destroyed and a liberated Europe has been re-established.'*

The big hit song of the summer of 1939 was 'There'll Always Be an England', first performed by Billy Scott-Coomber and his Singing Grenadiers in May. Its patriotic message caught the mood of the nation:

> Red, white and blue, what does it mean to you?
> Surely you're proud, shout it aloud: Britons, awake!
> The Empire too, we can depend on you.
> Freedom remains, these are the chains nothing can break.[98]

In August 1939, the song was everywhere. The South Shields Tattoo ended with a local singer accompanied by massed bands; in the film *Discoveries*, it was sung by boy soprano Glyn Davies, surrounded by hundreds of uniformed servicemen; dance band leader Billy Cotton closed his performance at the Winter Garden in Eastbourne with it and 'nearly brought the house down'.[99]

'The spirit of that song is running through England today like quicksilver,' declared Lieutenant J. Ernest Chapel of Bath. He'd been out walking near the village of Priddy in Somerset when he

---

* He did not. In May 1940 he resigned, replaced by Winston Churchill at the head of another coalition government. Chamberlain died six months later.

came across a young boy, sitting on a gate singing 'There'll Always Be an England' to himself, and had been touched to the quick by the sentiment. 'We are awake. The soul of our forefathers has stirred us into action,' Chapel wrote to the *Somerset Guardian*. 'We're mighty, and we'll be mightier yet, for the soul of that boy when he was singing that song was the echo of the tremendous fighting spirit of the great British race. Come what may from the Dictators, they'll rue the day. England is prepared, and ready, aye ready.'[100]

LIBERTY

Perhaps we can say that England as a whole, though suffering vast changes, has survived more recognisably than any other country. She is more than the ghost of her former self – she has a good deal still left of the substance.

James Hilton, *To You, Mr Chips*, 1938[1]

Does Adolf wear pyjamas or a nightshirt?
Does he take his teeth out when he goes to bed?
Is that unruly lock of hair a detachable affair
Which he hangs up on the bedpost overhead?

Tommy Handley, 'A Very Little Nazi', 1939[2]

Sally Gray and Lupino Lane doing the Lambeth Walk, 1939

Lupino Lane, born in the East End into what he claimed was the world's 'oldest theatrical family',[3] made his stage debut at the age of four in 1896, on a bill headed by male impersonator Vesta Tilley, though it wasn't until 1902 that he turned professional. In the 1920s and 30s he established himself as a popular stage and screen actor in both Britain and America; he appeared in D. W. Griffith's *Isn't Life Wonderful* (1924), and in 1935 he had a West End hit with the musical comedy *Twenty to One*, in which he played Bill Snibson, a cockney bookmaker.

That character was popular enough to be revived for a new musical, *Me and My Girl*, written by Noel Gay with book and lyrics by Douglas Furber and L. Arthur Rose. After a try-out in the provinces, it opened in London at the Victoria Palace Theatre in the run-up to Christmas 1937, and was initially a commercial disaster. 'We were losing £1,500 a week,' Lane later recalled.[4] That changed at the start of January 1938, when Jack Payne's band had to pull out of a radio broadcast and the BBC hurriedly arranged to relay a performance of *Me and My Girl* instead. 'Next day the box-office receipts jumped 400 per cent.'[5] The show went on to run for over 1,600 performances, was featured at the Royal Command Variety Show, broadcast on television, and filmed as *The Lambeth Walk* (1939).

The movie took its title from the show's big song, a simple and instantly catchy tune that was closer to the world of British dance bands than to jazz, and cried out to be whistled cheerily by postmen and plumbers. The lyrics were even simpler, notable for the shout of 'Oi!' and for the happy-go-lucky middle-eight: 'Everything free and easy; do as you darn well pleasey.' It was entirely in the spiritual tradition of the music hall, full of warm, communal conviviality.*

---

* There had been an earlier music-hall song titled 'The Lambeth Walk' (1899), sung by Alec Hurley, a cockney comedian (and Marie Lloyd's second husband) with whom Lane had worked.

Accompanying the song was the only truly successful British dance of the interwar years, though it was very different from the American imports. Where the Charleston had been a frenetic display of youthful vigour, the Lambeth Walk was a more relaxed affair, a rhythmic, swaying strut with swinging arms, the occasional patting of the knees and, on the 'Oi!' the right thumb jerked upwards. It took just a minute or two to learn, and it was so undemanding that it was all-inclusive, transcending class, sex and age. Pretty much anyone could do this dance – and they did. A contemporary report noted that it was being danced 'in Mayfair ballrooms, suburban dance halls, cockney parties and village hops'.[6] The king and queen were fans, and Mussolini was said to have learned the steps.

The song sold 350,000 copies of sheet music in Britain in its first year – happily for Noel Gay, its publisher as well as composer. Lupino Lane recorded a version of course, and so did many bands, including those of Billy Cotton, Michael Flome,* Carroll Gibbons, Phil Green, Harry Leader, Ronnie Munro and Billy Thorburn. Best of all was the jaunty jazz of trumpeter Nat Gonella – the closest Britain had to Louis Armstrong – and his Georgians. 'The Lambeth Walk' caught a public need for light escapism at a time when the world was lurching towards conflict. *The Times* predicted that it would 'be the "Tipperary" of the next World War'.[7]

When Charles Madge and Tom Harrisson of the Mass Observation project surveyed the nation in 1938, they concluded that this was a uniquely British creation, separate from both America and Europe: 'Lambeth walkers are free to express themselves without the hypnosis of a jazz-moan or a Führer.'[8] Yet it was Britain's biggest cultural export in that year of Munich and beyond; 'it is still going strong from China to Peru, from the Bank to Mandalay', marvelled the papers in early 1939.[9] In America it was recorded by Joseph Rines and his Hotel St. Regis Orchestra, by banjoist Eddie Peabody and his Dizzy Strings, by singer Eddie Cantor and vocal group the Mills

---

* Flome was killed in a traffic accident in London during a blackout in 1944.

Brothers, and by the two most acclaimed bandleaders: Artie Shaw and Duke Ellington. There was also a version by Europe's greatest jazz group, the Quintet of the Hot Club of France with Django Reinhardt and Stephane Grappelli. It was translated into a multitude of languages – even into Esperanto ('Venu al le Lambeth ter,' it went)[10] – and in Sweden singer Harry Brandelius had a hit with 'Hemma I Våran Kåk Dansas Det Lambeth Walk' ('At Home in Our Cabin, We Dance the Lambeth Walk').

It was popular, too, in Germany. 'The word "Oi!" has become the loudest battle-cry on the ballroom floors,'[11] reported the *Berliner Tageblatt* in January 1939.* That was in the context of a month's residency by Henry Hall and his band at the Scala in Berlin, for which – in deference to local prejudice – he had undertaken not to play any music by Jewish composers. 'There is, after all, plenty of Aryan music I can play,' he said. 'We are in the show business and not in the political field.'[12] So he played 'The Lambeth Walk', and it went down a storm.

It wasn't Jewish, and it wasn't black, so it wasn't officially suppressed, despite Hitler's disapproval of jazz, and bandleader Heinz Wehner, whose taste for swing was deemed suspect by the authorities, was permitted to release a version with his Großen Tanzorchester.† But there was a great deal of hostility in some Nazi quarters. It was denounced as 'bestial stamping'[13] and for having 'negroid tendencies'.[14] 'This is degenerate music and the people who dance it are also degenerate,' said *Der SA-Mann*, newspaper of the Brownshirts.[15] The song and the dance were banned at the Shrovetide Carnival festivities in Munich and at the University of Heidelberg – where Joseph Goebbels had been awarded his PhD – while Hermann Göring forbade Luftwaffe bands from playing

---

* The *Berliner Tageblatt*, one of Germany's great liberal papers, was closed by the Nazis later that month.
† Despite official disapproval, Wehner was popular, and during the war he was posted to Norway and then the Eastern Front to entertain the troops. He was last seen in Poland in 1945, and is assumed to have been killed in action.

it, and airmen from dancing it while in uniform; it presented an 'undignified picture not in keeping with the serious tasks of the Air Force', he decreed.[16]

The real problem, perhaps, was the very inclusivity that made it so successful, its implicit spirit of democracy and celebration of liberty. The cover of the *Radio Times* for 17 September 1939 had a photograph of an old man outside a small row of slightly rickety, thatched cottages in long shadows, with rolling downs behind; the caption read: 'There'll always be an England.' That was one image of the nation, the romanticised rural idyll that stirred atavistic dreams. As journalist H. V. Morton had written in his travelogue *In Search of England* (1927), the 'village that symbolises England sleeps in the subconsciousness of many a townsman'.[17] 'The Lambeth Walk' offered a complementary alternative, an urban declaration of cheerful resilience. 'Do as you darn well pleasey' spoke of a people free of an overbearing state, an anomaly in an increasingly authoritarian world.

'There is nothing free and easy in Nazi Germany,' said the *Liverpool Echo*; 'the Lambeth Walk must seem out of place in the land of the goose step.'[18] And Labour leader Clement Attlee reached for the same comparison. 'I understand that Hitler regards the Lambeth Walk as too democratic a dance for Germany,' he said. 'All they can do there is the goose step.'[19] In 1942 the Ministry of Information released a short propaganda film, *Schichlegruber Doing the Lambeth Walk*, in which Charles A. Ridley had painstakingly cut the tune to footage from Leni Riefenstahl's *Triumph of the Will* of Hitler and goosestepping Nazis, looping and reversing the film to ridiculous effect. It was very funny, and Goebbels was said to have added Ridley to his hit list of people to be arrested after the invasion of Britain.[20]

ii

At 8.15 p.m. on Wednesday 12 July 1939, BBC radio unveiled a new variety show, *It's That Man Again*. Its premise was that this was a transmission from a rival commercial station, broadcasting from a ship. There was music from Jack Harris's London Casino Band, and a couple of regular features, but at the heart of the show was comedian Tommy Handley.

Born in Liverpool in 1892, Handley had started in entertainment in an army concert party during the Great War, and then moved through different formats in the years of peace, including seaside Pierrots, musical comedy, revue, farce, pantomime and variety. He was best known for a sketch titled 'The Disorderly Room', a knockabout parody of army life featuring popular songs of the day to which new lyrics had been added. A performance of the skit at the Royal Command Variety Show in 1924 was relayed live by the BBC, his first appearance on radio.

In the fifteen years since, he'd become a familiar voice, one of the very few radio comics from those early days who was still broadcasting, though he was never a really big name. Even when he got his starring vehicle with *It's That Man Again*, it was only scheduled to run for six fortnightly episodes, and didn't manage that. The title of the show came from a phrase in increasingly common usage. When the *Daily Express* headlined an article in May 1939 IT'S THAT MAN AGAIN,[21] readers were expected to know that it referred to Adolf Hitler. It was ironic, then, that the radio series was cancelled after four shows because That Man had invaded Poland.

The show returned on 19 September with a new format, having truncated its name to *ITMA*, in parody of wartime abbreviations. Gone was the radio-ship conceit, with Handley now in a desk job at the Office of Twerps. The running time was cut from forty-five minutes to thirty, Jack Hylton replaced Jack Harris, and once the musical and other items were discounted, there were eighteen and a half minutes of scripted comedy. 'In this time,' noted the show's writer, Ted Kavanagh, 'we tried for at least one hundred potential laughs' – one every eleven seconds.[22] The result was a rapid-fire barrage of puns, non sequiturs and nonsense, with an ever-increasing roster of one-dimensional – but not cliched – characters whose job was to interrupt Handley, to deliver their catchphrase and to leave. Kavanagh talked of trying to write cartoons in sound, which was a fair description of the chaotic, often surreal, world that Handley inhabited, and which he just about managed to keep from collapsing in on itself.*

The regulations that had previously prevented BBC comics from making jokes about current affairs and foreign governments had been abandoned in the case of Germany, and *ITMA* took full advantage. In the first wartime episode, Handley referenced *Mein Kampf*, Joseph Goebbels and the goose step within the first thirty-five words. Mostly, though, the humour was aimed at the interfering busybodies and pettifogging bureaucrats who were starting to proliferate. Handley was the Minister of Aggravation and Mysteries, locking horns with the Ministry of Mothballs, the Ministry of Mis-Construction and the Office of Internal Disintegration. 'I'll sign everything that prohibits anything. That's what I'm here for,' he declared. 'I, the Minister of Aggravation, have power to confiscate, complicate and commandeer.'

Laughing at authority wasn't the most obvious way of building national unity at a time of peril, but the illogical and unpredictable system of censorship in Britain allowed for such humour. The first wartime *ITMA* script was submitted and, said Kavanagh, 'came back stamped in red "PROGRAMME CENSORED", without a single word deleted or altered'.[23] And, of course, the show did make a major contribution to the war effort. The targets were instantly recognisable and the jokes acted as a safety valve for public frustration. By the time of its fourth series, broadcast in 1941, *ITMA* was attracting an audience of sixteen million, the most popular variety show the BBC had ever produced, and Handley was as big a radio star as anyone would ever be.

---

* The catchphrases multiplied over the show's run and many passed into common usage: 'Can I do you now, sir?'; 'It's being so cheerful as keeps me going'; 'This is Funf speaking'; 'Most irregular, most irregular'; 'Don't forget the diver'; 'I don't mind if I do'; 'Friday? Friday!'; 'After you, Claude – No, after you, Cecil'; 'I go – I come back'; 'TTFN' (ta-ta for now).

There were still restrictions on what the BBC deemed suitable for broadcast. On another show, comedian Tommy Trinder had one of his gags banned, a joke about a man walking down White-hall and asking a passer-by which side of the road the War Office was on. 'Ours, I hope,' was the reply.[24] But the fact remained that Britain was very different to most of Europe, to – in the words of novelist James Hilton, bestselling author of *Lost Horizon* and *Goodbye, Mr Chips* – 'the polychromed shirtwearers of the Continent who not only cannot laugh but dare not allow laughter'.[25]

None of the dictatorships would have permitted Billy Russell to guy Air Raid Precaution wardens as 'those RIP chaps'.[26] Nor would they have tolerated Robb Wilton, whose bumbling logic, delivered in a slow Lancashire accent, gently ridiculed the very idea of home defence: 'The Missus said, she said, "Well, what do you *do* in the Home Guards?" I said, "I've got to stop Hitler's army landing." She said, "What, *you*?" I said, "No, there's Harry Bates and Charlie Evans," I said. "There's seven or eight of us altogether..."'[27]

That spirit of irreverence was integral to British culture. More than that, it was seen as integral to the cause of freedom in this age of dictators. One of the most popular fictional characters in the immediate post-war years had been Bindle, an easy-going, easy-drinking cockney created by Herbert Jenkins in 1916, a man much given to malapropisms, practical jokes and homespun philosophy. Bindle had been rejected for service in the Great War on medical grounds (he had 'various veins'), but he knew why Britain was fighting. 'We got a fine ole country and a good king, an' we can tell a archbishop to go to 'ell if we want to wi'out gettin' pinched for it,' he explains to his mates; 'an' when yer got all them things – an' there ain't no other country wot 'as – then it's worth 'avin' a scrap now an' then to keep 'em.'*

Despite all the changes that had come to the country in the

---

* After his debut in *Bindle* (1916), a further four volumes of his adventures followed, as well as six silent movies (all 1926), and *The Temperance Fete* (1932), the latter with George Robey in his first talkie.

years since the Armistice, that remained an article of faith for the British people. The impertinence of Tommy Handley, thumbing his nose at officialdom, was an expression of liberty. And that was worth fighting for.

That first wartime series of *ITMA* ended in February 1940, with Tommy Handley singing 'We'll Meet Again', a song that had been first heard the previous December on a record by Vera Lynn, accompanied by Arthur Young on the Novachord.* The show then went out on tour around the variety theatres. By the time it returned to radio the following year, the country felt very different, reshaped by Dunkirk, the Battle of Britain, the Blitz.

During the years of peace, the British tendency to stand apart, aloof even, from Europe had been much criticised by those who inclined towards internationalism and progress. There was insufficient commitment to the League of Nations; Britain was smug and arrogant in its assumption of superiority; its culture was parochial and backward, always looking to the glories of the past rather than facing the challenges of modernism and modernity. But in June 1940, as France fell under Nazi occupation, just as Austria, Belgium, Czechoslovakia and others had fallen – as Greece, Hungary, Ukraine and more would later fall – in such a context, that separation was looking priceless, keeping alive a flicker of hope that European civilisation might yet survive.

With the surrender of France, only Britain and its empire were left in the arena, facing both Nazi Germany and Fascist Italy. David Low's cartoon in the *Evening Standard* showed a Tommy on the cliffs of Dover, surrounded by stormy seas, raising a defiant fist to incoming bombers. 'Very well, alone,' ran the caption, and the sentiment was echoed elsewhere. 'Well, we fight alone,' wrote the *Daily Mirror*'s star columnist Cassandra. 'We alone defend the conscience of the world.'[28]

---

* The first polyphonic synthesiser on the market, described in the press as 'an electrical musical instrument which looks like a piano, but can simulate the sound of almost every other instrument'. 'We'll Meet Again' was Britain's first electronic hit.

At the Trocadero, the Renaissance-themed cinema in Elephant and Castle, south London, a matinee screening of the newly released comedy *Old Mother Riley in Society* was interrupted. The film stopped, the house lights came up, and Denis Norden, the gangly eighteen-year-old assistant manager, ventured out on stage. 'Ladies and gentlemen, I have to inform you that France has fallen,' he announced with all the solemnity he could muster. 'Britain is now fighting the war alone.' A shocked silence descended on the auditorium, as the enormity of the situation sank in. Then came a shout from the back: 'Put the bleeding picture back on.'[29]

Meanwhile, film-maker George Pearson, now working on wartime documentaries for the GPO Film Unit, was in a village pub and overheard a group of labourers talking about the fall of France. The discussion was concluded by an old farmhand. 'Well, now we know where we are,' he said. 'Give me another pint, Joe.'[30]

FICTION AND FILMS

The following novels were read, and films watched, in the preparation of this book.

Fiction

Margery Allingham, *Police at the Funeral* (William Heinemann, 1931).

——, *Sweet Danger* (William Heinemann, 1933).

——, *Dancers in Mourning* (William Heinemann, 1936).

——, *The Fashion in Shrouds* (William Heinemann, 1938).

Eric Ambler, *The Dark Frontier* (Hodder & Stoughton, 1936).

——, *The Mask of Dimitrios* (Hodder & Stoughton, 1939).

Michael Arlen, *The Green Hat* (William Collins Sons, 1924).

Enid Bagnold, *National Velvet* (William Heinemann, 1935).

Margaret Baillie-Saunders, *Herself MP* (Hutchinson, 1928).

Beachcomber (J. B. Morton), *Mr Thake: His Life and Letters* (Geoffrey Bles, 1929).

Francis Beeding, *The One Sane Man* (Hodder & Stoughton, 1934).

——, *The Eight Crooked Trenches* (Hodder & Stoughton, 1938).

E. F. Benson, *Miss Mapp* (Hutchinson, 1922).

——, *The Inheritor* (Hutchinson, 1930).

Reginald Berkeley, *Cassandra* (Victor Gollancz, 1931).

Nicholas Blake, *Thou Shell of Death* (Collins, 1936).

Lynn Brock, *The Deductions of Col. Gore* (William Collins Sons, 1924).

John Buchan, *The Thirty-Nine Steps* (William Blackwood, 1915).

——, *Greenmantle* (Hodder & Stoughton, 1916).

——, *Mr Standfast* (Hodder & Stoughton, 1919).

——, *Huntingtower* (Hodder & Stoughton, 1922).

——, *The Three Hostages* (Hodder & Stoughton, 1924).

——, *The Dancing Floor* (Hodder & Stoughton, 1926).

——, *The House of the Four Winds* (Hodder & Stoughton, 1935).

John Bude, *The Lake District Murder* (Skeffington & Son, 1935).

——, *The Cornish Coast Murder* (Skeffington & Son, 1935).

——, *The Sussex Downs Murder* (Skeffington & Son, 1936).

Leslie Charteris, *The Happy Highwayman* (Hodder & Stoughton, 1933).

——, *The Saint Goes On* (Hodder & Stoughton, 1934).

James Hadley Chase, *No Orchids for Miss Blandish* (Robert Hale, 1939).

Peter Cheyney, *Don't Get Me Wrong* (William Collins Sons, 1939).

Agatha Christie, *The Mysterious Affair at Styles* (John Lane, 1920).

——, *The Secret Adversary* (Bodley Head, 1922).

——, *The Man In the Brown Suit* (Bodley Head, 1924).

——, *The Murder of Roger Ackroyd* (William Collins Sons, 1926).

——, *The Big Four* (William Collins Sons, 1927).

——, *The Thirteen Problems* (Collins, 1932).

——, *One, Two, Buckle My Shoe* (William Collins Sons, 1940).

Joan Conquest, *Desert Love* (Werner Laurie, 1920).

John Creasey, *Introducing the Toff* (Long, 1938).

Freeman Wills Croft, *Mystery In the Channel* (William Collins Sons, 1931).

——, *The 12.30 from Croydon* (Hodder & Stoughton, 1934).

Aleister Crowley, *Diary of a Drug Fiend* (Collins, 1922).

Warwick Deeping, *Kitty* (Cassell, 1927).

O. Douglas, *Penny Plain* (Hodder & Stoughton, 1920).

Arthur Conan Doyle, *His Last Bow: Some Reminiscences of Sherlock Holmes* (John Murray, 1917).

——, *The Land of Mist* (Hutchinson & Co., 1926).

John Drinkwater, *Oliver Cromwell* (Sidgwick & Jackson, 1921).

J. Jefferson Farjeon, *Mystery in White: A Christmas Crime Story* (Collins, 1937).

John Ferguson, *Stealthy Terror* (John Lane, 1917).

W. B. M. Ferguson, *Crackerjack* (John Long, 1936).

E. M. Forster, *A Passage to India* (Edward Arnold, 1924).

S. Fowler-Wright, *The Island of Captain Sparrow* (Victor Gollancz, 1928).

John Galsworthy, *To Let* (William Heinemann, 1921).

W. L. George, *The Confession of Ursula Trent* (Chapman & Hall, 1921).

Bruce Graeme, *Blackshirt* (T. Fisher Unwin, 1925).

——, *The Return of Blackshirt* (Ernest Benn, 1927).

Graham Greene, *Brighton Rock* (William Heinemann, 1938).

Hubert Griffith, *Tunnel Trench* (Allen & Unwin, 1924).

Radclyffe Hall, *The Well of Loneliness* (Jonathan Cape, 1928).

Mavis Doriel Hay, *Murder Underground* (Skeffington & Son, 1934).

——, *The Santa Klaus Murder* (Skeffington & Son, 1936).

Georgette Heyer, *Footsteps in the Dark* (Longmans, 1932).

——, *Death in the Stocks* (Longmans, Green & Co., 1935).

James Hilton, *Lost Horizon* (Macmillan, 1933).

——, *Goodbye, Mr Chips* (Hodder & Stoughton, 1934).

——, *We Are Not Alone* (Macmillan & Co., 1937).

——, *To You, Mr Chips* (Hodder & Stoughton, 1938).

Sydney Horler, *Tiger Standish* (John Long, 1932).

——, *Tiger Standish Comes Back* (Hutchinson, 1934).

Geoffrey Household, *Rogue Male* (Chatto & Windus, 1939).

Aldous Huxley, *Crome Yellow* (Chatto & Windus, 1921).

——, *Antic Hay* (Chatto & Windus, 1923).

——, *Point Counter Point* (Chatto & Windus, 1928).

——, *Brave New World* (Chatto & Windus, 1932).

Michael Innes, *Hamlet, Revenge!* (Gollancz, 1937).

Herbert Jenkins, *Bindle: Some Chapters in the Life of Joseph Bindle* (Herbert Jenkins, 1916).

James Joyce, *Ulysses* (Shakespeare & Company, 1922).

D. H. Lawrence, *Lady Chatterley's Lover* (Tipografia Giuntina, 1928).

Rosamund Lehmann, *Dusty Answer* (Chatto & Windus, 1927).

A. G. Macdonell, *England, Their England* (Macmillan, 1933).

——, *Lords and Masters* (Macmillan, 1936).

Ngaio Marsh, *A Man Lay Dead* (William Collins Sons, 1934).

——, *Death in a White Tie* (Geoffrey Bles, 1938).

A. E. W. Mason, *The Prisoner in the Opal* (Hodder & Stoughton, 1928).

Nancy Mitford, *Highland Fling* (Thornton Butterworth, 1931).

R. H. Mottram, *The English Miss* (Chatto & Windus, 1928).

George Orwell, *Keep the Aspidistra Flying* (Victor Gollancz, 1936).

——, *Coming Up for Air* (Victor Gollancz, 1939).

John Cowper Powys, *A Glastonbury Romance* (Simon & Schuster, 1932).

Terence Rattigan, *After the Dance* (first staged 1939).

Harriet Rutland, *Knock, Murderer, Knock!* (Skeffington & Son, 1938).

Sapper (Herman McNeile), *Bulldog Drummond* (Hodder & Stoughton, 1920).

——, *The Black Gang* (Hodder & Stoughton, 1922).

——, *Jim Maitland* (Hodder & Stoughton, 1923).

Dorothy L. Sayers, *Clouds of Witness* (T. Fisher Unwin, 1926).

——, *The Unpleasantness at the Bellona Club* (Ernest Benn, 1928).

——, *Murder Must Advertise* (Victor Gollancz, 1933).

May Sinclair, *Life and Death of Harriett Frean* (Macmillan, 1922).

Olaf Stapledon, *Odd John* (Methuen, 1935).

G. H. Teed, *The Black Eagle* (*Union Jack*, 1923) – collected in David Stuart Davies (ed.), *The Casebook of Sexton Blake* (Wordsworth Editions, 2009).

Josephine Tey (originally published as by Gordon Daviot), *The Man in the Queue* (Peter Davies, 1929).

Emily Temple Thurston, from the play by Ernest Temple Thurston, *The Wandering Jew* (Putnam, 1934).

Barbara Euphan Todd, *Worzel Gummidge Again* (Burns Oates, 1937).

Basil Tozer, *The Story of a Terrible Life: The Amazing Career of a Notorious Procuress* (T. Werner Laurie, 1928).

Edgar Wallace, *Jack O' Judgment* (Ward, Lock & Co., 1920)

——, *The Mind of Mr. J. G. Reeder* (Hodder & Stoughton, 1925).

Evelyn Waugh, *Decline and Fall* (Chapman & Hall, 1928).

——, *Vile Bodies* (Chapman & Hall, 1930).

——, *Scoop* (Chapman & Hall, 1938).

Dennis Wheatley, *The Devil Rides Out* (Hutchinson & Co., 1934).

T. H. White, *Farewell Victoria* (Collins, 1934).

——, *The Sword in the Stone* (Collins, 1938).

Ellen Wilkinson, *The Division Bell Mystery* (George G. Harrap, 1932).

Valentine Williams (originally published as by Douglas Valentine), *The Man with the Clubfoot* (Herbert Jenkins, 1918).

P. G. Wodehouse, *The Inimitable Jeeves* (Herbert Jenkins, 1923).

——, *Meet Mr Mulliner* (Herbert Jenkins, 1927).

——, *The Code of the Woosters* (Herbert Jenkins, 1938).

Virginia Woolf, *Orlando: A Biography* (Hogarth Press, 1928).

P. C. Wren, *Beau Geste* (John Murray, 1924).

E. H. Young, *Miss Mole* (Jonathan Cape, 1930).

Films

The Amateur Gentleman (Thornton Freeland, Criterion Films, 1936).

Big Fella (J. Elder Wills, British Lion, 1937).

Blackmail (Alfred Hitchcock, British International Pictures, 1929).

Blighty (Adrian Brunel, Gainsborough Pictures, 1927).

Bulldog Drummond (F. Richard Jones, Samuel Goldwyn Productions, 1929).

Bulldog Jack (Walter Forde, Gaumont-British, 1935).

The Camels Are Coming (Tim Whelan, Gainsborough Pictures, 1934).

Champagne (Alfred Hitchcock, British International Pictures, 1928).

The Constant Nymph (Adrian Brunel, Gainsborough Pictures, 1928).

Crackerjack (Albert de Courville, Gainsborough Pictures, 1938).

Crime Unlimited (Ralph Ince, First National, 1935).

Crown v. Stevens (Michael Powell, First National, 1936).

A Cuckoo in the Nest (Tom Walls, Gaumont-British, 1933).
The Dark Eyes of London (Walter Summers, John Argyle Productions, 1939).
Death at Broadcasting House (Reginald Denham, Phoenix Films, 1934).
Dishonour Bright (Tom Walls, Cecil Films, 1936).
The Divorce of Lady X (Tim Whelan, London Films, 1938).
Doctor Syn (Roy William Neill, British Gaumont, 1937).
Downhill (Alfred Hitchcock, Gainsborough Pictures, 1927).
Drake of England (Arthur B. Woods, British International Pictures, 1935).
The Drum (Zoltán Korda, London Films, 1938).
Elephant Boy (Robert J. Flaherty & Zoltán Korda, London Films, 1937).
Elstree Calling (Adrian Brunel, British International Pictures, 1930).
Evergreen (Victor Saville, Gaumont-British, 1934).
Everything Is Thunder (Milton Rosmer, Gaumont-British, 1936).
The Face at the Window (George King, George King Productions, 1939).
Falling for You (Robert Stevenson & Jack Hulbert, Gainsborough Pictures, 1933).
Fire Over England (William K. Howard, London Film Productions, 1937).
First a Girl (Victor Saville, Gaumont-British, 1935).
The Four Feathers (Zoltán Korda, London Films, 1939).
The Four Just Men (Walter Forde, ABFD, 1939).
Friday the Thirteenth (Victor Saville, Gainsborough Pictures, 1933).
Girls Will Be Boys (Marcel Varnel, British International Pictures, 1934).
The Green Cockatoo (William Cameron Menzies, Devonshire Films, 1937).
High Treason (Maurice Elvey, Gaumont-British, 1929).
His Lordship Regrets (Maclean Rogers, RKO Pictures, 1938).
I Was a Spy (Victor Saville, Gaumont-British, 1933).
Inquest (Roy Boulting, Charter Films, 1939).
Inspector Hornleigh (Eugene Forde, Twentieth Century Fox, 1938).
The Iron Duke (Victor Saville, Gaumont-British, 1934).
Jack's the Boy (Walter Forde, Gainsborough Pictures, 1932).
Jack of All Trades (Robert Stevenson & Jack Hulbert, Gainsborough Pictures, 1936).
Jericho (Thornton Freeland, Buckingham Films, 1937).
Kate Plus Ten (Reginald Denham, Richard Wainwright Productions, 1938).
Kitty (Victor Saville, Burlington Films, 1929).
The Lady Vanishes (Alfred Hitchcock, Gainsborough Pictures, 1938).
Little Friend (Berthold Viertel, Gaumont-British, 1934).
The Lodger: A Story of the London Fog (Alfred Hitchcock, Gainsborough Pictures, 1927).
Love from a Stranger (Rowland V. Lee, Trafalgar Films, 1937).

Man of the Moment (Monty Banks, First National Pictures, 1935).
The Man Without Desire (Adrian Brunel, Atlas Biocraft, 1923).
The Man Who Changed His Mind (Robert Stevenson, Gainsborough Pictures, 1936).
The Man Who Could Work Miracles (Lothar Mendes, London Films, 1937).
The Man Who Knew too Much (Alfred Hitchcock, Gaumont-British, 1934).
Maria Marten, or The Murder in the Red Barn (Milton Rosmer, George King Productions, 1935).
Me and Marlborough (Victor Saville, Gaumont-British, 1935).
Men Are Not Gods (Walter Reisch, British Lion Film Corporation, 1936).
Moscow Nights (Anthony Asquith, Denham Films/London Films, 1935).
Music Hall (John Baxter, Real Art Productions, 1934).
My Old Dutch (Sinclair Hill, Gainsborough Pictures, 1934).
Nell Gwyn (Herbert Wilcox, British National Pictures, 1926).
The Night of the Party (Michael Powell, Gaumont-British, 1934).
Off the Dole (Arthur Mertz, Mancunian Film Company, 1935).
Oh, Mr Porter (Marcel Varnel, Gainsborough Pictures, 1938).
O-Kay for Sound (Marcel Varnel, Gainsborough Pictures, 1937).
Old Mother Riley (Oswald Mitchell, Butcher's Film Service, 1937).
Over the Moon (Thornton Freeland, London Films, 1939).
The Passing of the Third Floor Back (Berthold Viertel, Gaumont-British, 1935).
The Phantom Light (Michael Powell, Gainsborough Pictures, 1935).
The Private Life of Don Juan (Alexander Korda, London Films, 1934).
The Private Life of Henry VIII (Alexander Korda, London Films, 1933).
Public Nuisance No. 1 (Marcel Varnel, Cecil Films, 1936).
The Rat (Graham Cutts, Gainsborough Pictures, 1925).
The Right Age to Marry (Maclean Rogers, George Smith Productions, 1935).
Road House (Maurice Elvey, Gaumont-British, 1934).
Sabotage (Alfred Hitchcock, Gaumont-British, 1936).
St Martin's Lane (Tim Whelan, Mayflower Pictures, 1938).
Sanders of the River (Zoltán Korda, London Films, 1935).
The Scarlet Pimpernel (Harold Young, London Films, 1934).
Schichlegruber Doing the Lambeth Walk (Charles A. Ridley, Ministry of Information, 1942).
Scrooge (Henry Edwards, Twickenham Film Studios, 1935).
Service for Ladies (Alexander Korda, Paramount British Pictures, 1932).
Seven Sinners (Albert de Courville, Gaumont-British, 1936).
Sexton Blake and the Hooded Terror (George King, George King Productions, 1938).
The Silent Passenger (Reginald Denham, Phoenix Films, 1935).

Silver Blaze (Thomas Bentley, Twickenham Film Distributors, 1937).

Sleeping Car (Anatole Litvak, Gaumont-British, 1933).

The Sleeping Cardinal (Leslie S. Hiscott, Twickenham Studios, 1931).

Something Always Happens (Michael Powell, Warner Brothers/First National Productions, 1934).

Song of Freedom (J. Edgar Wills, Hammer Films, 1936).

The Speckled Band (Jack Raymond, British & Dominions Film Corporation, 1931).

Storm in a Teacup (Ian Dalrymple & Victor Savile, London Films, 1937).

The Tell Tale Heart (Brian Desmond Hurst, Blattner Studios, 1934).

There Goes the Bride (Albert de Courville, Gainsborough Pictures, 1932).

They Drive by Night (Arthur B. Woods, Warner Brothers/First National Productions, 1938).

Things Are Looking Up (Albert de Courville, Gaumont-British, 1935).

Things to Come (Alexander Korda, London Films, 1936).

This Man Is News (David MacDonald, Paramount British Pictures, 1938).

Thunder in the City (Marion Gering, Atlantic Film Company, 1937).

Trunk Crime (Roy Boulting, Charter Films, 1939).

Tudor Rose (Robert Stevenson, Gaumont-British, 1936).

The Tunnel (Maurice Elvey, Gaumont-British, 1935).

Vessel of Wrath (Erich Pommer, Mayflower Pictures, 1938).

Victoria the Great (Herbert Wilcox, Imperator Film Productions, 1937).

Walter Finds a Father (Joseph Jay Bamberger & William Bowman, Zodiac Films, 1921).

Young and Innocent (Alfred Hitchcock, Gaumont-British, 1937).

REFERENCES

1   Arthur Conan Doyle, 'His Last Bow: the War Service of Sherlock Holmes', *His Last Bow*.

2   Ellen Wilkinson, *The Division Bell Mystery* Chapter 17.

Prologue

1   John Drinkwater, *Oliver Cromwell* p. 24.

2   Herbert Rule, Fred Holt & George Carney, 'Stony Broke in No Man's Land' (Chas Austin Music Publishing, 1921).

3   *Times* 7 November 1919.

4   *Dundee Courier* 12 November 1919.

5   *Manchester Guardian* 12 November 1919;

6   *Yorkshire Post and Leeds Intelligencer* 12 November 1919.

7   *Hull Daily Mail* 12 November 1919.

8   Ibid.

9   *Sheffield Independent* 12 November 1919.

10 *Evening Mail* 12 November 1919.

11 *Essex Newsman* 15 November 1919.

12 *Cheshire Observer* 15 November 1919.

13 *Lincolnshire Echo* 12 November 1919.

14 *Tewkesbury Register* 12 January 1918.

15 *Birmingham Daily Gazette* 7 January 1920.

16 *Daily Mirror* 28 February 1919.

17 *Hampshire Advertiser* 18 January 1919.

18 *Sketch* 16 September 1925

19 *Western Mail* 26 November 1921.

20 *Daily News* (London) 3 March 1925.

21 *Observer* 4 May 1924.

22 John Buchan, *The Dancing Floor* Chapter 3.

23 *Dundee Courier* 11 November 1936.

24 *Sunday Post* 3 January 1926.

25 Harry Lauder & William Dillon, 'The End of the Road' (Zonophone, 1924).
26 *Graphic* 13 April 1929.
27 *Lewisham Borough News* 23 April 1930.
28 *Derby Daily Telegraph* 24 April 1930.
29 Stuart Ball & Ian Holliday (eds), *Conservatives and the Public Since the 1880s* (Routledge, 2013) p. 49.
30 *Sunday Sun* (Newcastle) 3 June 1934
31 *Liverpool Echo* 16 November 1936.
32 *Daily Herald* 19 February 1934.
33 *Daily Mirror* 15 July 1936.
34 *Aberdeen Press and Journal* 28 December 1932.
35 *Cornishman* 8 February 1934.
36 *Western Mail* 2 November 1925.
37 *Aberdeen Press and Journal* 22 September 1925.
38 *Manchester Evening News* 5 November 1926.
39 *Grimsby Daily Telegraph* 6 November 1926
40 Dennis Bardens, *Famous Cases of Norman Birkett K.C.* (Robert Hale, 1963) p. 44.
41 *Westminster Gazette* 24 March 1927.
42 David Hendy, *The BBC: A People's History* (Profile Books, 2022) p. 156.
43 Melba Cuddy-Keane, *Virginia Woolf, the Intellectual and the Public Sphere* (Cambridge University Press, 2003) p. 19.
44 *Daily Mirror* 31 October 1930.
45 *Marylebone Mercury* 25 July 1925.

1: Sickness and Cures

1   Arthur Conan Doyle, *The Land of Mist* Chapter 2.
2   P. C. Wren, *Beau Geste* Part 2 Chapter 2.
3   Arthur Mee, *Enchanted Land: Half-a-Million Miles in the King's England* (Hodder & Stoughton, 1936) p. 144.
4   *Northern Whig* 20 August 1923.
5   *Diss Express* 19 July 1918.
6   *Hull Daily Mail* 28 June 1918.
7   *Birmingham Mail* 29 June 1918.
8   *Leinster Reporter* 13 July 1918.
9   *Daily Mirror* 24 June 1918.
10 *Daily Record* 3 July 1918.
11 *Middlesex County Times* 8 October 1919.
12 *Times* 31 January 1919.

13 Lew Brown, Robert King & Ray Henderson, 'Why Did I Kiss that Girl?' (Keith Prowse & Co. Ltd, 1924).

14 *Times* 18 December 1918.

15 *Gloucestershire Echo* 10 May 1919.

16 *Sheffield Daily Telegraph* 26 November 1927.

17 Ibid. 8 March 1921.

18 *Hull Daily Mail* 2 December 1921.

19 Matthew Engel, *Tickle the Public: One Hundred Years of the Popular Press* (Victor Gollancz, 1996) p. 102.

20 *South Gloucestershire Gazette* 4 March 1922.

21 *Times* 9 June 1921; Paul Ferris, *Sex and the British: A Twentieth-Century History* (Michael Joseph, 1993) pp. 77–8.

22 *Westminster Gazette* 7 June 1921.

23 Asa Briggs, *A Social History of England* (Weidenfeld & Nicolson, 1983 – revised edition: Pelican 1987) p. 306.

24 *Daily Herald* 27 September 1924.

25 *Nottingham and Midland Catholic News* 19 February 1927.

26 *Coventry Evening Telegraph* 13 November 1930.

27 *Sunderland Daily Echo and Shipping Gazette* 24 October 1929.

28 *Derby Daily Telegraph* 12 July 1920; *London Daily Chronicle* 11 July 1929.

29 *Gloucester Citizen* 20 January 1930.

30 *Daily News* (London) 5 February 1929.

31 *London Daily Chronicle* 3 February 1930.

32 *Daily Express* 12 November 1919.

33 *Western Daily Press* 24 October 1923; *Dundee Courier* 19 October 1923.

34 *Birmingham Weekly Mercury* 16 February 1930.

35 Ibid.; *People* 5 October 1930.

36 *Birmingham Weekly Mercury* 25 January 1931.

37 Montague Summers, *The Geography of Witchcraft* (Kegan Paul, 1927) p. 184.

38 *Sketch* 22 October 1919.

39 Jeremy Lewis, *Cyril Connolly: A Life* (Jonathan Cape, 1997) p. 143.

40 *Nottingham and Midland Catholic News* 26 August 1922.

41 K. Wingfield, *Guidance from Beyond* (Philip Allan & Co., 1923) p. 105.

42 Ibid. p. 20.

43 Arthur Conan Doyle, *The Sign of the Four* (Spencer Blackett, 1890) Chapter 2.

44 *Westminster Gazette* 12 January 1921.

45 *Dundee Courier* 1 June 1933.

46   *Nairnshire Telegraph and General Advertiser for the Northern Counties* 11 July 1933.

47   *Edinburgh Evening News* 20 October 1933.

48   *Sunday Express*, 24 August 1930.

49   *Dudley Chronicle* 1 December 1932; *Cornish Guardian* 4 June 1931.

50   *Sheffield Independent* 6 April 1923.

51   *Belfast Telegraph* 20 March 1923.

52   *Grimsby Daily Telegraph* 3 February 1936.

53   *Truth* 12 February 1936.

54   *John Bull* 17 April 1937.

55   Robert Graves & Alan Hodge, *The Long Week-End: A Social History of Great Britain 1918–1939* (Faber & Faber, 1940) p. 15.

56   *Daily News* (London) 10 August 1922.

57   *Belfast Telegraph* 3 March 1923.

58   *Dumfries and Galloway Standard* 25 March 1939.

59   *North Wilts Herald* 12 April 1935.

60   *Daily News* (London) 27 November 1929.

61   *Sphere* 28 October 1922.

62   *Northern Whig* 6 June 1933.

63   Charles Fort, *The Book of the Damned* (Boni & Liveright, 1919) Chapter 2.

64   *Graphic* Saturday 30 May 1931.

65   *Western Mail* 25 June 1921.

66   Ibid. 2 November 1921.

67   *Liverpool Echo* 1 November 1921.

68   *Lancashire Evening Post* 12 September & 24 October 1924.

69   *Westminster Gazette* 16 May 1924.

70   Ethel Mannin, *Confessions and Impressions* (Jarrolds, 1930) pp. 121–2.

71   *Daily News* (London) 11 & 12 August 1927.

72   Gary D. Schmidt, *Hugh Lofting* (Twayne, 1992) p. 6.

73   *Nottingham Evening Post* 10 December 1929.

74   *Westminster Gazette* 2 December 1927.

75   *Aberdeen Press and Journal* 8 November 1932.

76   Ibid. 13 December 1928.

77   *Illustrated London News* 20 October 1928.

78   Richard S. Grayson, 'The British Government and the Channel Tunnel, 1919–39', *Journal of Contemporary History* Vol. 31 No. 1 (1996) p. 127.

79   Ibid. p. 129.

80   Ibid. p. 125.

81 *Oxford Chronicle and Reading Gazette* 23 March 1923; *Nottingham Evening Post* 27 April 1923; *West Bridgford Advertiser* 28 April 1923.

82 *People* 29 April 1923; *Sphere* 5 May 1923.

83 *Gloucestershire Echo* 24 September 1924.

84 *Western Morning News* 3 November 1925

85 *Roscommon Herald* 15 November 1924.

86 *Gloucester Journal* 8 November 1924.

2: Rebellions and Reassurance

1 John Buchan, *The Three Hostages* Chapter 4.

2 R. P. Weston & Bert Lee, 'She Was Poor But She Was Honest' (Regal Records, 1930).

3 *Acton Gazette* 27 November 1914.

4 *Justice* 24 July 1919.

5 *Dortmunder General-Anzeiger*, reported *Globe* 30 August 1919.

6 *Lancashire Evening Post* 30 June 1919.

7 *Graphic* 10 May 1919.

8 *Yarmouth Independent* 4 January 1919.

9 *Manchester Guardian* 21 July 1919.

10 *Western Daily Press* 21 July 1919.

11 *Manchester Guardian* 21 July 1919.

12 *Dundee Courier* 5 August 1919.

13 *Evening Telegraph* 22 July 1919.

14 *Derby Daily Telegraph* 23 July 1919.

15 Lucas Chancel, Thomas Piketty, Emmanuel Saez & Gabriel Zucman, *World Inequality Report 2022* (World Inequality Lab, 2021) p. 223.

16 *Dundee Courier* 6 December 1918.

17 Robert J. Scally, *The Origins of the Lloyd George Coalition: The Politics of Social-Imperialism 1900–1918* (Princeton University Press, 1975) p. 354.

18 *People* 18 May 1924.

19 Aneurin Bevan, *In Place of Fear* (William Heinemann, 1952) pp. 20–21.

20 Robert Rhodes James, *The British Revolution Volume 2: From Asquith to Chamberlain 1914–89* (Hamish Hamilton, 1977) p. 153.

21 Allen Hutt, *British Trade Unionism: A Short History* (Lawrence & Wishart, 1941 – revised and enlarged edition 1974) p. 96.

22 *Times* 30 May 1919.

23 Manny Shinwell, *Lead with the Left: My First Ninety-Six Years* (Cassell, 1981) p. 66.

24 Allen Hutt, *British Trade Unionism: A Short History* (Lawrence & Wishart, 1941 – revised and enlarged edition 1974) p. 85.

25 Edward Scobie, *Black Britannia: A History of Blacks in Britain* (Johnson Publishing Company Inc., 1972) p. 158.

26 *Dundee Courier* 13 June 1919.

27 *Times* 5 August 1919.

28 *Aberdeen Press and Journal* 5 April 1920.

29 *Tamworth Herald* 27 September 1919.

30 *Western Daily Press* 30 December 1919.

31 *Irish Times* 1 May 1920.

32 Hansard 14 December 1921.

33 Ibid.

34 *Times* 14 December 1926.

35 Ibid. 6 October 1921.

36 *Hampshire Independent* 14 October 1921.

37 *Times* 17 October 1930.

38 *Daily Echo* (Northampton) 6 November 1925.

39 *Lancashire Evening Post* 17 October 1929.

40 Alan Jenkins, *The Twenties* (William Heinemann, 1974) p. 86.

41 *Newcastle Daily Chronicle* 4 December 1931.

42 Lord Longford, *Avowed Intent: An Autobiography* (Little, Brown & Co., 1994) p. 52.

43 *Western Times* 26 October 1923.

44 A. J. P. Taylor, *English History 1914–1945* (Oxford University Press, 1965) p. 205.

45 Matthew Parris, *Great Parliamentary Scandals: Four Centuries of Calumny, Smear and Innuendo* (Robson Books, 1997) p. 93.

46 *Forward* (Glasgow) 10 November 1917; *Carluke and Lanark Gazette* 8 June 1918.

47 Parris, *Great Parliamentary Scandals* p. 95.

48 James, *The British Revolution Volume 2* p. 163.

49 Hansard 16 February 1923.

50 Malcolm Pearce & Geoffrey Stewart, *British Political History 1867–1995: Democracy and Decline* (Routledge, 1992 – 2nd edition, 1996) p. 392.

51 *Daily Herald* 31 July 1920.

52 *Communist* (London) 20 January 1921.

53 *Globe* 8 November 1920; *Pall Mall Gazette* 12 November 1920.

54 *Communist* (London) 20 January 1921.

55 Andrew Thorpe, 'The Membership of the Communist Party of Great Britain, 1920–1945', *Historical Journal* Vol. 43 No. 3 (2000).

56 *Exeter and Plymouth Gazette* 10 January 1921.

57 *Scotsman* 23 August 1920.

58   *London Daily Chronicle* 21 July 1924.
59   *Workers' Dreadnought* 7 August 1920.
60   *Sheffield Daily Telegraph* 18 January 1924.
61   *Halifax Evening Courier* 8 December 1923.
62   Shinwell, *Lead with the Left* p. 81.
63   *Cornishman* 8 October 1924.
64   David Marquand, *Britain since 1918: The Strange Career of British Democracy* (Wiedenfeld & Nicolson, 2008) p. 84.
65   Quoted *Exeter and Plymouth Gazette* 13 September 1924.
66   *Suffolk and Essex Free Press* 25 September 1924.
67   Shinwell, *Lead with the Left* p. 86.
68   Matthew Engel, *Tickle the Public: One Hundred Years of the Popular Press* (Victor Gollancz, 1996) p. 103.
69   Ibid. p. 103.
70   *Nottingham and Midland Catholic News* 29 November 1924.
71   Maurice Cowling, *The Impact of Labour, 1920–1924: The Beginning of Modern British Politics* (Cambridge University Press, 1971) p. 359.
72   Kevin Hickson (ed.), *The Political Thought of the Conservative Party since 1945* (Palgrave Macmillan, 2005) p. 71.
73   *Oxford Chronicle and Reading Gazette* 1 February 1924.

3: Sound and Vision

1   *Manchester Guardian* 28 April 1932.
2   *Holyhead Mail and Anglesey Herald* 5 June 1925.
3   *Morning Leader* 26 October 1906.
4   Sam Mayo & Worton David, 'I Can't Forget the Days When I Was Young' (J. Albert & Son, 1917).
5   *Kensington Post* 15 September 1922.
6   *Western Gazette* 20 October 1922.
7   *Sheffield Independent* 13 October 1922.
8   *Daily News* (London) 9 October 1922.
9   *Pall Mall Gazette* 9 October 1922.
10   *Sunday Illustrated* 8 October 1922.
11   *Dial* Vol. 73 No. 6, December 1922.
12   *Edinburgh Evening News* 9 October 1922.
13   *Westminster Gazette* 9 October 1922.
14   *Birmingham Daily Gazette* 9 October 1922.
15   *Weekly Dispatch* (London) 29 June 1919.
16   Henry Hall, *Here's to the Next Time* (Odhams Press, 1955) p. 41.

17   *Aberdeen Press and Journal* 6 November 1926.

18   Flotsam & Jetsam, 'Only a Few of Us Left' (Columbia Records, 1928).

19   *Huddersfield Daily Examiner* 6 January 1928.

20   *Daily News* (London) 25 February 1926.

21   *Illustrated Sporting and Dramatic News* 27 December 1921.

22   *Kentish Express* 9 April 1927.

23   *Daily Mirror* 11 May 1928.

24   *Bioscope* 29 March 1928.

25   Ibid. 8 August 1928.

26   H. Llewellyn Smith (ed.), *New Survey of London Life and Labour: Volume I: Forty Years of Change* (King, 1930) p. 291.

27   *Times* 12 April 1913.

28   *Bioscope* 20 April 1916.

29   *Pall Mall Gazette* 29 September 1921.

30   *Staffordshire Sentinel* 14 July 1931.

31   Jeffrey Richards, *The Age of the Dream Palace: Cinema and Society in Britain 1930–1939* (Routledge, 1984) p. 64.

32   *Call* (London) 4 September 1919.

33   *Framlingham Weekly News* 15 September 1928.

34   Richards, *The Age of the Dream Palace* p. 60.

35   *Weekly Dispatch* (London) 17 August 1919.

36   *Sheerness Times Guardian* 10 January 1929.

37   *Daily News* (London) 28 May 1923.

38   *Sunday Mirror* 27 May 1923.

39   George Pearson, *Flashback: An Autobiography of a British Film Maker* (George Allen & Unwin, 1957) p. 113.

40   *Sketch* 27 December 1922.

41   *Era* 5 December 1923.

42   Quoted in advert *Perthshire Advertiser* 12 March 1927.

43   Richards, *The Age of the Dream Palace* p. 63.

44   *Daily News* (London) 18 July 1931.

45   *Eastbourne Chronicle* 1 September 1928.

46   *Kinematograph Weekly* 30 January 1930.

47   *Picturegoer* 13 June 1931.

48   Pearson, *Flashback* p. 192.

49   *Stage* 27 June 1929.

50   *London Daily Chronicle* 3 February 1930.

51   *Daily Mirror* 2 December 1929.

52   *Hartlepool Northern Daily Mail* 20 December 1930.

53 *Western Gazette* 8 January 1932. See also Jane Duffus, *Yeovil Cinemas Through Time* (Amberley, 2013).

54 Denis Norden, *Clips from a Life* (Fourth Estate, 2008) p. 18.

55 *Daily News* (London) 5 April 1929.

56 W. Sydney Robinson, *The Last Victorians: A Daring Reassessment of Four Twentieth Century Eccentrics* (Robson Press, 2014) p. 132.

57 David Hendy, *The BBC: A People's History* (Profile Books, 2022) p. 76.

58 Robinson, *The Last Victorians* p. 189.

59 Ibid. p. 161.

60 *Nottingham Evening Post* 17 January 1930.

61 Susan Briggs, *Those Radio Times* (Weidenfeld & Nicolson, 1981) p. 149.

62 Hendy, *The BBC* p. 141.

63 Asa Briggs, *The History of Broadcasting in the United Kingdom, Volume II: The Golden Age of Wireless* (Oxford University Press, 1995) p. 54.

64 Robinson, *The Last Victorians* p. 171.

65 Ibid. p. 166.

66 Briggs, *Those Radio Times* p. 148.

67 *Reynolds's Newspaper* 28 February 1932.

68 Briggs, *Those Radio Times* p. 150.

69 Ronald Blythe, *The Age of Illusion: Some Glimpses of Britain between the Wars 1919–1940* (Hamish Hamilton, 1963) p. 48.

70 Briggs, *Those Radio Times* p. 24.

71 *St. Andrews Citizen* 1 October 1927.

72 A. J. Davies, *To Build a New Jerusalem: The Labour Movement from the 1880s to the 1990s* (Michael Joseph, 1992) p. 90.

73 *Scotsman* 17 October 1924.

74 *Hull Daily Mail* 17 October 1924; *Daily News* (London) 17 October 1924; *Liverpool Echo* 17 October 1924.

75 *St. Andrews Citizen* 1 October 1927.

76 Briggs, *Those Radio Times* p. 147.

77 *Daily News* (London) 17 January 1924.

78 Briggs, *Those Radio Times* p. 119.

79 *Cornish Guardian* 4 March 1927.

80 Roger Wilmut, *Kindly Leave the Stage: The Story of Variety 1919–1960* (Methuen, 1985) p. 101.

81 H. M. Burnaby & N. Long, 'We Can't Let You Broadcast That' (Columbia Records, 1933).

82 Hendy, *The BBC* p. 56.

83 Briggs, *Those Radio Times* p. 143.

84 *Evening Despatch* 28 July 1934.

85 *Birmingham Daily Post* 6 January 1928.

86 *Stage* 9 August 1928.

87 *Bystander* 28 July 1926.

88 *Yorkshire Evening Post* 28 December 1933.

89 *Scotsman* 27 May 1929.

90 *Nottingham Journal* 8 November 1938.

91 Robert Lynd, *Life's Little Oddities* (J. M. Dent and Sons, 1941) p. 64.

92 *Huddersfield Daily Examiner* 6 January 1928.

93 Briggs, *Those Radio Times* p. 136.

94 *Lincolnshire Echo* 8 October 1934.

95 *Liverpool Daily Post* 14 February 1935.

96 Letter dated 29 October 1924, National Archives HO4/11557.

97 Memorandum dated 16 April 1928, National Archives CAB/24/194.

98 Tony Currie, *The Radio Times Story* (Kelly Publications, 2001) p. 4.

99 Briggs, *Those Radio Times* p. 78.

100 *Birmingham Mail* 7 May 1925.

101 *Hinckley Guardian and South Leicestershire Advertiser* 12 June 1925.

102 *Kensington News and West London Times* 5 June 1925.

103 Harry Stanley, *Can You Hear Me, Mother? Sandy Powell's Lifetime of Music Hall* (Jupiter Books, 1975) p. 76.

104 *Western Daily Press* 4 February 1926.

105 *St. Andrews Citizen* 1 October 1927.

4: Highs and Hangovers

1 Sydney Horler, *Tiger Standish Comes Back* Chapter 2.

2 Robert Hewison, *Footlights! A Hundred Years of Cambridge Comedy* (Methuen, 1983) p. 76.

3 *Birmingham Daily Gazette* 5 April 1919.

4 Bob Stanley, *Let's Do It: The Birth of Pop* (Faber & Faber, 2022) p. 76.

5 *Hull Daily Mail* 29 October 1919.

6 *Birmingham Mail* 20 September 1919.

7 *Chelsea News and General Advertiser* 3 December 1920.

8 Stanley Damerell & William Hargreaves, 'John Willie's Jazz Band' (Edison Bell, 1926).

9 Ray Pallett, *They Called Him Al: A Musical Life of Al Bowlly* (BearManor Media, 2015) Chapter 4.

10 *Daily Mirror* 2 December 1932

11 *Shields Daily News* 8 October 1925.

12 Alan Jenkins, *The Twenties* (William Heinemann, 1974) p. 145.

13 *Weekly Dispatch* (London) 3 April 1927
14 Billy Cotton, *I Did It My Way* (George G. Harrap, 1970) p. 106.
15 *Eastern Post* 22 July 1922.
16 *Daily Herald* 14 February 1935.
17 Jack Payne, *This Is Jack Payne* (Sampson Low, Martson & Co., 1932) p. 32.
18 *Western Mail* 16 March 1932.
19 *Sunday Post* 23 August 1925.
20 *Nottingham Evening Post* 1 August 1925.
21 *Dundee Evening Telegraph* 14 October 1926.
22 *Western Mail* 14 January 1928.
23 *Daily Herald* 3 August 1932.
24 *Daily News* (London) 17 June 1933.
25 Jenkins, *The Twenties* p. 49.
26 *Britannia and Eve* 1 October 1929.
27 *Sunderland Daily Echo and Shipping Gazette* 14 May 1929.
28 Cotton, *I Did It My Way* p. 99.
29 *Lancashire Evening Post* 3 July 1925.
30 *Leeds Mercury* 20 April 1925.
31 *Aberdeen Press and Journal* 28 May 1925.
32 *Bystander* 18 March 1925.
33 *Daily Mirror* 23 June 1924.
34 Jenkins, *The Twenties* p. 56.
35 *Daily Sketch* 5 October 1925.
36 *Newcastle Journal* 18 August 1927.
37 *Birmingham Mail* 6 October 1925.
38 *Northern Whig* 10 October 1925.
39 *Portsmouth Evening News* 21 October 1925; *Nuneaton Chronicle* 30 October 1925.
40 *Aberdeen Press and Journal* 31 July 1924.
41 *Nelson Leader* 12 March 1920.
42 *Daily Mirror* 17 May 1929.
43 *Streatham News* 1 November 1929.
44 *Tatler* 8 April 1925.
45 Ibid. 10 September 1930.
46 *Dial* Vol. 73 No. 6 (December 1922).
47 *Hampshire Advertiser* 7 September 1935.
48 *Freeman's Journal* 9 February 1924.
49 *Gentlewoman* 17 October 1925.
50 *Exeter and Plymouth Gazette* 4 May 1926.

51 *Times* 1 May 1926.

52 *Sphere* 22 May 1926.

53 Jim Godbolt, *A History of Jazz in Britain, 1919–50* (Quartet Books, 1984) p. 24.

54 *Times* 1 May 1926.

55 *Royal Academy Annual Report 1926* p. 13.

56 Jeffrey Richards, *The Age of the Dream Palace: Cinema and Society in Britain 1930–1939* (Routledge, 1984) p. 64.

57 *Weekly Dispatch* (London) 30 November 1924.

58 *Leicester Daily Mercury* 25 August 1925.

59 *Sunday Mirror* 1 March 1925.

60 *Dundee Courier* 24 April 1925.

61 Jenkins, *The Twenties* p. 148.

62 *Britannia and Eve* 1 January 1931.

63 *Bystander* 25 September 1935.

64 Douglas Byng, 'I'm One of the Queens of England' (Zonophone, 1930).

65 Roger Wilmut, *Kindly Leave the Stage: The Story of Variety 1919–1960* (Methuen, 1985) p. 70.

66 *Era* 1 May 1929.

67 Hansard 15 August 1921.

68 Patrick Macnee & Marie Cameron, *Blind in One Ear* (Harrap, 1988) p. 27.

69 *London Daily Chronicle* 12 April 1927.

70 *Hull Daily Mail* 24 August 1928.

71 *Daily Herald* 21 August 1928.

72 Ibid. 20 August 1928.

73 Ibid.

74 *Tatler* 15 August 1928.

75 *Truth* 15 August 1928.

76 Jean Bobby Noble, *Masculinities without Men? Female Masculinity in Twentieth-Century Fictions* (University of British Columbia Press, 2004) p. 26.

77 Paul Ferris, *Sex and the British: A Twentieth-Century History* (Michael Joseph, 1993) p. 109.

78 Edward J. Bristow, *Vice and Vigilance: Purity Movements in Britain since 1700* (Gill & Macmillan, 1977) p. 224.

79 Macnee & Cameron, *Blind in One Ear* p. 13.

80 *Manchester Guardian* 22 November 1928.

81 *Liverpool Daily Post* 15 December 1928.

82 *John Bull* 20 October 1928.

83 *Yorkshire Post and Leeds Intelligencer* 11 December 1929.

84 *Bystander* 17 July 1929.

85 *Reynolds's Newspaper* 11 August 1929.

86 *Evening Despatch* 3 March 1937.

87 Introduction to *The Letters of D. H. Lawrence* (Heinemann, 1932).

88 *Graphic* 22 December 1928; *Daily Mirror* 10 December 1928; *Sphere* 15 December 1928; *Birmingham Daily Post* 4 December 1928; *Liverpool Echo* 6 December 1928.

89 *Sheffield Daily Telegraph* 13 December 1928.

90 *Illustrated London News* 2 February 1929.

91 *Nottingham Journal* 27 December 1929.

92 *Daily News* (London) 26 November 1929.

93 Ibid. 21 January 1931.

94 *Liverpool Echo* 27 September 1929.

95 *Graphic* 28 December 1929.

96 National Archives CAB/24/206.

97 *Grey River Argus* (New Zealand) 30 June 1920.

5: Confrontation and Coalition

1   May Sinclair, *Life and Death of Harriett Frean* Chapter 4.

2   British Pathé, 1936.

3   *Daily News* (London) 18 January 1926.

4   *Berwick Advertiser* 21 January 1926.

5   *Gloucester Citizen* 18 January 1926.

6   *Dundee Courier* 20 February 1924.

7   *Atherstone News and Herald* 22 January 1926.

8   *Daily News* (London) 18 January 1926.

9   Quoted in *Nottingham Evening Post* 18 January 1926.

10 Ibid.

11 *Western Morning News* 18 January 1926.

12 *Weekly Dispatch* (London) 17 January 1926.

13 *Cornish Guardian* 22 January 1926.

14 David Boyd Haycock, *A Crisis of Brilliance: Five Young British Artists and the Great War* (Old Street Publishing, 2009) p. 307.

15 *Daily Herald* 10 September 1925.

16 *Evesham Standard & West Midland Observer* 21 November 1925.

17 *Newmarket Journal* 5 December 1925.

18 Nan Sloane, *The Women in the Room: Labour's Forgotten History* (I. B. Tauris, 2018) p. 220.

19 *Liverpool Journal of Commerce* 26 October 1925.

20 Roy Hattersley, *Borrowed Time: The Story of Britain Between the Wars* (Little, Brown, 2007) p. 124.

21 *Campbeltown Courier* 8 May 1926.

22 *Portsmouth Evening News* 3 May 1926.

23 *Ballymena Weekly Telegraph* 15 May 1926.

24 Matthew Engel, *Tickle the Public: One Hundred Years of the Popular Press* (Victor Gollancz, 1996) p. 108.

25 *Newcastle Daily Chronicle* 3 May 1926.

26 Lord Boothby, *My Yesterday, Your Tomorrow* (Hutchinson & Co., 1962) p. 118.

27 *Western Daily Press* 10 May 1926.

28 *Daily Herald* 4 May 1926.

29 *Freedom* (London) April/May 1926.

30 *British Gazette* 6 May 1926.

31 Andrew Boyle, *Only the Wind Will Listen: Reith of the BBC* (Hutchinson, 1972) p. 200.

32 Roy Jenkins, *Baldwin* (Collins, 1987) p. 103.

33 Margaret Morris, *The General Strike* (Journeyman Press, 1976) p. 251.

34 David Hendy, *The BBC: A People's History* (Profile Books, 2022) p. 117.

35 Asa Briggs, *A Social History of England* (Weidenfeld & Nicolson, 1983 – revised edition: Pelican 1987) p. 309.

36 *Leeds Mercury* 18 June 1926.

37 *Liverpool Daily Post* 6 August 1912

38 J. Ramsay MacDonald, *Syndicalism: A Critical Examination* (Constable & Co., 1912) p. 62.

39 *London Daily Chronicle* 25 May 1926.

40 Manny Shinwell, *Lead with the Left: My First Ninety-Six Years* (Cassell, 1981) p. 88.

41 Allen Hutt, *British Trade Unionism: A Short History* (Lawrence & Wishart, 1941 – revised and enlarged edition 1974) p. 116.

42 *Coventry Evening Telegraph* 6 September 1928.

43 Robert Rhodes James, *The British Revolution Volume 2: From Asquith to Chamberlain 1914–89* (Hamish Hamilton, 1977) p. 198.

44 Alan Jenkins, *The Twenties* (William Heinemann, 1974) p. 92.

45 *Northampton Chronicle and Echo* 17 June 1922.

46 *The Progressive Magazine* Vol. 4 (Wisconsin, 1922) p. 262.

47 Chris Horrie, *Tabloid Nation: From the Birth of the Daily Mirror to the Death of the Tabloid* (André Deutsch, 2003) p. 31.

48 Charles Wintour, *The Rise and Fall of Fleet Street* (Hutchinson, 1989) p. 28.

49 Engel, *Tickle the Public* pp. 104–5.

50 Sir Oswald Mosley, *My Life* (Nelson, 1968) p. 288.

51 Hugh Cudlipp, *Walking on the Water* (Bodley Head, 1976) p. 57.

52 Tom Driberg, *Ruling Passions* (Jonathan Cape, 1977) p. 103.

53 Harry J. Greenwall, *I Hate Tomorrow: An Autobiographical Experiment* (Book Club, 1940) p. 217.

54 *John Bull* 2 May 1936.

55 *People* 18 May 1924.

56 Hattersley, *Borrowed Time* p. 369.

57 Christopher Burgess, *From the Political Pipe to Devil Eyes: A History of the British Election Poster from 1910–1997* (PhD thesis, University of Nottingham, 2004).

58 John D. Fair, 'The Second Labour Government and the Politics of Electoral Reform, 1929–1931' (*Albion* Autumn 1981) p. 278.

59 Trevor Wilson (ed.), *The Political Diaries of C. P. Scott, 1911–1928* (Collins, 1970) p. 274.

60 *Daily Express* 31 January 1931.

61 *Scotsman* 18 February 1930.

62 *Daily Mail* 19 February 1930.

63 *Scotsman* 18 March 1931.

64 *Exeter and Plymouth Gazette* 18 March 1931

65 *Gloucester Citizen* 17 March 1931

66 *Daily Herald* 18 March 1931.

67 Philip Williamson & Edward Baldwin (eds), *Baldwin Papers: A Conservative Statesman 1908–1947* (Cambridge University Press, 2004) p. 258.

68 *Daily News* (London) 18 March 1931.

69 *Newcastle Daily Chronicle* 4 December 1931.

70 *Daily Herald* 24 June 1929; *Truth* 10 July 1929; A. J. Davies, *To Build a New Jerusalem: The Labour Movement from the 1880s to the 1990s* (Michael Joseph, 1992) p. 77.

71 Malcolm Pearce & Geoffrey Stewart, *British Political History 1867–1995: Democracy and Decline* (Routledge, 1992 – 2nd edition, 1996) p. 361.

72 Andrew Adonis, *Ernest Bevin: Labour's Churchill* (Biteback Publishing, 2020).

73 *Yorkshire Evening Post* 4 October 1937.

74 *Clarion* 24 October 1924.

75 Matthew Worley, *Oswald Mosley and the New Party* (Palgrave Macmillan, 2010) p. 5.

76 Ibid. p. 131.

77 James Crotty, *Keynes Against Capitalism: His Economic Case for Liberal Socialism* (Routledge, 2019) p. 122.

78 Ian Mikardo, *Back-Bencher* (Weidenfeld & Nicolson, 1988) p. 47.

79 *Western Mail* 8 October 1930; *Reynolds's Newspaper* 12 October 1930.

80 Pearce & Stewart, *British Political History 1867–1995* p. 272.

81 John D. Fair, 'The Second Labour Government and the Politics of Electoral Reform, 1929–1931' (*Albion* Autumn 1981) p. 297.

82 Vernon Bogdanor, *The Monarchy and the Constitution* (Oxford University Press, 1995) p. 108.

83 Pearce & Stewart, *British Political History 1867–1995* p. 268.

84 Davies, *To Build a New Jerusalem* p. 95.

85 *Daily Herald* 19 February 1934.

86 *Sheffield Independent* 4 July 1934.

87 John Buchan, *Memory Hold-the-Door* (Hodder & Stoughton, 1940) p. 237.

88 Alan Jenkins, *The Twenties* (William Heinemann, 1974) p. 86.

89 *Western Morning News* 24 June 1932.

90 *Yorkshire Evening Post* 21 September 1932.

91 *Dundee Evening Telegraph* 27 August 1924.

92 Kyla Thomas & David Gunnell, 'Suicide in England and Wales 1861–2007: a time-trends analysis', *International Journal of Epidemiology* Vol 39 No 6 (2010).

93 George Orwell, *The Road to Wigan Pier* (Victor Gollancz, 1937) Chapter 5.

94 *Leeds Mercury* 1 August 1935.

95 *Daily Herald* 7 September 1931.

96 W. F. Deedes, *Dear Bill: W. F. Deedes Reports* (Macmillan, 1997) p. 40.

97 *Shields Daily Gazette* 4 April 1934.

98 *Daily Mirror* 28 September 1936.

99 J. B. Priestley, *English Journey* (William Heinemann, 1934) Chapter 9, Section 5.

100 *Daily Mirror* 18 May 1936; *Daily Herald* 9 April 1937.

101 Ethel Mannin, *Confessions and Impressions* (Jarrolds, 1930) p. 174.

102 Nicholas Crafts & Peter Fearon (eds), *The Great Depression of the 1930s: Lessons for Today* (Oxford University Press, 2013) p. 3.

6: Peace and Comfort

1   Francis Beeding, *The One Sane Man* (Hodder & Stoughton, 1934) Prologue.
2   *Evening Despatch* 19 September 1929.
3   *Sunday Sun* (Newcastle) 5 February 1933.
4   *Daily News* (London) 14 October 1931.
5   *Evening Despatch* 14 October 1931.
6   *Scotsman* 14 October 1931.
7   *Evening Despatch* 14 October 1931.
8   *Hull Daily Mail* 15 October 1931.
9   *Sphere* 7 November 1931.
10 *Staffordshire Sentinel* 9 February 1933.
11 *Sheffield Daily Telegraph* 27 October 1931.
12 *Dundee Evening Telegraph* 10 April 1933.
13 *Cherwell*, October 1933.
14 Robert Hewison, *Footlights! A Hundred Years of Cambridge Comedy* (Methuen, 1983) p. 74.
15 Paul Ferris, *Sir Huge: The Life of Huw Wheldon* (Michael Joseph, 1990) p. 14.
16 *Daily Herald* 20 February 1933; *North Devon Journal* 23 March 1933; *Dundee Evening Telegraph* 10 April 1933.
17 *Dundee Evening Telegraph* 10 April 1933.
18 Peter Shore, *Leading the Left* (Weidenfeld & Nicolson, 1993) p. 17.
19 Roy Hattersley, *Borrowed Time: The Story of Britain Between the Wars* (Little, Brown, 2007) p. 182.
20 *Daily Express* 8 May 1940.
21 *Larne Times* 31 October 1931.
22 *Daily Herald* 3 July 1934.
23 Ethel Mannin, *Confessions and Impressions* (Jarrolds, 1930) p. 170–72.
24 *Manchester Guardian* 9 May 1940.
25 Clement Attlee (ed. Frank Field), *Attlee's Great Contemporaries: The Politics of Character* (Continuum, 2009) p. 62.
26 Sir Oswald Mosley, *My Life* (Nelson, 1968) p. 222.
27 *Daily Herald* 3 July 1934.
28 *Halifax Evening Courier* 29 October 1931.
29 Attlee, *Attlee's Great Contemporaries* p. 62.
30 *Irish Weekly and Ulster Examiner* 6 August 1932.
31 Raymond Postgate, *The Life of George Lansbury* (Longmans, Green & Co., 1951) p. 238.
32 *Gloucester Citizen* 11 December 1933.

33 *Daily Herald* 3 July 1934.
34 George Lansbury, *My England* (Selwyn & Blount, 1934) pp. 63 & 106.
35 *Clarion* 23 June 1934.
36 *Diss Express* 5 July 1935.
37 Mosley, *My Life* p. 222.
38 *Western Mail* 5 October 1933.
39 *Manchester Guardian* 16 October 1934.
40 *Derbyshire Advertiser and Journal* 14 November 1924.
41 *Lincoln Leader and County Advertiser* 1 December 1923.
42 John Buchan, *Memory Hold-the-Door* (Hodder and Stoughton, 1940) p. 144.
43 David Hendy, *The BBC: A People's History* (Profile Books, 2022) p. 39.
44 Western Daily Press 20 March 1931.
45 *Sunderland Daily Echo and Shipping Gazette* 28 September 1929.
46 *Manchester Guardian* 30 January 1923.
47 *Daily Express* 15 February 1923.
48 *Daily Express* 4 May 1931.
49 *Nottingham Journal* 17 December 1930.
50 *Hampstead News* 15 March 1934.
51 *Leicester Daily Mercury* 6 October 1933.
52 *Scotsman* 17 April 1933.
53 *Yorkshire Post and Leeds Intelligencer* 24 July 1933.
54 *Leicester Evening Mail* 13 September 1933.
55 *Hartlepool Northern Daily Mail* 23 June 1931.
56 *Yorkshire Post and Leeds Intelligencer* 31 January 1933.
57 *Daily Mirror* 30 September 1930.
58 *Illustrated London News* 3 June 1933.
59 *West Sussex Gazette* 6 July 1933.
60 *Western Mail* 2 March 1933.
61 *Yorkshire Evening Post* 20 July 1934.
62 *Nottingham Journal* 29 October 1923.
63 *Daily News* 31 July 1933.
64 *Daily Herald* 16 January 1934.
65 *Daily Express* 18 September 1935.
66 *West Sussex Gazette* 6 July 1933.
67 Hansard 13 April 1933.
68 Robert Rhodes James, *The British Revolution Volume 2: From Asquith to Chamberlain 1914–89* (Hamish Hamilton, 1977) p. 245.
69 *Dundee Evening Telegraph* 3 April 1933.
70 *Daily Mirror* 5 November 1925.

71 *Era* 12 October 1927

72 *Skegness News* 29 June 1938.

73 *Holloway Press* 10 June 1933.

74 *Worthing Gazette* 6 March 1935.

75 *Leeds Mercury* 25 November 1939.

76 *Reading Standard* 6 April 1934.

77 Jeffrey Richards (ed.), *The Unknown 1930s: An Alternative History of the British Cinema 1929–1939* (I. B. Tauris, 1998) p. 141.

78 Ibid. p. 144.

79 *Yorkshire Post and Leeds Intelligencer* 8 February 1936.

80 *Era* 28 February 1934.

81 Ralph Butler, Harry Tilsley & Horatio Nicholls, 'Let's All Go to the Music Hall' (Rex Records, 1934).

82 *Liverpool Echo* 22 June 1934.

83 *Dundee Evening Telegraph* 26 November 1934.

84 *Coventry Evening Telegraph* 8 September 1934.

85 *Leeds Mercury* 21 November 1905.

86 Chris Hopkins, *Walter Greenwood's Love on the Dole: Novel, Play, Film* (Liverpool University Press, 2018) p. 143.

87 Richards, *The Unknown 1930s* p. 81.

88 *Bolton News* 24 March 2020.

89 George Orwell, *The Road to Wigan Pier* (Victor Gollancz, 1937) Chapter 5.

90 *Sunday Mirror* 15 December 1935.

91 *Bystander* 20 December 1939.

92 *Daily Mirror* 30 January 1939.

93 *Mercury* (Tasmania) 25 February 1939.

94 *Weekly Dispatch* (London) 12 February 1928.

95 Joan Moules, *Gracie Fields: A Biography* (Robert Hale Ltd, 1981) p. 72.

96 *Gracie in the Theatre* (HMV, 1933).

97 *Edinburgh Evening News* 2 October 1937.

98 *Britannia and Eve* 1 October 1937.

99 *Hull Daily Mail* 23 January 1937.

100 *Shields Daily News* 14 July 1938.

101 *Kinematograph Weekly* 28 July 1938.

102 Moules, *Gracie Fields* p. 62.

103 *Western Daily Press* 14 June 1939.

104 Arthur Le Clerk, 'What Can You Give a Nudist on His Birthday?' (HMV, 1934).

105 *Bystander* 12 January 1938.

106 *Birmingham Mail*, quoted in advert in *Kinematograph Weekly* 20 September 1934.
107 Howard Flynn, 'Looking on the Bright Side' (HMV, 1932).
108 *Leeds Mercury* 12 February 1936.
109 *Daily Herald* 23 August 1933.
110 *Daily Herald* 9 May 1934.
111 *Birmingham Daily Gazette* 27 September 1937.
112 Barry Took, *Laughter in the Air : An Informal History of British Radio Comedy* (Robson Books, 1976) p. 90.
113 Maureen Owen, *The Crazy Gang* (Weidenfeld & Nicolson, 1986) p. 91.
114 Arthur Askey, *Before Your Very Eyes* (Woburn Press, 1975) p. 100.
115 *Marylebone Mercury* 30 April 1938.
116 *Era* 23 March 1932.
117 *Daily Mirror* 3 March 1937.
118 *Birmingham Daily Gazette* 8 March 1935.
119 Henry Hall, *Here's to the Next Time* (Odhams Press, 1955) p. 37.
120 *Sunday Sun* (Newcastle) 26 September 1937.
121 Harry Parr Davies, 'Smile When You Say Goodbye' (Rex, 1937).
122 Hall, *Here's to the Next Time* p. 154.

7: Leisure and Libraries

1 Edgar Wallace, 'The Poetical Policeman', *The Mind of Mr J. G. Reeder*.
2 *Trunk Crime* (1939) directed Roy Boulting, screenplay Francis Miller.
3 *Western Daily Press* 25 March 1931.
4 *Dundee Evening Telegraph* 30 December 1931.
5 *Portsmouth Evening News* 23 September 1932.
6 *Daily Herald* 14 June 1923.
7 *Aberdeen Press and Journal* 30 September 1936.
8 *Daily News* (London) 30 June 1934.
9 *Era* 9 May 1934.
10 *Aberdeen Press and Journal* 30 September 1936.
11 *Western Daily Press* 19 February 1930.
12 *Flintshire County Herald* 24 August 1934
13 Martin Pugh, *We Danced All Night: A Social History of Britain Between the Wars* (Vintage, 2009) p. 233.
14 *Newark Advertiser* 20 May 1936.
15 *Daily News* (London) 19 June 1939.
16 *London Daily Chronicle* 14 September 1929.
17 Ibid.

18 *Daily News* (London) 5 March 1928.
19 *London Daily Chronicle* 31 May 1929.
20 *John Bull* 30 January 1932.
21 Arthur Askey, *Before Your Very Eyes* (Woburn Press, 1975) p. 65.
22 Robert Self, *The Neville Chamberlain Diary Letters Volume Three: The Heir Apparent, 1928–33* (Ashgate Publishing, 2002) p. 72.
23 Charles Wintour, *The Rise and Fall of Fleet Street* (Hutchinson, 1989) p. 57.
24 Roy Hattersley, *Borrowed Time: The Story of Britain Between the Wars* (Little, Brown, 2007) p. 373.
25 *People* 5 March 1933; *Daily Herald* 20 March 1933.
26 Charles Wintour, *The Rise and Fall of Fleet Street* (Hutchinson, 1989) p. 56.
27 *Daily News* (London) 17 March 1933.
28 *John Bull* 30 December 1933.
29 *Daily News* (London) 4 December 1933.
30 *Halifax Evening Courier* 22 January 1934.
31 *Aberdeen Press and Journal* 31 October 1934.
32 John Steel, *Journalism and Free Speech* (Routledge, 2012) p. 156.
33 James Curran, Anthony Smith & Pauline Wingate, *Impacts and Influences: Media Power in the Twentieth Century* (Routledge, 1987) p. 29.
34 *Bookseller* 14 April 1933.
35 Ibid. 16 February 1939.
36 Ibid. 30 September 1932.
37 *Yorkshire Evening Post* 8 December 1932.
38 *Leeds Mercury* 18 July 1934.
39 Zachary Lesser (ed.), *The Book in Britain: A Historical Introduction* (Wiley Blackwell, 2019).
40 *Sheffield Independent* 31 January 1936.
41 Much of the following material – indeed this whole section – is indebted to Joseph McAleer, *Popular Reading and Publishing in Britain 1914–1950* (Clarendon Press, 1992).
42 *Daily Mirror* 6 August 1936.
43 Quoted in advert, *Truth* 21 April 1909.
44 *Reading Mercury* 5 August 1939.
45 Colin Watson, *Snobbery with Violence: English Crime Stories and Their Audience* (Eyre & Spottiswoode, 1971) p. 78.
46 *Sheffield Independent* 6 July 1931.
47 *Times* 11 February 1932.

48 William Vivian Butler, *The Durable Desperadoes* (Macmillan, 1973) p. 162.

49 Martin Edwards, *The Golden Age of Murder* (HarperCollins, 2015) p. 233.

50 Ngaio Marsh, *Death in a White Tie* (1938); Margery Allingham, *Police at the Funeral* (1931).

51 P. G. Wodehouse, *Meet Mr Mulliner* (1927).

52 *Kinematograph Weekly* 30 March 1939.

53 *Picturegoer* 19 September 1931.

54 John Buchan, *The Three Hostages* (1924).

55 Leslie Charteris, *The Happy Highwayman* (1933).

8: Outsiders and Incomers

1   E. H. Young, *Miss Mole* (Jonathan Cape, 1930) Chapter 28.

2   *The Drum* (1938) directed Zoltan Korda, screenplay Lajos Bíró, from a story by A. E. W. Mason.

3   *John Bull* 9 August 1924.

4   *Reynolds's Newspaper* 29 June 1930.

5   *Daily Mirror* 5 July 1930.

6   Lawrence James, *The Middle Class: A History* (Little, Brown, 2006) p. 418.

7   *Daily Herald* 30 June 1930.

8   *Belfast Telegraph* 30 June 1930.

9   *Sheffield Independent* 11 September 1930.

10 *Birmingham Weekly Mercury* 10 July 1932.

11 James, *The Middle Class* pp. 418–19.

12 *Chelsea News and General Advertiser* 24 February 1933.

13 *Nottingham Evening Post* 27 February 1933.

14 *Fulham Chronicle* 3 March 1933.

15 *West London Observer* 3 March 1933.

16 *Daily Mirror* 14 January 1938.

17 *Birmingham Daily Gazette* 26 October 1928.

18 *West Ham and South Essex Mail* 7 September 1934.

19 *Dundee Courier* 23 October 1937.

20 *Thanet Advertiser* 6 August 1937.

21 *Western Daily Press* 14 January 1938.

22 *Holloway Press* 12 February 1938.

23 *Portsmouth Evening News* 3 November 1937.

24 *Evening Despatch* 26 October 1937.

25 *Daily Herald* 23 October 1937.

26 *Illustrated Sporting and Dramatic News* 7 February 1931.

27 *Evening Herald* (Dublin) 26 August 1930.

28 *Britannia and Eve* 1 November 1934.

29 *Burton Observer and Chronicle* 21 July 1938.

30 *Era* 24 June 1936.

31 *Birmingham Weekly Mercury* 5 April 1936.

32 Billy Hill, *Boss of Britain's Underworld* (Naldrett Press, 1955) p. 28.

33 Christopher Josiffe, 'British Voodoo: The Black Art of Rollo Ahmed' (*Fortean Times* 316/317, July & August 2014); *Liverpool Daily Post* 21 October 1937; *Northern Whig* 5 January 1938.

34 *Northern Whig* 5 January 1938.

35 *Liverpool Echo* 15 September 1928.

36 *Daily Herald* 20 May 1930.

37 *Sheffield Daily Telegraph* 20 May 1930.

38 *London Daily Chronicle* 20 May 1930.

39 *Leeds Mercury* 21 May 1930.

40 *Era* 16 September 1936.

41 *Daily Mirror* 28 January 1928.

42 *Belfast Telegraph* 30 January 1928.

43 *Daily News* (London) 30 January 1928.

44 *Belfast Telegraph* 30 January 1928.

45 *Lincolnshire Echo* 8 July 1932.

46 Charlotte Breese, *Hutch* (Bloomsbury Publishing, 1990) p. 113.

47 *Western Mail* 11 June 1936.

48 *Montrose Standard* 19 June 1936.

49 *Eastbourne Chronicle* 30 October 1937.

50 *Newcastle Daily Chronicle* 14 May 1927.

51 *Manchester Evening News* 4 February 1932.

52 *Sketch* 18 August 1926.

53 *Clarion* 1 October 1928.

54 Sybille Beford, *Aldous Huxley, a Biography – Volume One: The Apparent Stability* (Chatto & Windus, 1973) p. 199.

55 Sir Oswald Mosley, *My Life* (Nelson, 1968) p. 225.

56 *Daily Herald* 14 May 1927.

57 Mosley, *My Life* p. 288.

58 *Daily Herald* 23 September 1932.

59 P. G. Wodehouse, *The Code of the Woosters*.

60 *Roscommon Herald* 15 August 1931.

61 *Daily Mail* 15 January 1934.

62 *Daily Mirror* 20 January 1934.

63 G. C. Webber, 'Patterns of Membership and Support for the British Union of Fascists', *Journal of Contemporary History* Vol. 19 No. 4 (1984).

64 *Daily Herald* 8 February 1936.

65 *Sheffield Independent* 5 October 1936.

66 *Daily News* (London) 30 September 1932.

67 *Daily Herald* 23 September 1932.

68 *Yorkshire Post and Leeds Intelligencer* 5 October 1936.

69 *Liverpool Daily Post* 14 April 1937.

70 *Weekly Dispatch* (London) 2 February 1930.

71 *Huddersfield Daily Examiner* 10 October 1935.

72 *Daily Herald* 16 January 1931.

73 Richard Nichols, *Radio Luxembourg: The Station of the Stars* (Comet, 1983) p. 22.

74 George Nobbs, *The Wireless Stars* (Wensum Books, 1972) p. 17.

75 *Daily News* (London) 31 December 1938.

76 *Nottingham Journal* 16 March 1934.

77 *Liverpool Daily Post* 7 May 1931.

78 *South London Observer* 31 March 1934.

79 *Evening Despatch* 20 April 1934.

80 *Sunday Sun* (Newcastle) 3 June 1934.

81 *Alderley & Wilmslow Advertiser* 11 May 1934.

82 *Daily Herald* 25 May 1934.

83 *Evening Despatch* 28 April 1934.

84 Ibid.

85 *Daily Herald* 1 June 1934.

86 *Aberdeen Press and Journal* 20 August 1934.

87 *Daily Mirror* 26 May 1934.

88 *Yorkshire Post and Leeds Intelligencer* 17 May 1934.

89 *Liverpool Daily Post* 17 May 1934.

90 *Scotsman* 6 January 1937.

91 *Daily News* (London) 11 September 1934.

92 *Country Life* 9 October 1942.

93 *Weekly Dispatch* (London) 7 June 1936.

94 *Daily News* (London) 27 May 1936.

95 Ibid. 12 June 1936.

96 *Edinburgh Evening News* 20 June 1936.

97 *Bystander* 17 June 1936.

98 *Liverpool Echo* 24 February 1932.

99 *Huddersfield and Holmfirth Examiner* 9 April 1932.

100 Peter Shore, *Leading the Left* (Weidenfeld & Nicolson, 1993) p. 33.

101 *Yorkshire Post* 2 October 1935.

102 *Edinburgh Evening News* 5 October 1936.

103 Hansard 22 May 1935.

104 Susan Briggs, *Those Radio Times* (Weidenfeld & Nicolson, 1981) pp. 133–4.

105 *Daily Mirror* 9 November 1935.

106 Manny Shinwell, *Lead with the Left: My First Ninety-Six Years* (Cassell, 1981) p. 106.

107 *Birmingham Daily Gazette* 21 November 1936.

108 *Newcastle Evening Chronicle* 23 September 1936.

109 *Birmingham Weekly Mercury* 22 September 1935.

110 Clement Attlee (ed. Frank Field), *Attlee's Great Contemporaries: The Politics of Character* (Continuum, 2009) p. 121.

111 A. J. Davies, *To Build a New Jerusalem: The Labour Movement from the 1880s to the 1990s* (Michael Joseph, 1992) p. 172.

112 Mosley, *My Life* p. 261.

113 Attlee, *Attlee's Great Contemporaries* p. 124.

114 Ibid. p. 126.

115 Alan Bullock, *The Life and Times of Ernest Bevin, Volume One: Trade Union Leader, 1881–1940* (Heinemann, 1960) p. 592.

116 Frank Joseph, *Mussolini's War: Fascist Italy's Military Struggles from Africa and Western Europe to the Mediterranean and Soviet Union 1935–45* (Helion & Company, 2010) p. 17.

117 Robert Rhodes James, *The British Revolution Volume 2: From Asquith to Chamberlain 1914–89* (Hamish Hamilton, 1977) p. 277.

118 *Weekly Dispatch* (London) 6 October 1935

119 *Spectator* 27 March 1936.

120 *Daily Mirror* 9 March 1936.

121 *Daily Express* 9 March 1936.

122 *Daily News* (London) 9 January 1939.

123 *Chester Chronicle* 19 September 1936.

124 Victor Gollancz, *More for Timothy* (Victor Gollancz, 1953) p. 357.

125 Stuart Samuels, 'The Left Book Club', *Journal of Contemporary History* Vol. 1 No. 2 (1966).

126 *Hastings and St Leonards Observer* 18 June 1938.

127 *The Record* (TGWU) December 1938.

128 *Derby Daily Telegraph* 11 November 1937.

129 Advert in *Daily News* (London) 10 February 1939.

9: Resignation and Resolve

1   *Storm in a Teacup* (London Films, 1937), directed Ian Dalrymple & Victor Savile, screenplay Donald Bull & Ian Dalrymple.

2   *The Lady Vanishes* (Gainsborough Pictures, 1938) directed Alfred Hitchcock, screenplay Sidney Gilliat & Frank Launder.

3   Thomas Patteson, *Instruments for New Music: Sound, Technology and Modernism* (University of California Press, 2016) p. 135

4   *Scotsman* 26 December 1934.

5   *Western Mail* 11 May 1935.

6   *Whitstable Times and Herne Bay Herald* 25 January 1936.

7   Harold Nicolson, *King George V* (Constable, 1952) p. 525.

8   *Daily News* (London) 24 January 1936.

9   Erik Levi, *Music in the Third Reich* (Palgrave Macmillan, 1994) p. 115.

10   *Sheffield Independent* 29 January 1936.

11   Sarah Bradford, *King George VI* (Weidenfeld and Nicolson, 1989) p. 204.

12   Keith Middlemass & John Barnes, *Baldwin: A Biography* (Weidenfeld & Nicolson, 1969) p. 970.

13   *Daily Mail* 19 November 1936.

14   *Daily Mirror* 19 November 1936.

15   *Cornishman* 17 December 1936.

16   *New York Journal* 26 October 1936.

17   *Galway Observer* 14 November 1936.

18   J. G. Lockhart, *Cosmo Gordon Lang* (Hodder & Stoughton, 1949) p. 598.

19   Roy Hattersley, *Borrowed Time: The Story of Britain Between the Wars* (Little, Brown, 2007) p. 106.

20   Michael Bloch, *The Reign and Abdication of Edward VIII* (Bantam Press, 1990) Chapter 5.

21   *Halifax Evening Courier* 12 December 1936.

22   *Times* 12 December 1936.

23   *People* 20 December 1936.

24   *Grimsby Daily Telegraph* 12 December 1936.

25   Patrick Macnee & Marie Cameron, *Blind in One Ear* (Harrap, 1988) p. 82.

26   *Liverpool Daily Post* 15 December 1936

27   W. Sydney Robinson, *The Last Victorians: A Daring Reassessment of Four Twentieth Century Eccentrics* (Robson Press, 2014) p. 181.

28   Albert Speer, *Inside the Third Reich* (Simon & Schuster, 1970) p. 72.

29   Robert Rhodes James, *The British Revolution Volume 2: From Asquith to Chamberlain 1914–89* (Hamish Hamilton, 1977) p. 301.

30   *John Bull* 2 May 1936.

31   *Belfast Telegraph* 14 December 1936.

32   *Sunday Express*, 24 August 1930.

33   *Londonderry Sentinel* 23 January 1937.

34   *Barrier Miner* (New South Wales) 8 February 1936.

35   David Arnold, *Gandhi* (Pearson Education, 2001) p. 153.

36   *Daily Mirror* 18 March 1931.

37   Harry J. Greenwall, *I Hate Tomorrow: An Autobiographical Experiment* (Book Club, 1940) p. 269.

38   *Yorkshire Post and Leeds Intelligencer* 31 January 1933.

39   Malcolm Pearce & Geoffrey Stewart, *British Political History 1867–1995: Democracy and Decline* (Routledge, 1992 – 2nd edition, 1996) p. 410.

40   The Editors of *Freedomways, Paul Robeson: The Great Forerunner* (International Publishers, 1998) pp. 75–76.

41   Jeffrey Richards, *The Age of the Dream Palace: Cinema and Society in Britain 1930–1939* (Routledge, 1984) p. 90.

42   *Common Cause* 24 December 1920.

43   *Kinematograph Weekly* 4 July 1935.

44   Richards, *The Age of the Dream Palace* p. 111.

45   *Yorkshire Post and Leeds Intelligencer* 26 February 1937.

46   *Sheffield Independent* 13 November 1937.

47   *Yorkshire Evening Post* 30 January 1937.

48   *Derby Daily Telegraph* 29 January 1937.

49   *Evening Despatch* 25 February 1937.

50   *Daily Mirror* 26 February 1937.

51   *Birmingham Daily Gazette* 26 February 1937.

52   Daniel Biltereyst & Roel Vande Winkel (eds), *Silencing Cinema: Film Censorship around the World* (Palgrave Macmillan, 2013).

53   Ibid.

54   G. L. Simons, *Pornography Without Prejudice* (Abelard-Schuman, 1972) p. 7.

55   Richards, *The Age of the Dream Palace* p. 97.

56   *John Bull* 23 July 1938.

57   *Daily Herald* 7 March 1932.

58   *Spectator* 24 April 1936.

59   David Dilks, *Neville Chamberlain, Volume 1: Pioneering and Reform 1869–1929* (Cambridge University Press, 1984) p. 519.

60   *Belfast Telegraph* 18 March 1939.

61   R. J. Q. Adams, *British Politics and Foreign Policy in the Age of Appeasement 1935–39* (Standford University Press, 1993) p. 7.

62   F. W. S. Craig (ed.), *The Most Gracious Speeches to Parliament 1900–1974* (Macmillan, 1975) p. 90.

63   *Daily Mirror* 1 May 1937.

64   Hansard 6 May 1937.

65   Walford Selby, 'Austria before the Anschluss and a View of Her Future Prospects' (*International Affairs* Vol. 21 No. 4, October 1945).

66   *Dundee Evening Telegraph* 12 March 1938.

67   Ibid.

68   Hansard 14 March 1938.

69   *Staffordshire Sentinel* 28 September 1938.

70   *Scotsman* 29 September 1938.

71   *Belfast News-Letter, Daily Mirror* 1 October 1938.

72   Denis Norden, *Coming to You Live! Behind-the-Scenes Memories of Forties and Fifties Television* (Methuen, 1985) p. 99.

73   Lord Home, *The Way the Wind Blows: An Autobiography* (Collins, 1976) pp. 64–6.

74   Robert J. Caputi, *Neville Chamberlain and Appeasement* (Susquehanna University Press, 2000) p. 25.

75   *Daily Mirror* 30 September 1938.

76   *Daily Express* 2 January 1939.

77   *Aberdeen Press and Journal* 30 December 1938.

78   *Belfast Telegraph* 18 March 1939.

79   *Kilmarnock Herald and North Ayrshire Gazette* 31 March 1939.

80   Richard Dannatt & Robert Lyman, *Victory to Defeat: The British Army 1918–1940* (Osprey Publishing, 2023) p. 261.

81   D. R. Thorpe, *Eden: The Life and Times of Anthony Eden, First Earl of Avon 1897–1977* (Chatto & Windus, 2003) p. 193.

82   Hansard 31 March 1939.

83   Ronald Frankau, 'There's Absolutely Nothing Wrong at All' (Parlophone, 1939).

84   *Western Morning News* 4 August 1939.

85   *Daily Gazette for Middlesbrough* 1 August 1939.

86   W. H. Auden, 'Musée des Beaux Arts' (*New Writing*, Spring 1939).

87   *Lewisham Borough News* 15 August 1939.

88   *Daily Mirror* 19 August 1939.

89   *Daily News* (London) 19 August 1939.

90   Prince of Wales's broadcast on BBC radio, 12 April 1935.

91   *Aberdeen Press and Journal* 8 August 1939.

92   *Daily Herald* 3 August 1939.
93   H. G. Wells, *The Fate of Homo Sapiens* (Secker & Warburg, 1939) pp. 217, 190, 140, 273.
94   *Daily News* (London) 21 August 1939.
95   Louise London, *Whitehall and the Jews, 1933–1948: British Immigration Policy, Jewish Refugees and the Holocaust* (Cambridge University Press, 2000).
96   *Daily News* (London) 25 August 1939.
97   *Shields Daily News* 26 August 1939.
98   Ross Parker & Hughie Charles, 'There'll Always Be an England' (Dash Music, 1939).
99   *Eastbourne Chronicle* 26 August 1939.
100 *Somerset Guardian and Radstock Observer* 11 August 1939.

Epilogue
1   James Hilton, *To You, Mr Chips* (1938) Chapter 1.
2   Max Lester, 'A Very Little Nazi' (Decca Records, 1939).
3   *Sunday Mirror* 4 September 1938.
4   Ibid. 11 September 1938.
5   Ibid. 18 September 1938.
6   Raphael Samuel, *Theatres of Memory: Past and Present in Contemporary Culture* (Verso, 2012) p. 390.
7   *Times* 18 October 1938.
8   Ibid. 20 January 1939.
9   *Bristol Evening Post* 27 May 1939.
10   *Daily Herald* 29 July 1938.
11   *Belfast Telegraph* 23 January 1939.
12   *Daily News* (London) 9 January 1939; *Nottingham Journal* 10 January 1939.
13   *Lancashire Evening Post* 30 January 1939.
14   *Reynolds's Newspaper* 4 December 1938.
15   *Daily Record* 7 January 1939.
16   *Daily News* (London) 25 March 1939.
17   H. V. Morton, *In Search of England* (Methuen, 1927) p. 2.
18   *Liverpool Echo* 25 January 1939.
19   *East End News and London Shipping Chronicle* 20 January 1939.
20   William Chapman Sharpe, *The Art of Walking: A History in 100* Images (Yale University Press, 2023) p. 153.
21   *Daily Express* 2 May 1939.

22 Ted Kavanagh, *Tommy Handley* (Hodder & Stoughton, 1949) p. 110.
23 Ibid. p. 103.
24 Roger Wilmut, *Kindly Leave the Stage: The Story of Variety 1919–1960* (Methuen, 1985) p. 155.
25 Hilton, *To You, Mr Chips* Chapter 1.
26 Wilmut, *Kindly Leave the Stage* p. 137.
27 Robb Wilton, 'The Day War Broke Out' (1942). See Malcom Atkin, *To the Last Man: The Home Guard in War and Popular Culture* (Pen & Sword Military, 2019).
28 *Daily Mirror* 18 June 1940.
29 Denis Norden, *Clips from a Life* (Fourth Estate, 2008) p. 16.
30 George Pearson, *Flashback: An Autobiography of a British Film Maker* (George Allen & Unwin, 1957) p. 202.

ACKNOWLEDGEMENTS

I've said this before, but Profile Books really are a terrifically good publishing house. And, as the Universal horror movies of the 1930s used to say, a good cast is worth repeating: editor, Jon Petre; managing editor, Georgina Difford; copy editor, Hugh Davis; typesetter, Jonathan Harley; Dahmicca Wright and Rosie Parnham in marketing; commercial director, Claire Beaumont, and Sian Gibson, Esther Waters and Sarah Bunce in sales; audio editors, Louisa Dunnigan and Audrey Kerr; proofreader, Seán Costello; publicist, Hannah Ross and indexer, Geraldine Beare. Above all, Nick Humphrey, who's a great editor. I'm indebted to Andrew Franklin and to Euan Thorneycroft at A. M. Heath for their faith in this project.

My thanks to Hugo Frey and Andrew Chandler at the University of Chichester, and to my students there, particularly Gerard Griffith, with whom I explored the Spanish Flu epidemic. Also, to those who helped point me to material or thoughts, including Dan Atkinson, Jennie Bird, Ben Blackwood, Jonathan Calder, Helen Campbell, Adenike Deane-Pratt, Stephanie Egerton, Ben Finlay, John Flaxman, Brian Freeborn, Tim Hague, Simon Matthews, York Membery and Joe Ryan. In particular, Sam Harrison and Anthony Teague have listened to me rambling on about this far beyond the call of duty and have contributed a great deal.

My late father's influence is all over this book – it was he who initiated me into the mysteries of Arthur Conan Doyle, Sandy Powell and the British dance band. (The latter also reminds me of Steve Konrad's enthusiasm, which I remember with fondness.) While I was writing, the last of my parents' generation in my family died. This book is an attempt to depict the world they were born into, and I'd like to remember them here: Donald, Dorothy, Eileen, Gordon, Iris, Olive, Pamela and Toots.

Lastly, but not leastly, Thamasin Marsh remains invaluable.

INDEX